JE CROIS EN MOI

MORIARTY
❧ THE PATRIOT ❧

BASED ON THE WORKS OF Sir Arthur Conan Doyle
STORYBOARDS BY Ryosuke Takeuchi
ART BY Hikaru Miyoshi

2

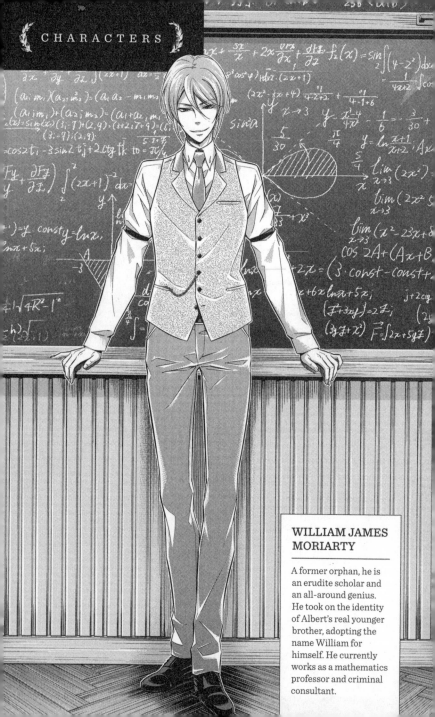

WILLIAM JAMES MORIARTY

A former orphan, he is an erudite scholar and an all-around genius. He took on the identity of Albert's real younger brother, adopting the name William for himself. He currently works as a mathematics professor and criminal consultant.

ALBERT JAMES MORIARTY

The eldest son of the deceased Count Moriarty. His primary occupation is working in London as a lieutenant colonel in the British Army.

LOUIS JAMES MORIARTY

William's younger brother. He's in charge of maintaining the family estate and assets.

SEBASTIAN MORAN

A master gunman. He's a former soldier and is quick to throw punches. He supports William as his confidant and right-hand man.

FRED PORLOCK

A young man with connections to a criminal network in England. He is proficient in covert operations and the art of disguise.

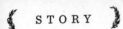

{ STORY }

It's the end of the 19th century, the golden age of the British Empire. The people have been divided into two groups—the ruling class and the laborers. Sick of the corrupted state of the nation, Albert, the son of a nobleman, conspires with his two adopted brothers to murder his entire family and destroy the evidence in a fire orchestrated to look like an accident. Playing the part of three orphaned noble boys, they inherit the name and entire estate of the late Count Moriarty. Thus they begin putting in motion their plan to rid the world of evil and create their ideal world.

As adults, William and Louis move to the city of Durham. There, William takes the case of a couple who want revenge on their tyrannical landowner, Baron Dublin. Baron Dublin's family has ruled there for generations, and his greed led to the death of the couple's child. William succeeds in performing the perfect crime—assassinating Baron Dublin after deviously manipulating the man into signing over his land to the couple and his tenants.

William's next case is the mysterious suicide of a dancer in a pub. He notices that one of the students at the university where he teaches has been skipping classes and takes it upon himself to investigate what's going on. After learning that Dudley Bale, a university employee, is behind his student's disappearance and the death of the girl from the pub, William gets rid of Bale by luring him into a trap and forcing him to jump to his death off the same bridge the dancer did.

CONTENTS

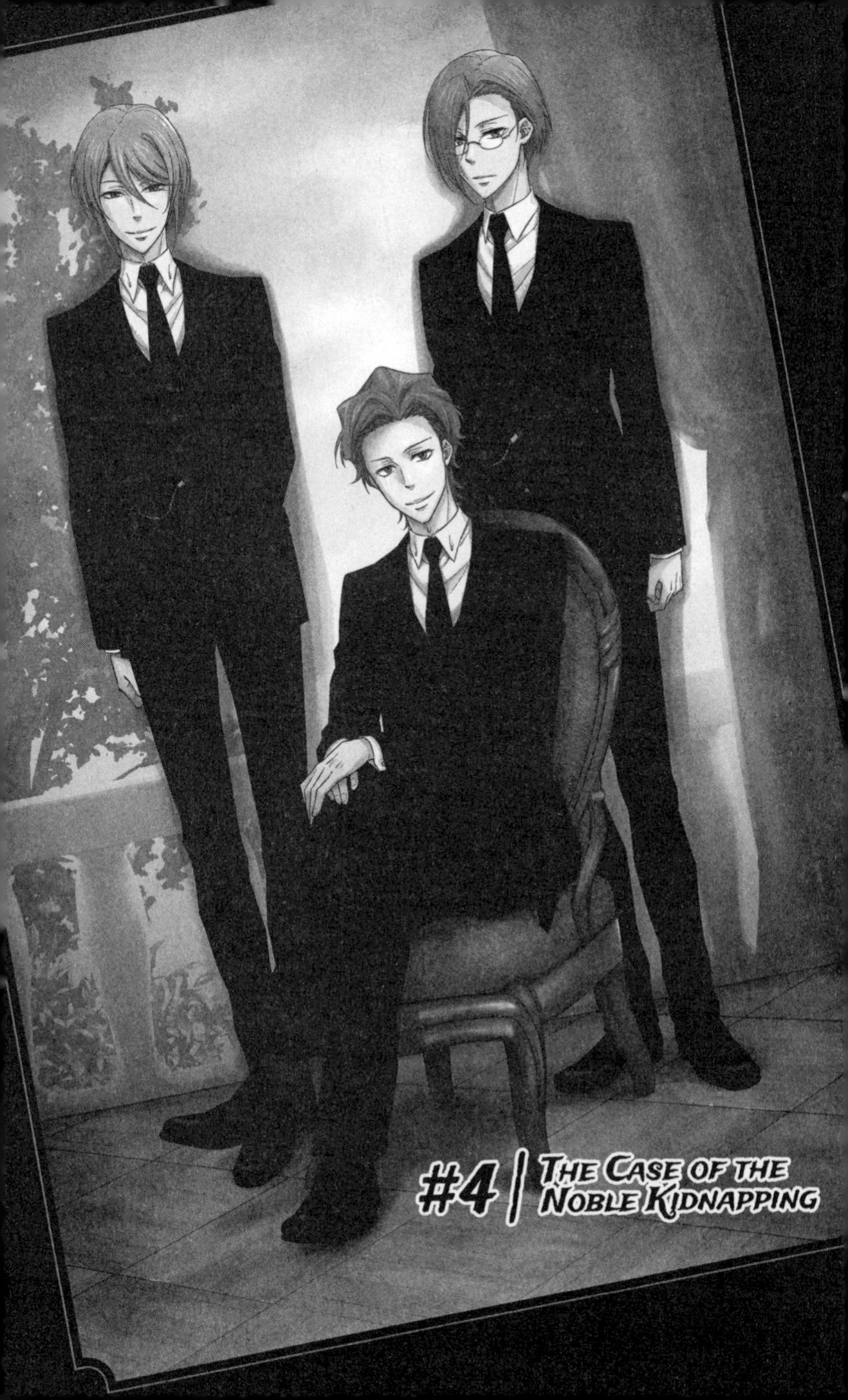
#4 The Case of the Noble Kidnapping

MORIARTY
THE PATRIOT

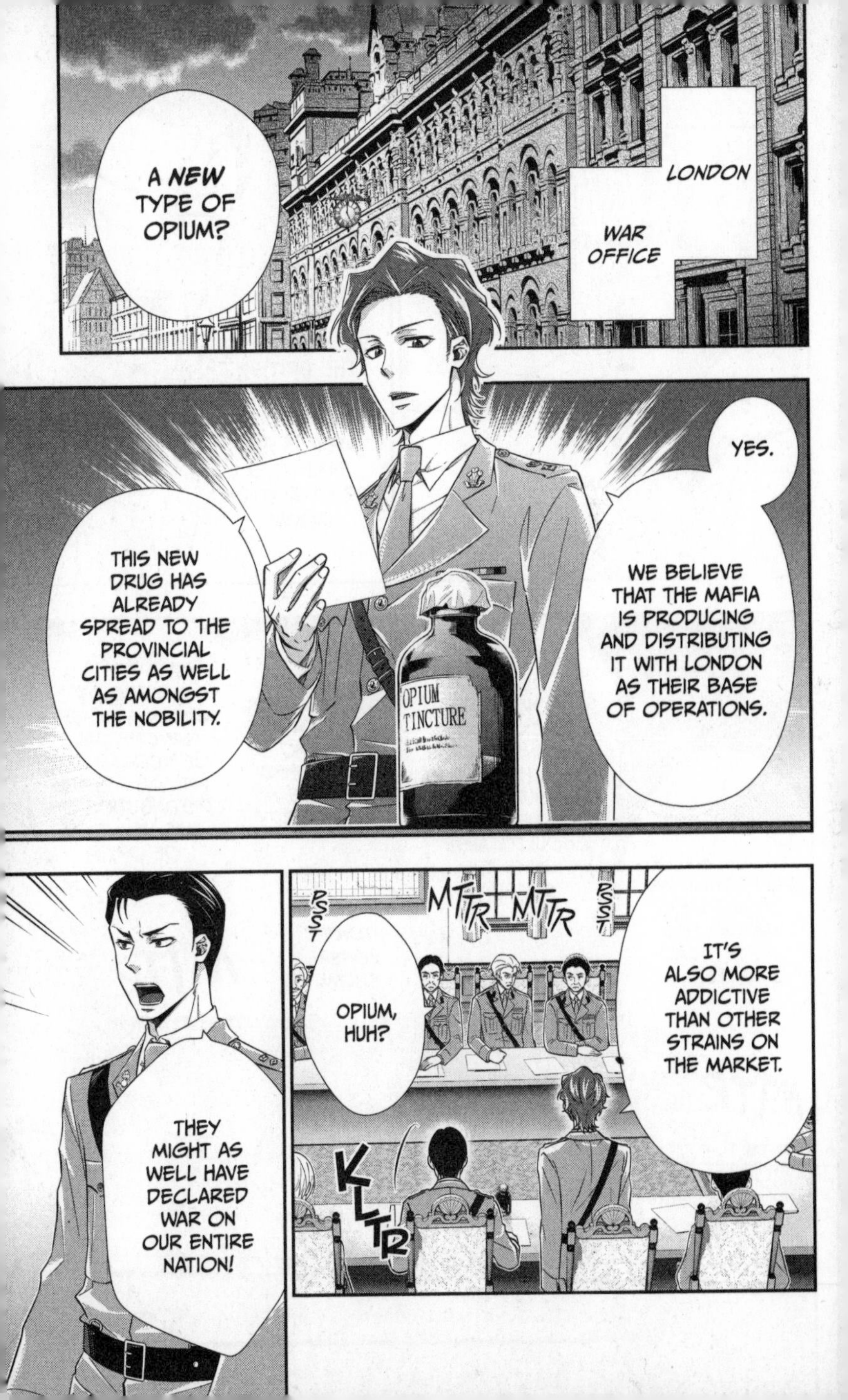
LONDON
WAR OFFICE
A NEW TYPE OF OPIUM?
YES.
WE BELIEVE THAT THE MAFIA IS PRODUCING AND DISTRIBUTING IT WITH LONDON AS THEIR BASE OF OPERATIONS.
OPIUM TINCTURE
THIS NEW DRUG HAS ALREADY SPREAD TO THE PROVINCIAL CITIES AS WELL AS AMONGST THE NOBILITY.
IT'S ALSO MORE ADDICTIVE THAN OTHER STRAINS ON THE MARKET.
PSST
MTTR MTTR
PSST
OPIUM, HUH?
KLTR
THEY MIGHT AS WELL HAVE DECLARED WAR ON OUR ENTIRE NATION!

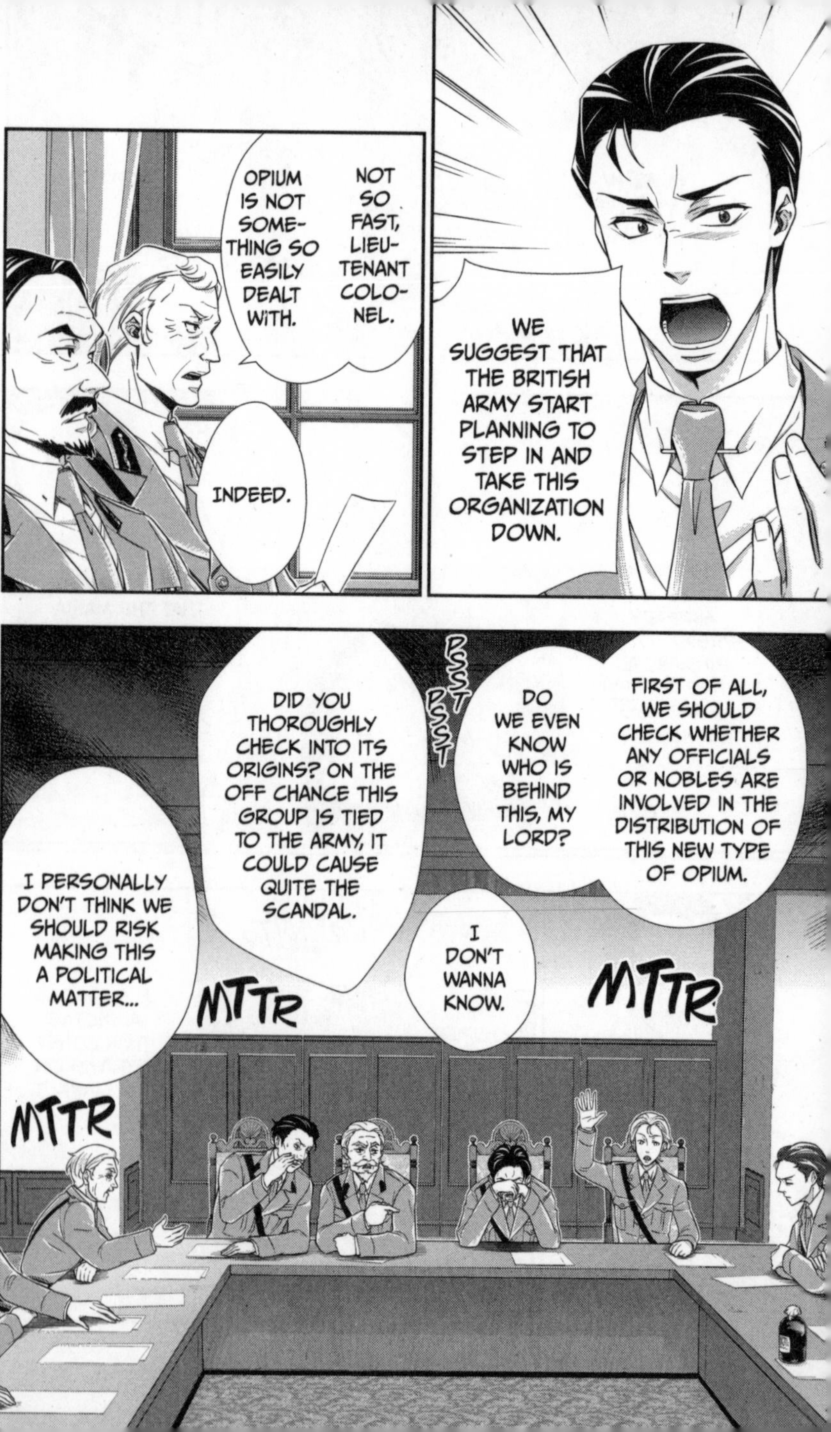
WE SUGGEST THAT THE BRITISH ARMY START PLANNING TO STEP IN AND TAKE THIS ORGANIZATION DOWN.
NOT SO FAST, LIEU-TENANT COLO-NEL.
OPIUM IS NOT SOME-THING SO EASILY DEALT WITH.
INDEED.
FIRST OF ALL, WE SHOULD CHECK WHETHER ANY OFFICIALS OR NOBLES ARE INVOLVED IN THE DISTRIBUTION OF THIS NEW TYPE OF OPIUM.
PSST PSST
DO WE EVEN KNOW WHO IS BEHIND THIS, MY LORD?
DID YOU THOROUGHLY CHECK INTO ITS ORIGINS? ON THE OFF CHANCE THIS GROUP IS TIED TO THE ARMY, IT COULD CAUSE QUITE THE SCANDAL.
MTTR
I DON'T WANNA KNOW.
MTTR
I PERSONALLY DON'T THINK WE SHOULD RISK MAKING THIS A POLITICAL MATTER...
MTTR

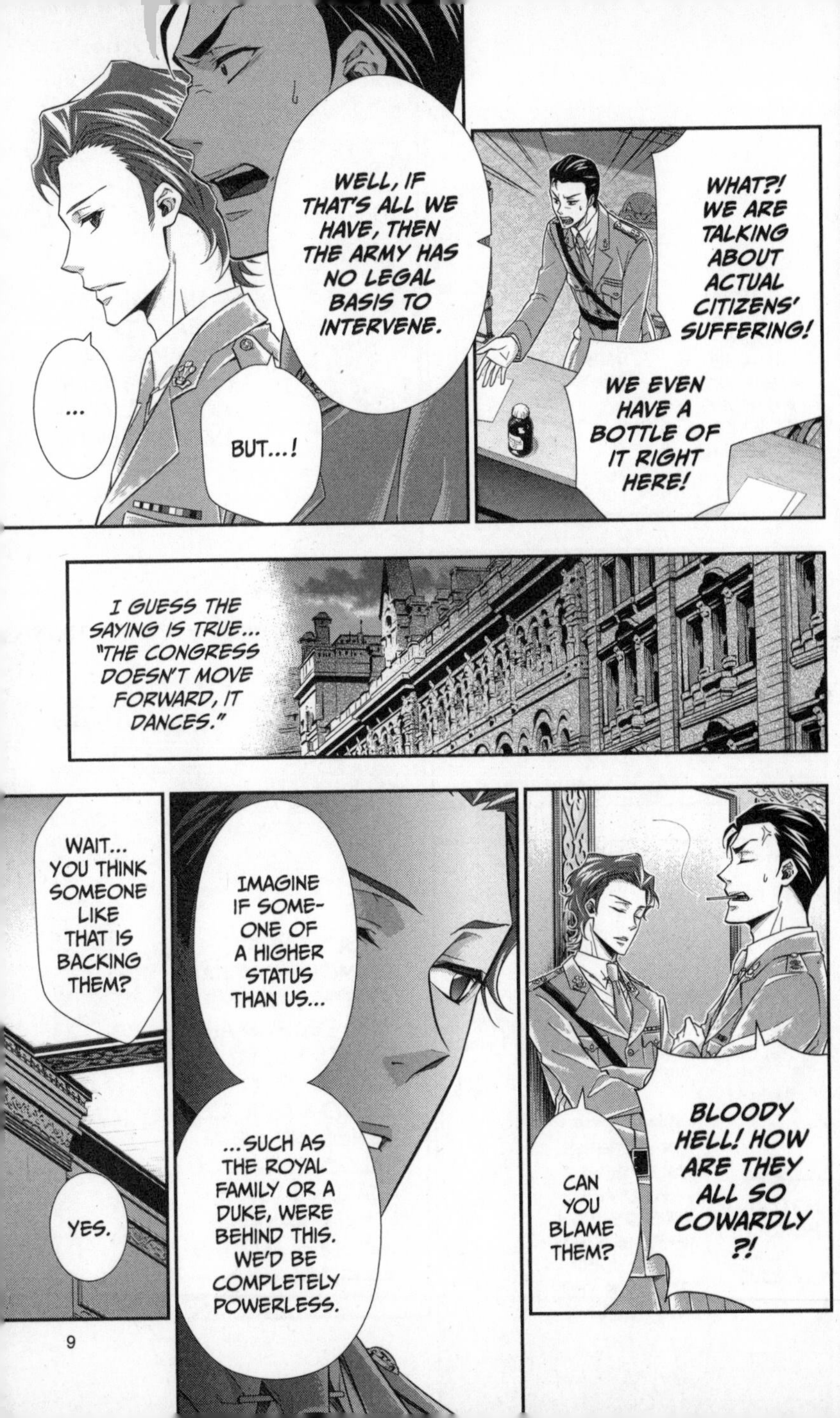
WHAT?! WE ARE TALKING ABOUT ACTUAL CITIZENS' SUFFERING!
WE EVEN HAVE A BOTTLE OF IT RIGHT HERE!
WELL, IF THAT'S ALL WE HAVE, THEN THE ARMY HAS NO LEGAL BASIS TO INTERVENE.
BUT...!
...
I GUESS THE SAYING IS TRUE... "THE CONGRESS DOESN'T MOVE FORWARD, IT DANCES."
BLOODY HELL! HOW ARE THEY ALL SO COWARDLY?!
CAN YOU BLAME THEM?
IMAGINE IF SOME-ONE OF A HIGHER STATUS THAN US...
...SUCH AS THE ROYAL FAMILY OR A DUKE, WERE BEHIND THIS. WE'D BE COMPLETELY POWERLESS.
WAIT... YOU THINK SOMEONE LIKE THAT IS BACKING THEM?
YES.

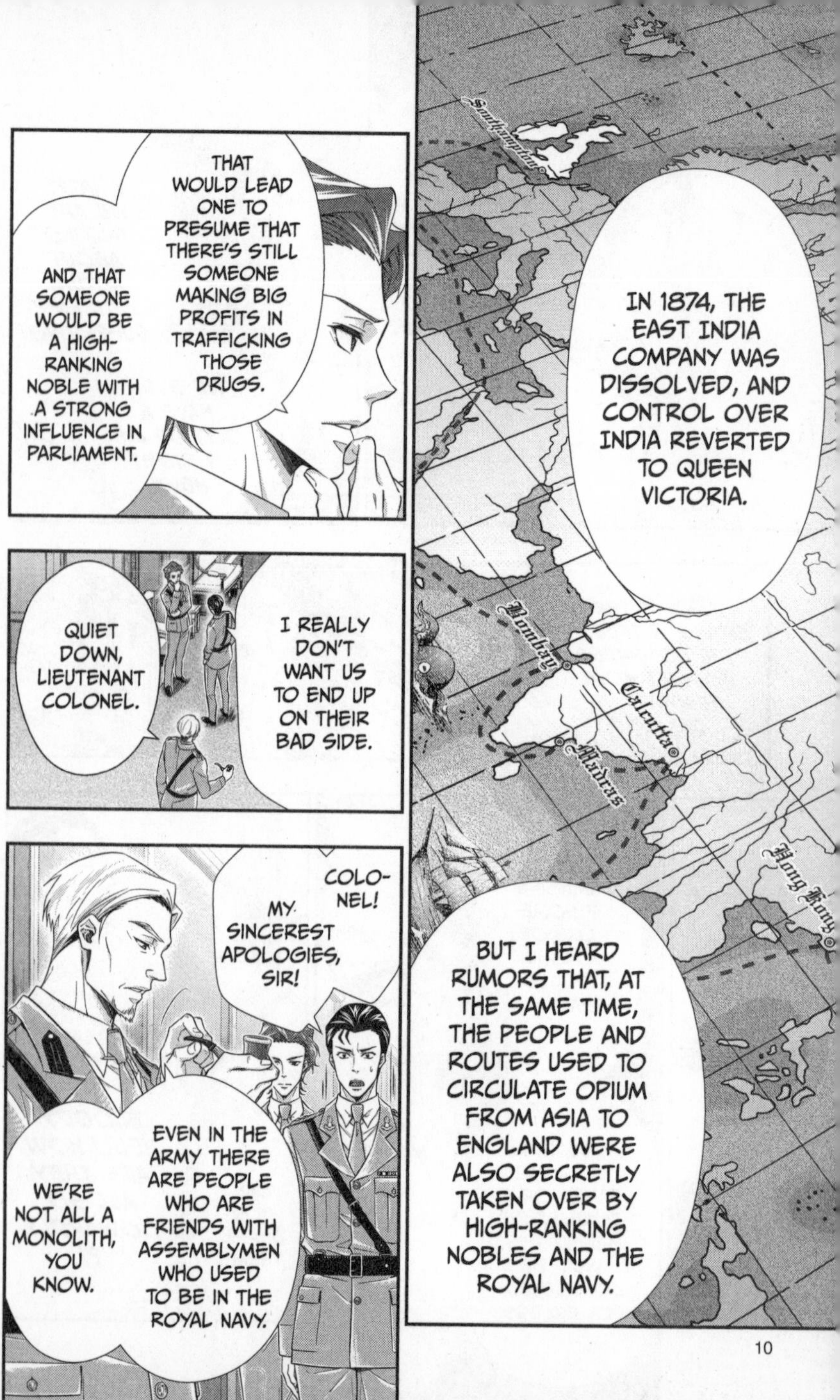
Southampton
IN 1874, THE EAST INDIA COMPANY WAS DISSOLVED, AND CONTROL OVER INDIA REVERTED TO QUEEN VICTORIA.
Bombay
Calcutta
Madras
Hong Kong
BUT I HEARD RUMORS THAT, AT THE SAME TIME, THE PEOPLE AND ROUTES USED TO CIRCULATE OPIUM FROM ASIA TO ENGLAND WERE ALSO SECRETLY TAKEN OVER BY HIGH-RANKING NOBLES AND THE ROYAL NAVY.
THAT WOULD LEAD ONE TO PRESUME THAT THERE'S STILL SOMEONE MAKING BIG PROFITS IN TRAFFICKING THOSE DRUGS.
AND THAT SOMEONE WOULD BE A HIGH-RANKING NOBLE WITH A STRONG INFLUENCE IN PARLIAMENT.
I REALLY DON'T WANT US TO END UP ON THEIR BAD SIDE.
QUIET DOWN, LIEUTENANT COLONEL.
COLONEL!
MY SINCEREST APOLOGIES, SIR!
EVEN IN THE ARMY THERE ARE PEOPLE WHO ARE FRIENDS WITH ASSEMBLYMEN WHO USED TO BE IN THE ROYAL NAVY.
WE'RE NOT ALL A MONOLITH, YOU KNOW.

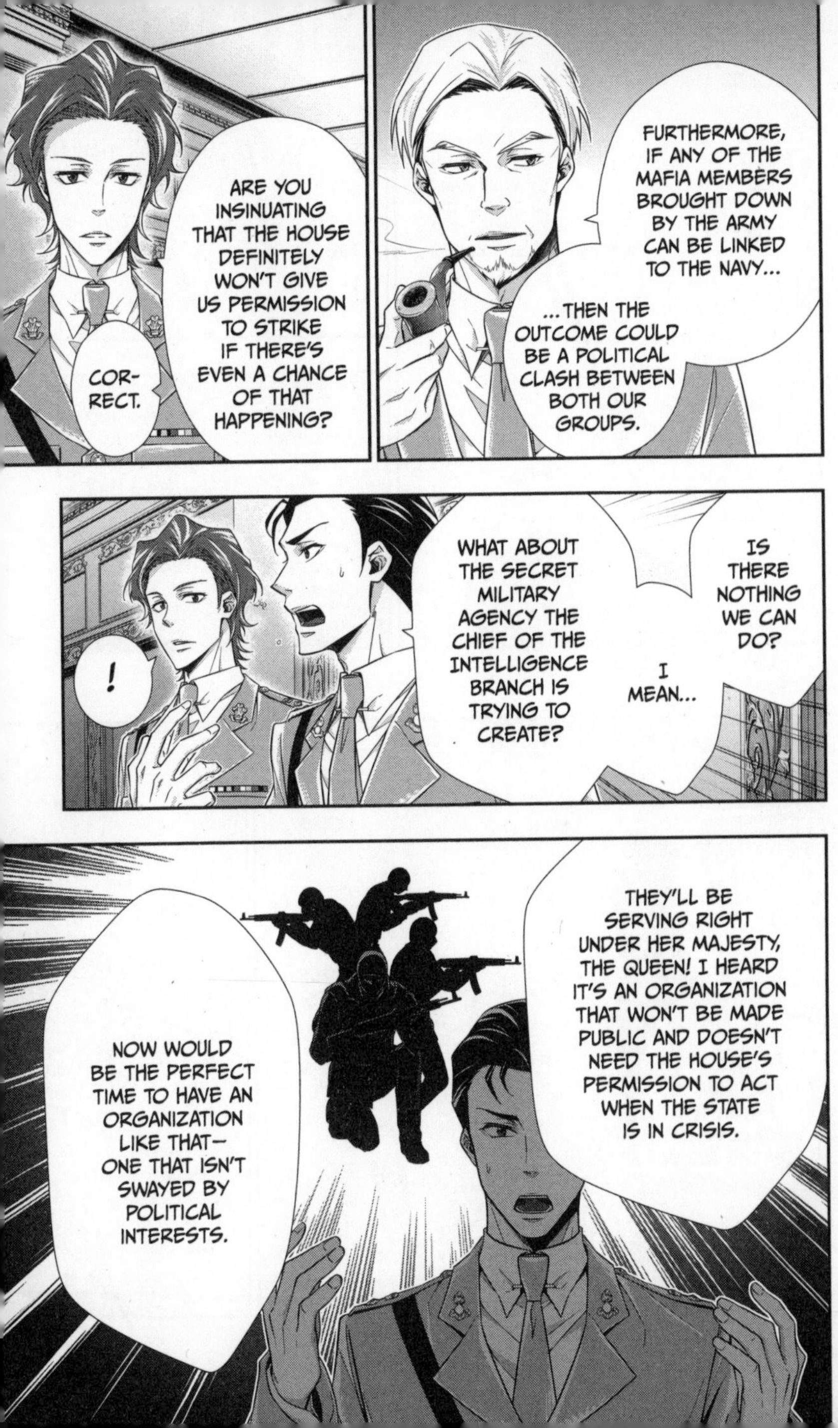
FURTHERMORE, IF ANY OF THE MAFIA MEMBERS BROUGHT DOWN BY THE ARMY CAN BE LINKED TO THE NAVY...
...THEN THE OUTCOME COULD BE A POLITICAL CLASH BETWEEN BOTH OUR GROUPS.
ARE YOU INSINUATING THAT THE HOUSE DEFINITELY WON'T GIVE US PERMISSION TO STRIKE IF THERE'S EVEN A CHANCE OF THAT HAPPENING?
COR-RECT.
IS THERE NOTHING WE CAN DO?
I MEAN...
WHAT ABOUT THE SECRET MILITARY AGENCY THE CHIEF OF THE INTELLIGENCE BRANCH IS TRYING TO CREATE?
!
THEY'LL BE SERVING RIGHT UNDER HER MAJESTY, THE QUEEN! I HEARD IT'S AN ORGANIZATION THAT WON'T BE MADE PUBLIC AND DOESN'T NEED THE HOUSE'S PERMISSION TO ACT WHEN THE STATE IS IN CRISIS.
NOW WOULD BE THE PERFECT TIME TO HAVE AN ORGANIZATION LIKE THAT—ONE THAT ISN'T SWAYED BY POLITICAL INTERESTS.

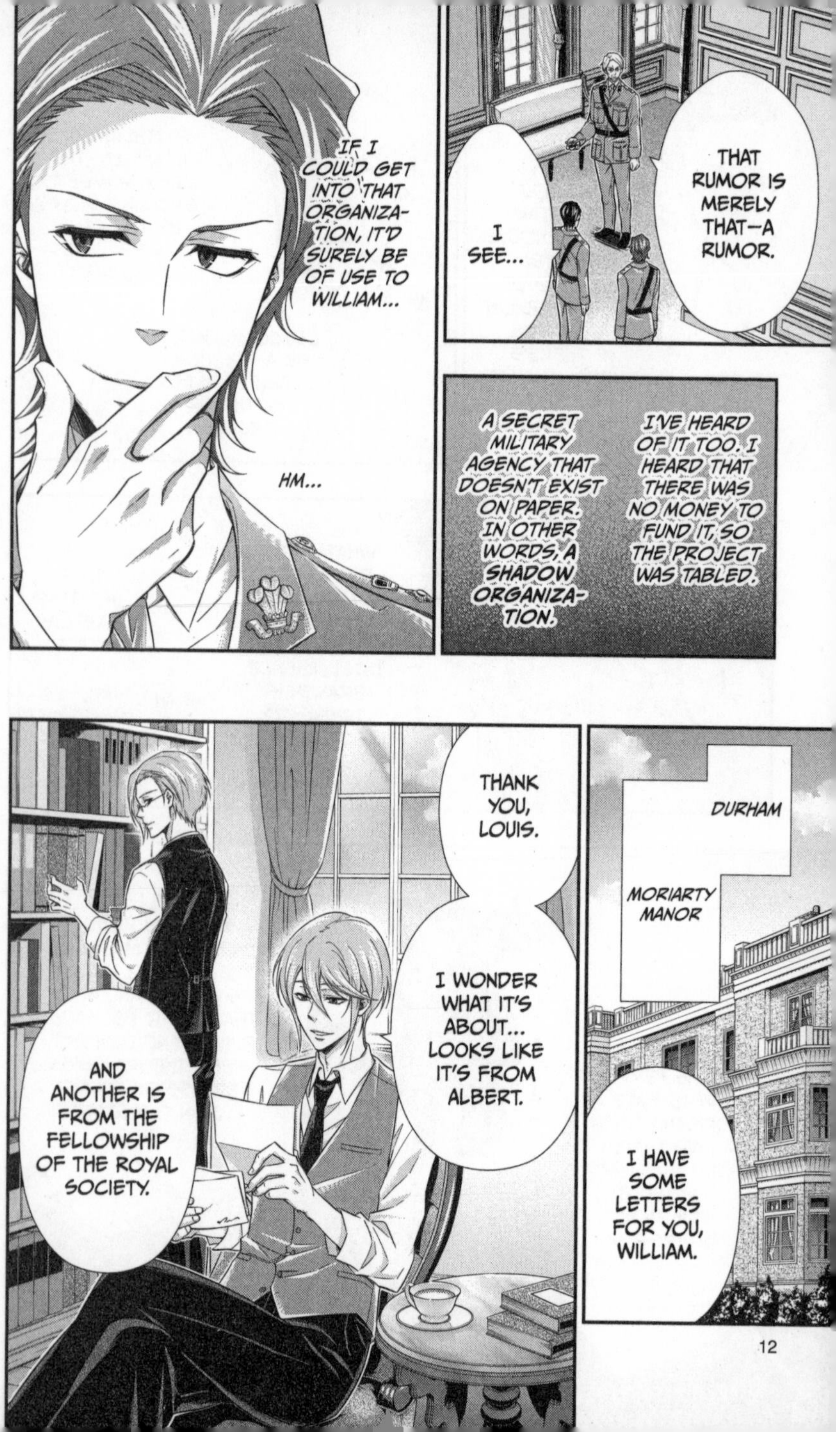
THAT RUMOR IS MERELY THAT—A RUMOR.
I SEE...
I'VE HEARD OF IT TOO. I HEARD THAT THERE WAS NO MONEY TO FUND IT, SO THE PROJECT WAS TABLED.
A SECRET MILITARY AGENCY THAT DOESN'T EXIST ON PAPER. IN OTHER WORDS, A SHADOW ORGANIZATION.
IF I COULD GET INTO THAT ORGANIZATION, IT'D SURELY BE OF USE TO WILLIAM...
HM...
DURHAM
MORIARTY MANOR
I HAVE SOME LETTERS FOR YOU, WILLIAM.
THANK YOU, LOUIS.
I WONDER WHAT IT'S ABOUT... LOOKS LIKE IT'S FROM ALBERT.
AND ANOTHER IS FROM THE FELLOWSHIP OF THE ROYAL SOCIETY.

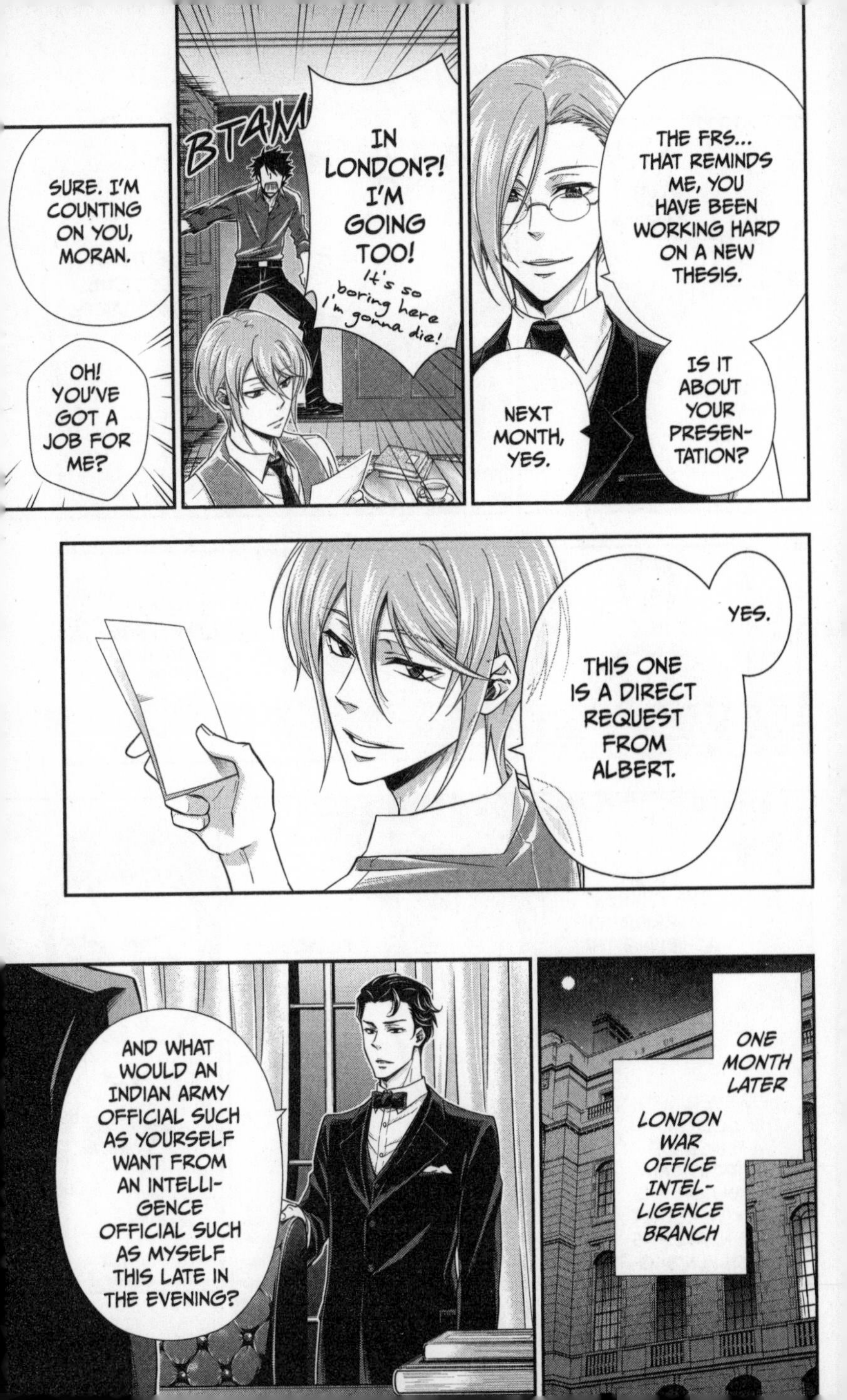
THE FRS... THAT REMINDS ME, YOU HAVE BEEN WORKING HARD ON A NEW THESIS.
IS IT ABOUT YOUR PRESENTATION?
NEXT MONTH, YES.
BTAM
IN LONDON?! I'M GOING TOO!
It's so boring here I'm gonna die!
SURE. I'M COUNTING ON YOU, MORAN.
OH! YOU'VE GOT A JOB FOR ME?
YES.
THIS ONE IS A DIRECT REQUEST FROM ALBERT.
ONE MONTH LATER
LONDON WAR OFFICE INTELLIGENCE BRANCH
AND WHAT WOULD AN INDIAN ARMY OFFICIAL SUCH AS YOURSELF WANT FROM AN INTELLIGENCE OFFICIAL SUCH AS MYSELF THIS LATE IN THE EVENING?

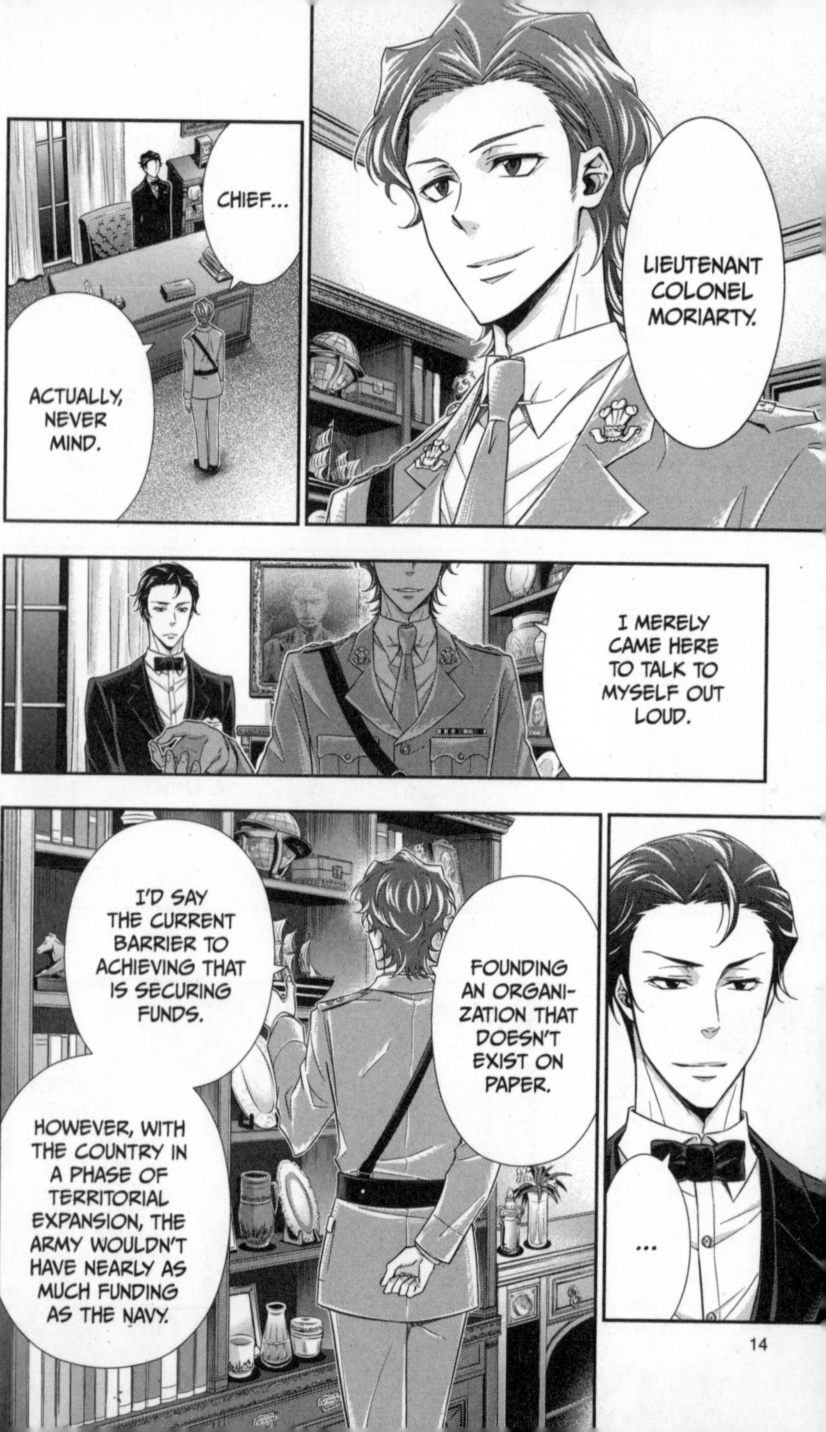
LIEUTENANT COLONEL MORIARTY.
CHIEF...
ACTUALLY, NEVER MIND.
I MERELY CAME HERE TO TALK TO MYSELF OUT LOUD.
...
FOUNDING AN ORGANI-ZATION THAT DOESN'T EXIST ON PAPER.
I'D SAY THE CURRENT BARRIER TO ACHIEVING THAT IS SECURING FUNDS.
HOWEVER, WITH THE COUNTRY IN A PHASE OF TERRITORIAL EXPANSION, THE ARMY WOULDN'T HAVE NEARLY AS MUCH FUNDING AS THE NAVY.

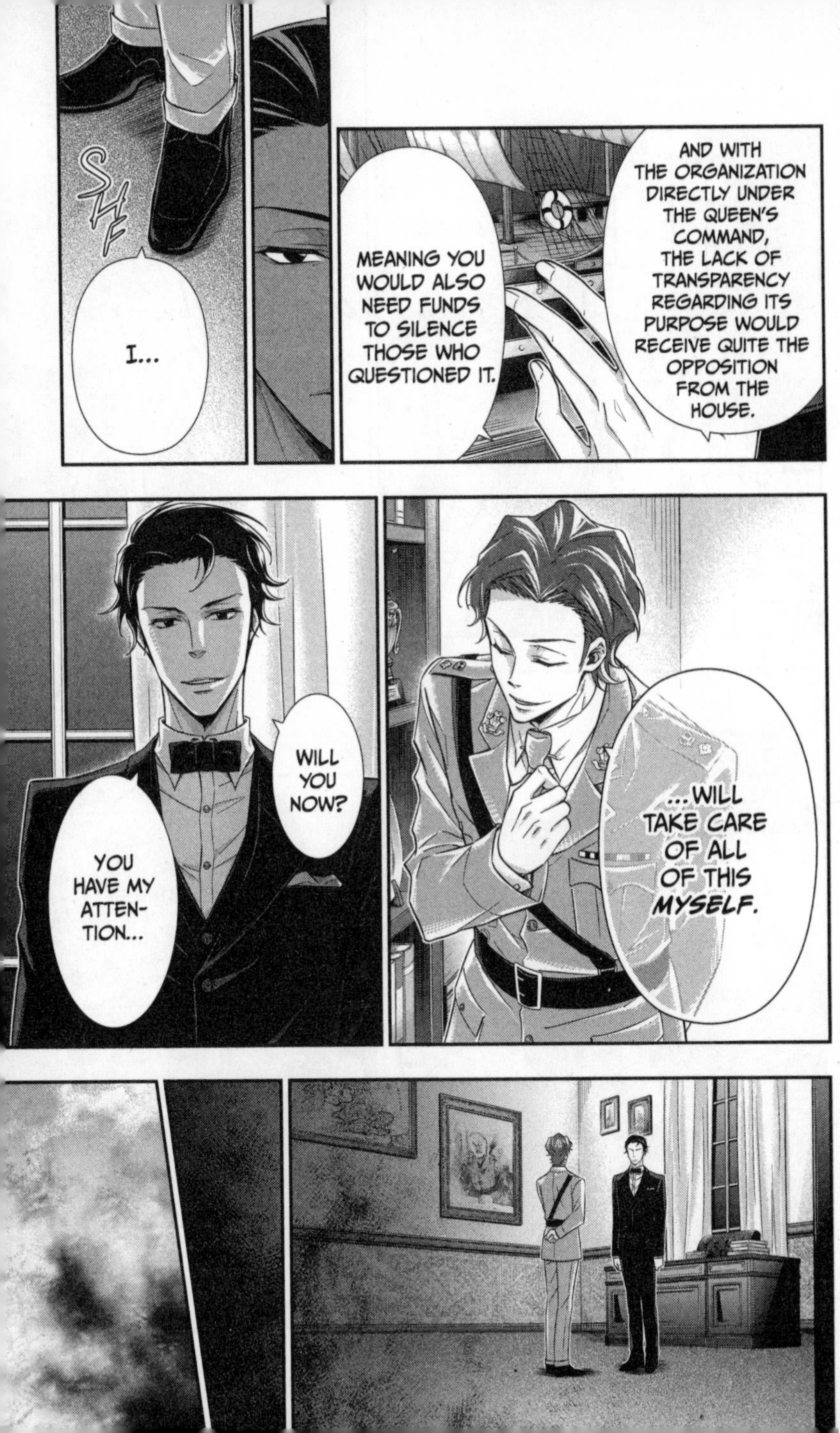
AND WITH THE ORGANIZATION DIRECTLY UNDER THE QUEEN'S COMMAND, THE LACK OF TRANSPARENCY REGARDING ITS PURPOSE WOULD RECEIVE QUITE THE OPPOSITION FROM THE HOUSE.
MEANING YOU WOULD ALSO NEED FUNDS TO SILENCE THOSE WHO QUESTIONED IT.
SHF
I...
...WILL TAKE CARE OF ALL OF THIS *MYSELF*.
WILL YOU NOW?
YOU HAVE MY ATTENTION...

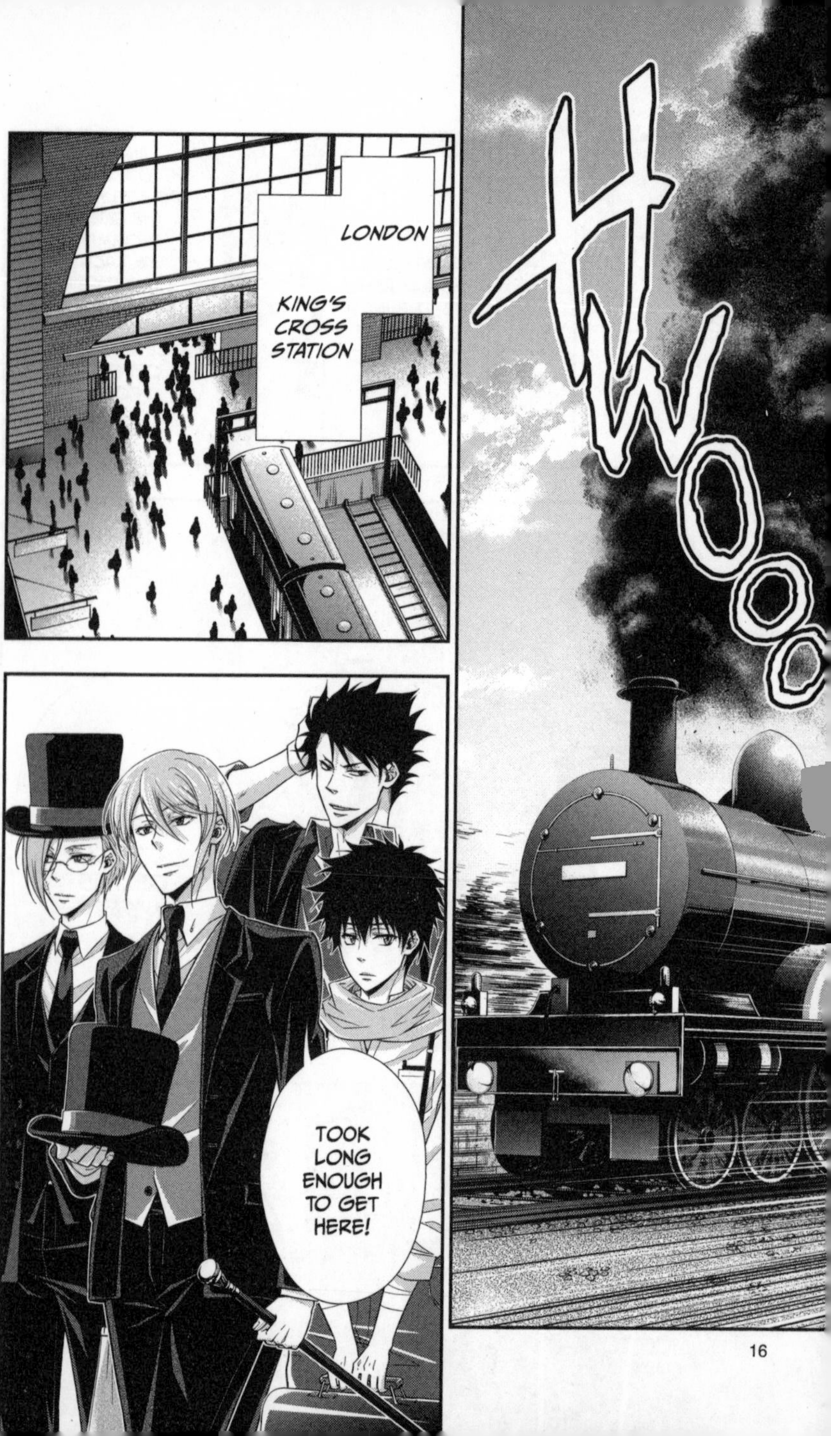
HWOOO
LONDON
KING'S CROSS STATION
TOOK LONG ENOUGH TO GET HERE!

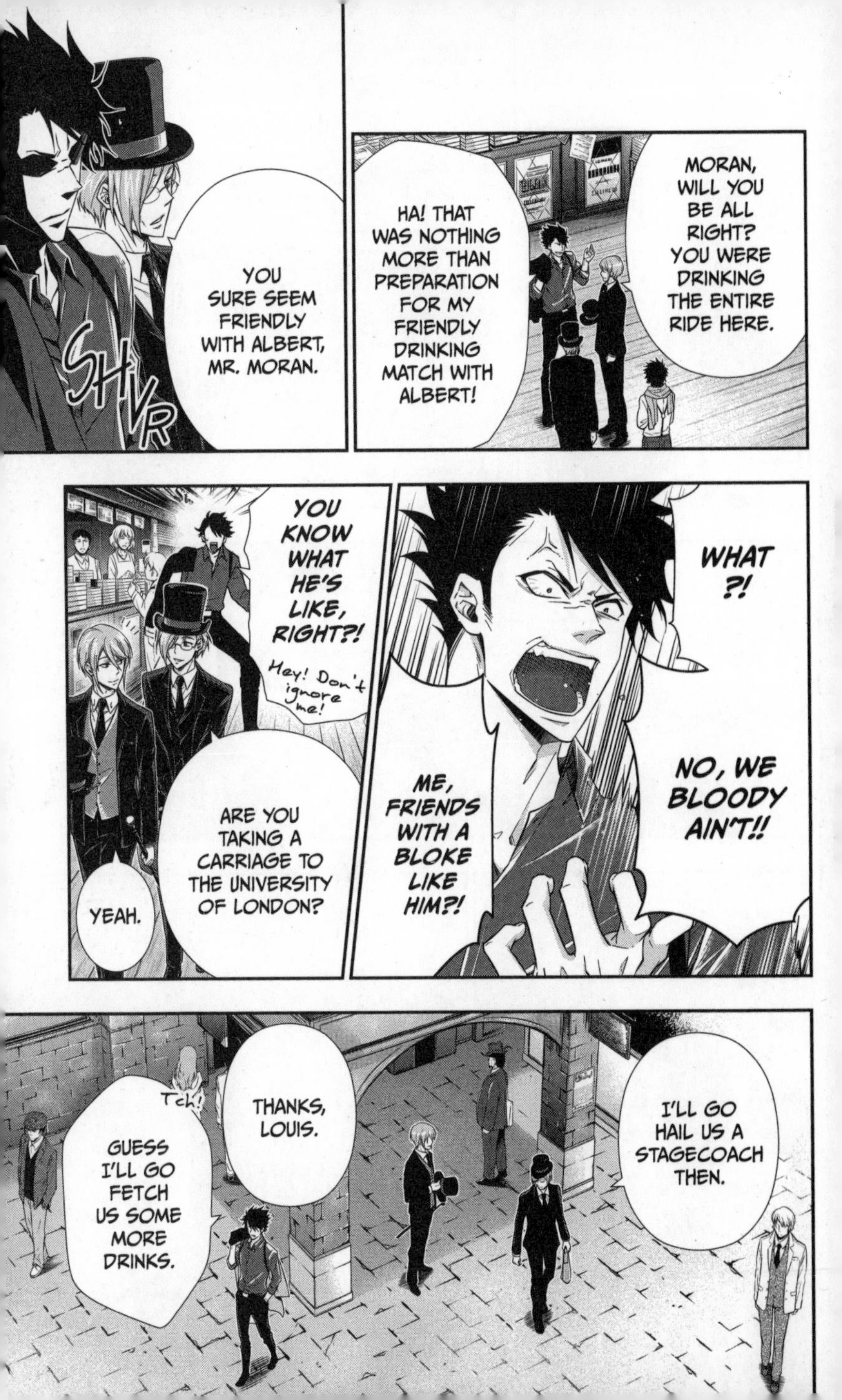
MORAN, WILL YOU BE ALL RIGHT? YOU WERE DRINKING THE ENTIRE RIDE HERE.
HA! THAT WAS NOTHING MORE THAN PREPARATION FOR MY FRIENDLY DRINKING MATCH WITH ALBERT!
YOU SURE SEEM FRIENDLY WITH ALBERT, MR. MORAN.
SHIVR
WHAT?!
NO, WE BLOODY AIN'T!!
ME, FRIENDS WITH A BLOKE LIKE HIM?!
YOU KNOW WHAT HE'S LIKE, RIGHT?!
Hey! Don't ignore me!
ARE YOU TAKING A CARRIAGE TO THE UNIVERSITY OF LONDON?
YEAH.
I'LL GO HAIL US A STAGECOACH THEN.
THANKS, LOUIS.
Tch!
GUESS I'LL GO FETCH US SOME MORE DRINKS.

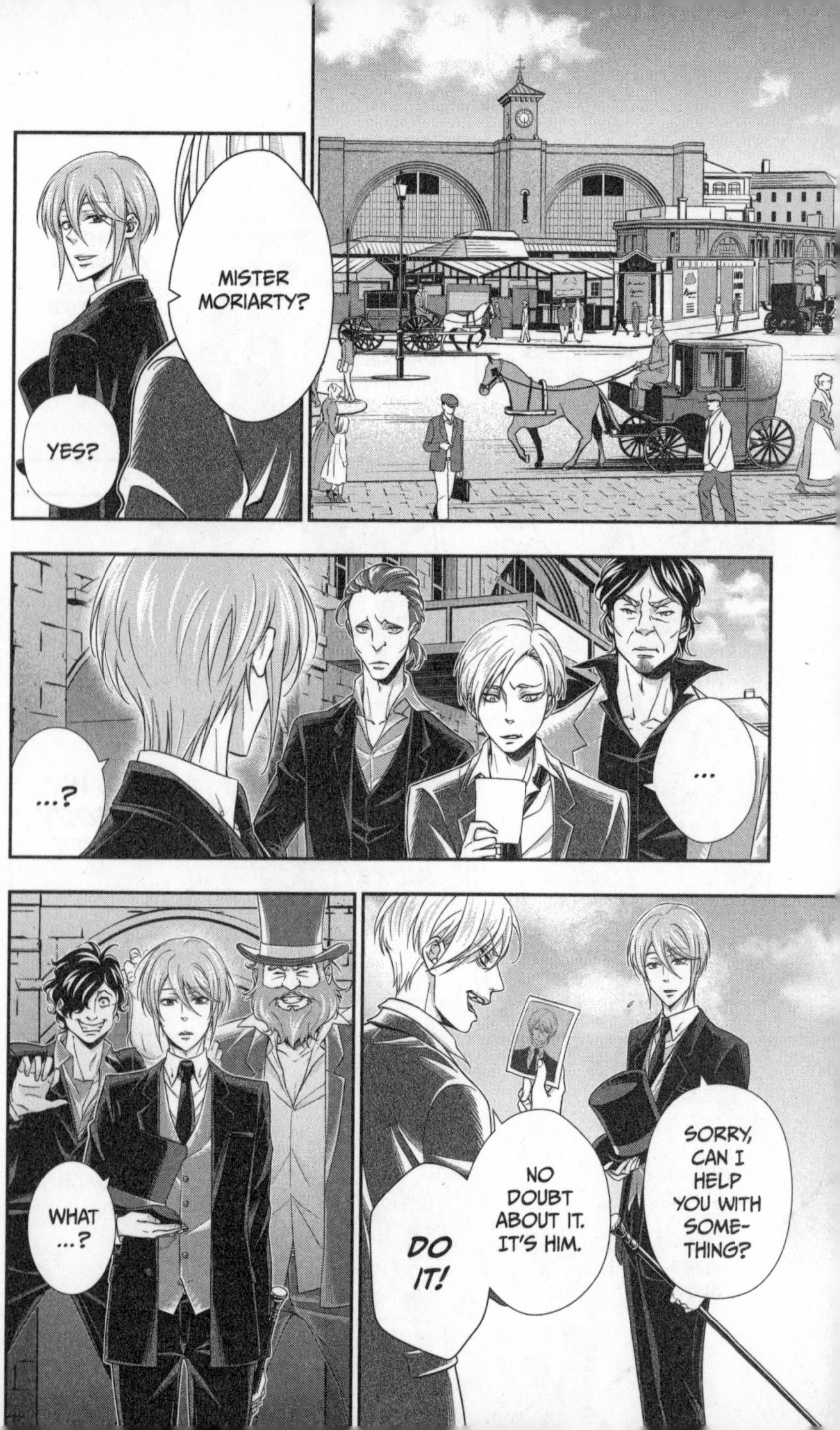
MISTER MORIARTY?
YES?
...
...?
SORRY, CAN I HELP YOU WITH SOME-THING?
NO DOUBT ABOUT IT. IT'S HIM.
DO IT!
WHAT ...?

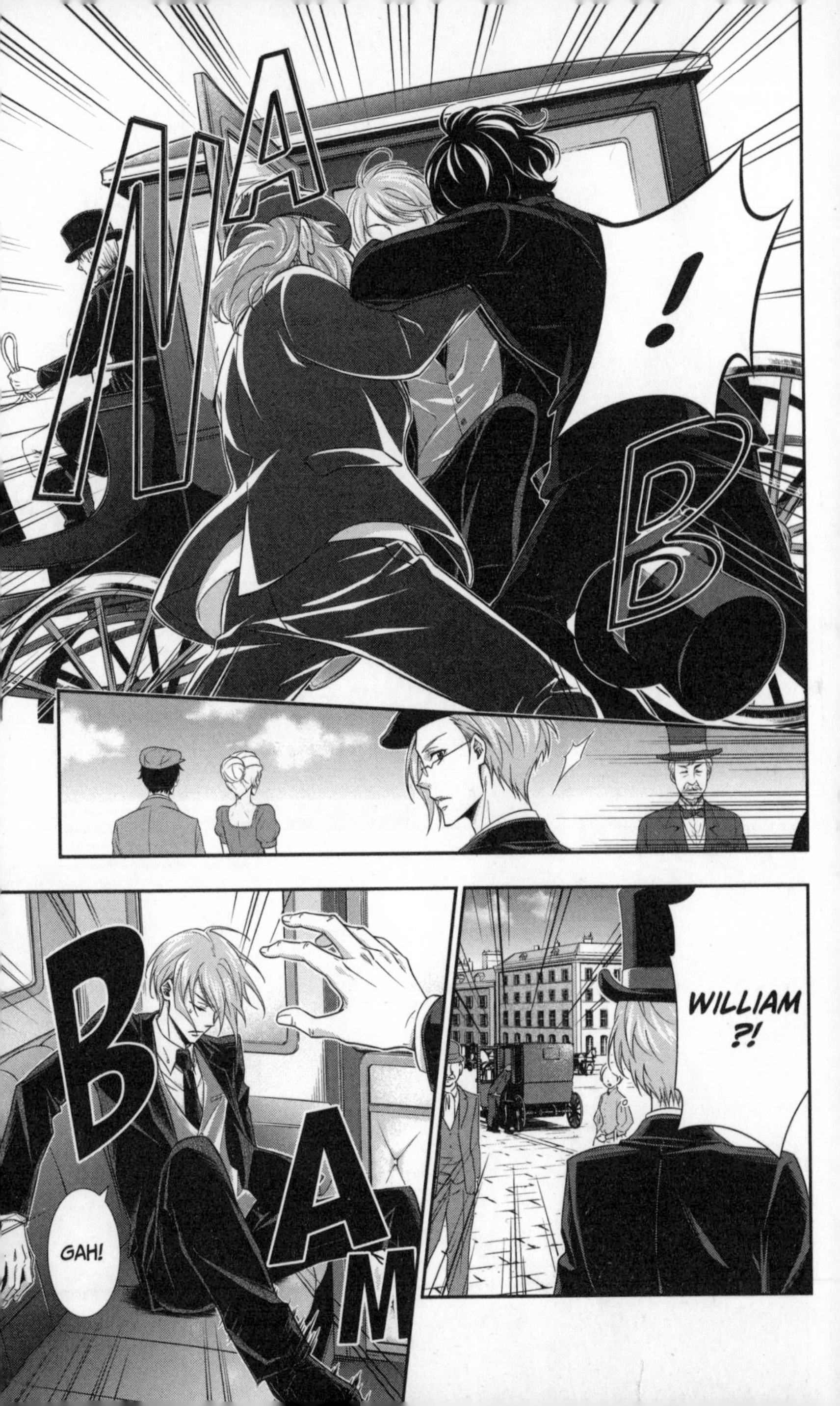
!
BAM
WILLIAM ?!
BAM
GAH!

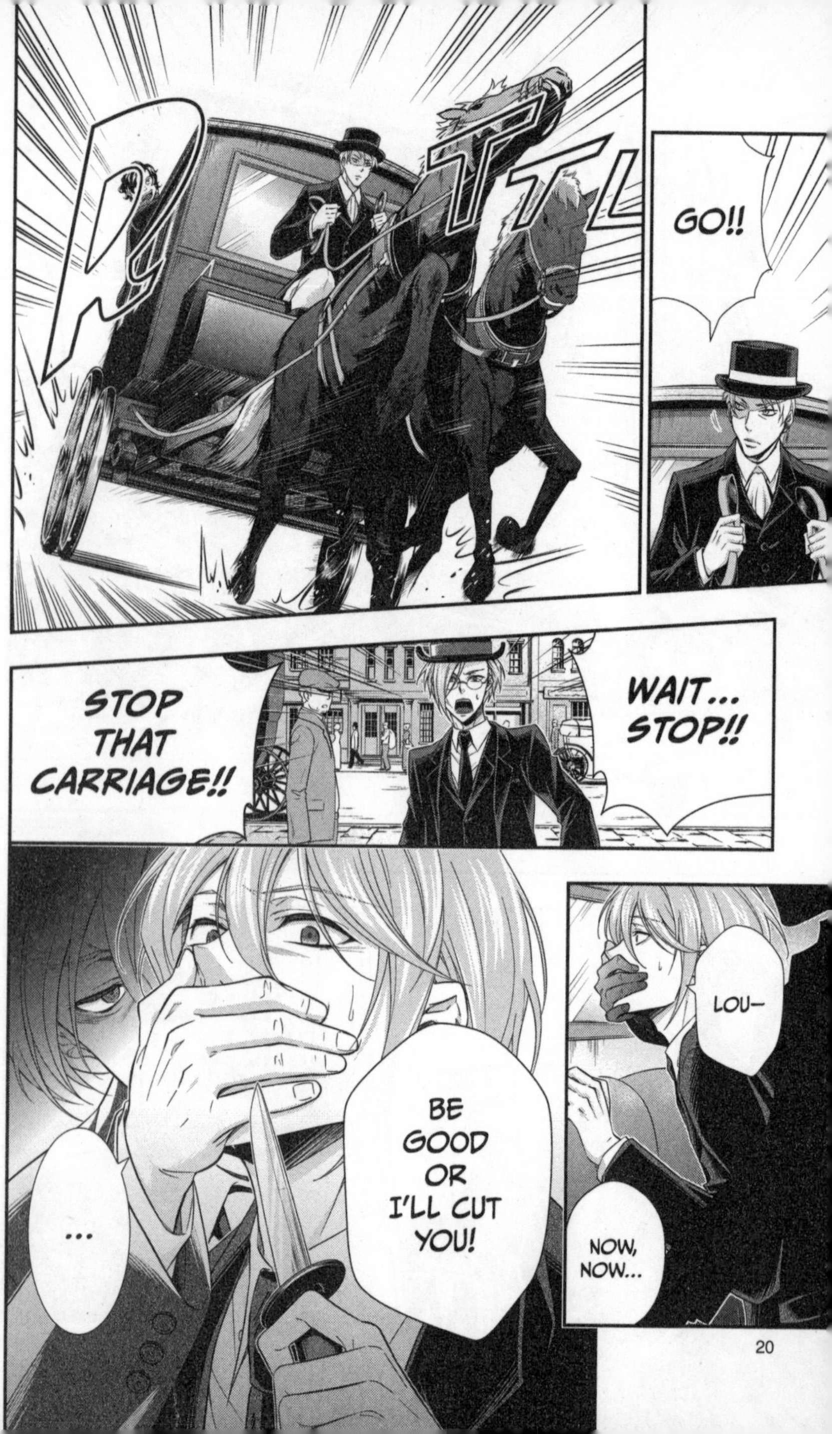
GO!!
WAIT... STOP!!
STOP THAT CARRIAGE!!
LOU—
NOW, NOW...
BE GOOD OR I'LL CUT YOU!
...

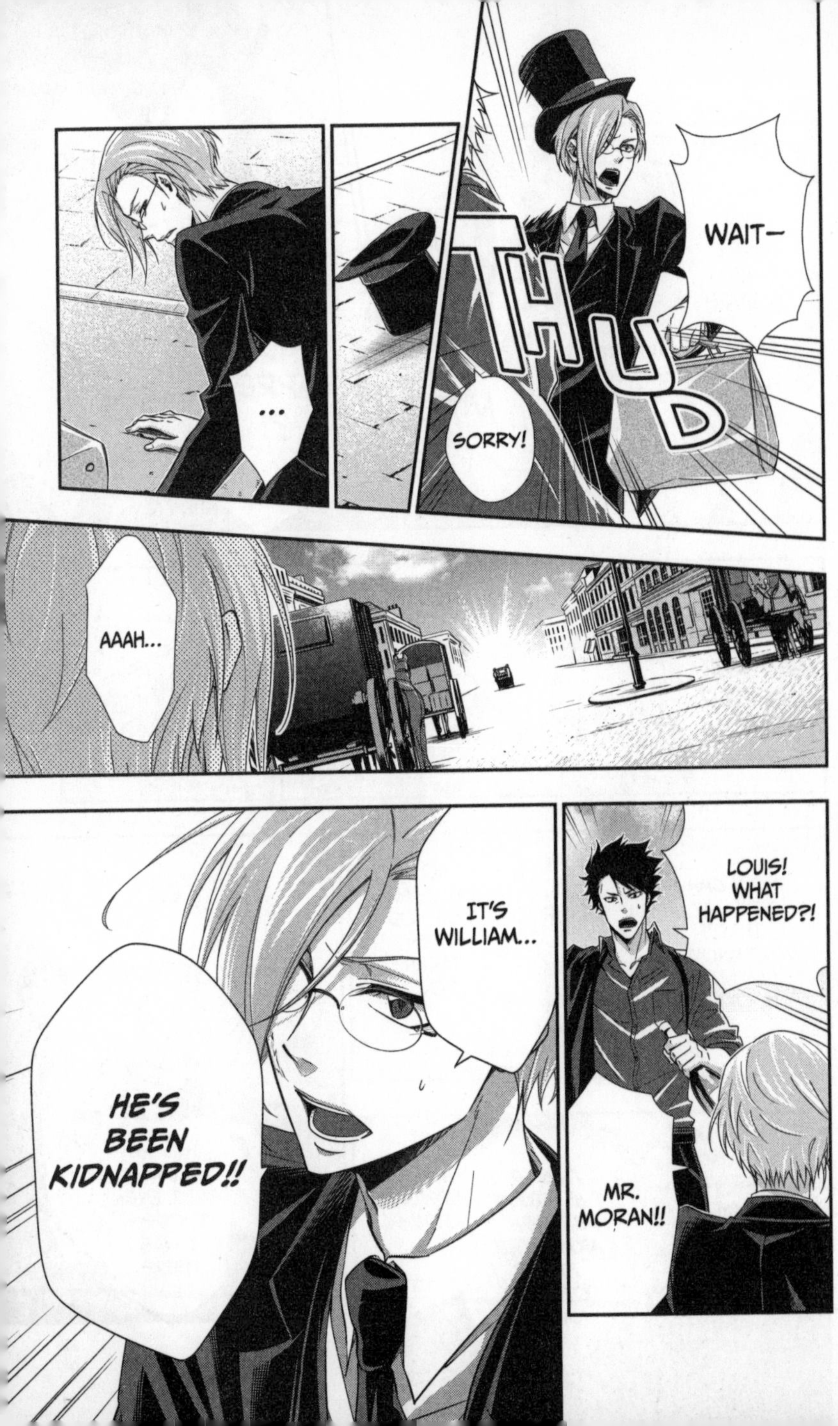
WAIT—
THUD
SORRY!
...
AAAH...
LOUIS! WHAT HAPPENED?!
MR. MORAN!!
IT'S WILLIAM...
HE'S BEEN KIDNAPPED!!

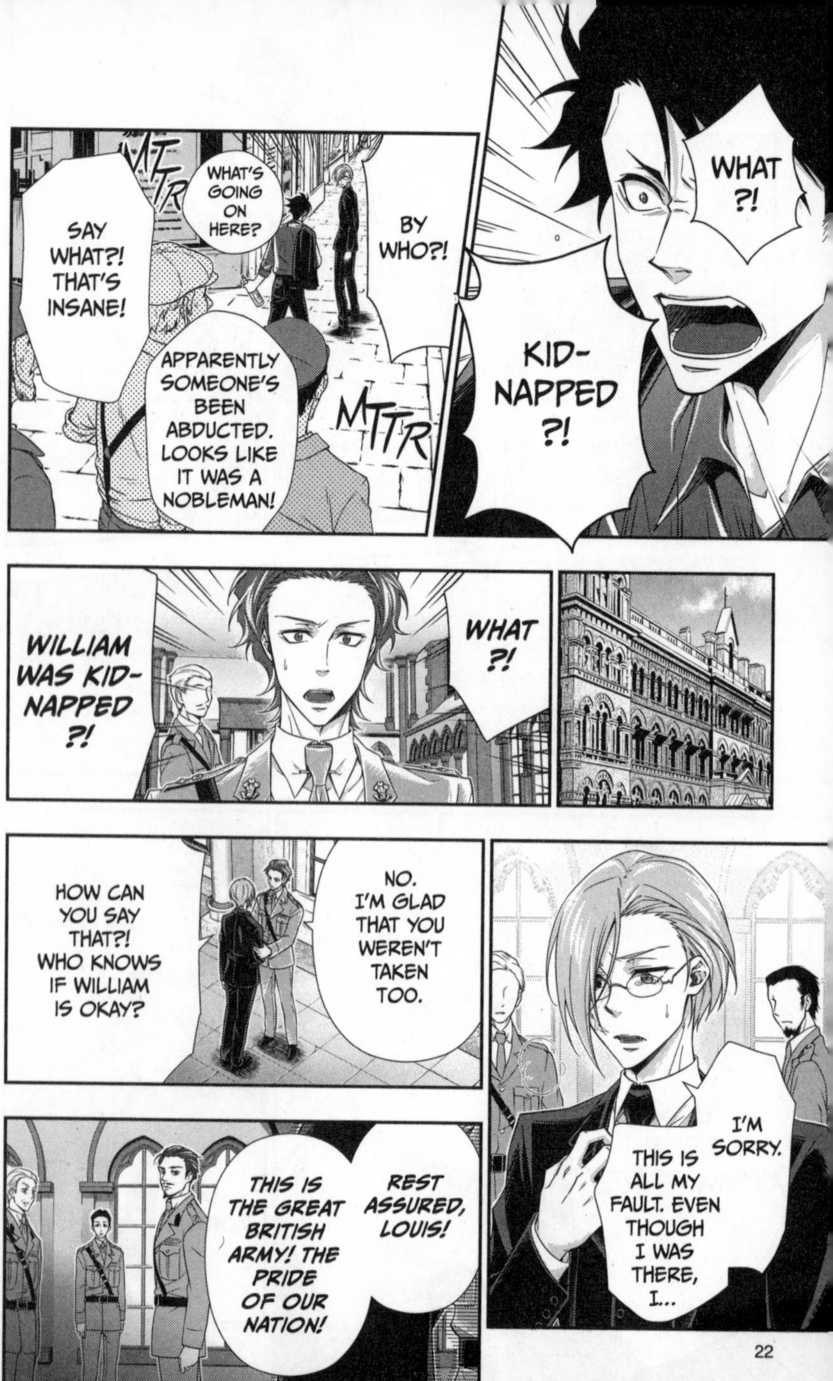
WHAT ?!
KID-NAPPED ?!
BY WHO?!
WHAT'S GOING ON HERE?
MTTR
SAY WHAT?! THAT'S INSANE!
APPARENTLY SOMEONE'S BEEN ABDUCTED. LOOKS LIKE IT WAS A NOBLEMAN!
MTTR
WHAT ?!
WILLIAM WAS KID-NAPPED ?!
I'M SORRY.
THIS IS ALL MY FAULT. EVEN THOUGH I WAS THERE, I...
NO. I'M GLAD THAT YOU WEREN'T TAKEN TOO.
HOW CAN YOU SAY THAT?! WHO KNOWS IF WILLIAM IS OKAY?
REST ASSURED, LOUIS!
THIS IS THE GREAT BRITISH ARMY! THE PRIDE OF OUR NATION!

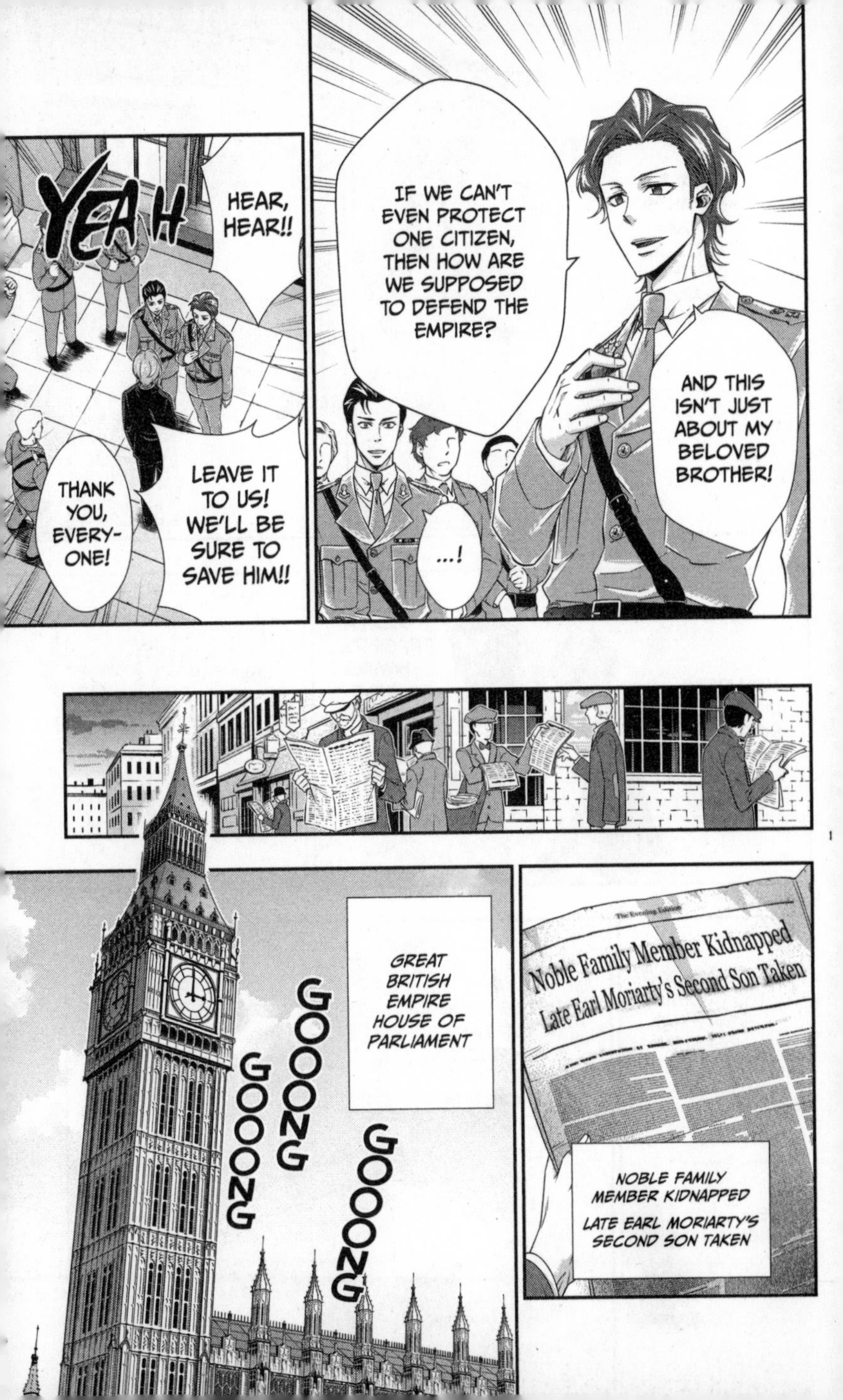
IF WE CAN'T EVEN PROTECT ONE CITIZEN, THEN HOW ARE WE SUPPOSED TO DEFEND THE EMPIRE?
AND THIS ISN'T JUST ABOUT MY BELOVED BROTHER!
...!
HEAR, HEAR!!
YEAH
LEAVE IT TO US! WE'LL BE SURE TO SAVE HIM!!
THANK YOU, EVERY-ONE!
The Evening Edition
Noble Family Member Kidnapped
Late Earl Moriarty's Second Son Taken
NOBLE FAMILY MEMBER KIDNAPPED
LATE EARL MORIARTY'S SECOND SON TAKEN
GREAT BRITISH EMPIRE HOUSE OF PARLIAMENT
GOOOONG
GOOOONG
GOOOONG

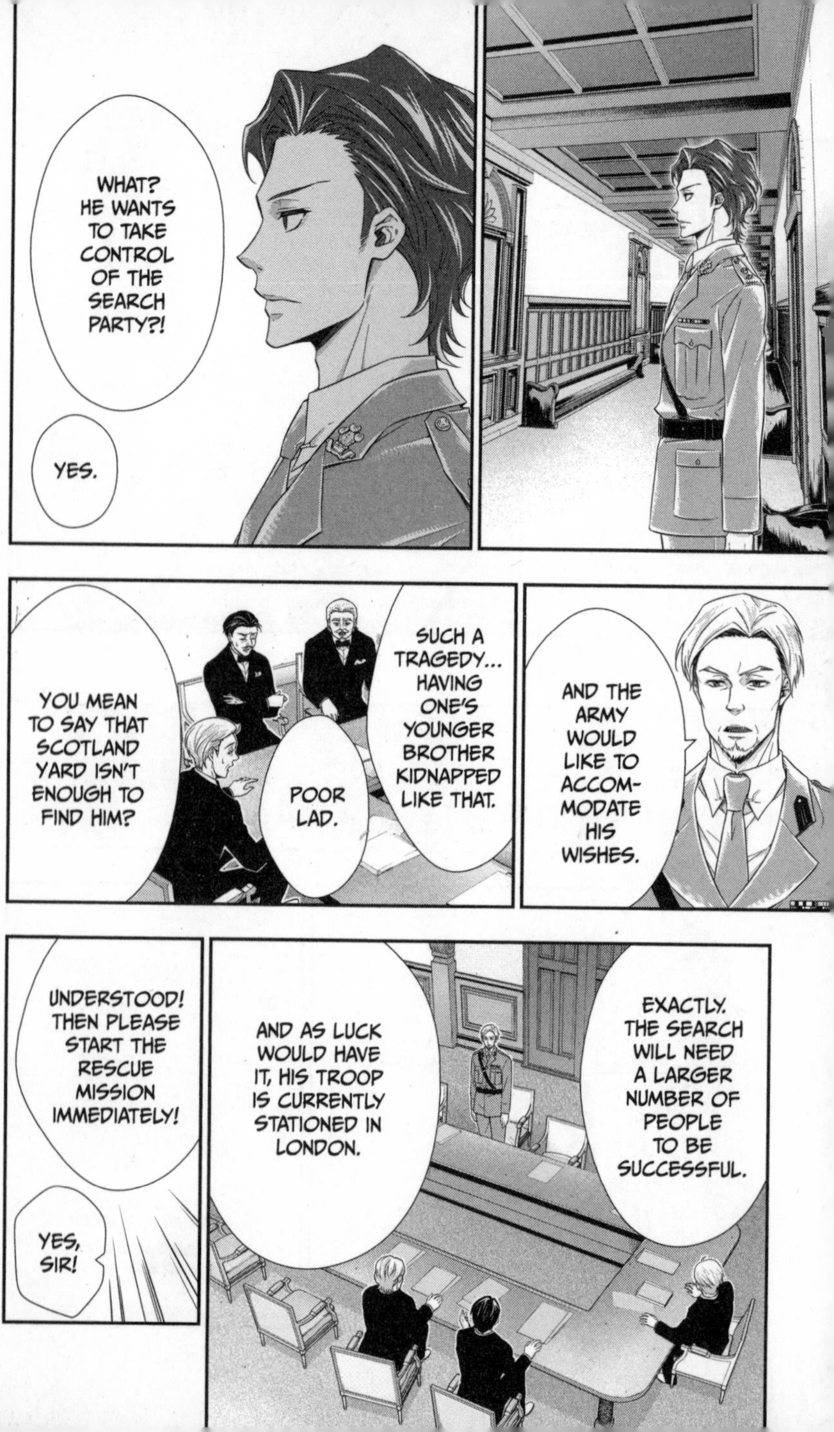

WHAT? HE WANTS TO TAKE CONTROL OF THE SEARCH PARTY?!
YES.
AND THE ARMY WOULD LIKE TO ACCOM-MODATE HIS WISHES.
SUCH A TRAGEDY... HAVING ONE'S YOUNGER BROTHER KIDNAPPED LIKE THAT.
POOR LAD.
YOU MEAN TO SAY THAT SCOTLAND YARD ISN'T ENOUGH TO FIND HIM?
EXACTLY. THE SEARCH WILL NEED A LARGER NUMBER OF PEOPLE TO BE SUCCESSFUL.
AND AS LUCK WOULD HAVE IT, HIS TROOP IS CURRENTLY STATIONED IN LONDON.
UNDERSTOOD! THEN PLEASE START THE RESCUE MISSION IMMEDIATELY!
YES, SIR!

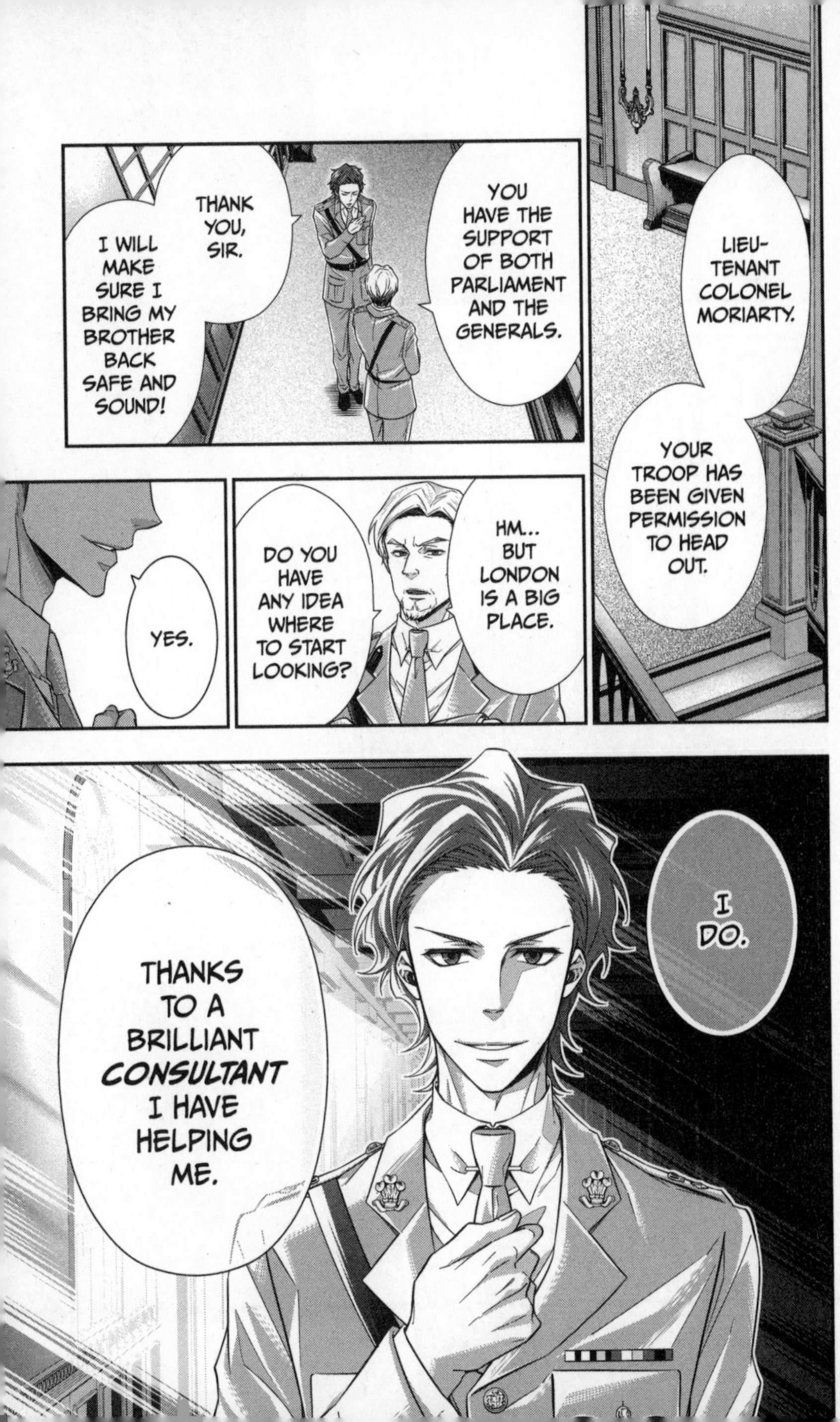
LIEU-TENANT COLONEL MORIARTY.
YOUR TROOP HAS BEEN GIVEN PERMISSION TO HEAD OUT.
YOU HAVE THE SUPPORT OF BOTH PARLIAMENT AND THE GENERALS.
THANK YOU, SIR.
I WILL MAKE SURE I BRING MY BROTHER BACK SAFE AND SOUND!
HM... BUT LONDON IS A BIG PLACE.
DO YOU HAVE ANY IDEA WHERE TO START LOOKING?
YES.
I DO.
THANKS TO A BRILLIANT *CONSULTANT* I HAVE HELPING ME.

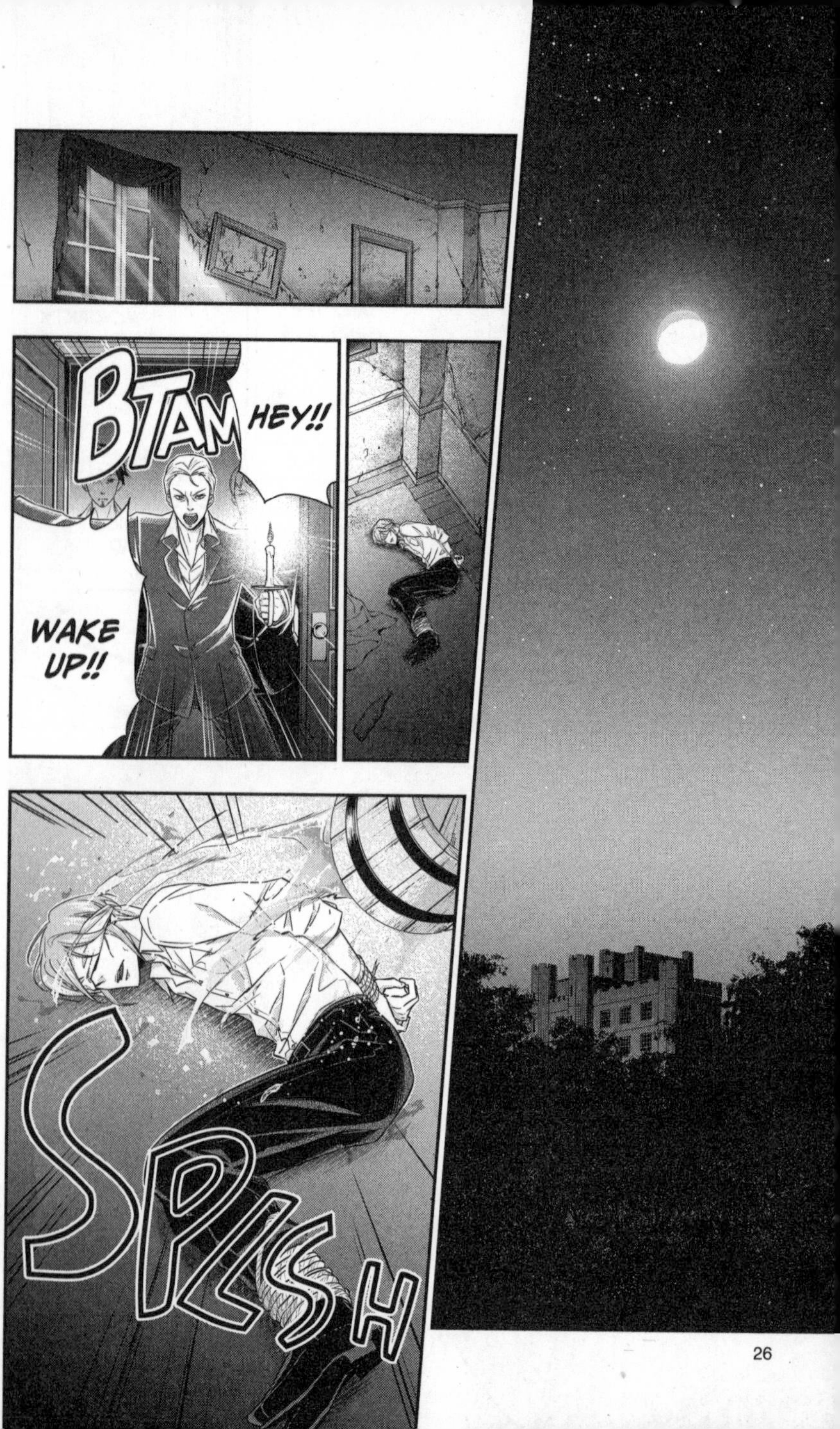
BTAM
HEY!!
WAKE UP!!
SPLSH

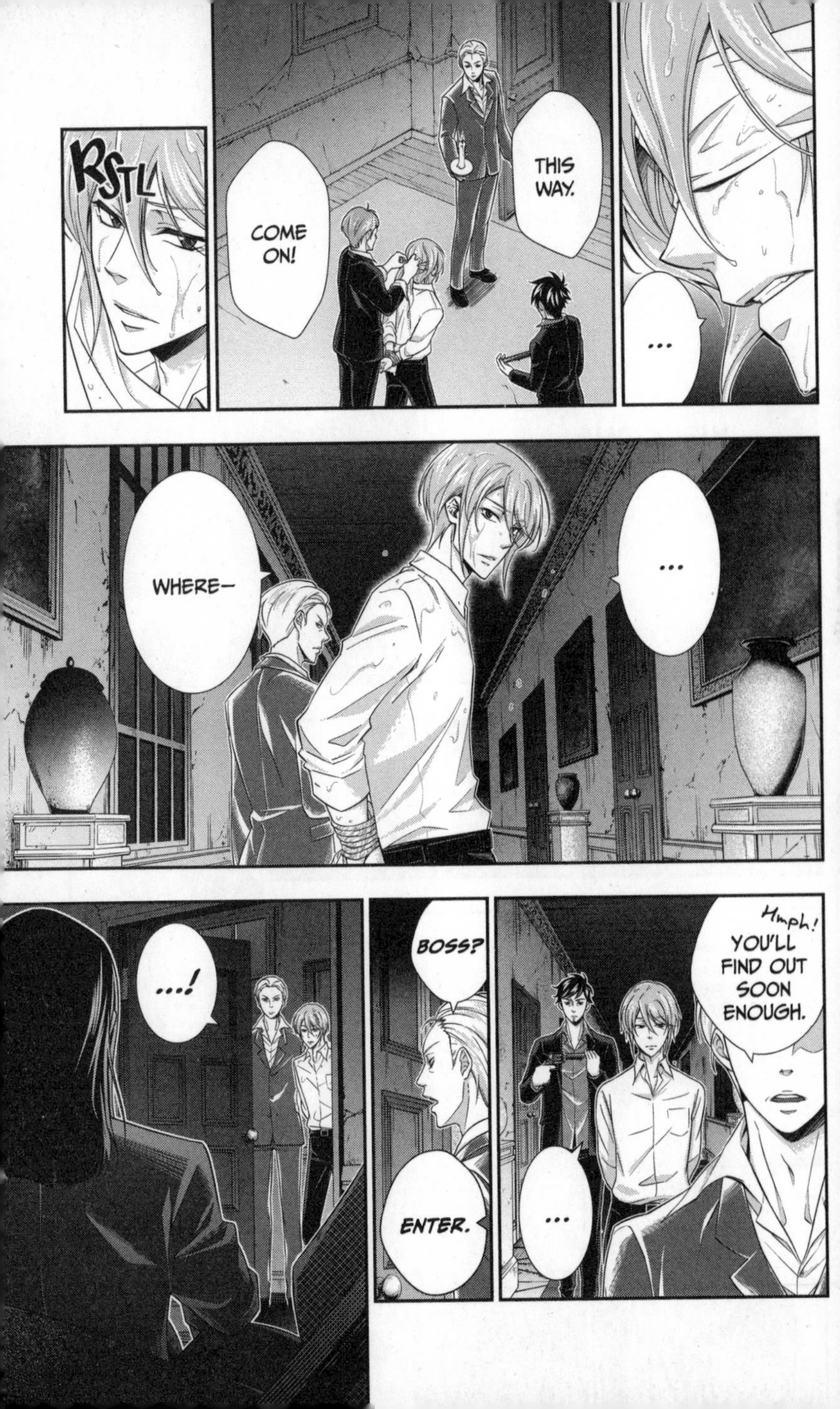
...
THIS WAY.
COME ON!
RSTL
...
WHERE—
Hmph! YOU'LL FIND OUT SOON ENOUGH.
...
BOSS?
ENTER.
...!

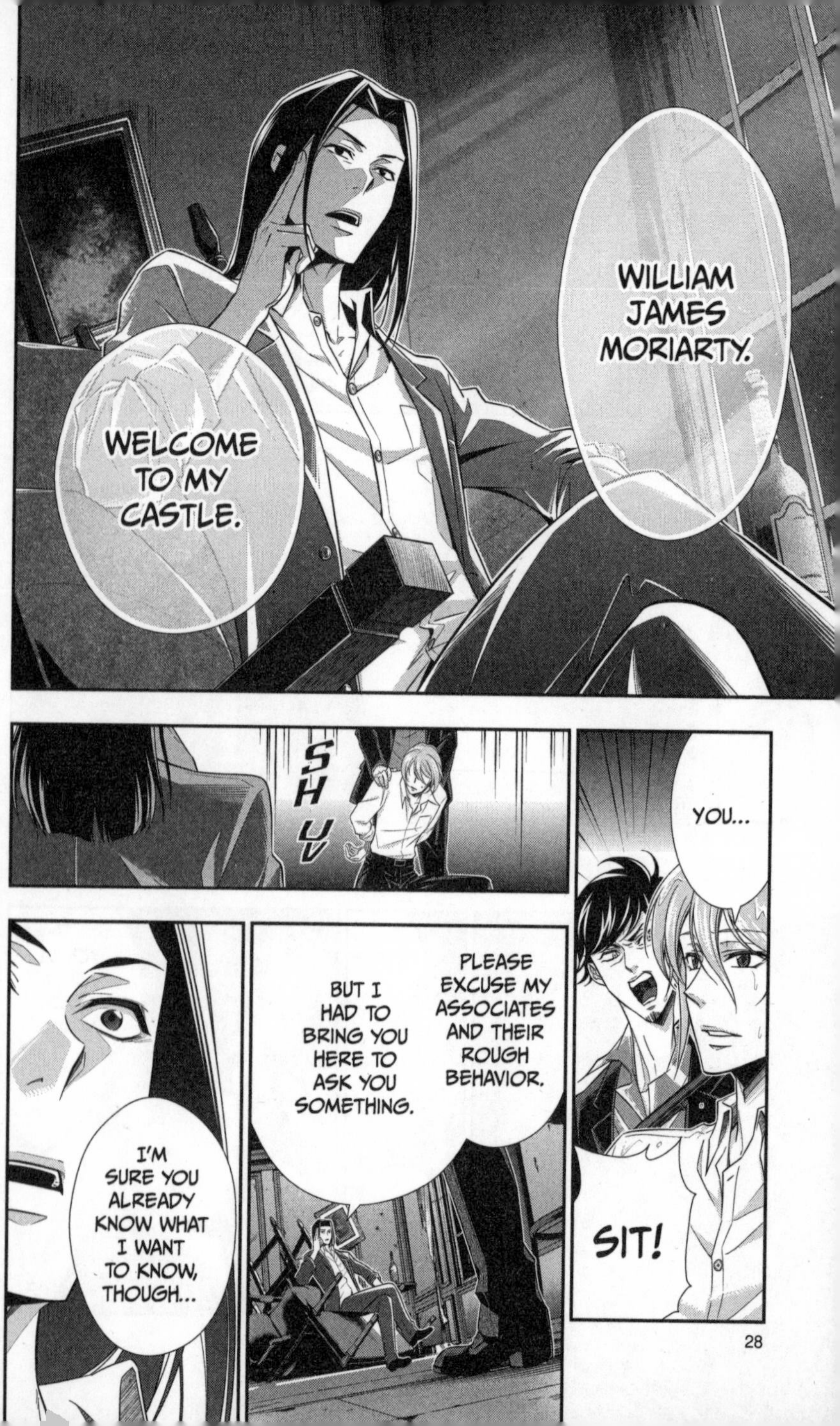
WILLIAM JAMES MORIARTY.
WELCOME TO MY CASTLE.
YOU...
SIT!
SHUV
PLEASE EXCUSE MY ASSOCIATES AND THEIR ROUGH BEHAVIOR.
BUT I HAD TO BRING YOU HERE TO ASK YOU SOMETHING.
I'M SURE YOU ALREADY KNOW WHAT I WANT TO KNOW, THOUGH...

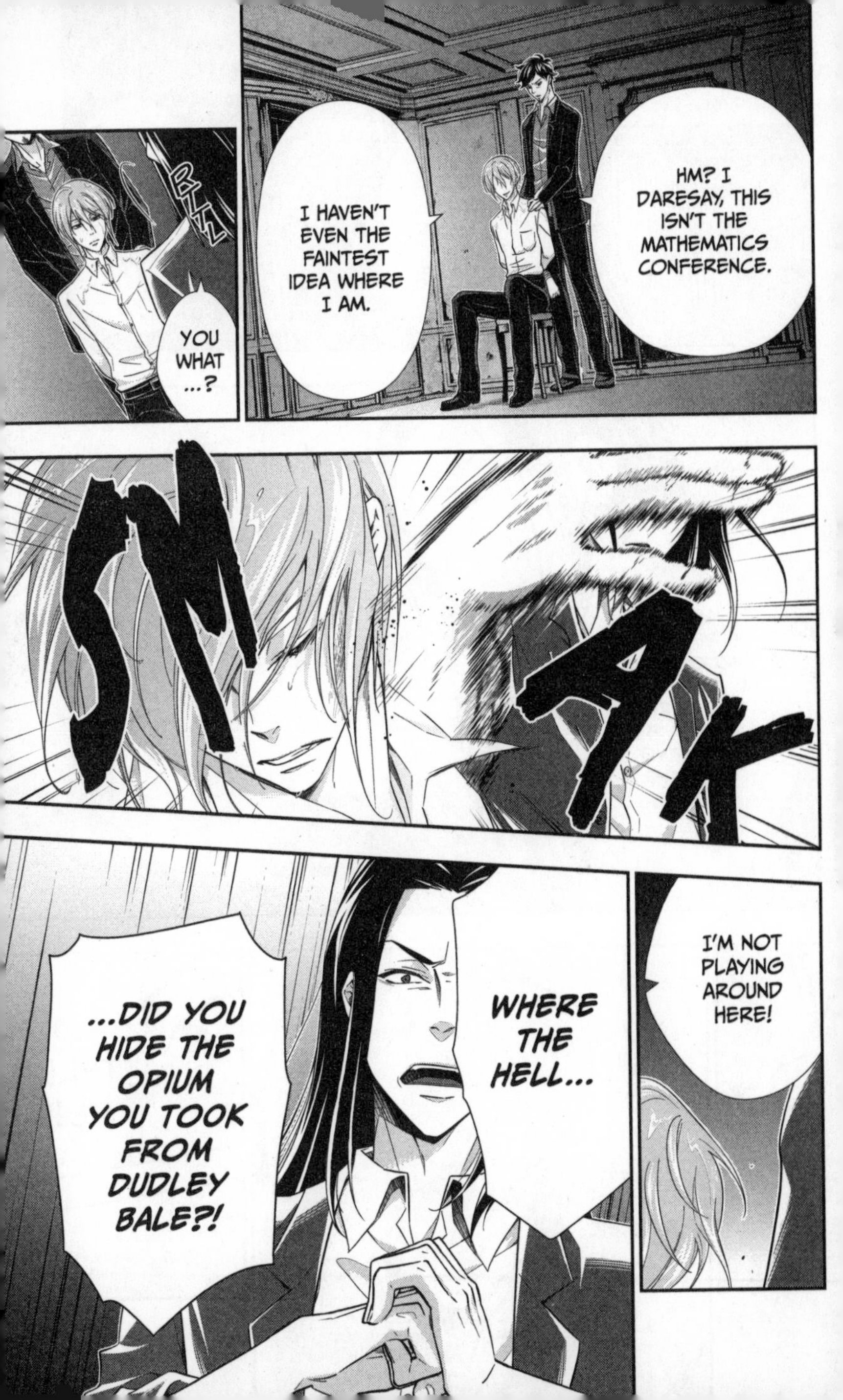
HM? I DARESAY, THIS ISN'T THE MATHEMATICS CONFERENCE.
I HAVEN'T EVEN THE FAINTEST IDEA WHERE I AM.
YOU WHAT ...?
SMAK
I'M NOT PLAYING AROUND HERE!
WHERE THE HELL...
...DID YOU HIDE THE OPIUM YOU TOOK FROM DUDLEY BALE?!

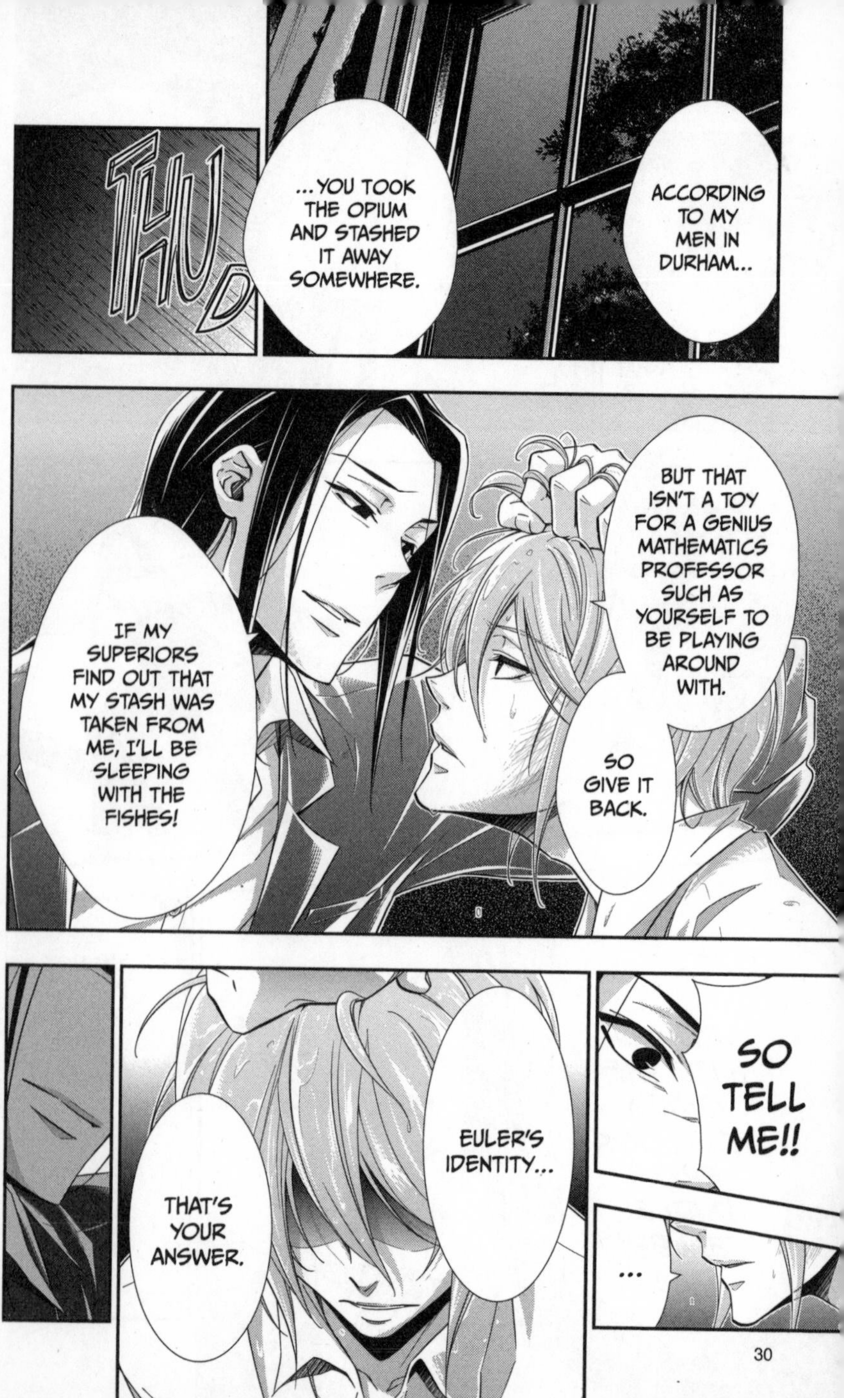
ACCORDING TO MY MEN IN DURHAM...
...YOU TOOK THE OPIUM AND STASHED IT AWAY SOMEWHERE.
THUD
BUT THAT ISN'T A TOY FOR A GENIUS MATHEMATICS PROFESSOR SUCH AS YOURSELF TO BE PLAYING AROUND WITH.
SO GIVE IT BACK.
IF MY SUPERIORS FIND OUT THAT MY STASH WAS TAKEN FROM ME, I'LL BE SLEEPING WITH THE FISHES!
SO TELL ME!!
...
EULER'S IDENTITY...
THAT'S YOUR ANSWER.

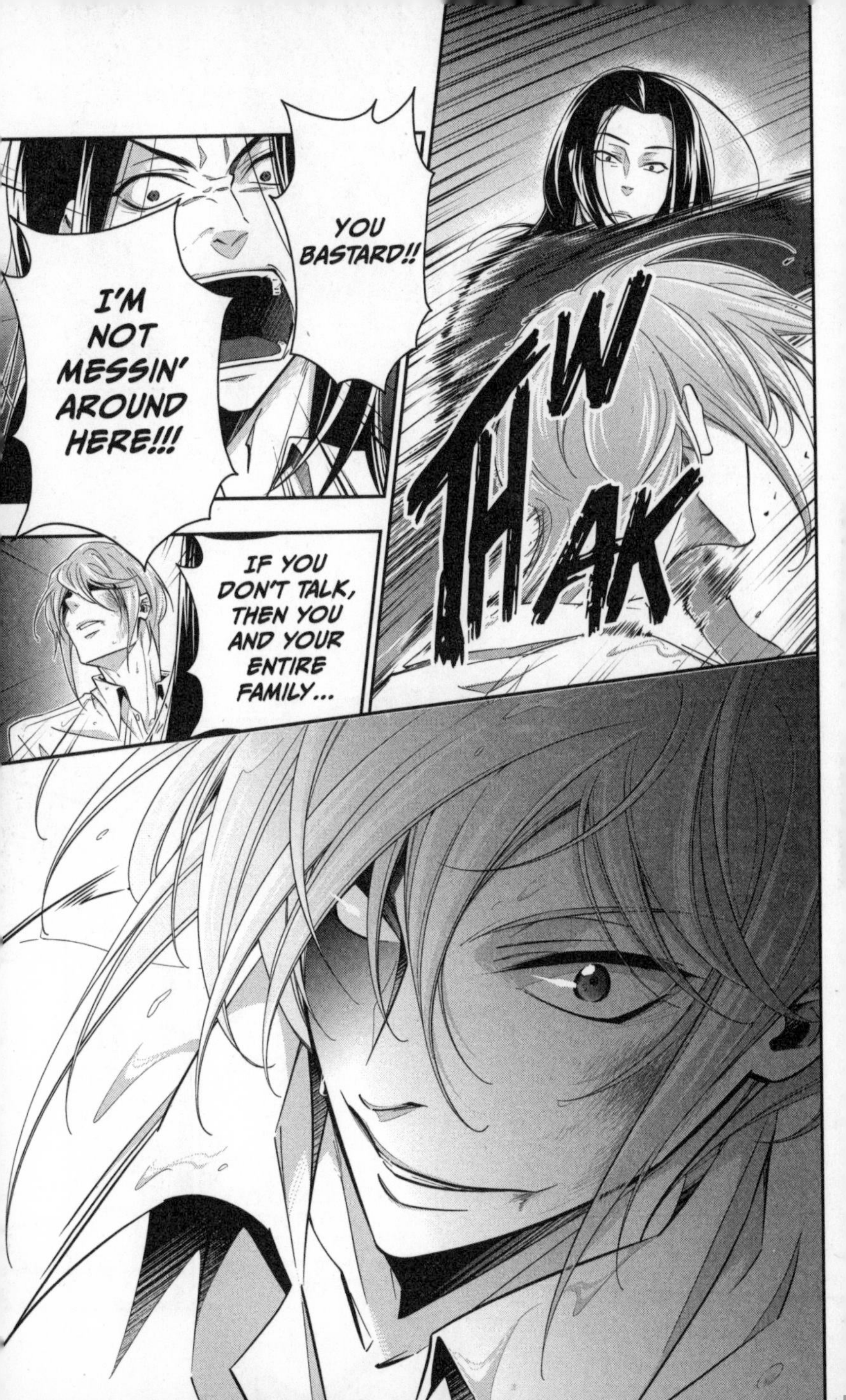
THWAK
YOU BASTARD!!
I'M NOT MESSIN' AROUND HERE!!!
IF YOU DON'T TALK, THEN YOU AND YOUR ENTIRE FAMILY...

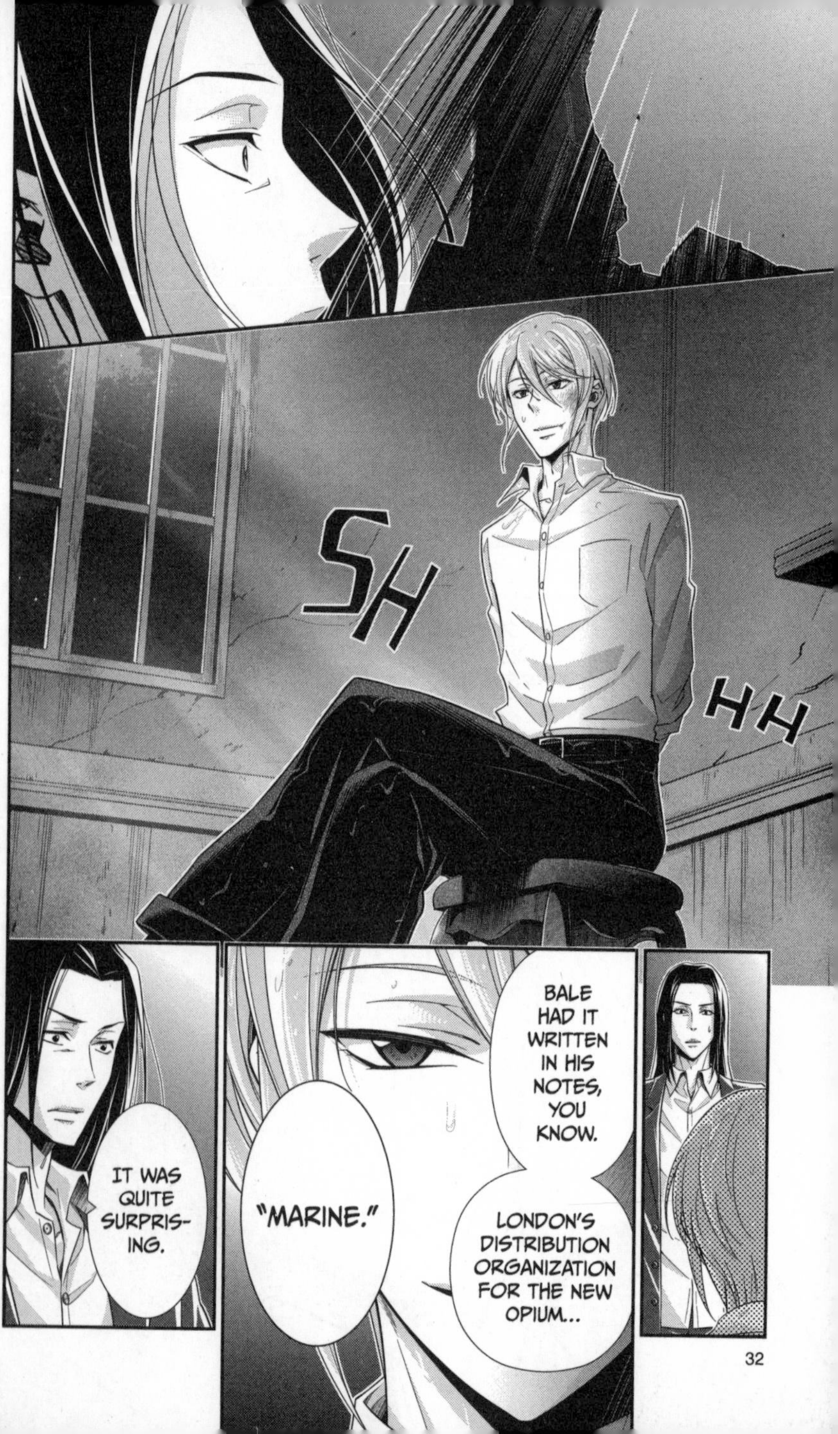
SH HH
BALE HAD IT WRITTEN IN HIS NOTES, YOU KNOW.
LONDON'S DISTRIBUTION ORGANIZATION FOR THE NEW OPIUM...
"MARINE."
IT WAS QUITE SURPRIS-ING.

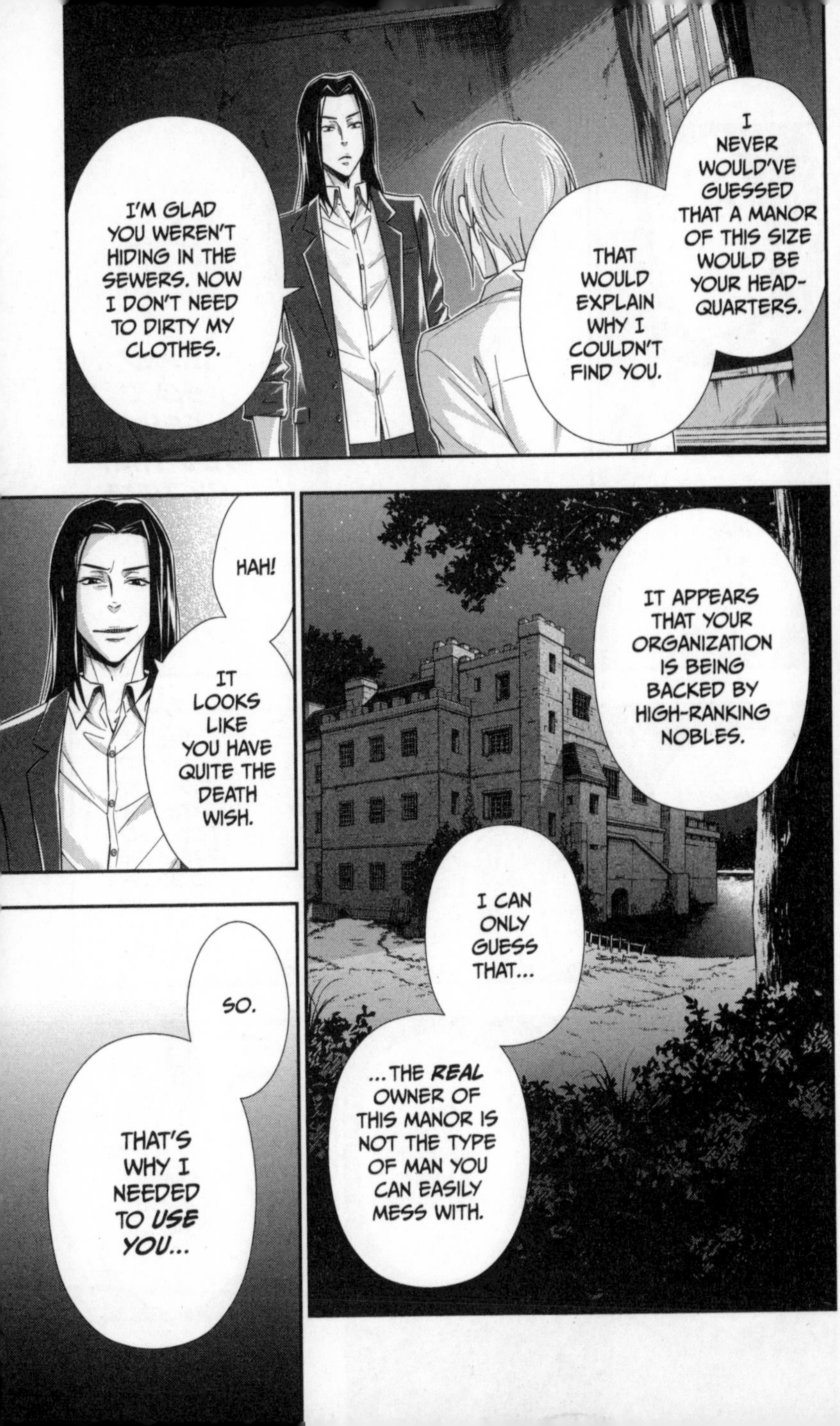
I NEVER WOULD'VE GUESSED THAT A MANOR OF THIS SIZE WOULD BE YOUR HEAD-QUARTERS.
THAT WOULD EXPLAIN WHY I COULDN'T FIND YOU.
I'M GLAD YOU WEREN'T HIDING IN THE SEWERS. NOW I DON'T NEED TO DIRTY MY CLOTHES.
IT APPEARS THAT YOUR ORGANIZATION IS BEING BACKED BY HIGH-RANKING NOBLES.
I CAN ONLY GUESS THAT...
...THE *REAL* OWNER OF THIS MANOR IS NOT THE TYPE OF MAN YOU CAN EASILY MESS WITH.
HAH!
IT LOOKS LIKE YOU HAVE QUITE THE DEATH WISH.
SO.
THAT'S WHY I NEEDED TO *USE YOU*...

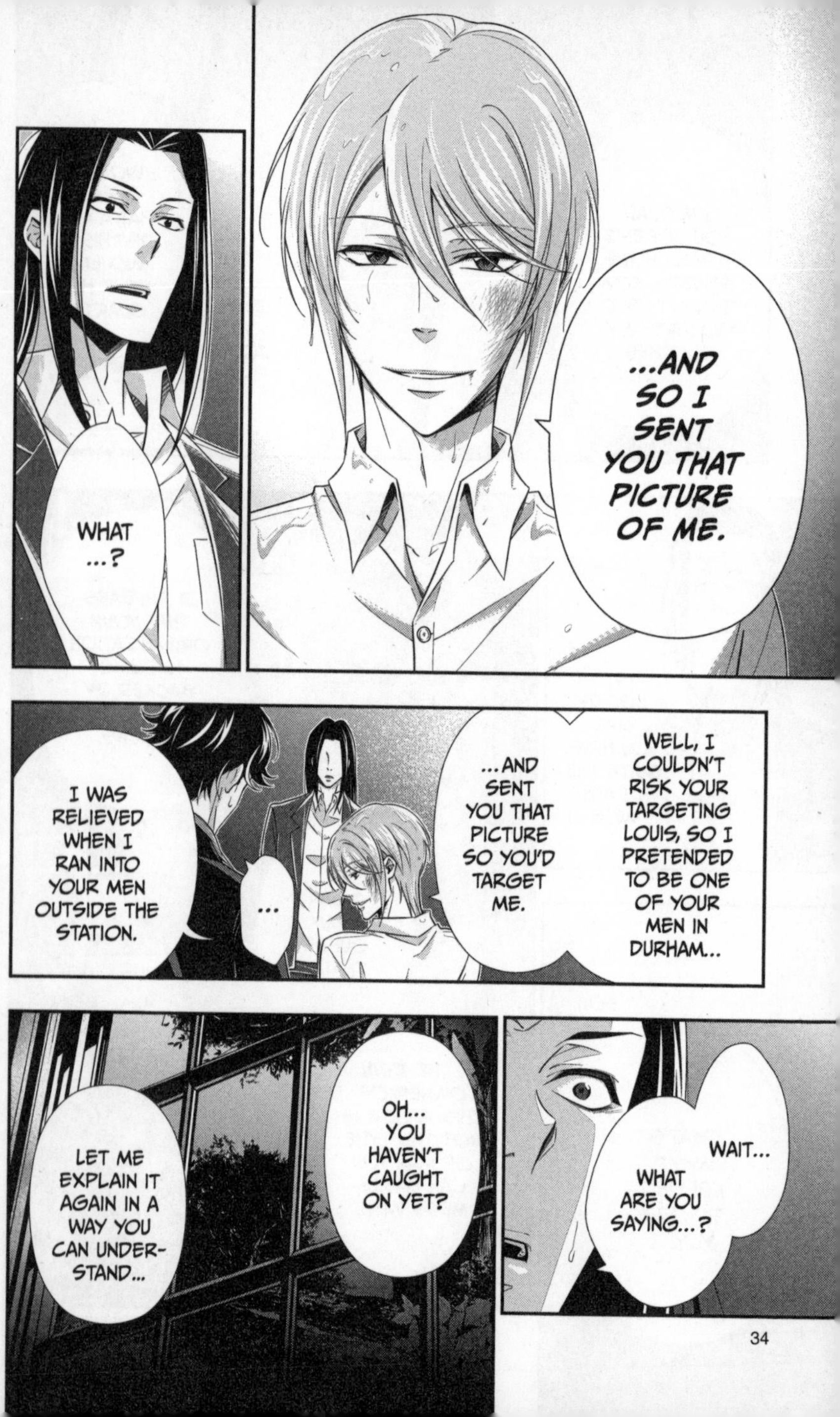
...AND SO I SENT YOU THAT PICTURE OF ME.
WHAT ...?
WELL, I COULDN'T RISK YOUR TARGETING LOUIS, SO I PRETENDED TO BE ONE OF YOUR MEN IN DURHAM...
...AND SENT YOU THAT PICTURE SO YOU'D TARGET ME.
...
I WAS RELIEVED WHEN I RAN INTO YOUR MEN OUTSIDE THE STATION.
WAIT...
WHAT ARE YOU SAYING...?
OH... YOU HAVEN'T CAUGHT ON YET?
LET ME EXPLAIN IT AGAIN IN A WAY YOU CAN UNDER-STAND...

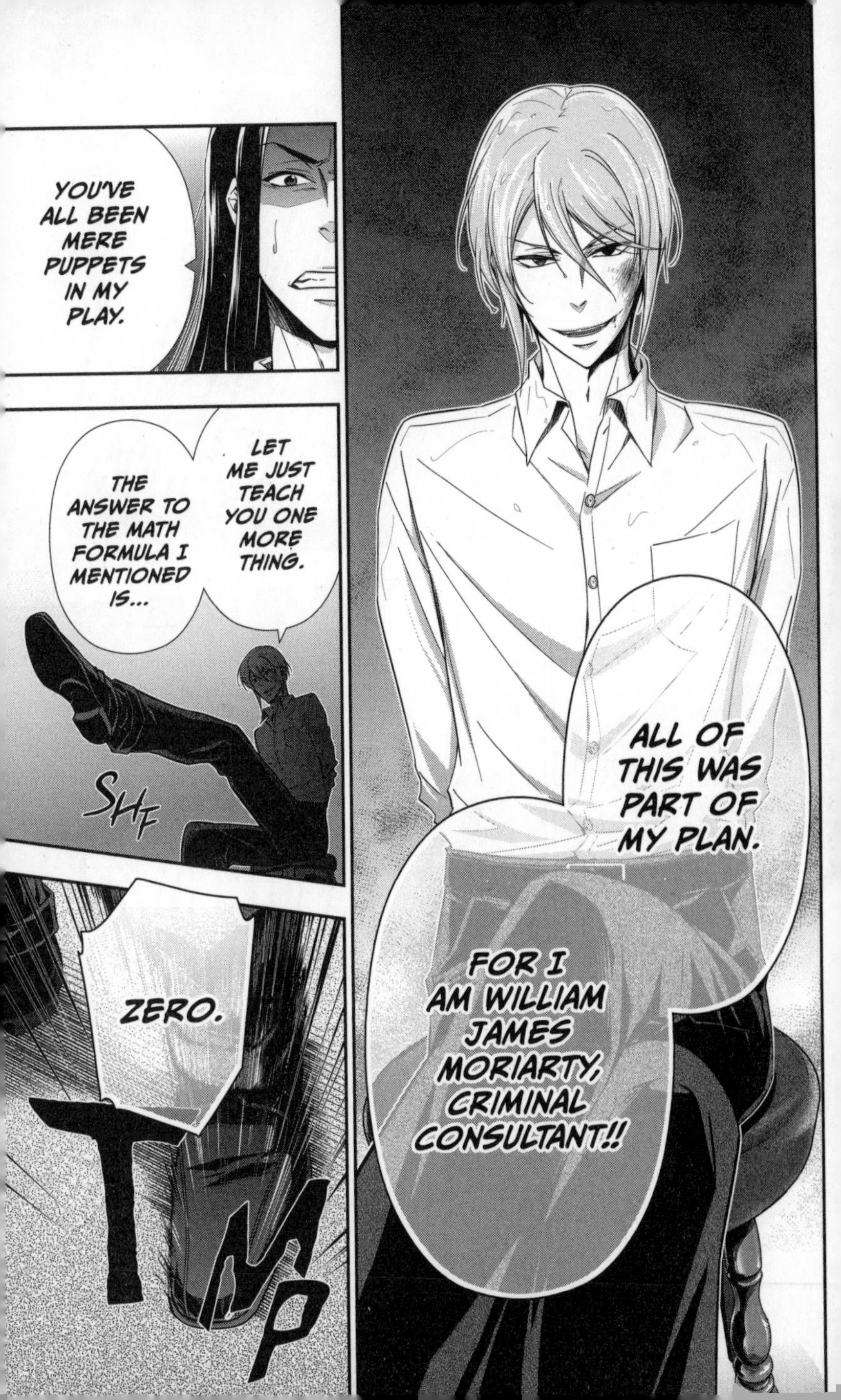
ALL OF THIS WAS PART OF MY PLAN.
FOR I AM WILLIAM JAMES MORIARTY, CRIMINAL CONSULTANT!!
YOU'VE ALL BEEN MERE PUPPETS IN MY PLAY.
LET ME JUST TEACH YOU ONE MORE THING.
THE ANSWER TO THE MATH FORMULA I MENTIONED IS...
SHF
ZERO.
TMP

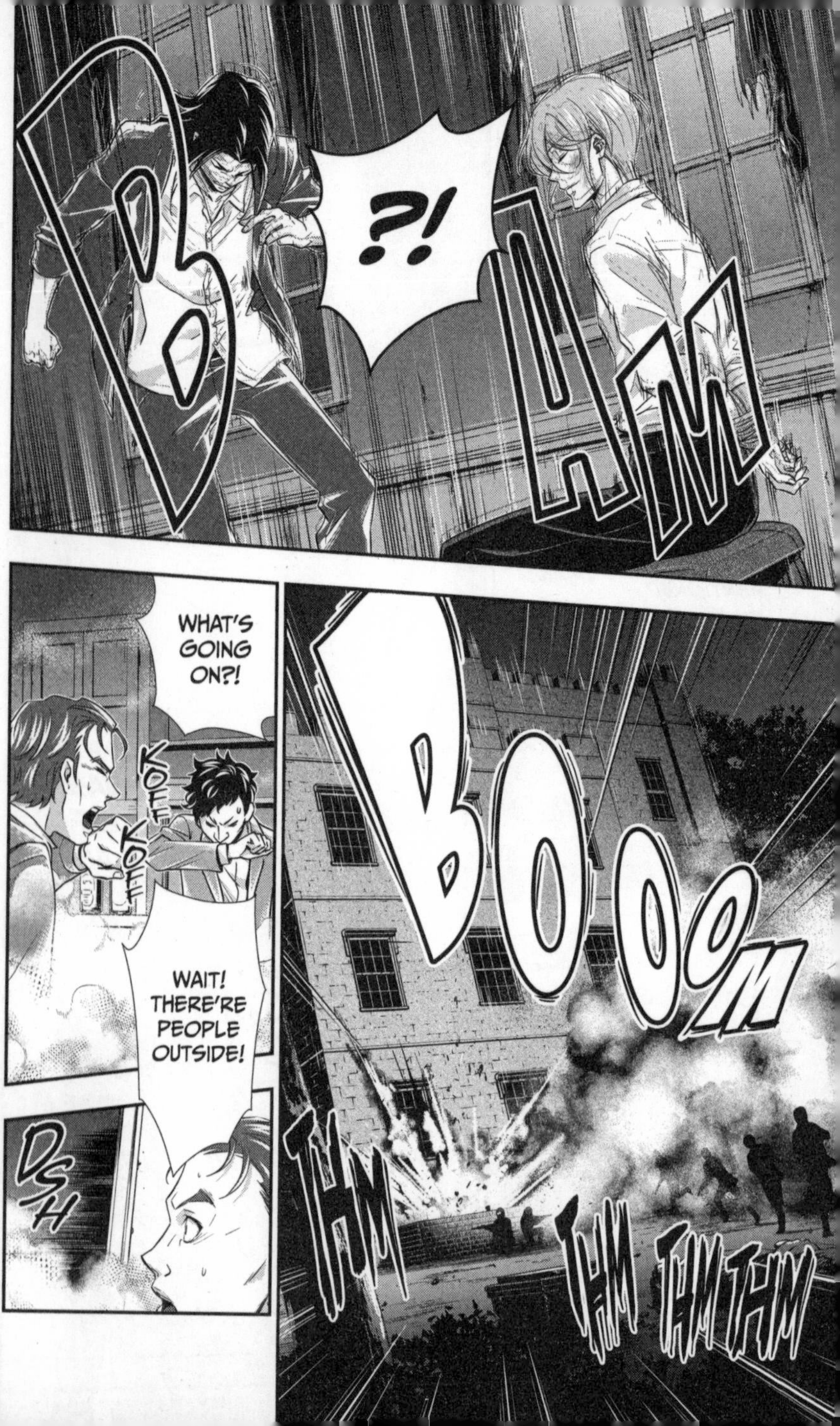
?!
BOOOM
THM THM THM THM
WHAT'S GOING ON?!
KOFF KOFF
WAIT! THERE'RE PEOPLE OUTSIDE!
DSH

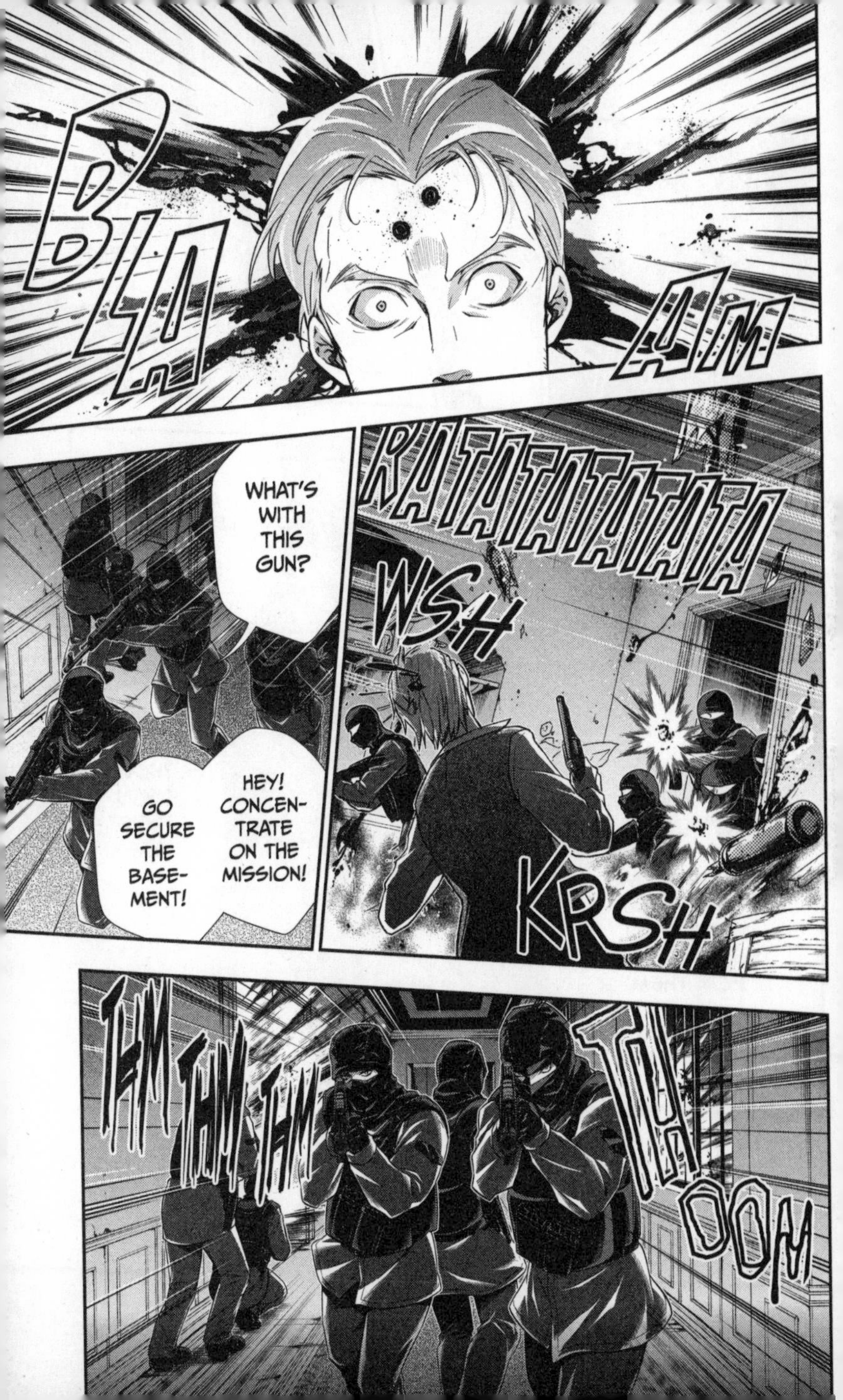
BLAAM
RATATATATATATA
WSH
KRSH
WHAT'S WITH THIS GUN?
HEY! CONCENTRATE ON THE MISSION!
GO SECURE THE BASEMENT!
THOOM
THM THM THM

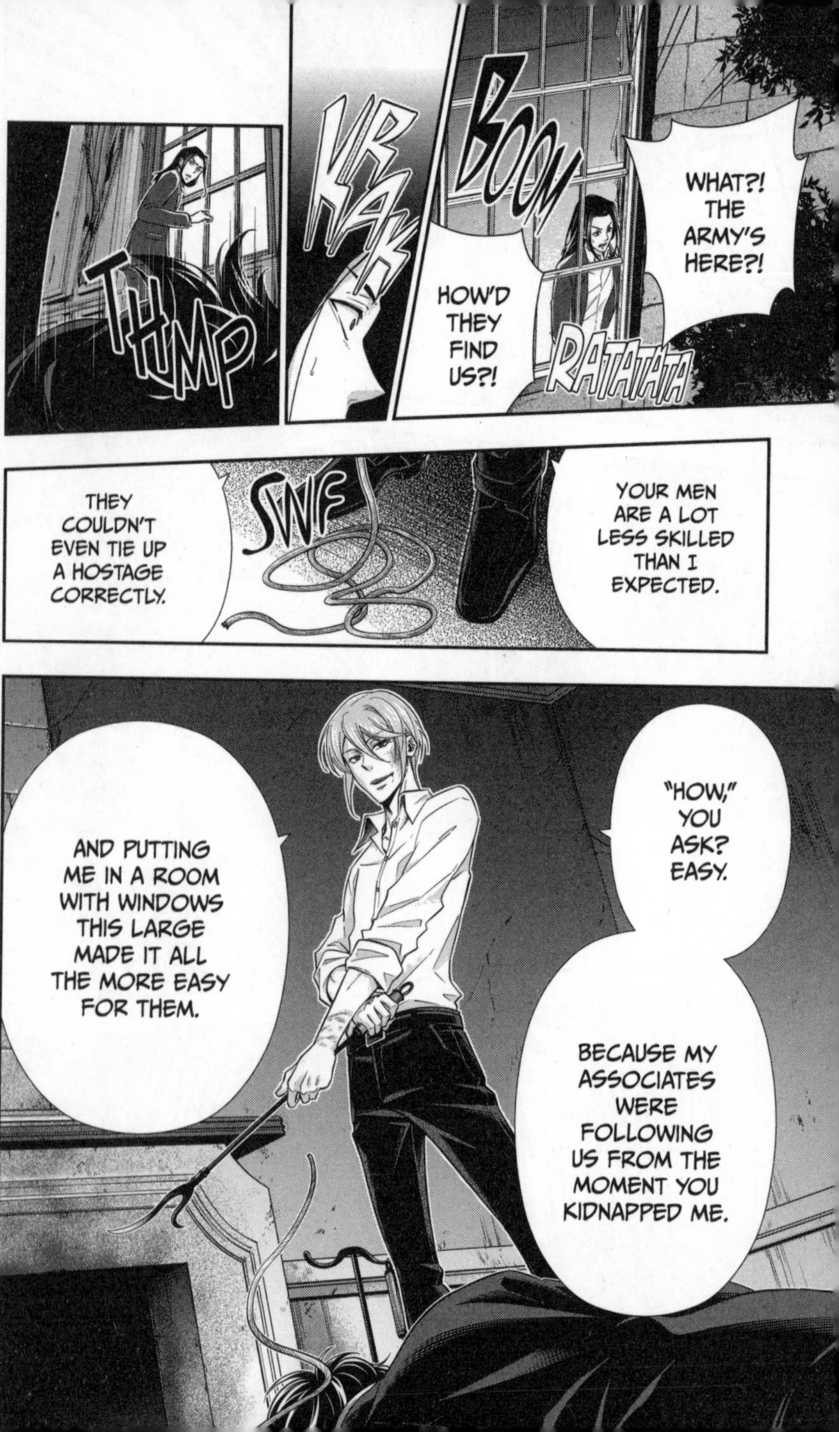
BOOM
WHAT?! THE ARMY'S HERE?!
HOW'D THEY FIND US?!
RATATATA
KRAK
THUMP
YOUR MEN ARE A LOT LESS SKILLED THAN I EXPECTED.
SWF
THEY COULDN'T EVEN TIE UP A HOSTAGE CORRECTLY.
"HOW," YOU ASK? EASY.
BECAUSE MY ASSOCIATES WERE FOLLOWING US FROM THE MOMENT YOU KIDNAPPED ME.
AND PUTTING ME IN A ROOM WITH WINDOWS THIS LARGE MADE IT ALL THE MORE EASY FOR THEM.

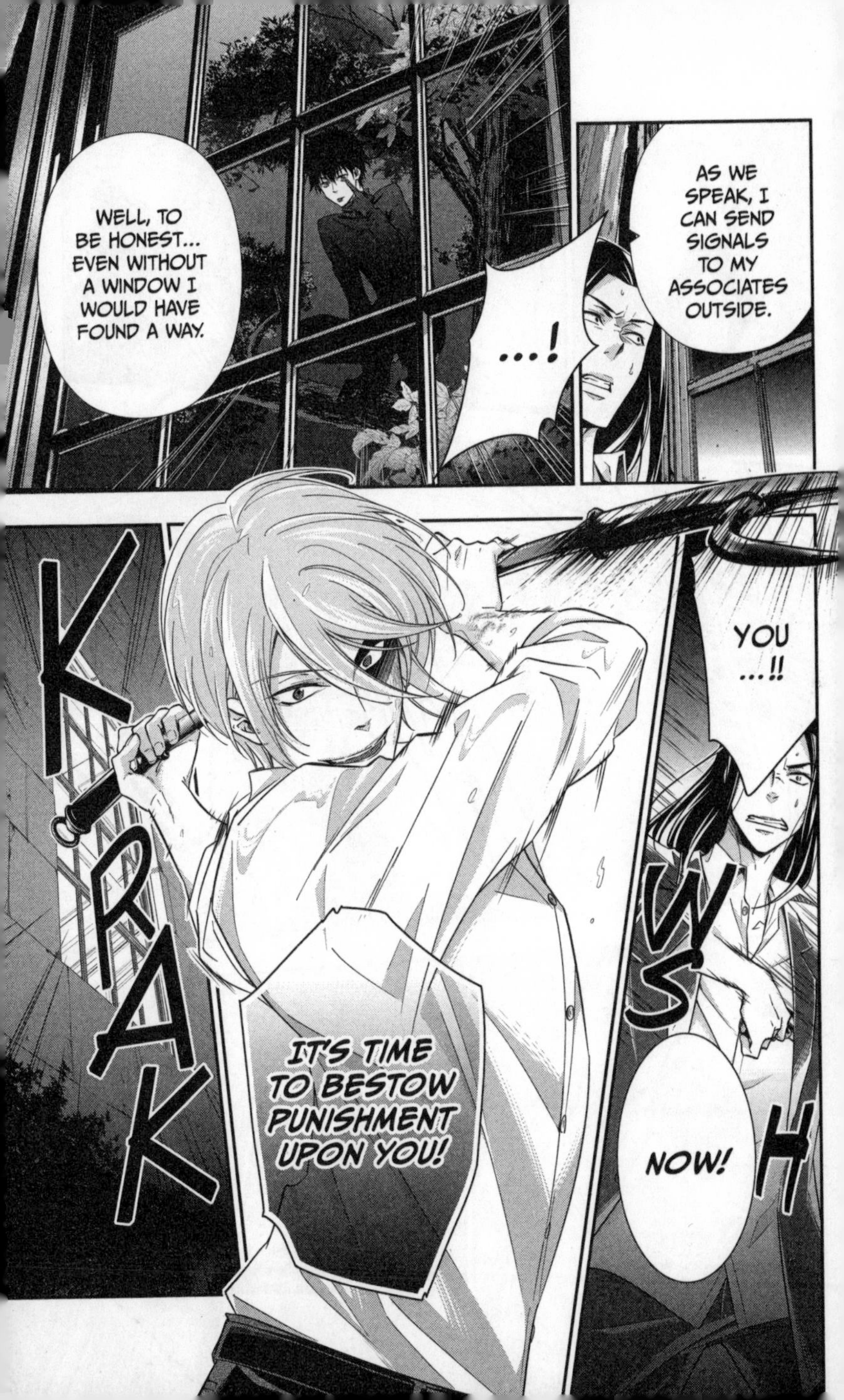
AS WE SPEAK, I CAN SEND SIGNALS TO MY ASSOCIATES OUTSIDE.
...!
WELL, TO BE HONEST... EVEN WITHOUT A WINDOW I WOULD HAVE FOUND A WAY.
YOU ...!!
WSH
NOW!
KRAK
IT'S TIME TO BESTOW PUNISHMENT UPON YOU!

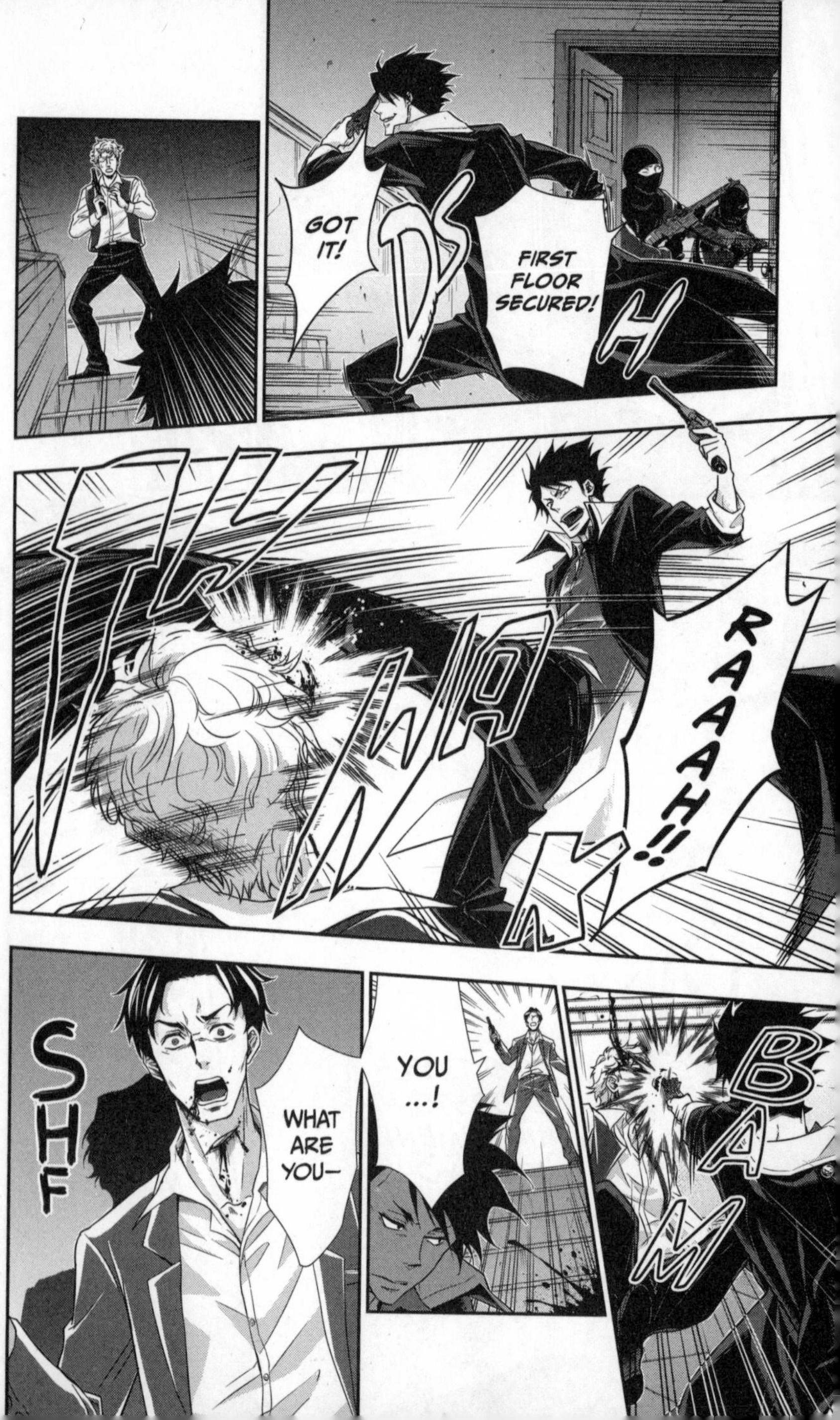
FIRST FLOOR SECURED!
DSH
GOT IT!
RAAAAH!!
WHAM
BAM
YOU ...!
WHAT ARE YOU—
SHF

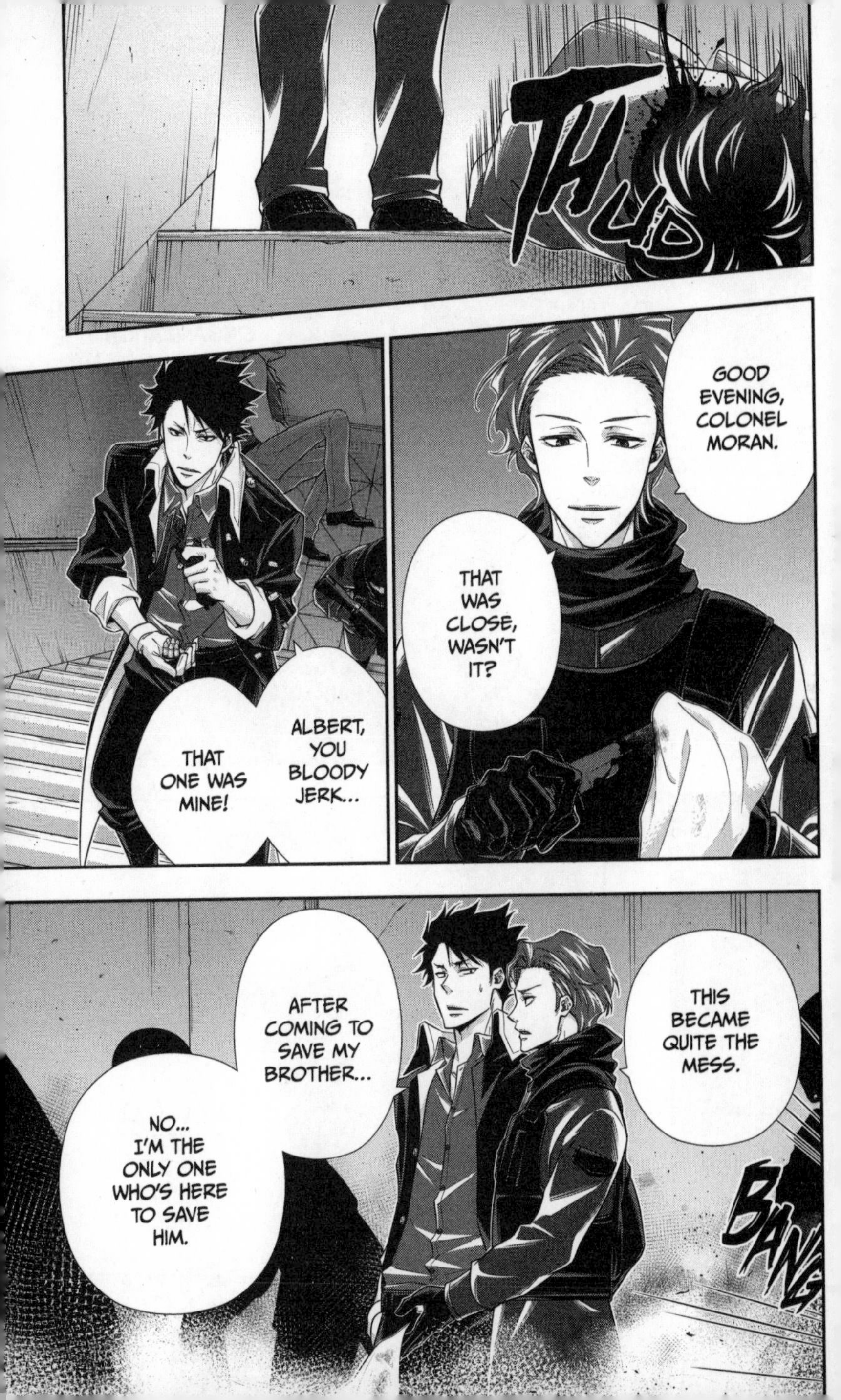
THUD
GOOD EVENING, COLONEL MORAN.
THAT WAS CLOSE, WASN'T IT?
ALBERT, YOU BLOODY JERK...
THAT ONE WAS MINE!
THIS BECAME QUITE THE MESS.
BANG
AFTER COMING TO SAVE MY BROTHER...
NO... I'M THE ONLY ONE WHO'S HERE TO SAVE HIM.

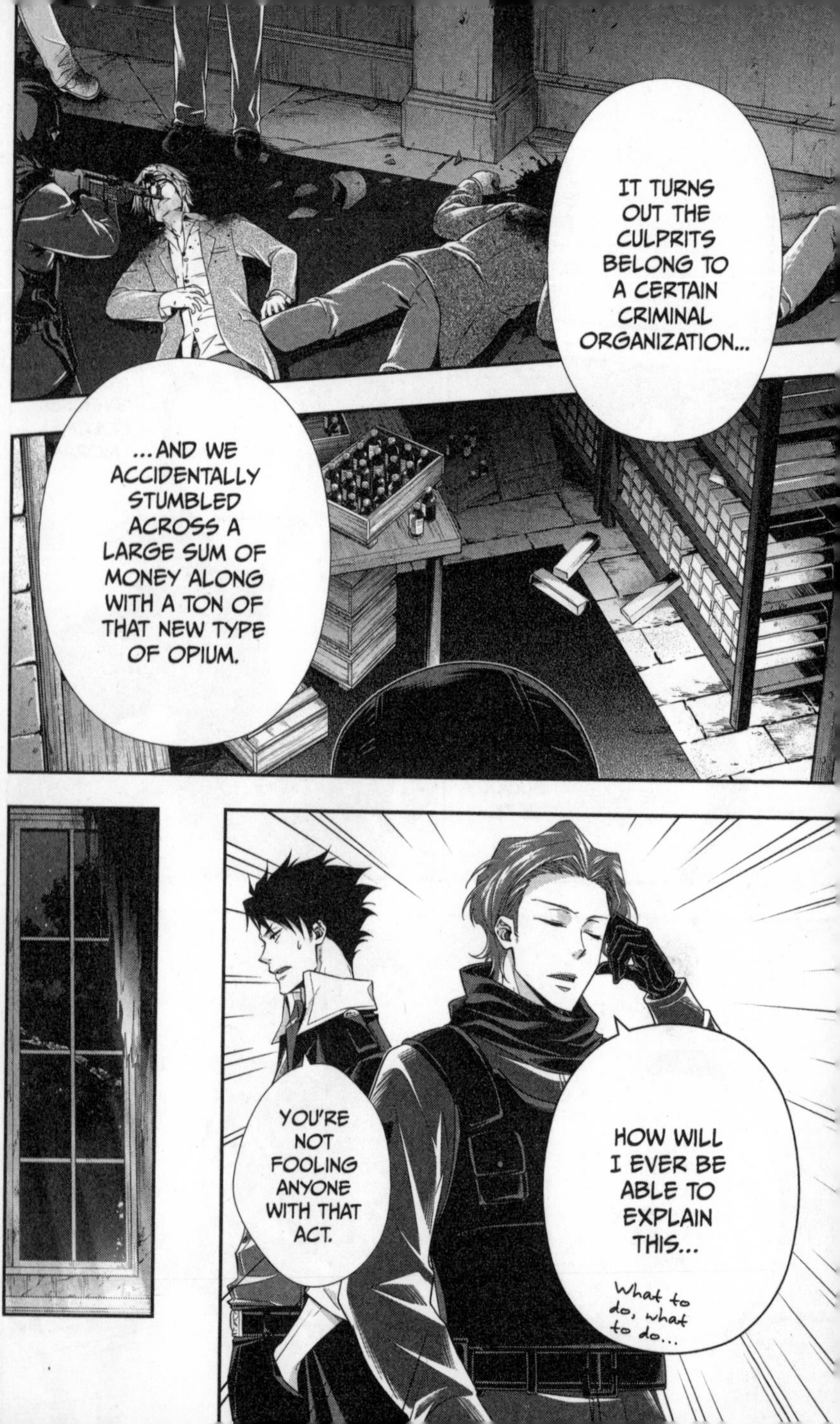
IT TURNS OUT THE CULPRITS BELONG TO A CERTAIN CRIMINAL ORGANIZATION...
...AND WE ACCIDENTALLY STUMBLED ACROSS A LARGE SUM OF MONEY ALONG WITH A TON OF THAT NEW TYPE OF OPIUM.
HOW WILL I EVER BE ABLE TO EXPLAIN THIS...
What to do, what to do...
YOU'RE NOT FOOLING ANYONE WITH THAT ACT.

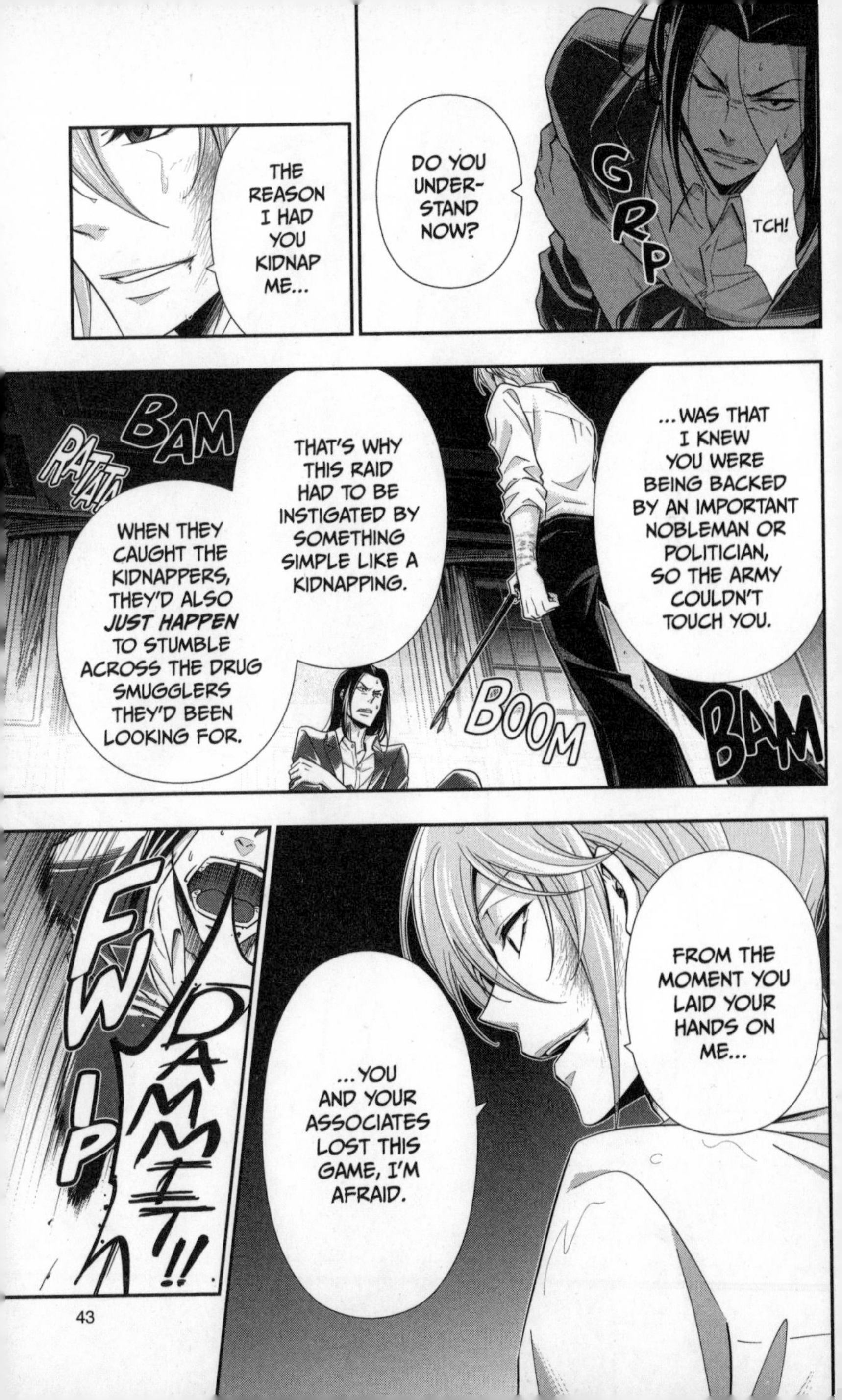
GRP
TCH!
DO YOU UNDER-STAND NOW?
THE REASON I HAD YOU KIDNAP ME...
...WAS THAT I KNEW YOU WERE BEING BACKED BY AN IMPORTANT NOBLEMAN OR POLITICIAN, SO THE ARMY COULDN'T TOUCH YOU.
BAM
BOOM
THAT'S WHY THIS RAID HAD TO BE INSTIGATED BY SOMETHING SIMPLE LIKE A KIDNAPPING.
WHEN THEY CAUGHT THE KIDNAPPERS, THEY'D ALSO *JUST HAPPEN* TO STUMBLE ACROSS THE DRUG SMUGGLERS THEY'D BEEN LOOKING FOR.
BAM
RATATA
FROM THE MOMENT YOU LAID YOUR HANDS ON ME...
...YOU AND YOUR ASSOCIATES LOST THIS GAME, I'M AFRAID.
FWIP
DAMMIT!!

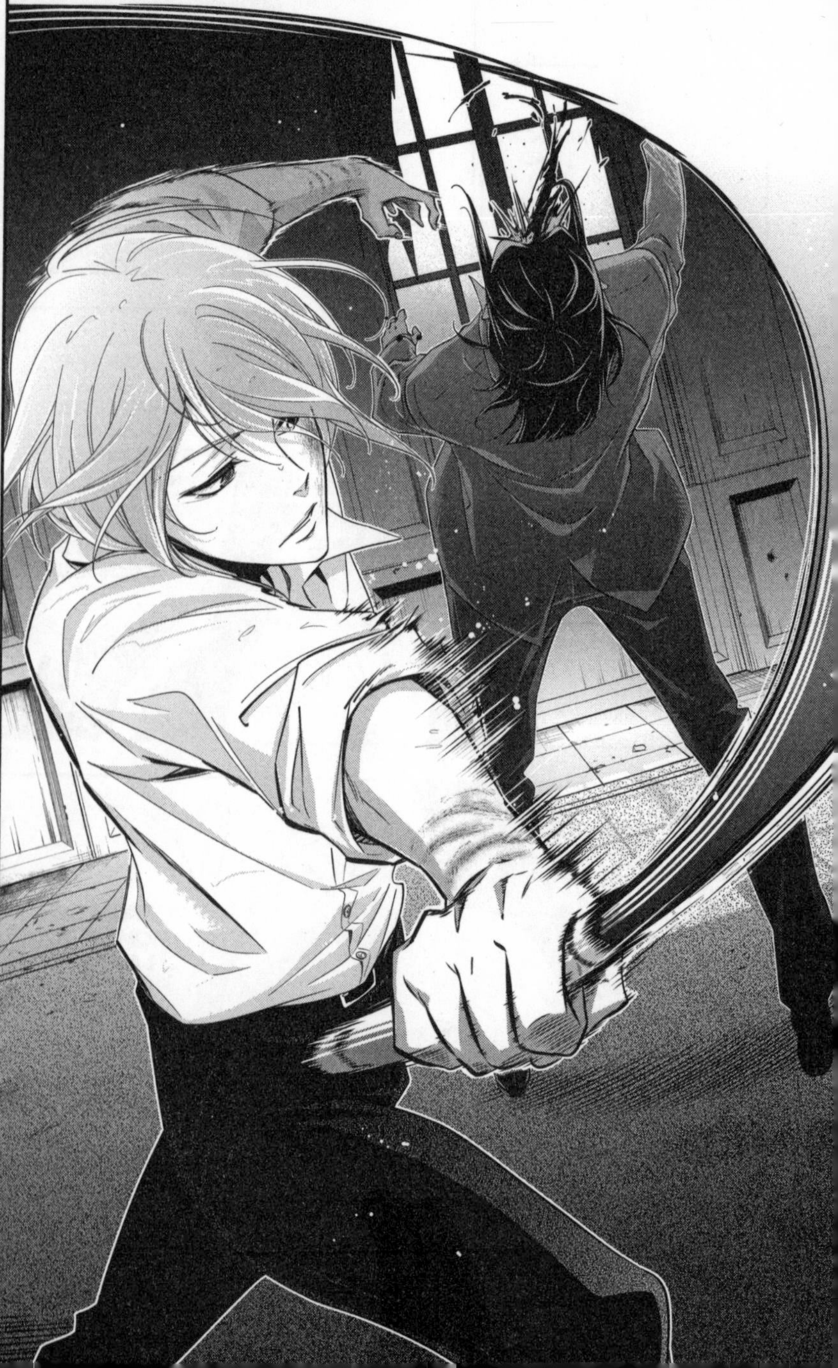

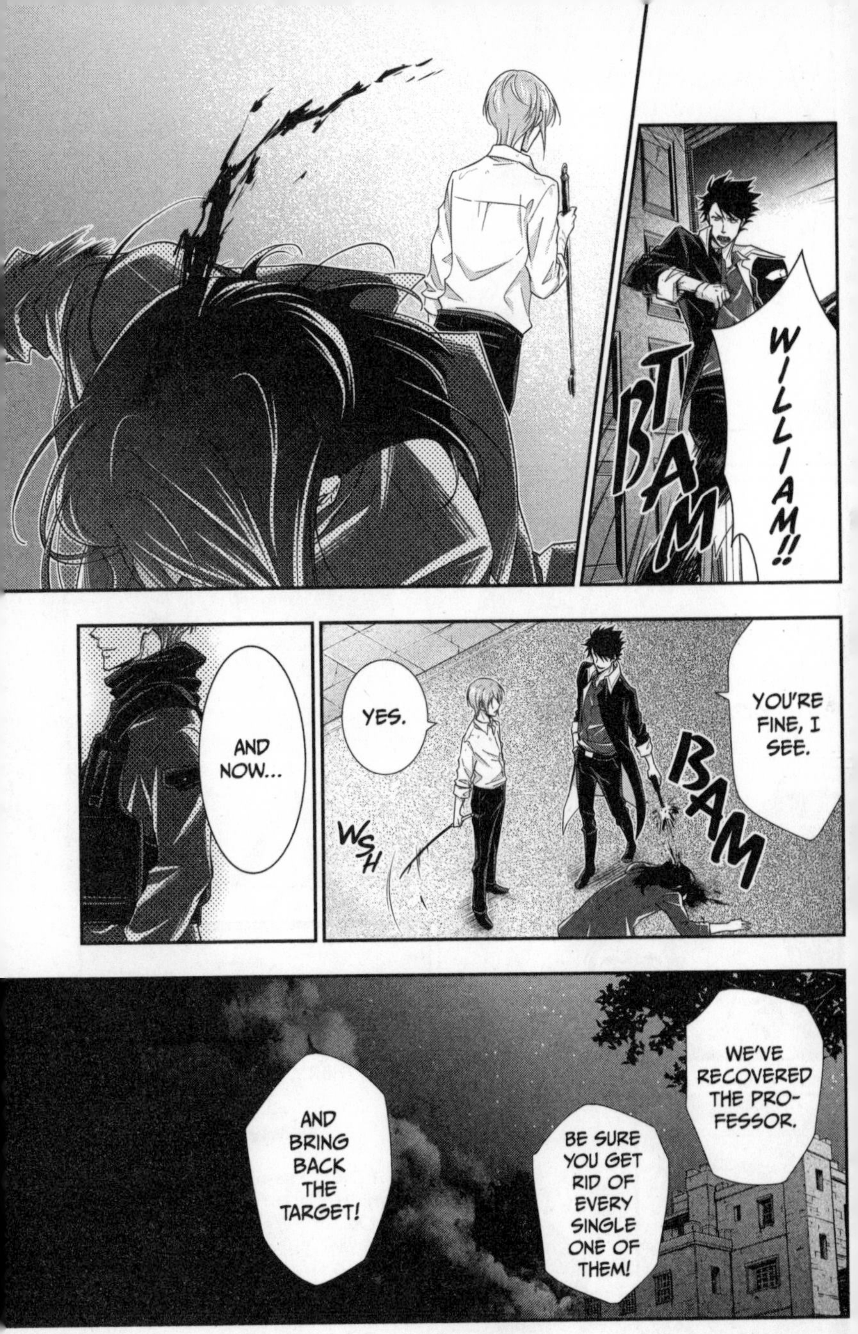
BTBAM
WILLIAM!!
YOU'RE FINE, I SEE.
BAM
YES.
WSH
AND NOW...
WE'VE RECOVERED THE PRO-FESSOR.
BE SURE YOU GET RID OF EVERY SINGLE ONE OF THEM!
AND BRING BACK THE TARGET!

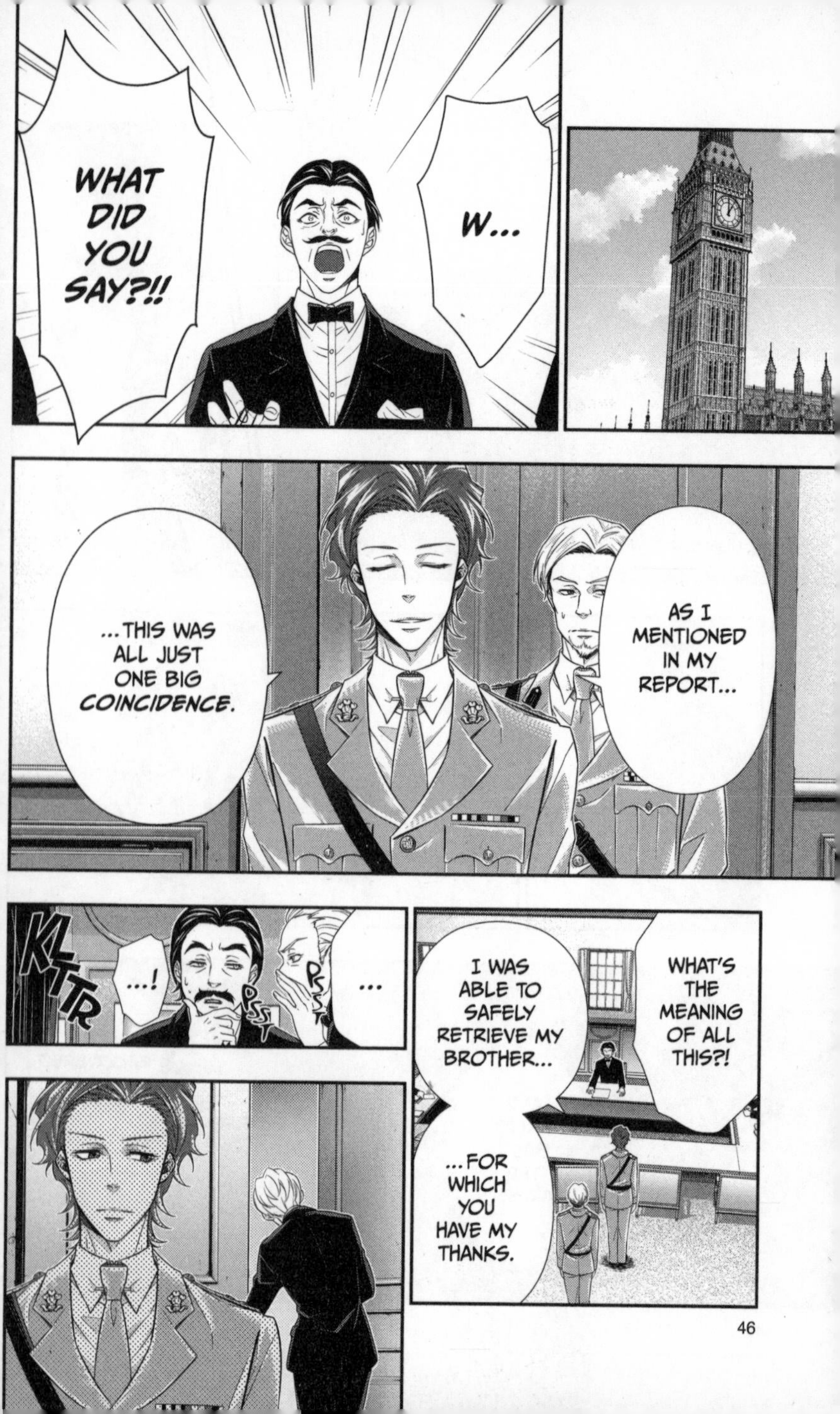
W...
WHAT DID YOU SAY?!!
AS I MENTIONED IN MY REPORT...
...THIS WAS ALL JUST ONE BIG COINCIDENCE.
WHAT'S THE MEANING OF ALL THIS?!
I WAS ABLE TO SAFELY RETRIEVE MY BROTHER...
...FOR WHICH YOU HAVE MY THANKS.
...
PSST
...!
KLTTR

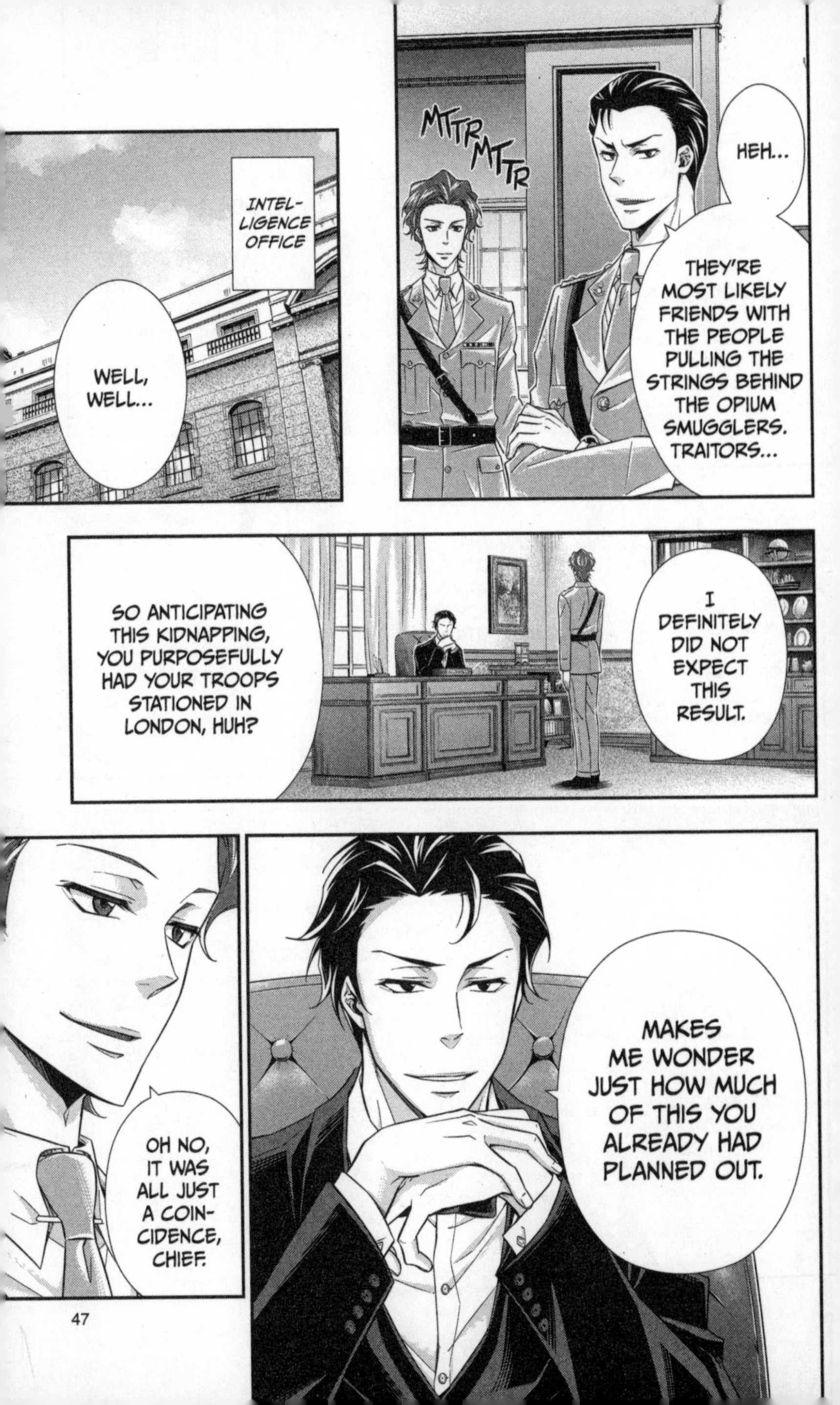
MTTR MTTR
HEH...
THEY'RE MOST LIKELY FRIENDS WITH THE PEOPLE PULLING THE STRINGS BEHIND THE OPIUM SMUGGLERS. TRAITORS...
INTEL-LIGENCE OFFICE
WELL, WELL...
I DEFINITELY DID NOT EXPECT THIS RESULT.
SO ANTICIPATING THIS KIDNAPPING, YOU PURPOSEFULLY HAD YOUR TROOPS STATIONED IN LONDON, HUH?
MAKES ME WONDER JUST HOW MUCH OF THIS YOU ALREADY HAD PLANNED OUT.
OH NO, IT WAS ALL JUST A COIN-CIDENCE, CHIEF.

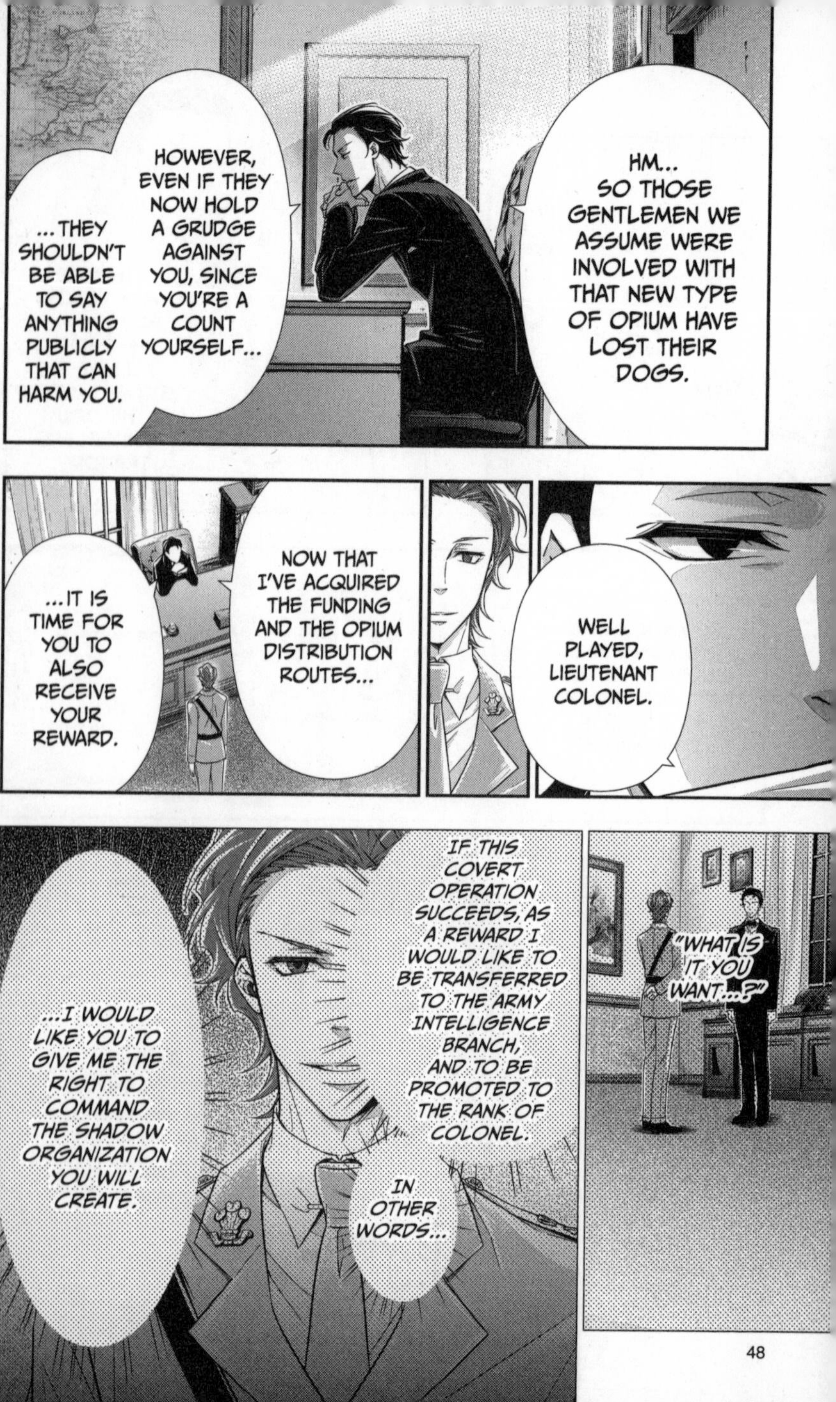
HM... SO THOSE GENTLEMEN WE ASSUME WERE INVOLVED WITH THAT NEW TYPE OF OPIUM HAVE LOST THEIR DOGS.
HOWEVER, EVEN IF THEY NOW HOLD A GRUDGE AGAINST YOU, SINCE YOU'RE A COUNT YOURSELF...
...THEY SHOULDN'T BE ABLE TO SAY ANYTHING PUBLICLY THAT CAN HARM YOU.
WELL PLAYED, LIEUTENANT COLONEL.
NOW THAT I'VE ACQUIRED THE FUNDING AND THE OPIUM DISTRIBUTION ROUTES...
...IT IS TIME FOR YOU TO ALSO RECEIVE YOUR REWARD.
"WHAT IS IT YOU WANT...?"
IF THIS COVERT OPERATION SUCCEEDS, AS A REWARD I WOULD LIKE TO BE TRANSFERRED TO THE ARMY INTELLIGENCE BRANCH, AND TO BE PROMOTED TO THE RANK OF COLONEL.
IN OTHER WORDS...
...I WOULD LIKE YOU TO GIVE ME THE RIGHT TO COMMAND THE SHADOW ORGANIZATION YOU WILL CREATE.

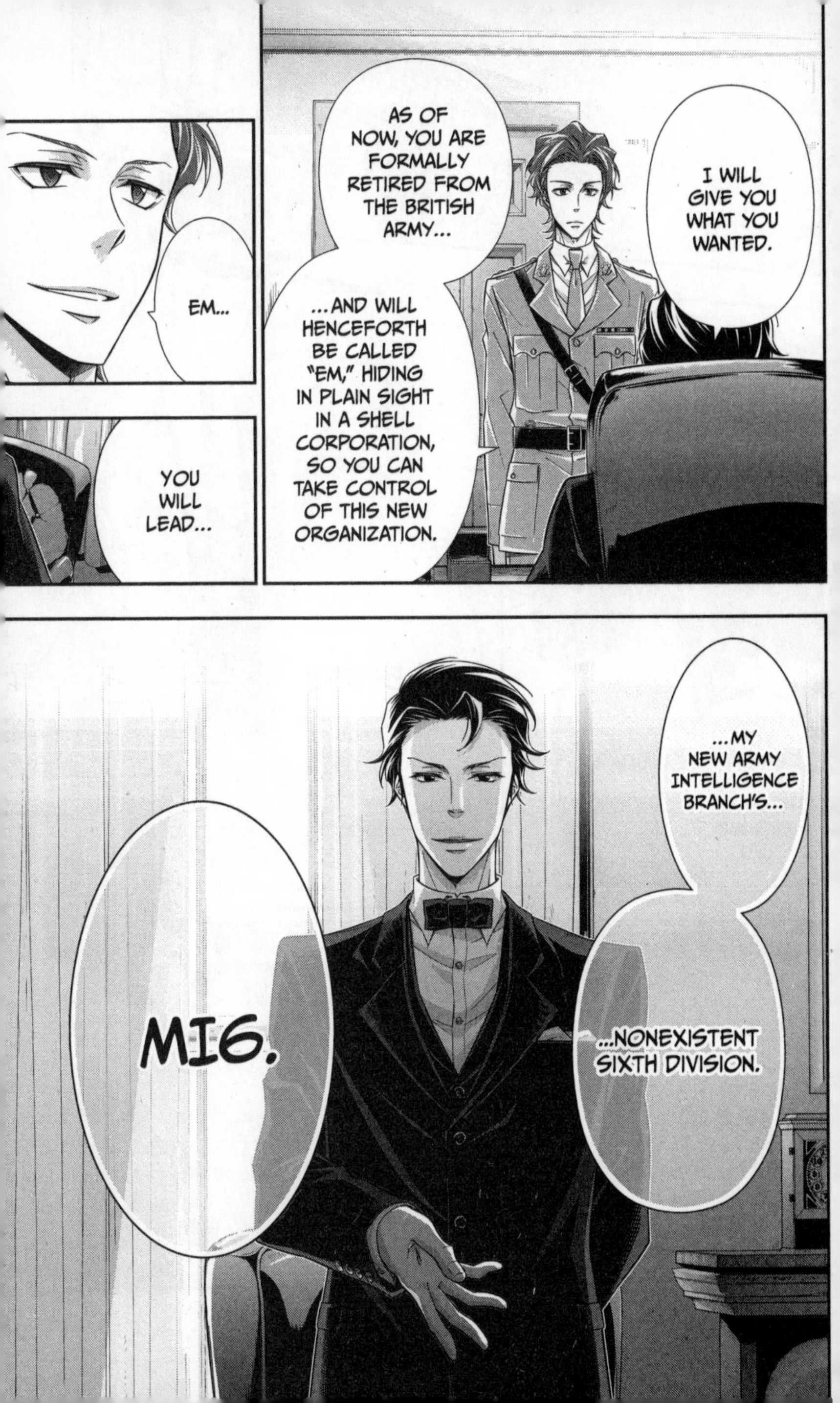
I WILL GIVE YOU WHAT YOU WANTED.
AS OF NOW, YOU ARE FORMALLY RETIRED FROM THE BRITISH ARMY...
...AND WILL HENCEFORTH BE CALLED "EM," HIDING IN PLAIN SIGHT IN A SHELL CORPORATION, SO YOU CAN TAKE CONTROL OF THIS NEW ORGANIZATION.
EM...
YOU WILL LEAD...
...MY NEW ARMY INTELLIGENCE BRANCH'S...
...NONEXISTENT SIXTH DIVISION.
MI6.

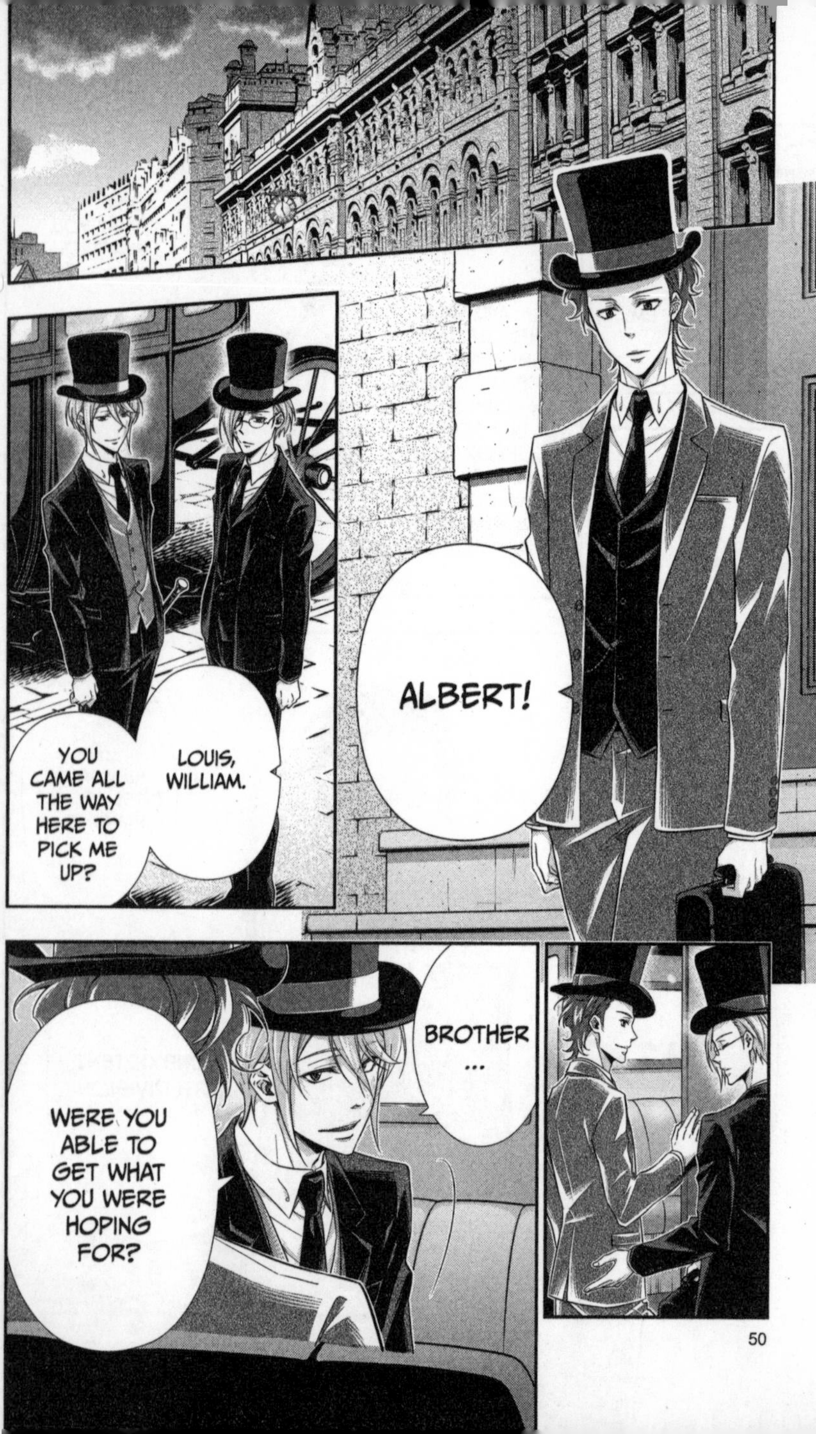
ALBERT!
LOUIS, WILLIAM.
YOU CAME ALL THE WAY HERE TO PICK ME UP?
BROTHER ...
WERE YOU ABLE TO GET WHAT YOU WERE HOPING FOR?

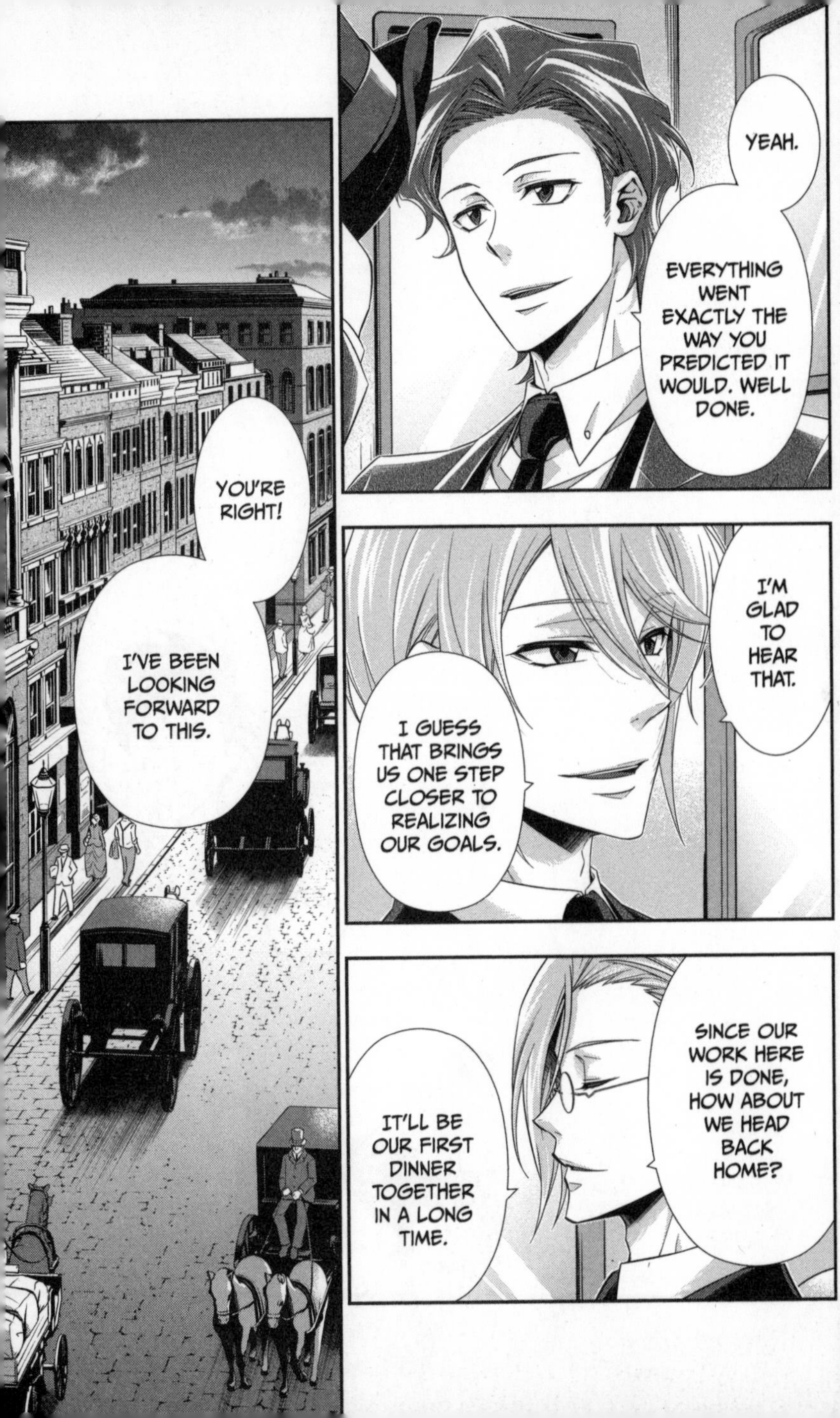
YEAH.
EVERYTHING WENT EXACTLY THE WAY YOU PREDICTED IT WOULD. WELL DONE.
I'M GLAD TO HEAR THAT.
I GUESS THAT BRINGS US ONE STEP CLOSER TO REALIZING OUR GOALS.
SINCE OUR WORK HERE IS DONE, HOW ABOUT WE HEAD BACK HOME?
IT'LL BE OUR FIRST DINNER TOGETHER IN A LONG TIME.
YOU'RE RIGHT!
I'VE BEEN LOOKING FORWARD TO THIS.

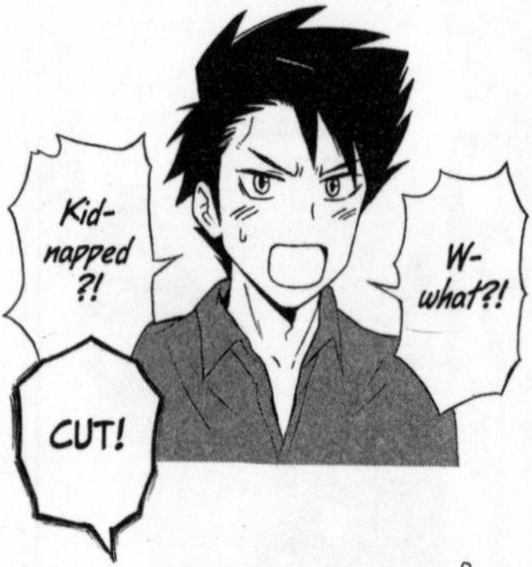
W-what?!
Kid-napped?!
CUT!
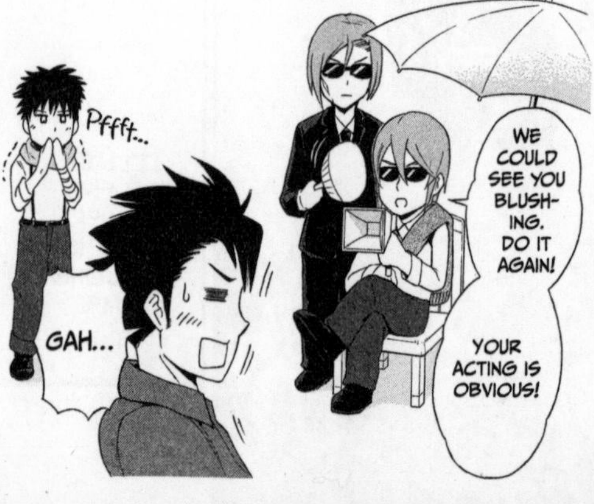
WE COULD SEE YOU BLUSH-ING. DO IT AGAIN!
YOUR ACTING IS OBVIOUS!
Pffft...
GAH...

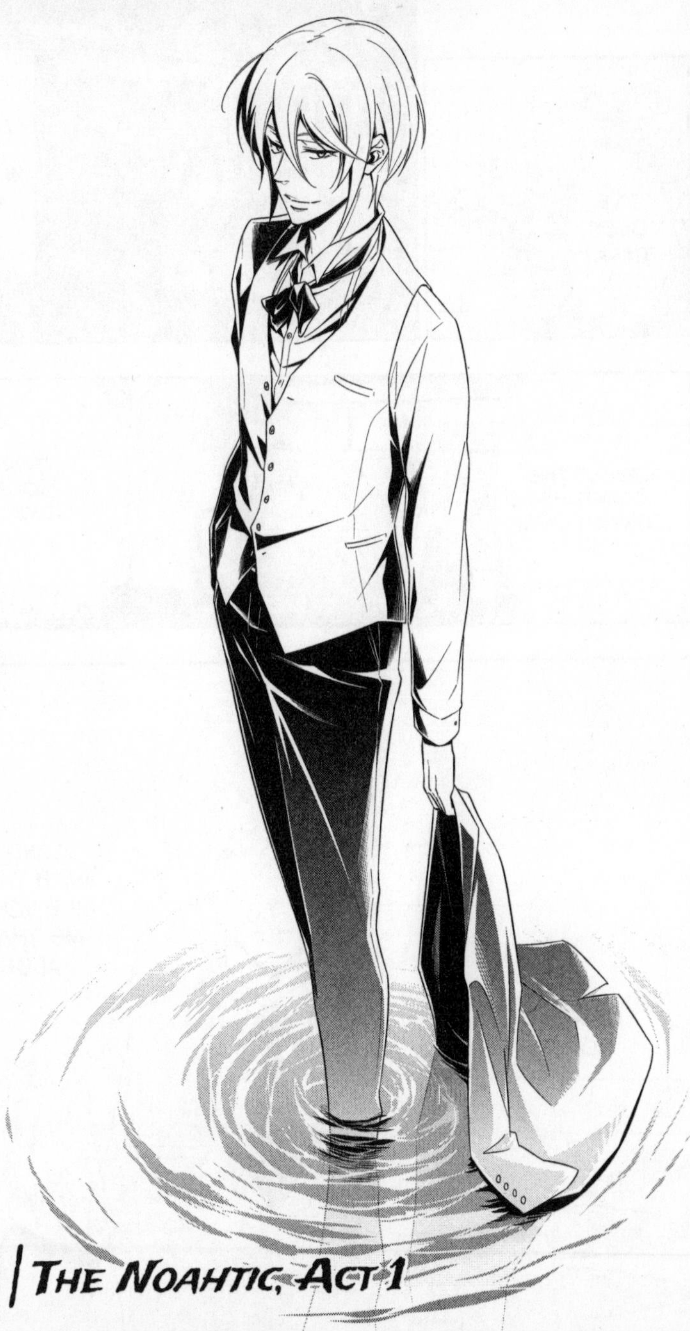

#5 | The Noahtic, Act 1

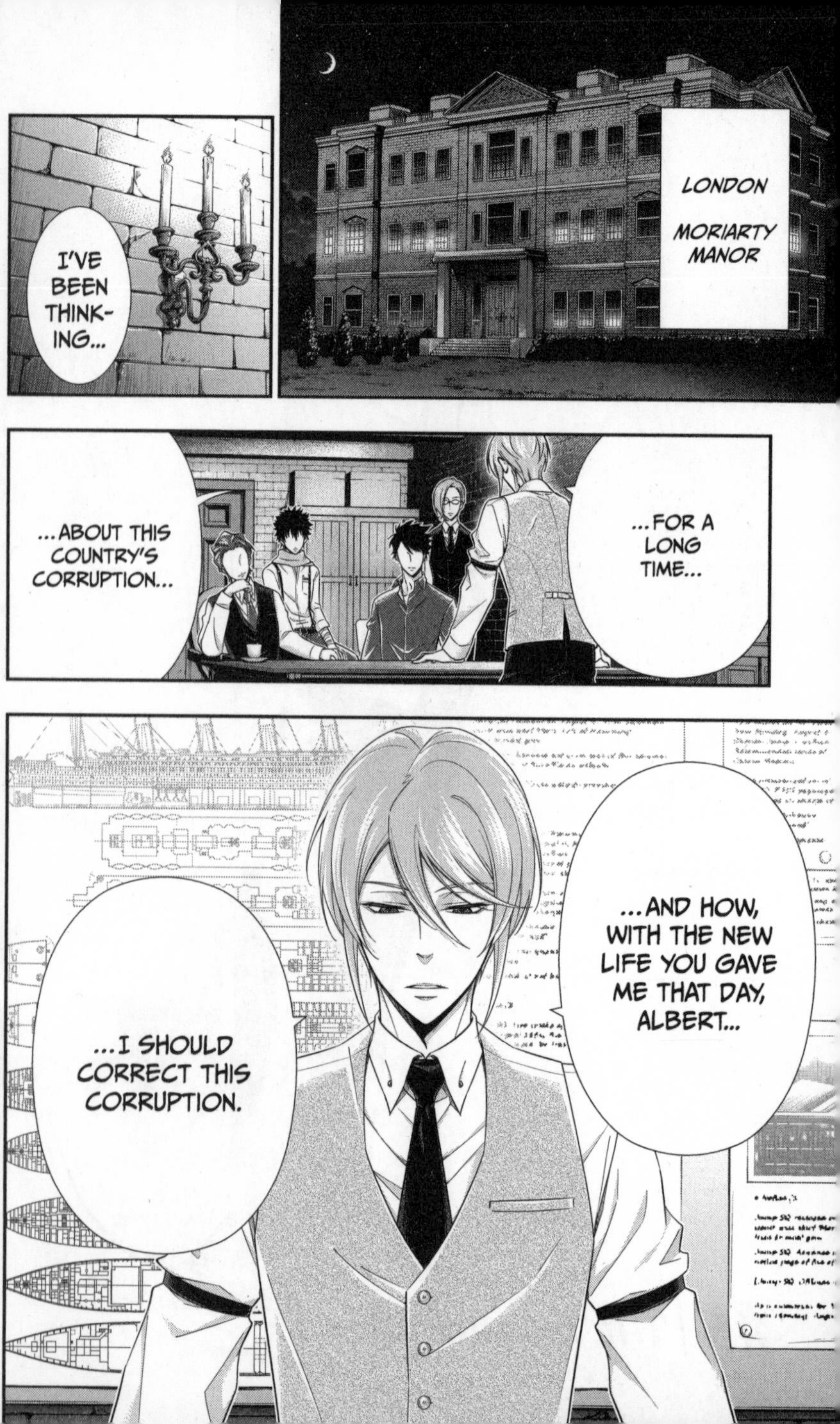
LONDON
MORIARTY MANOR
I'VE BEEN THINKING...
...FOR A LONG TIME...
...ABOUT THIS COUNTRY'S CORRUPTION...
...AND HOW, WITH THE NEW LIFE YOU GAVE ME THAT DAY, ALBERT...
...I SHOULD CORRECT THIS CORRUPTION.

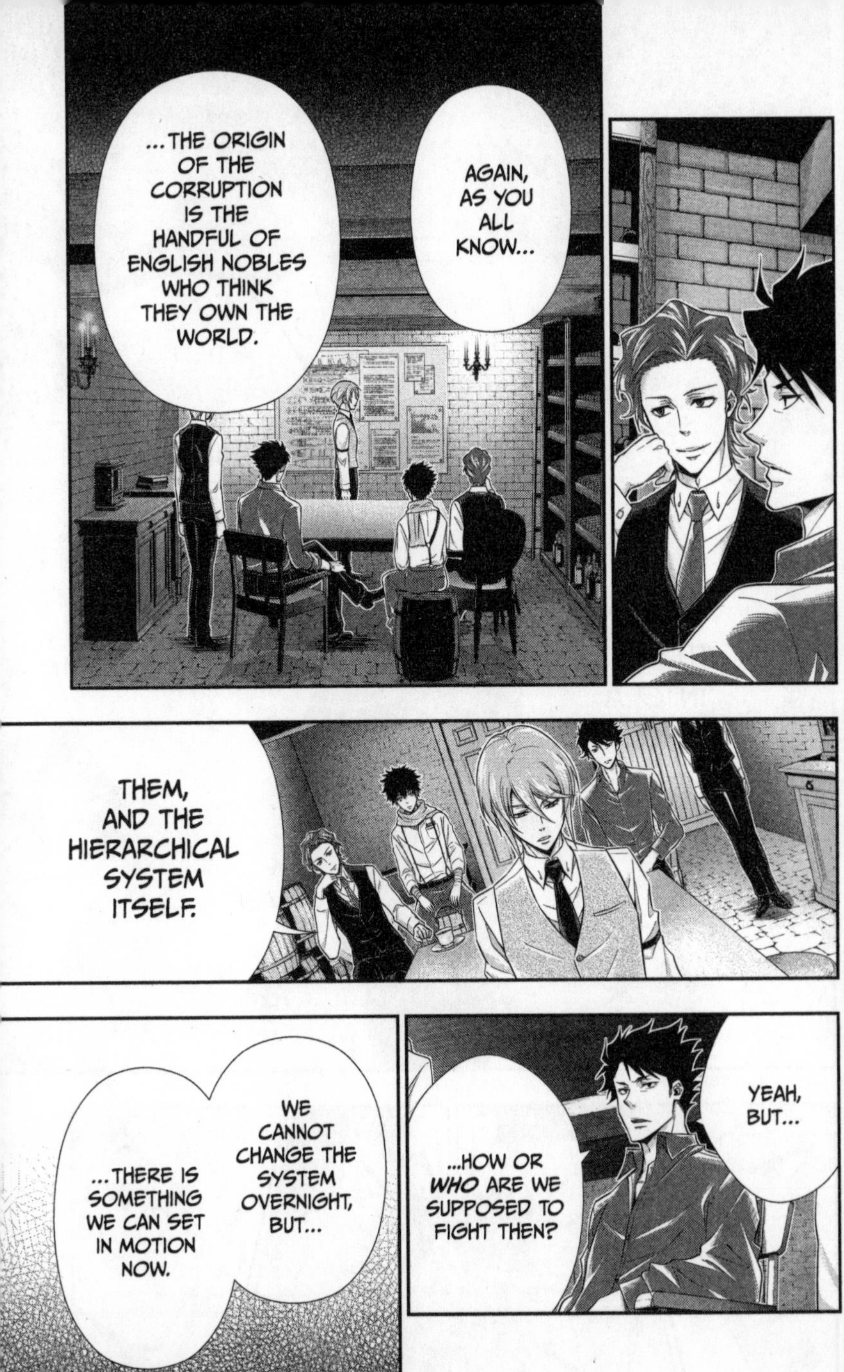
AGAIN, AS YOU ALL KNOW...
...THE ORIGIN OF THE CORRUPTION IS THE HANDFUL OF ENGLISH NOBLES WHO THINK THEY OWN THE WORLD.
THEM, AND THE HIERARCHICAL SYSTEM ITSELF.
YEAH, BUT...
...HOW OR *WHO* ARE WE SUPPOSED TO FIGHT THEN?
WE CANNOT CHANGE THE SYSTEM OVERNIGHT, BUT...
...THERE IS SOMETHING WE CAN SET IN MOTION NOW.

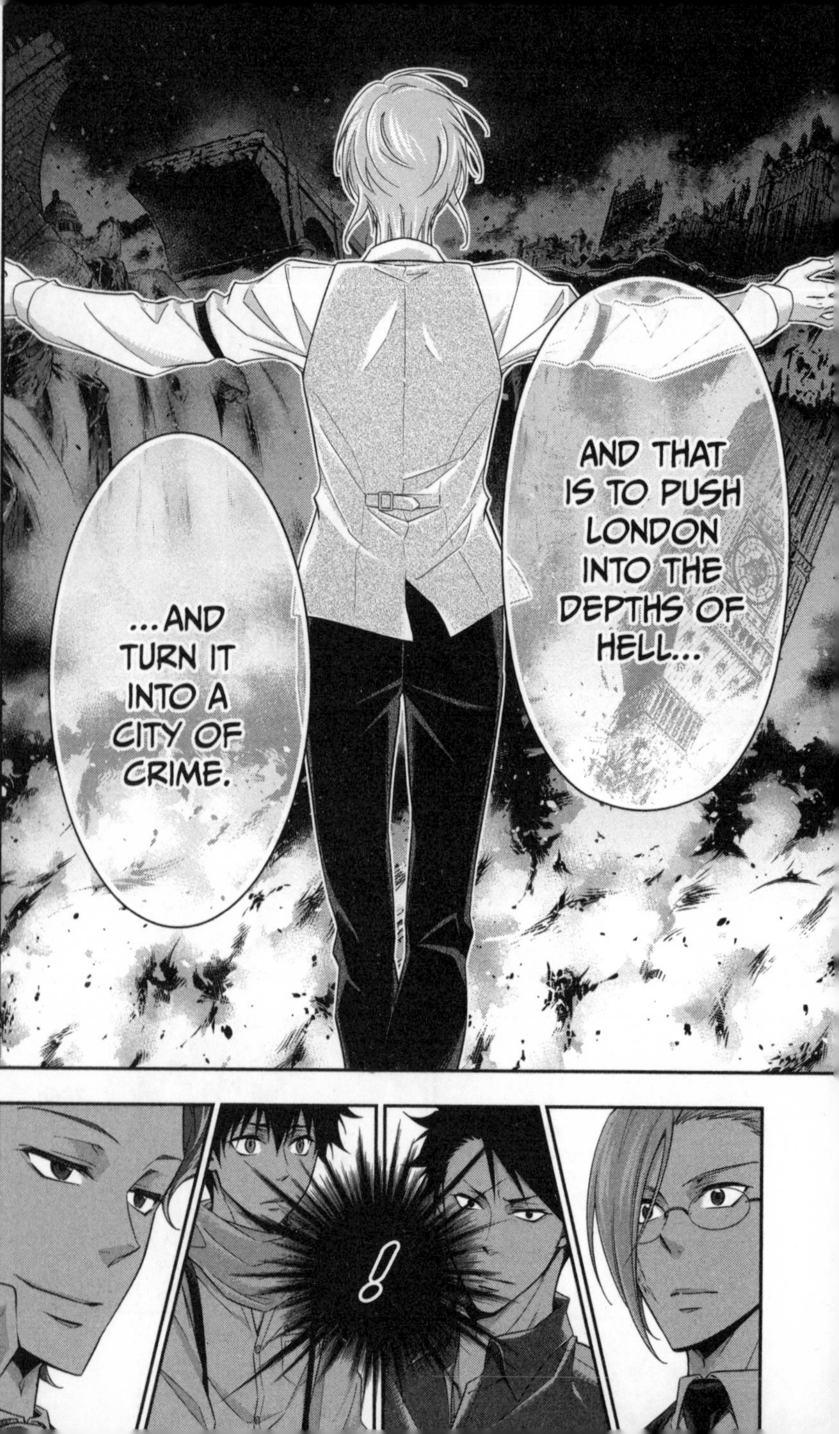
AND THAT IS TO PUSH LONDON INTO THE DEPTHS OF HELL...
...AND TURN IT INTO A CITY OF CRIME.
!

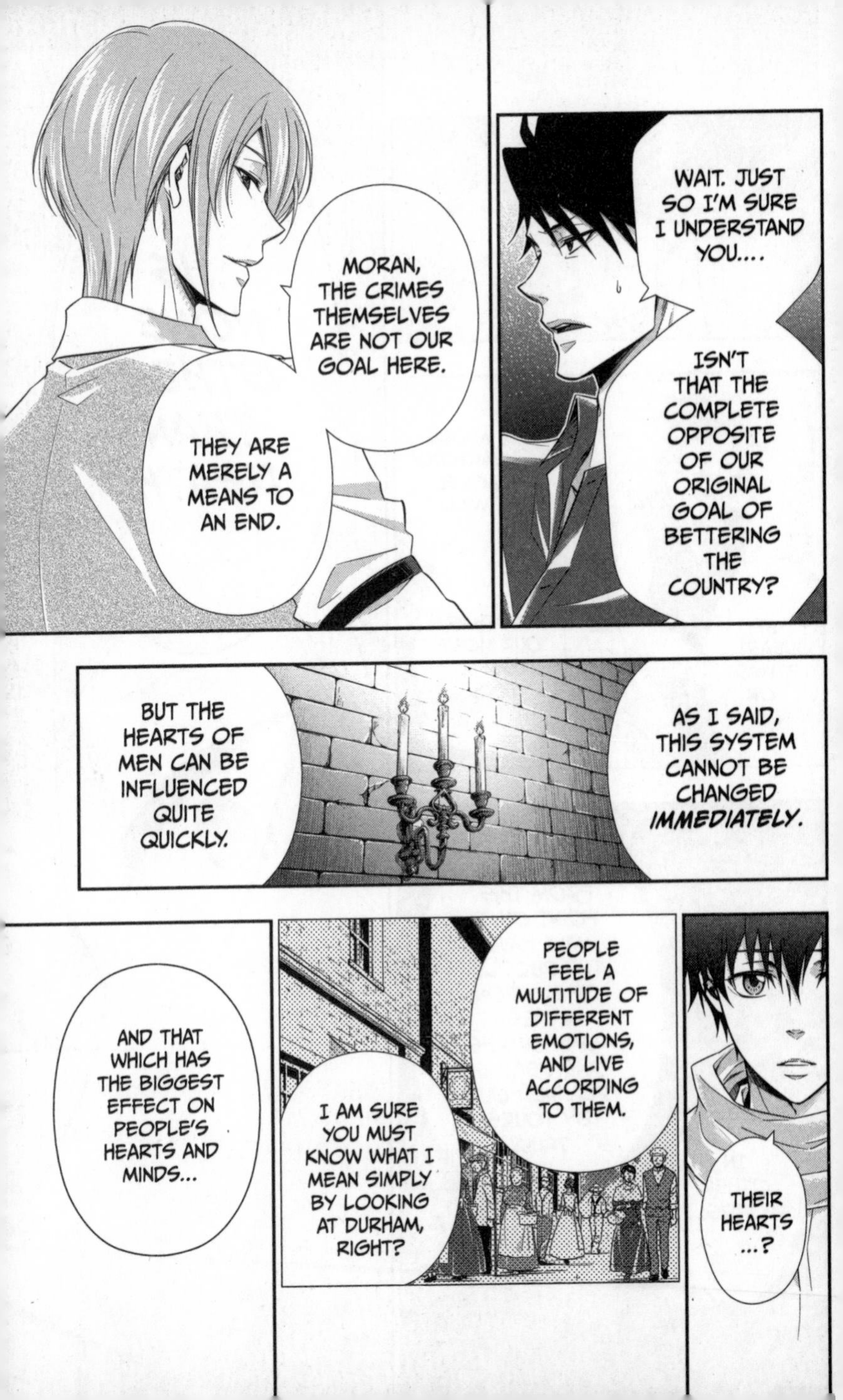
WAIT. JUST SO I'M SURE I UNDERSTAND YOU....
ISN'T THAT THE COMPLETE OPPOSITE OF OUR ORIGINAL GOAL OF BETTERING THE COUNTRY?
MORAN, THE CRIMES THEMSELVES ARE NOT OUR GOAL HERE.
THEY ARE MERELY A MEANS TO AN END.
AS I SAID, THIS SYSTEM CANNOT BE CHANGED *IMMEDIATELY*.
BUT THE HEARTS OF MEN CAN BE INFLUENCED QUITE QUICKLY.
THEIR HEARTS ...?
PEOPLE FEEL A MULTITUDE OF DIFFERENT EMOTIONS, AND LIVE ACCORDING TO THEM.
I AM SURE YOU MUST KNOW WHAT I MEAN SIMPLY BY LOOKING AT DURHAM, RIGHT?
AND THAT WHICH HAS THE BIGGEST EFFECT ON PEOPLE'S HEARTS AND MINDS...

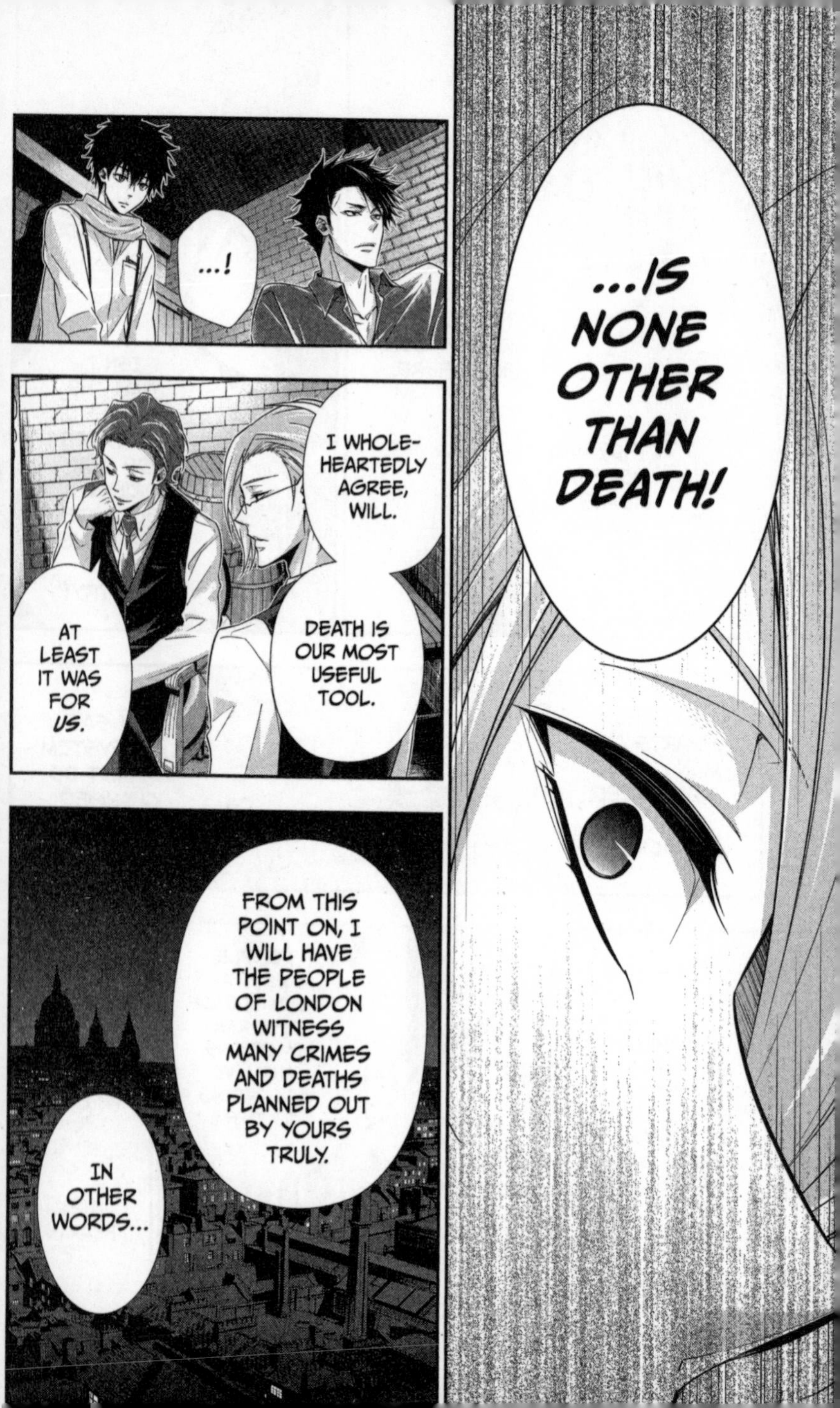
...!
I WHOLE-HEARTEDLY AGREE, WILL.
DEATH IS OUR MOST USEFUL TOOL.
AT LEAST IT WAS FOR US.
FROM THIS POINT ON, I WILL HAVE THE PEOPLE OF LONDON WITNESS MANY CRIMES AND DEATHS PLANNED OUT BY YOURS TRULY.
IN OTHER WORDS...
...IS NONE OTHER THAN DEATH!

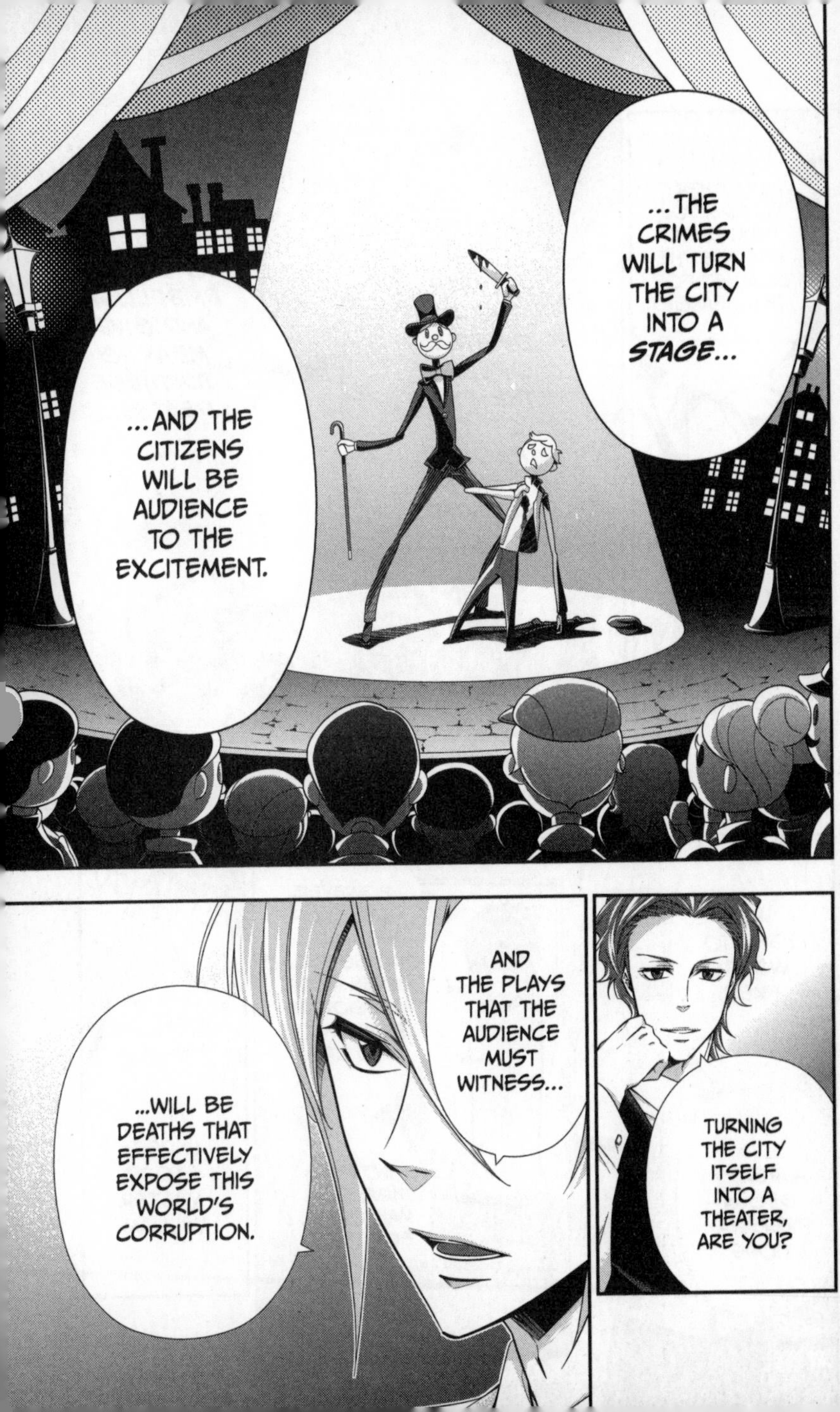
...THE CRIMES WILL TURN THE CITY INTO A *STAGE*...
...AND THE CITIZENS WILL BE AUDIENCE TO THE EXCITEMENT.
TURNING THE CITY ITSELF INTO A THEATER, ARE YOU?
AND THE PLAYS THAT THE AUDIENCE MUST WITNESS...
...WILL BE DEATHS THAT EFFECTIVELY EXPOSE THIS WORLD'S CORRUPTION.

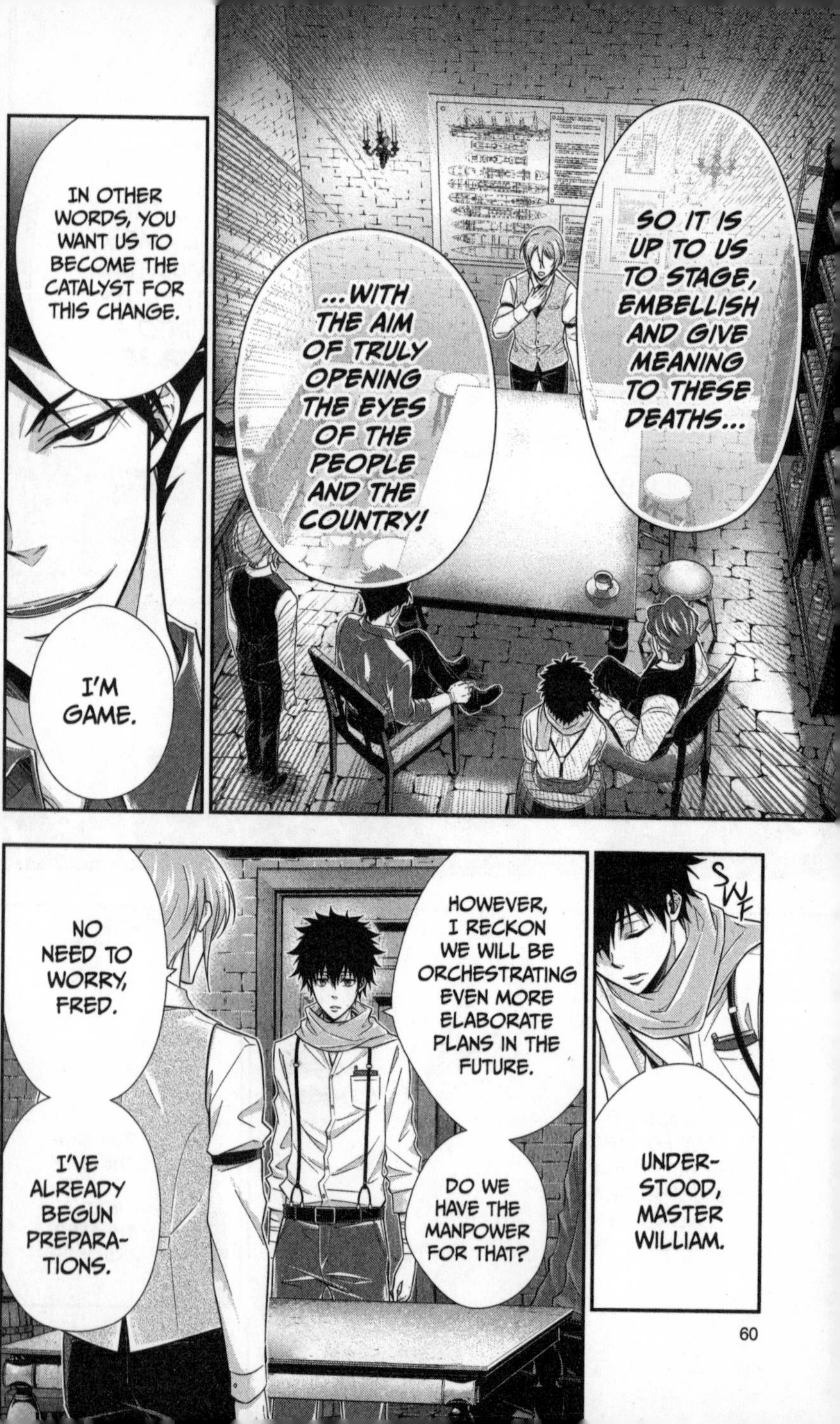
SO IT IS UP TO US TO STAGE, EMBELLISH AND GIVE MEANING TO THESE DEATHS...
...WITH THE AIM OF TRULY OPENING THE EYES OF THE PEOPLE AND THE COUNTRY!
IN OTHER WORDS, YOU WANT US TO BECOME THE CATALYST FOR THIS CHANGE.
I'M GAME.
SWF
UNDER-STOOD, MASTER WILLIAM.
HOWEVER, I RECKON WE WILL BE ORCHESTRATING EVEN MORE ELABORATE PLANS IN THE FUTURE.
DO WE HAVE THE MANPOWER FOR THAT?
NO NEED TO WORRY, FRED.
I'VE ALREADY BEGUN PREPARA-TIONS.

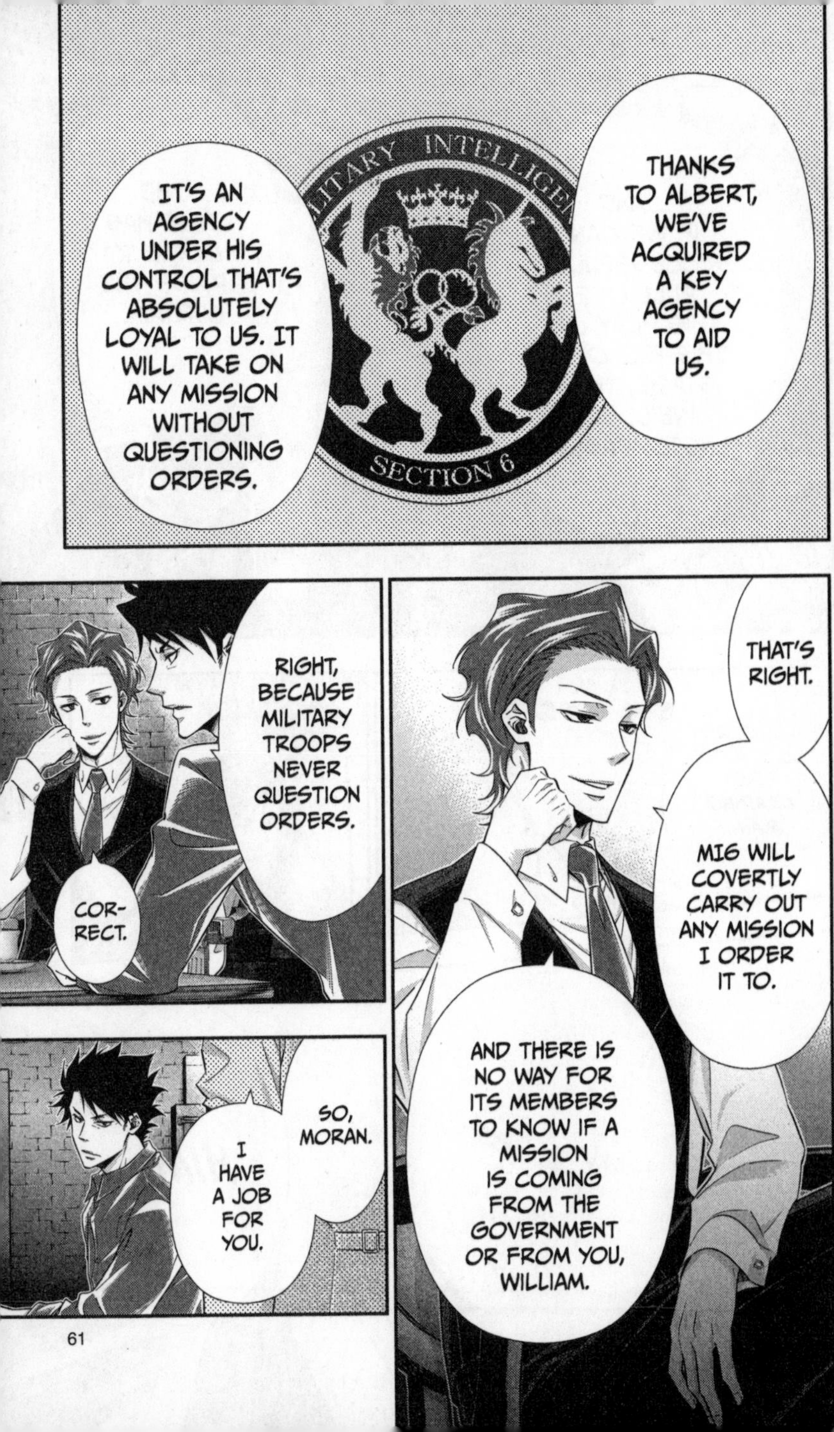
THANKS TO ALBERT, WE'VE ACQUIRED A KEY AGENCY TO AID US.
IT'S AN AGENCY UNDER HIS CONTROL THAT'S ABSOLUTELY LOYAL TO US. IT WILL TAKE ON ANY MISSION WITHOUT QUESTIONING ORDERS.
SECTION 6
THAT'S RIGHT.
MI6 WILL COVERTLY CARRY OUT ANY MISSION I ORDER IT TO.
AND THERE IS NO WAY FOR ITS MEMBERS TO KNOW IF A MISSION IS COMING FROM THE GOVERNMENT OR FROM YOU, WILLIAM.
RIGHT, BECAUSE MILITARY TROOPS NEVER QUESTION ORDERS.
COR-RECT.
SO, MORAN.
I HAVE A JOB FOR YOU.

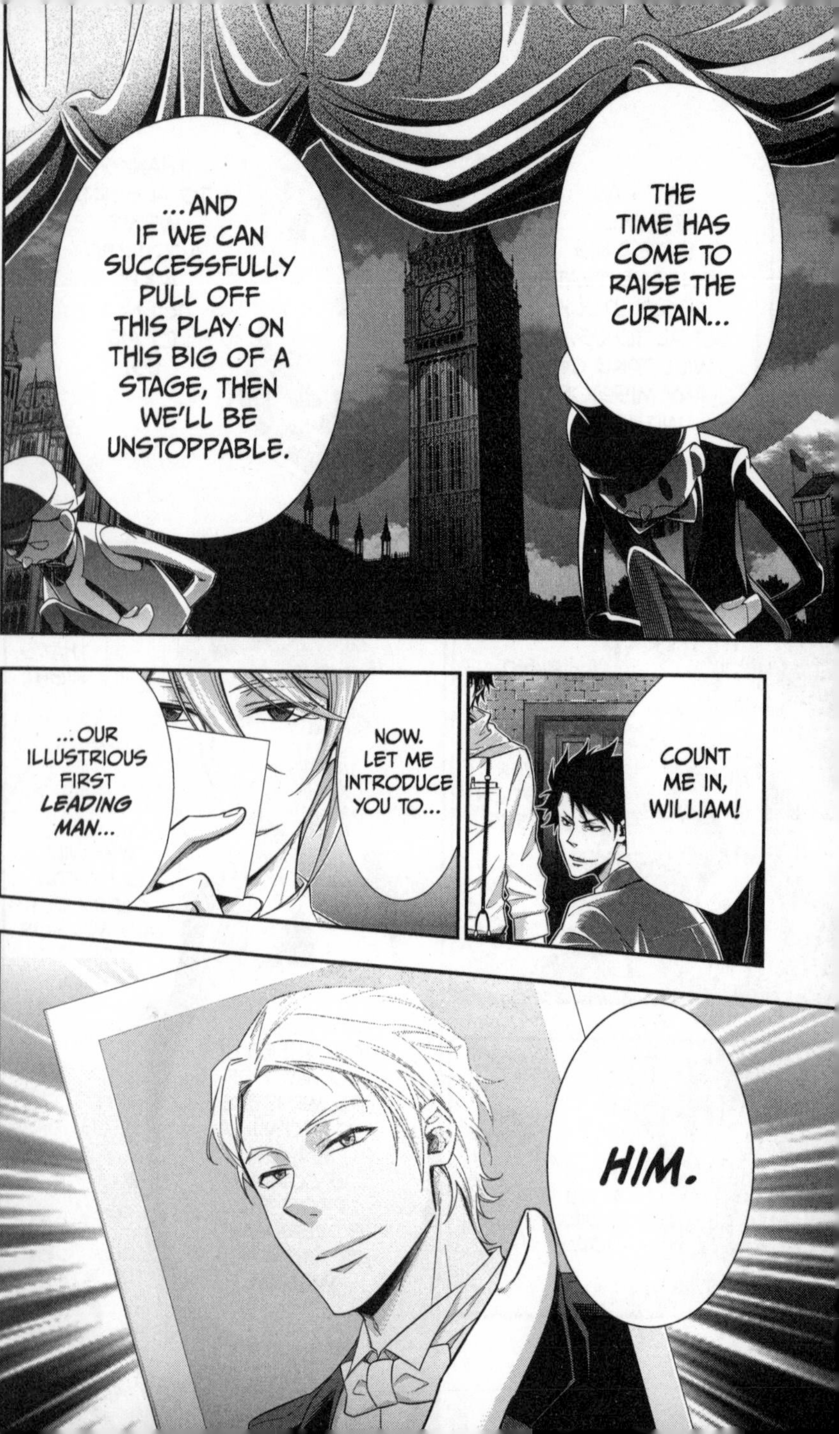
THE TIME HAS COME TO RAISE THE CURTAIN...
...AND IF WE CAN SUCCESSFULLY PULL OFF THIS PLAY ON THIS BIG OF A STAGE, THEN WE'LL BE UNSTOPPABLE.
COUNT ME IN, WILLIAM!
NOW. LET ME INTRODUCE YOU TO...
...OUR ILLUSTRIOUS FIRST *LEADING MAN*...
HIM.

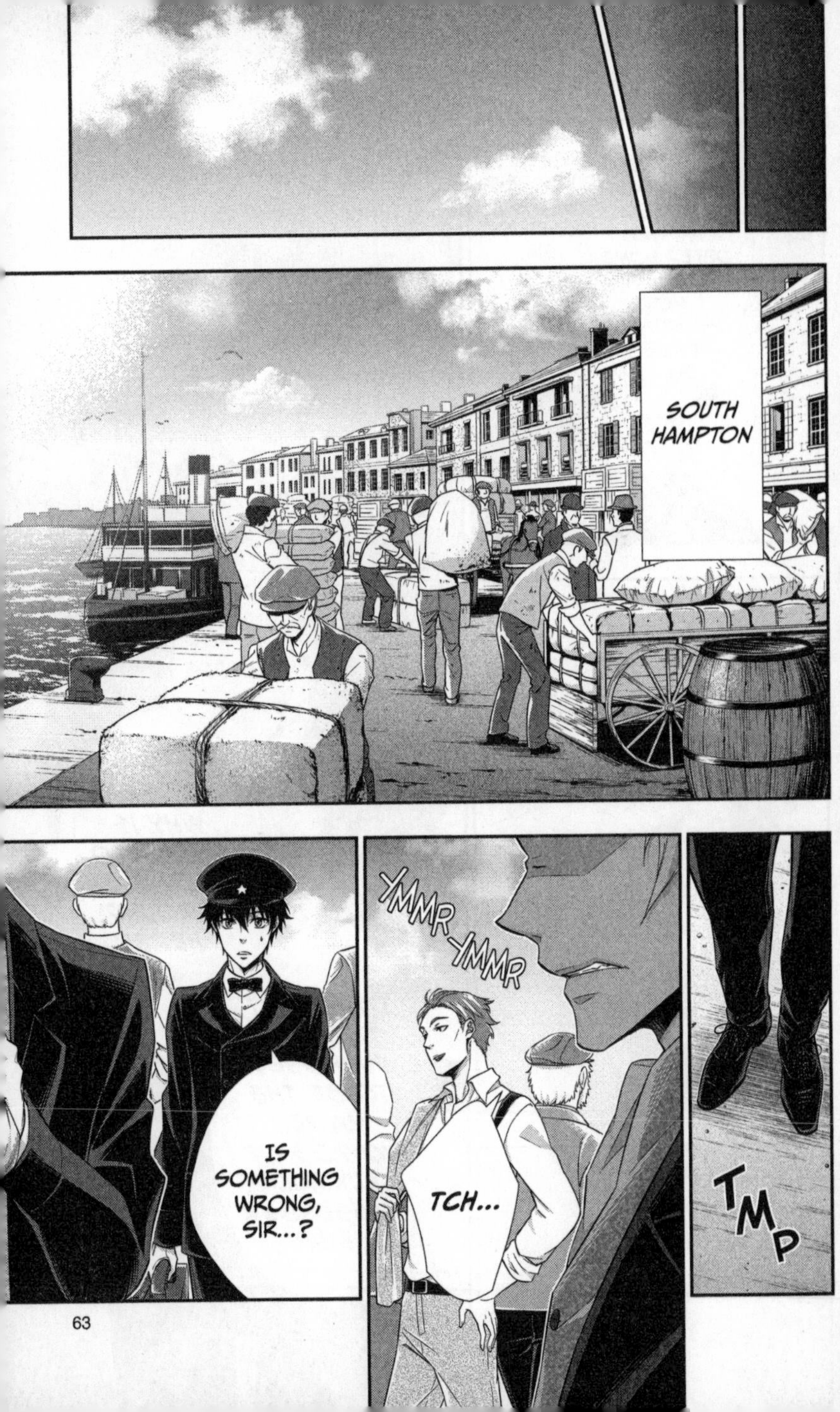
SOUTH HAMPTON
TMP
YMMR-YMMR
TCH...
IS SOMETHING WRONG, SIR...?

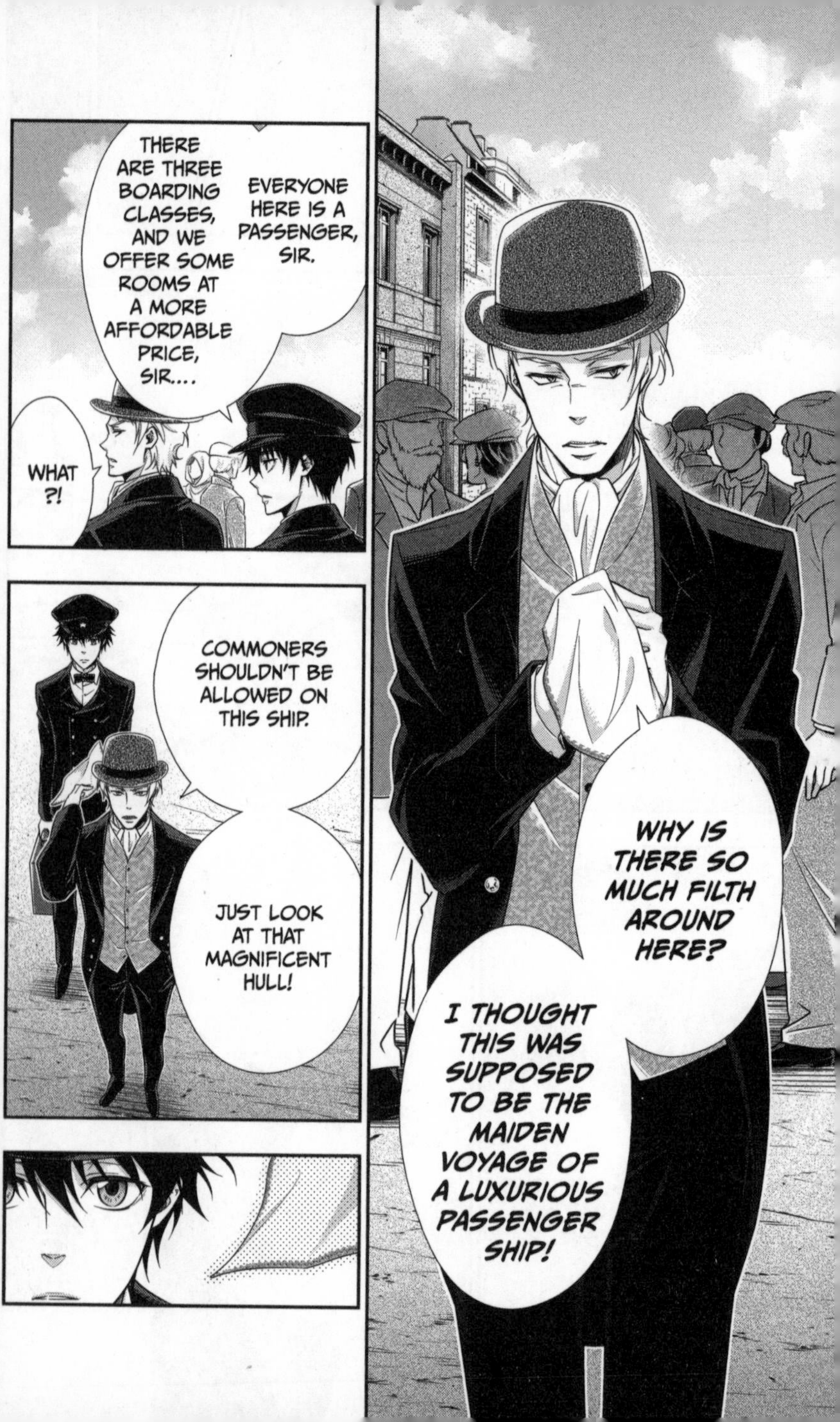
WHY IS THERE SO MUCH FILTH AROUND HERE?
I THOUGHT THIS WAS SUPPOSED TO BE THE MAIDEN VOYAGE OF A LUXURIOUS PASSENGER SHIP!
EVERYONE HERE IS A PASSENGER, SIR.
THERE ARE THREE BOARDING CLASSES, AND WE OFFER SOME ROOMS AT A MORE AFFORDABLE PRICE, SIR....
WHAT?!
COMMONERS SHOULDN'T BE ALLOWED ON THIS SHIP.
JUST LOOK AT THAT MAGNIFICENT HULL!

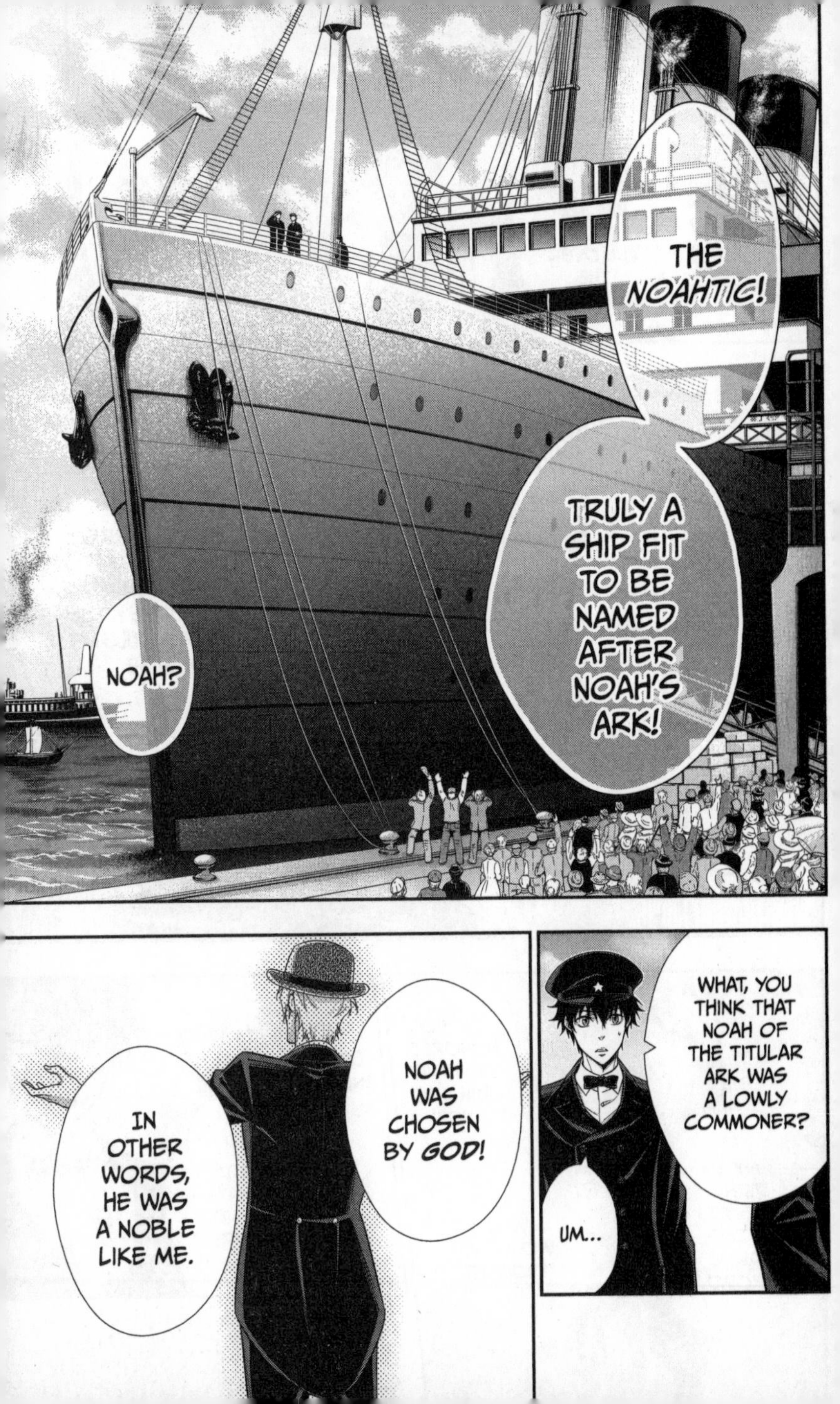
THE NOAHTIC!
TRULY A SHIP FIT TO BE NAMED AFTER NOAH'S ARK!
NOAH?
WHAT, YOU THINK THAT NOAH OF THE TITULAR ARK WAS A LOWLY COMMONER?
UM...
NOAH WAS CHOSEN BY GOD!
IN OTHER WORDS, HE WAS A NOBLE LIKE ME.

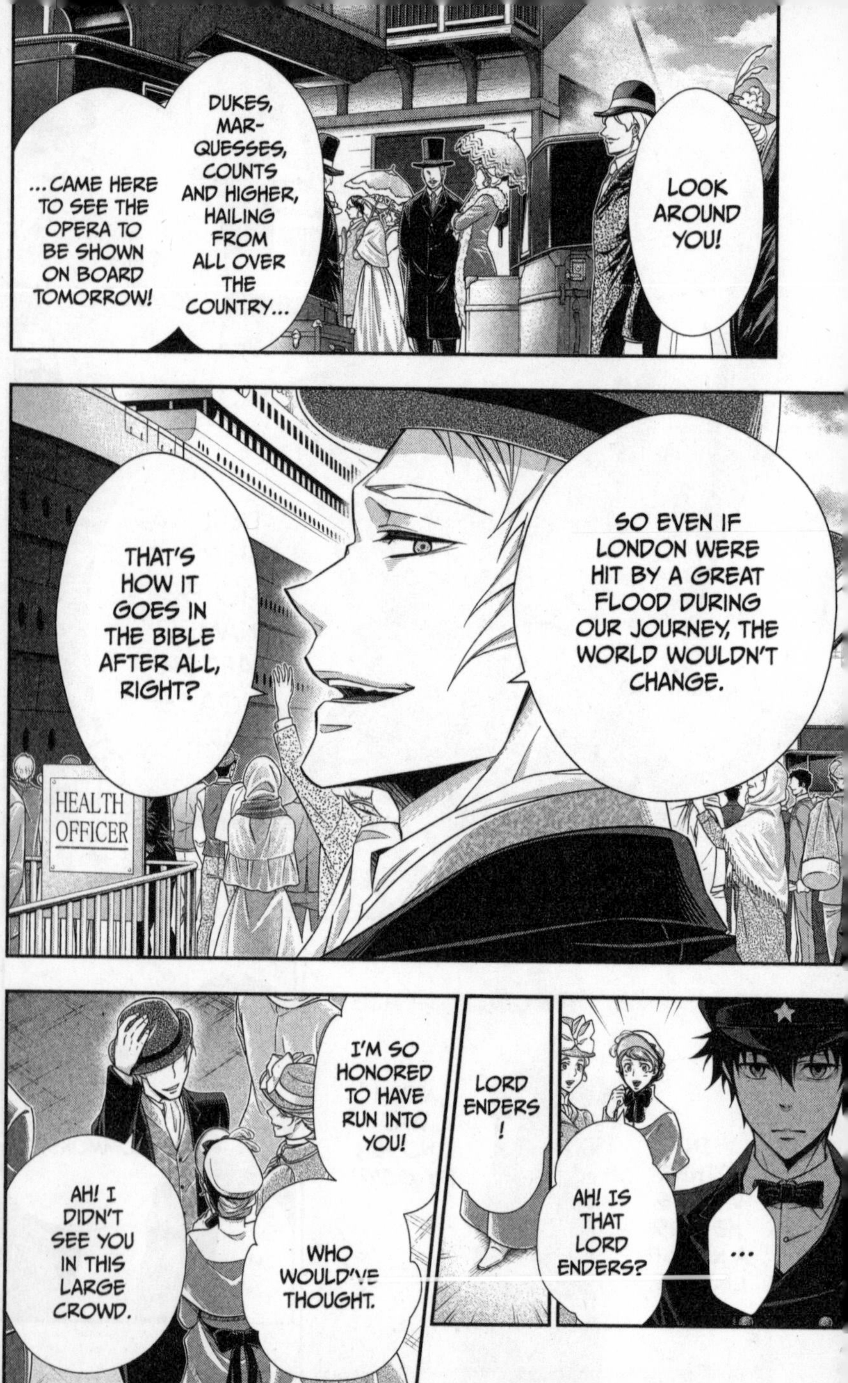
LOOK AROUND YOU!
DUKES, MARQUESSES, COUNTS AND HIGHER, HAILING FROM ALL OVER THE COUNTRY...
...CAME HERE TO SEE THE OPERA TO BE SHOWN ON BOARD TOMORROW!
SO EVEN IF LONDON WERE HIT BY A GREAT FLOOD DURING OUR JOURNEY, THE WORLD WOULDN'T CHANGE.
THAT'S HOW IT GOES IN THE BIBLE AFTER ALL, RIGHT?
HEALTH OFFICER
AH! IS THAT LORD ENDERS?
...
LORD ENDERS!
I'M SO HONORED TO HAVE RUN INTO YOU!
WHO WOULD'VE THOUGHT.
AH! I DIDN'T SEE YOU IN THIS LARGE CROWD.

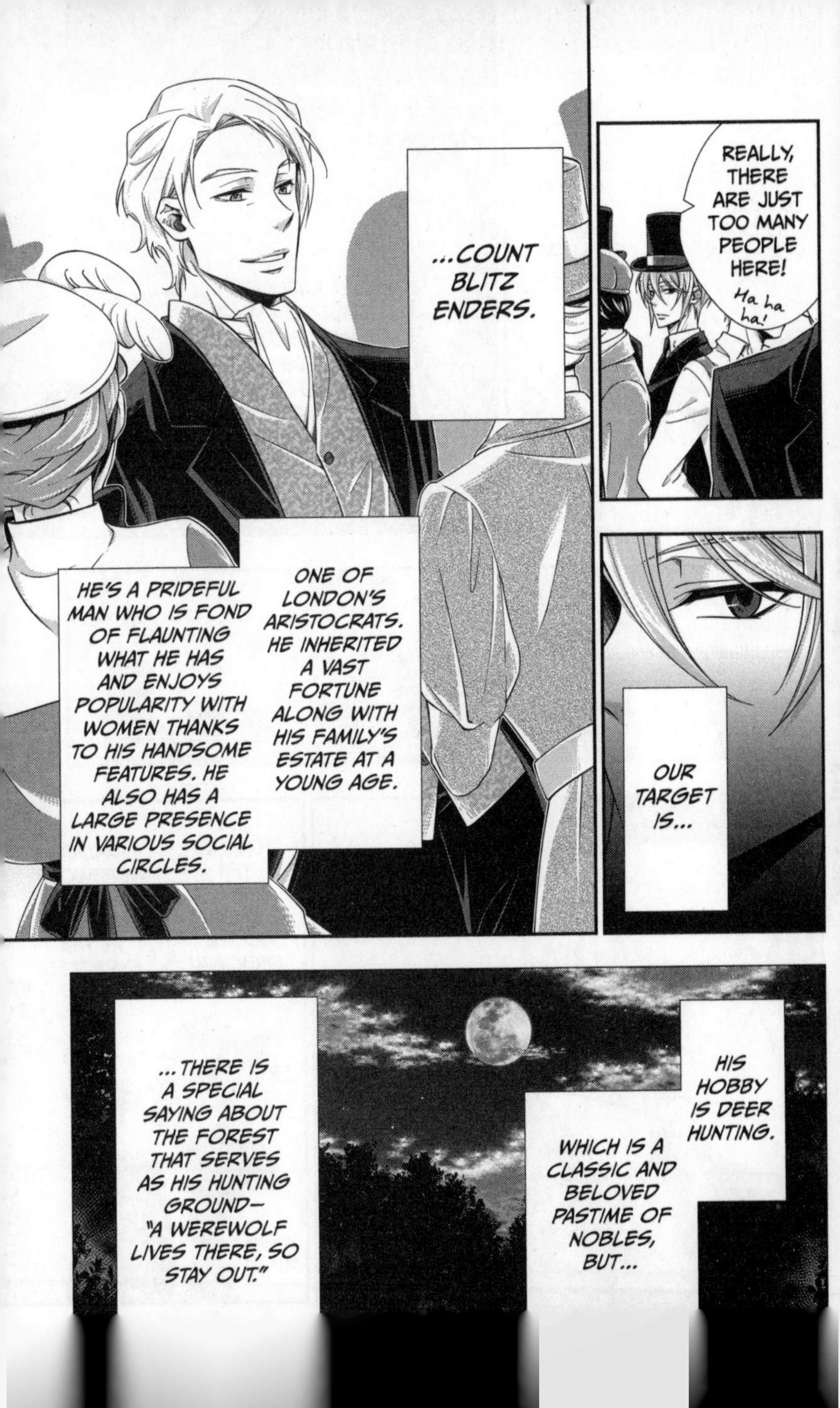
REALLY, THERE ARE JUST TOO MANY PEOPLE HERE!
Ha ha ha!
OUR TARGET IS...
...COUNT BLITZ ENDERS.
ONE OF LONDON'S ARISTOCRATS. HE INHERITED A VAST FORTUNE ALONG WITH HIS FAMILY'S ESTATE AT A YOUNG AGE.
HE'S A PRIDEFUL MAN WHO IS FOND OF FLAUNTING WHAT HE HAS AND ENJOYS POPULARITY WITH WOMEN THANKS TO HIS HANDSOME FEATURES. HE ALSO HAS A LARGE PRESENCE IN VARIOUS SOCIAL CIRCLES.
HIS HOBBY IS DEER HUNTING.
WHICH IS A CLASSIC AND BELOVED PASTIME OF NOBLES, BUT...
...THERE IS A SPECIAL SAYING ABOUT THE FOREST THAT SERVES AS HIS HUNTING GROUND— "A WEREWOLF LIVES THERE, SO STAY OUT."

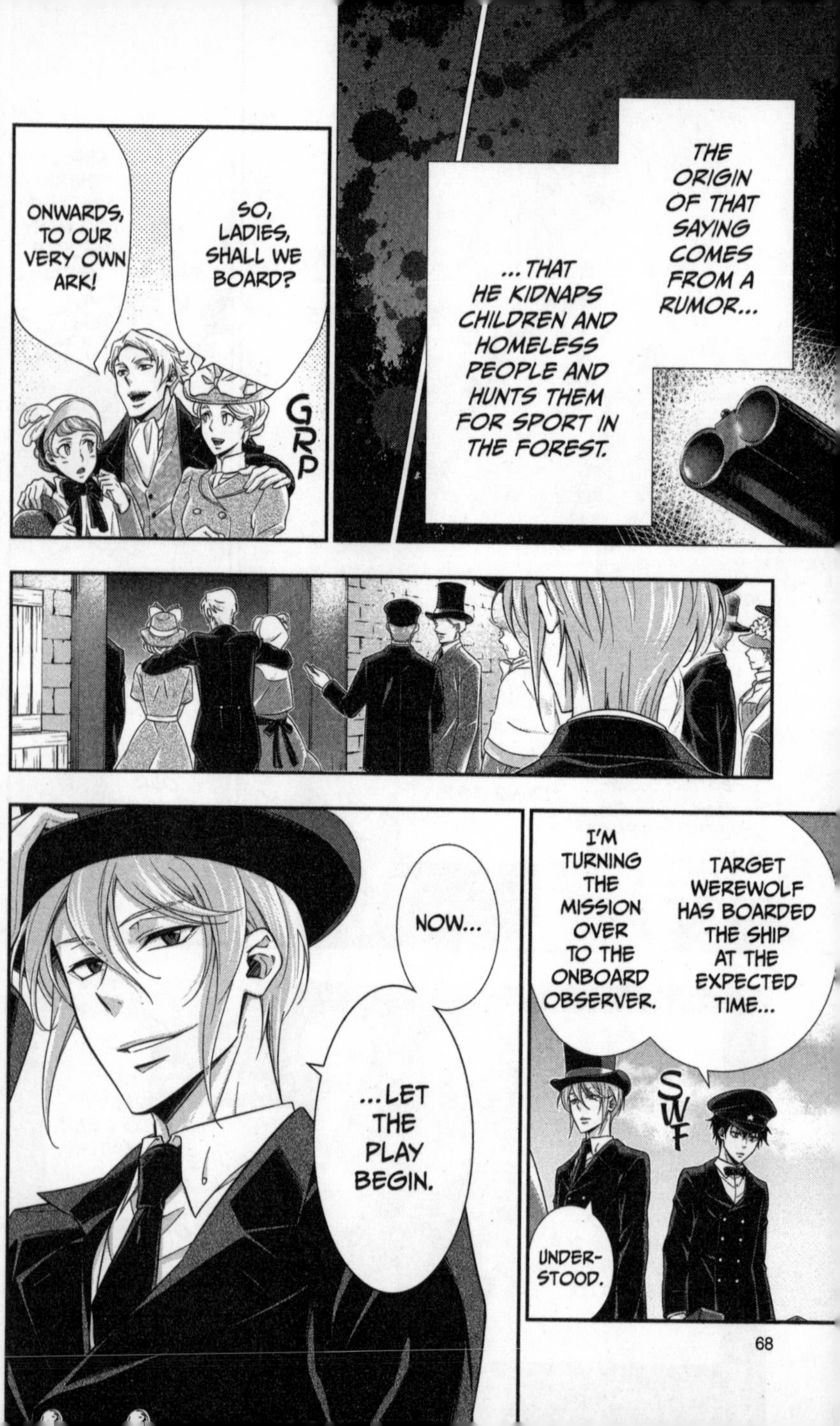
THE ORIGIN OF THAT SAYING COMES FROM A RUMOR...
...THAT HE KIDNAPS CHILDREN AND HOMELESS PEOPLE AND HUNTS THEM FOR SPORT IN THE FOREST.
SO, LADIES, SHALL WE BOARD?
ONWARDS, TO OUR VERY OWN ARK!
GRP
TARGET WEREWOLF HAS BOARDED THE SHIP AT THE EXPECTED TIME...
I'M TURNING THE MISSION OVER TO THE ONBOARD OBSERVER.
SWF
UNDER-STOOD.
NOW...
...LET THE PLAY BEGIN.

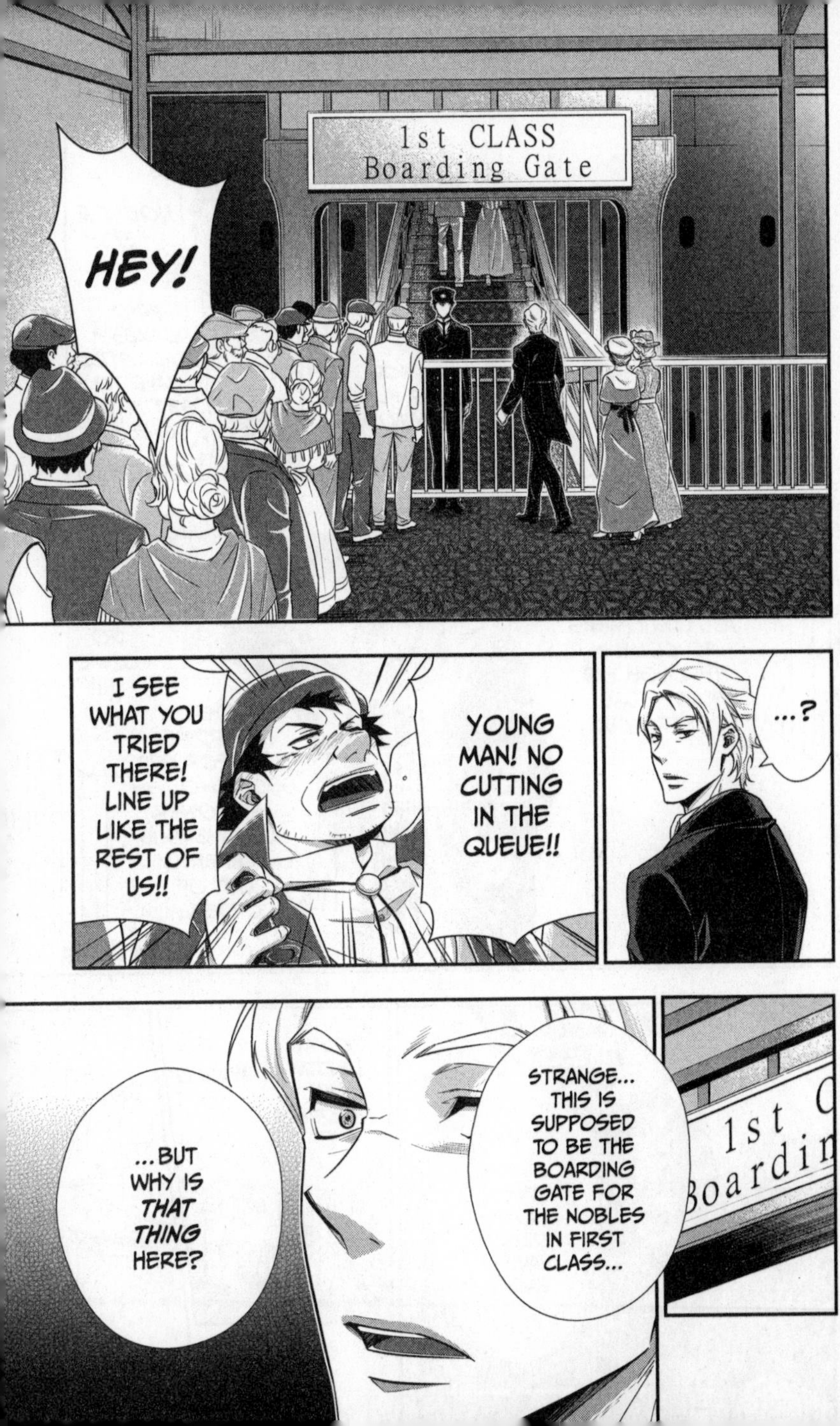
1st CLASS Boarding Gate
HEY!
...?
YOUNG MAN! NO CUTTING IN THE QUEUE!!
I SEE WHAT YOU TRIED THERE! LINE UP LIKE THE REST OF US!!
STRANGE... THIS IS SUPPOSED TO BE THE BOARDING GATE FOR THE NOBLES IN FIRST CLASS...
...BUT WHY IS *THAT THING* HERE?

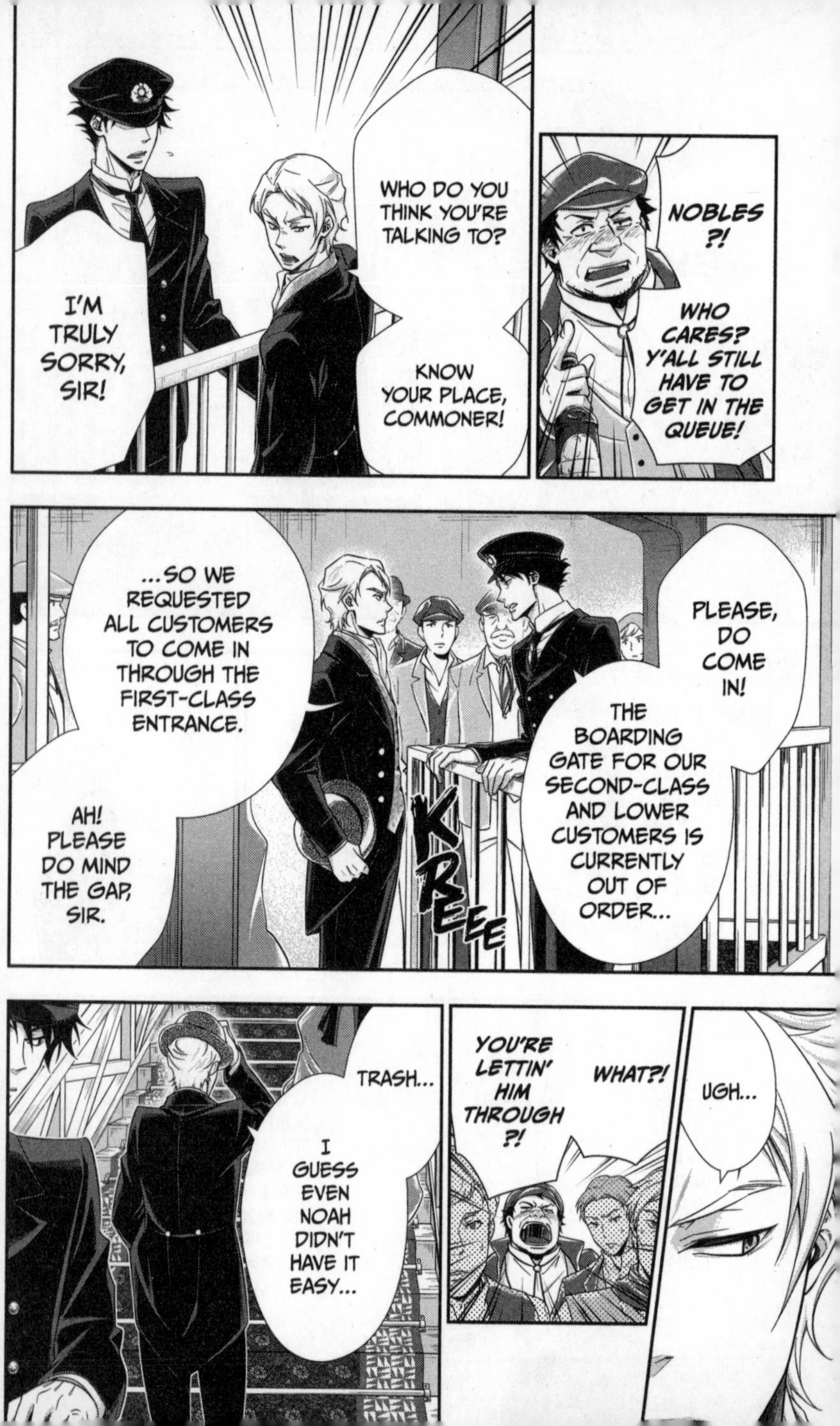
NOBLES ?!
WHO CARES? Y'ALL STILL HAVE TO GET IN THE QUEUE!
WHO DO YOU THINK YOU'RE TALKING TO?
KNOW YOUR PLACE, COMMONER!
I'M TRULY SORRY, SIR!
PLEASE, DO COME IN!
THE BOARDING GATE FOR OUR SECOND-CLASS AND LOWER CUSTOMERS IS CURRENTLY OUT OF ORDER...
...SO WE REQUESTED ALL CUSTOMERS TO COME IN THROUGH THE FIRST-CLASS ENTRANCE.
KREEE
AH! PLEASE DO MIND THE GAP, SIR.
UGH...
WHAT?!
YOU'RE LETTIN' HIM THROUGH ?!
TRASH...
I GUESS EVEN NOAH DIDN'T HAVE IT EASY...

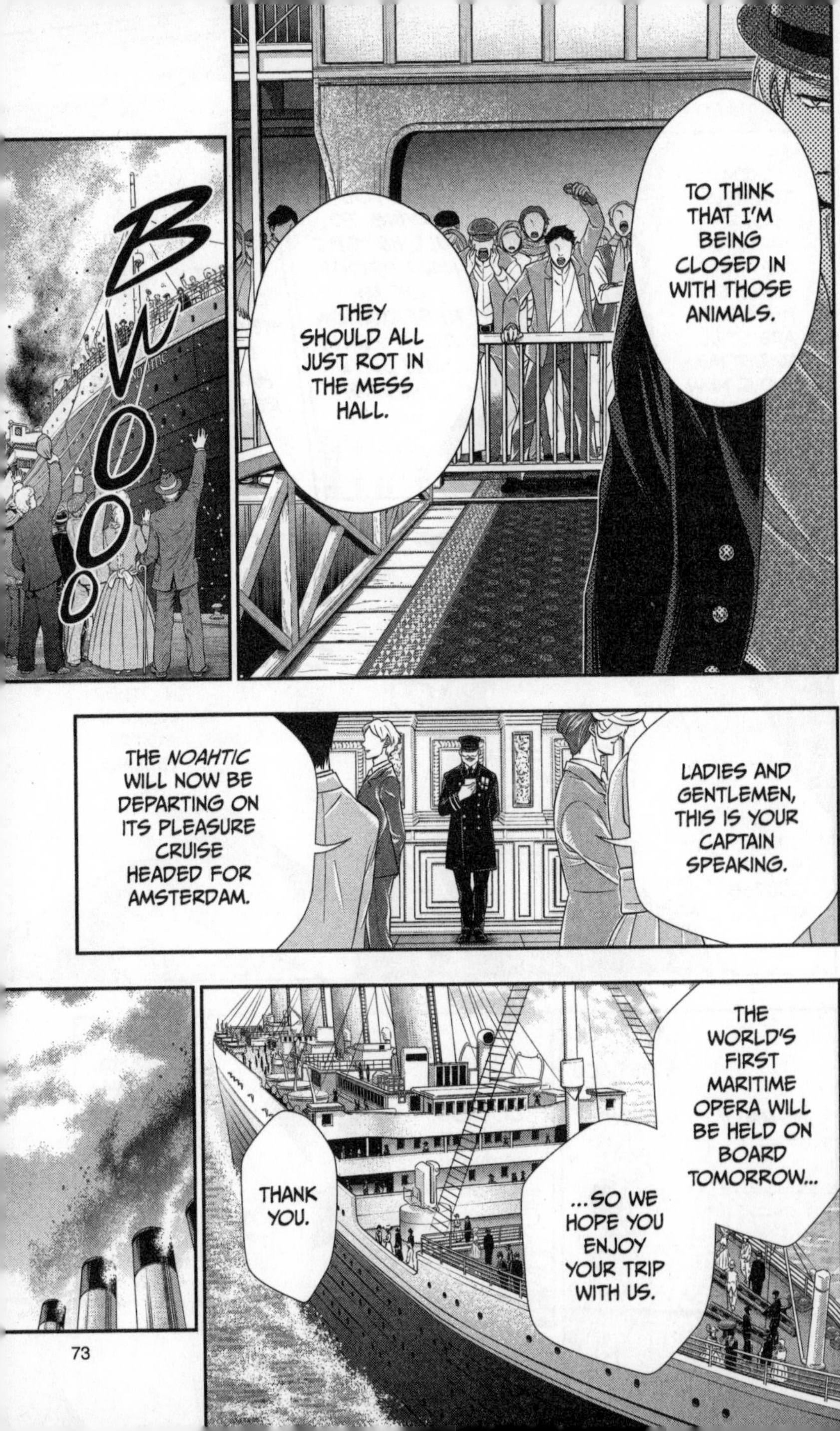
TO THINK THAT I'M BEING CLOSED IN WITH THOSE ANIMALS.
THEY SHOULD ALL JUST ROT IN THE MESS HALL.
BWOOOO
LADIES AND GENTLEMEN, THIS IS YOUR CAPTAIN SPEAKING.
THE *NOAHTIC* WILL NOW BE DEPARTING ON ITS PLEASURE CRUISE HEADED FOR AMSTERDAM.
THE WORLD'S FIRST MARITIME OPERA WILL BE HELD ON BOARD TOMORROW...
...SO WE HOPE YOU ENJOY YOUR TRIP WITH US.
THANK YOU.

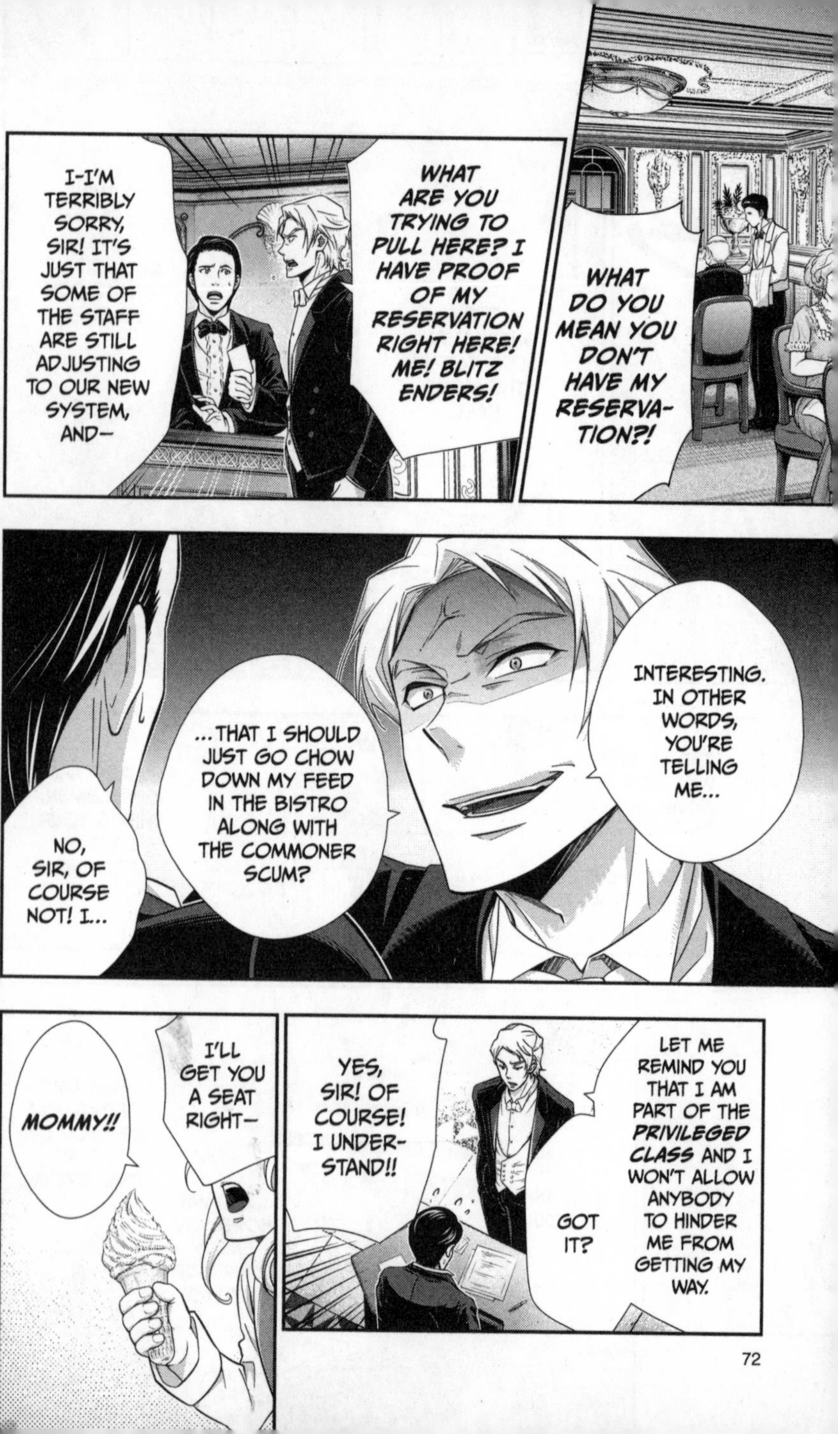
WHAT DO YOU MEAN YOU DON'T HAVE MY RESERVATION?!
WHAT ARE YOU TRYING TO PULL HERE? I HAVE PROOF OF MY RESERVATION RIGHT HERE! ME! BLITZ ENDERS!
I-I'M TERRIBLY SORRY, SIR! IT'S JUST THAT SOME OF THE STAFF ARE STILL ADJUSTING TO OUR NEW SYSTEM, AND—
INTERESTING. IN OTHER WORDS, YOU'RE TELLING ME...
...THAT I SHOULD JUST GO CHOW DOWN MY FEED IN THE BISTRO ALONG WITH THE COMMONER SCUM?
NO, SIR, OF COURSE NOT! I...
LET ME REMIND YOU THAT I AM PART OF THE PRIVILEGED CLASS AND I WON'T ALLOW ANYBODY TO HINDER ME FROM GETTING MY WAY.
GOT IT?
YES, SIR! OF COURSE! I UNDERSTAND!!
I'LL GET YOU A SEAT RIGHT—
MOMMY!!

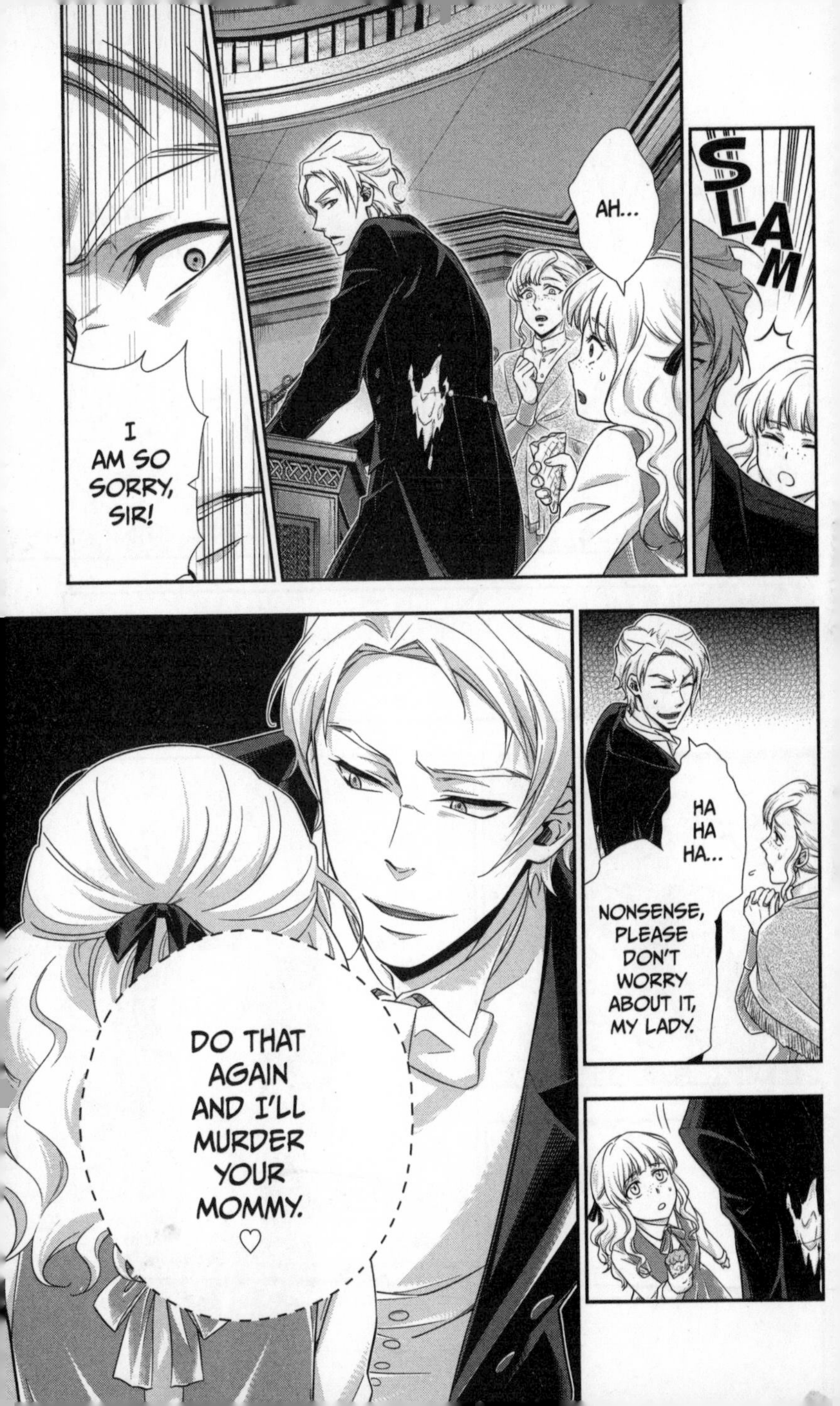
SLAM
AH...
I AM SO SORRY, SIR!
HA HA HA...
NONSENSE, PLEASE DON'T WORRY ABOUT IT, MY LADY.
DO THAT AGAIN AND I'LL MURDER YOUR MOMMY. ♡

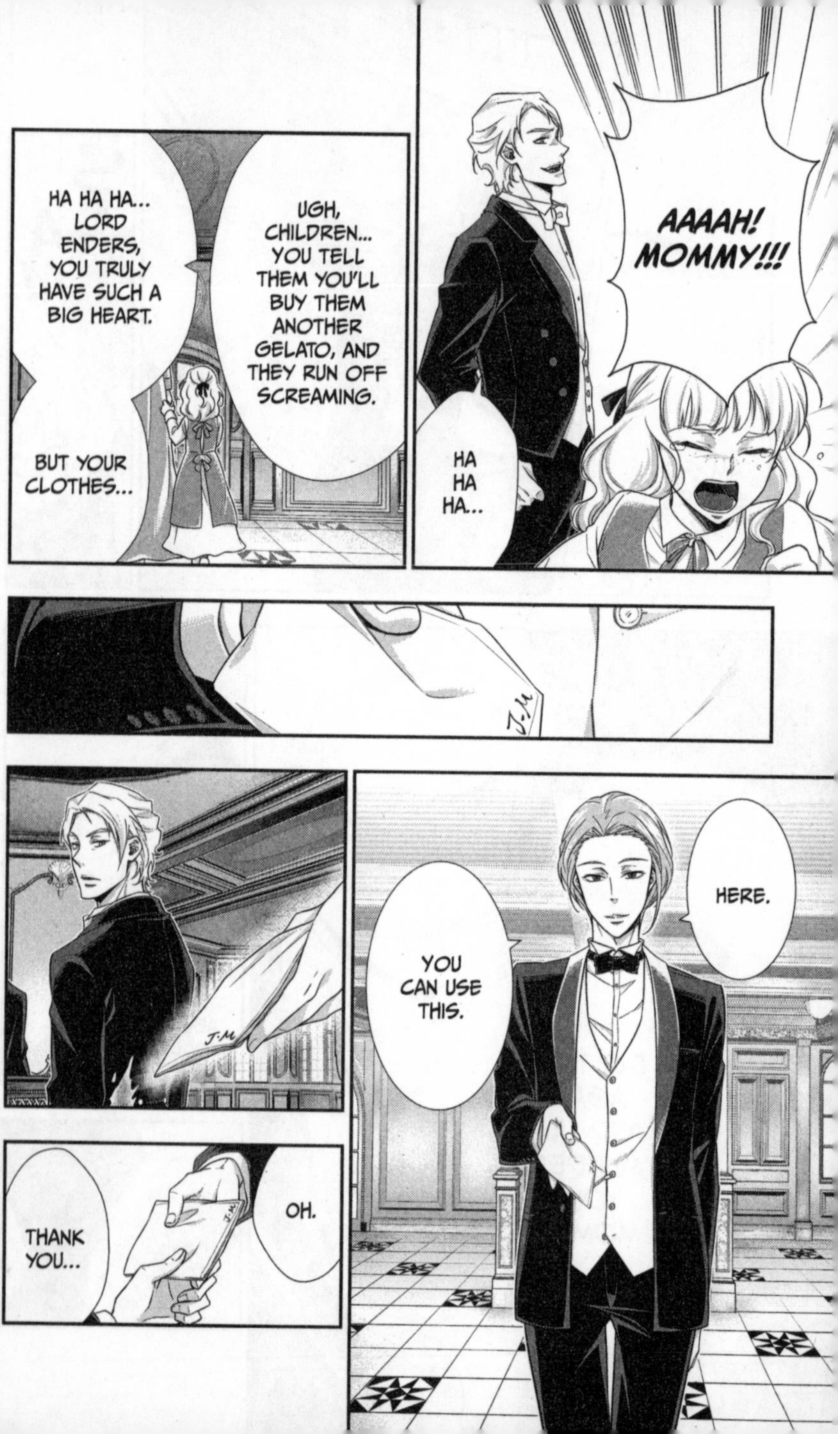
AAAAH! MOMMY!!!
HA HA HA...
UGH, CHILDREN... YOU TELL THEM YOU'LL BUY THEM ANOTHER GELATO, AND THEY RUN OFF SCREAMING.
HA HA HA... LORD ENDERS, YOU TRULY HAVE SUCH A BIG HEART.
BUT YOUR CLOTHES...
HERE.
YOU CAN USE THIS.
OH.
THANK YOU...

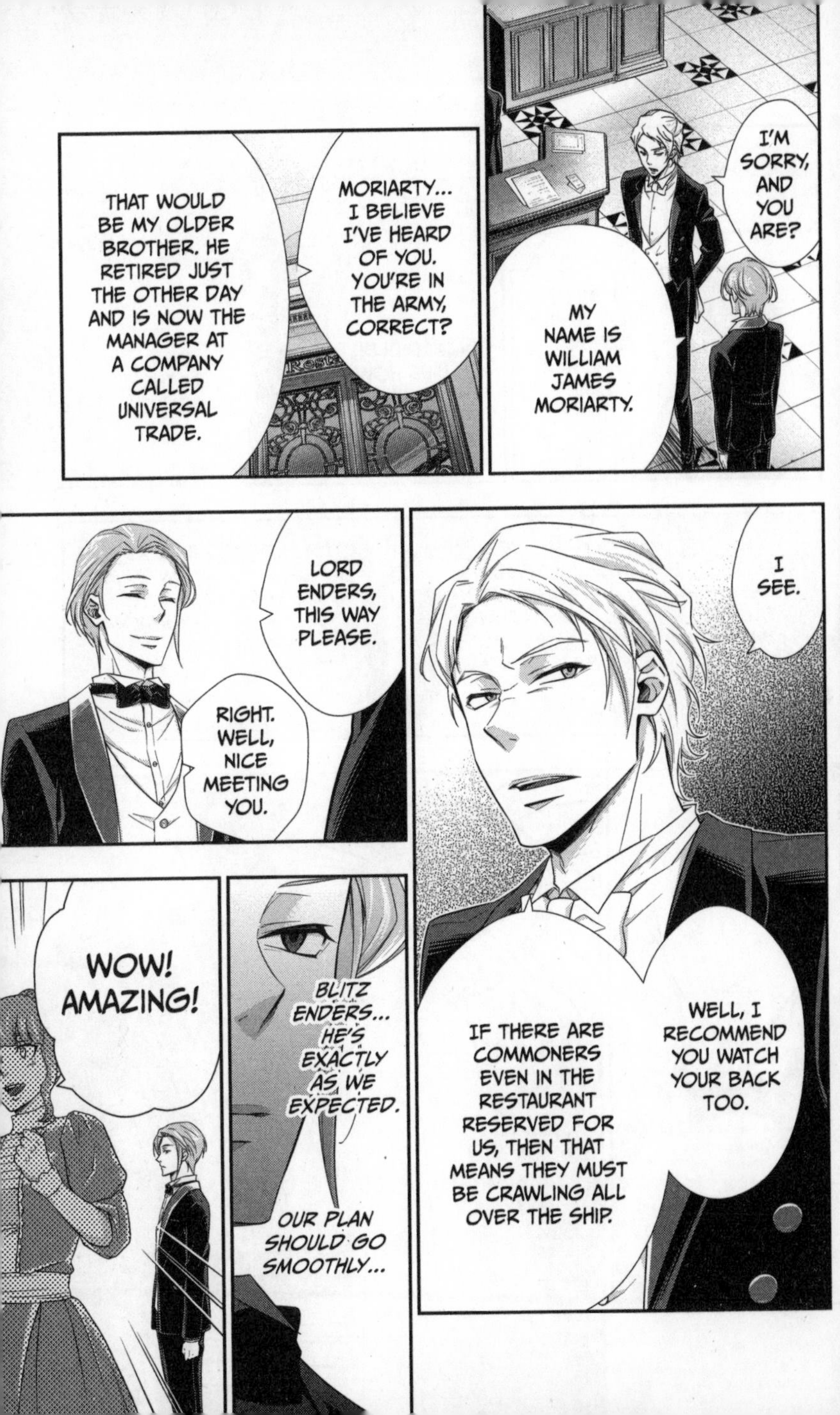
I'M SORRY, AND YOU ARE?
MY NAME IS WILLIAM JAMES MORIARTY.
MORIARTY... I BELIEVE I'VE HEARD OF YOU. YOU'RE IN THE ARMY, CORRECT?
THAT WOULD BE MY OLDER BROTHER. HE RETIRED JUST THE OTHER DAY AND IS NOW THE MANAGER AT A COMPANY CALLED UNIVERSAL TRADE.
I SEE.
WELL, I RECOMMEND YOU WATCH YOUR BACK TOO.
IF THERE ARE COMMONERS EVEN IN THE RESTAURANT RESERVED FOR US, THEN THAT MEANS THEY MUST BE CRAWLING ALL OVER THE SHIP.
LORD ENDERS, THIS WAY PLEASE.
RIGHT. WELL, NICE MEETING YOU.
BLITZ ENDERS... HE'S EXACTLY AS WE EXPECTED.
OUR PLAN SHOULD GO SMOOTHLY...
WOW! AMAZING!

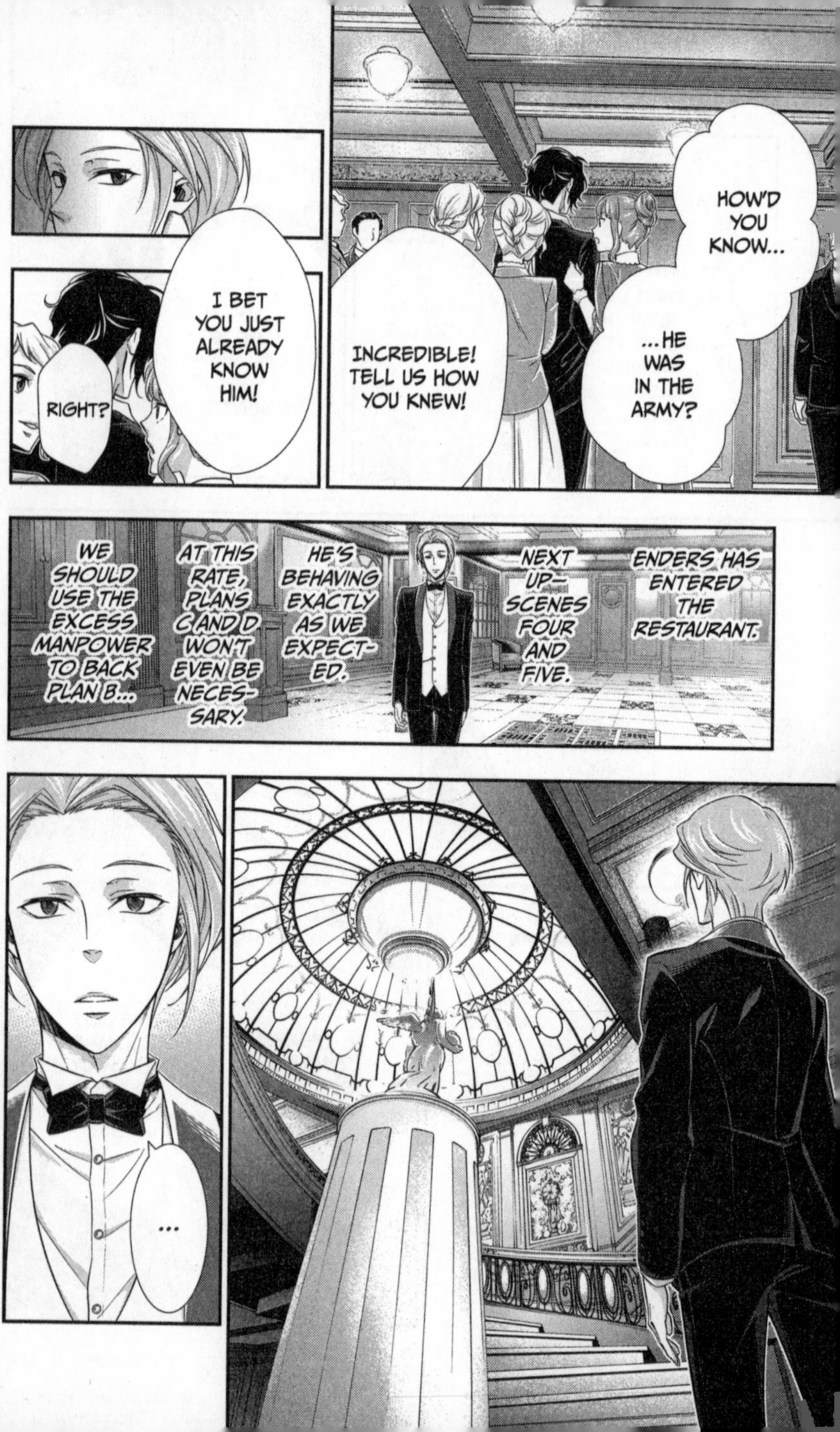
HOW'D YOU KNOW...
...HE WAS IN THE ARMY?
INCREDIBLE! TELL US HOW YOU KNEW!
I BET YOU JUST ALREADY KNOW HIM!
RIGHT?
ENDERS HAS ENTERED THE RESTAURANT.
NEXT UP—SCENES FOUR AND FIVE.
HE'S BEHAVING EXACTLY AS WE EXPECTED.
AT THIS RATE, PLANS C AND D WON'T EVEN BE NECESSARY.
WE SHOULD USE THE EXCESS MANPOWER TO BACK PLAN B...
...

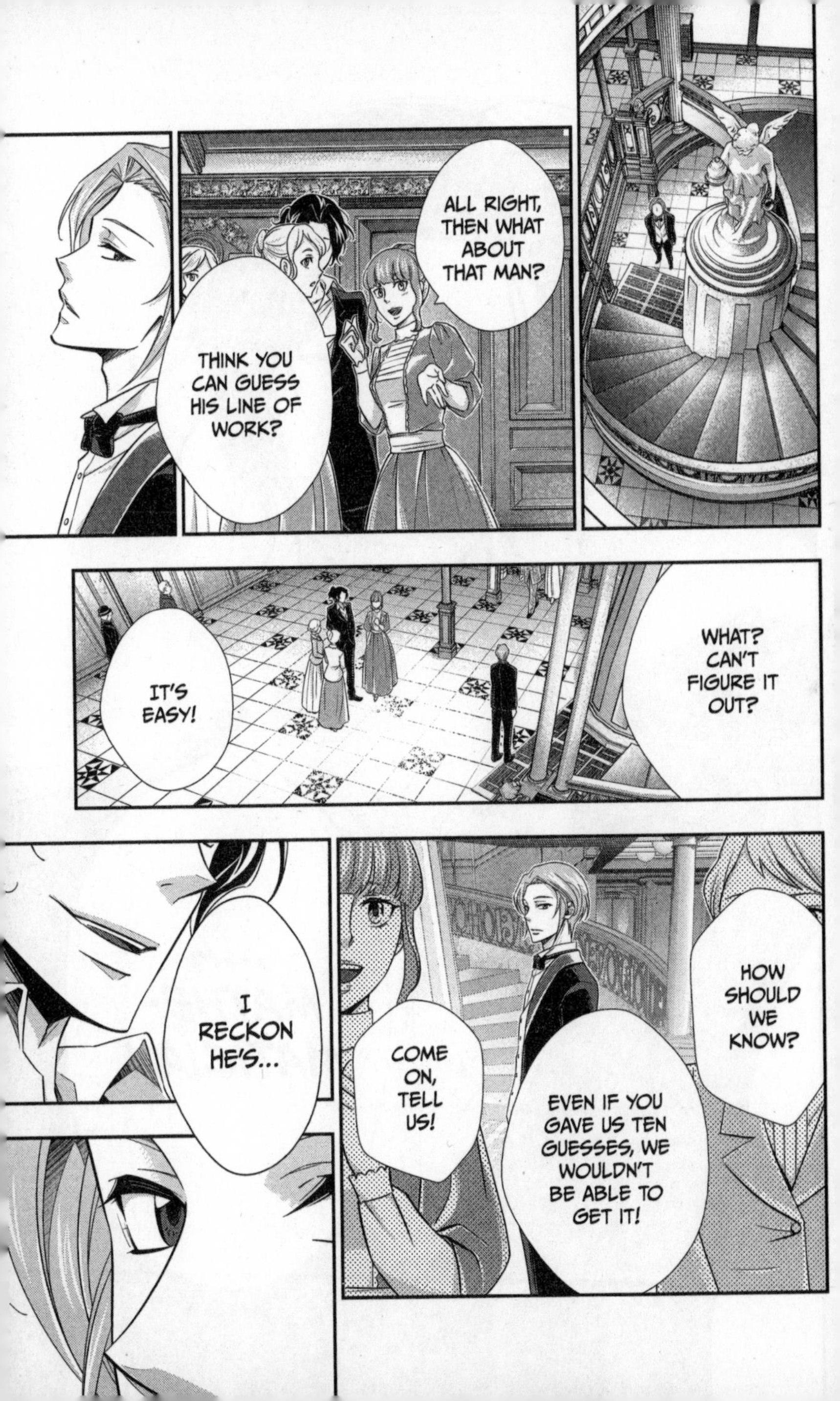
ALL RIGHT, THEN WHAT ABOUT THAT MAN?
THINK YOU CAN GUESS HIS LINE OF WORK?
WHAT? CAN'T FIGURE IT OUT?
IT'S EASY!
HOW SHOULD WE KNOW?
EVEN IF YOU GAVE US TEN GUESSES, WE WOULDN'T BE ABLE TO GET IT!
COME ON, TELL US!
I RECKON HE'S...

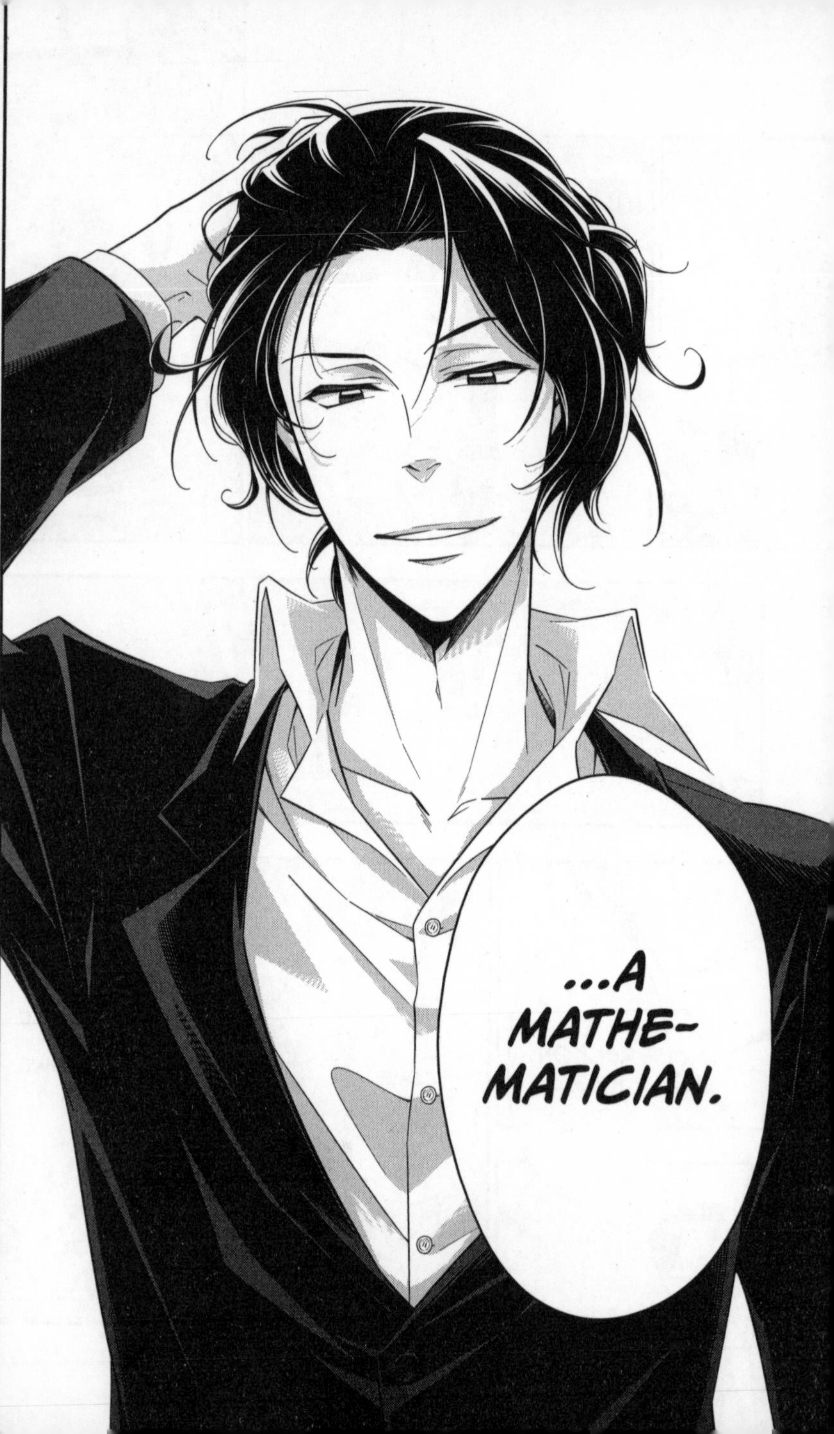
...A MATHE-MATICIAN.

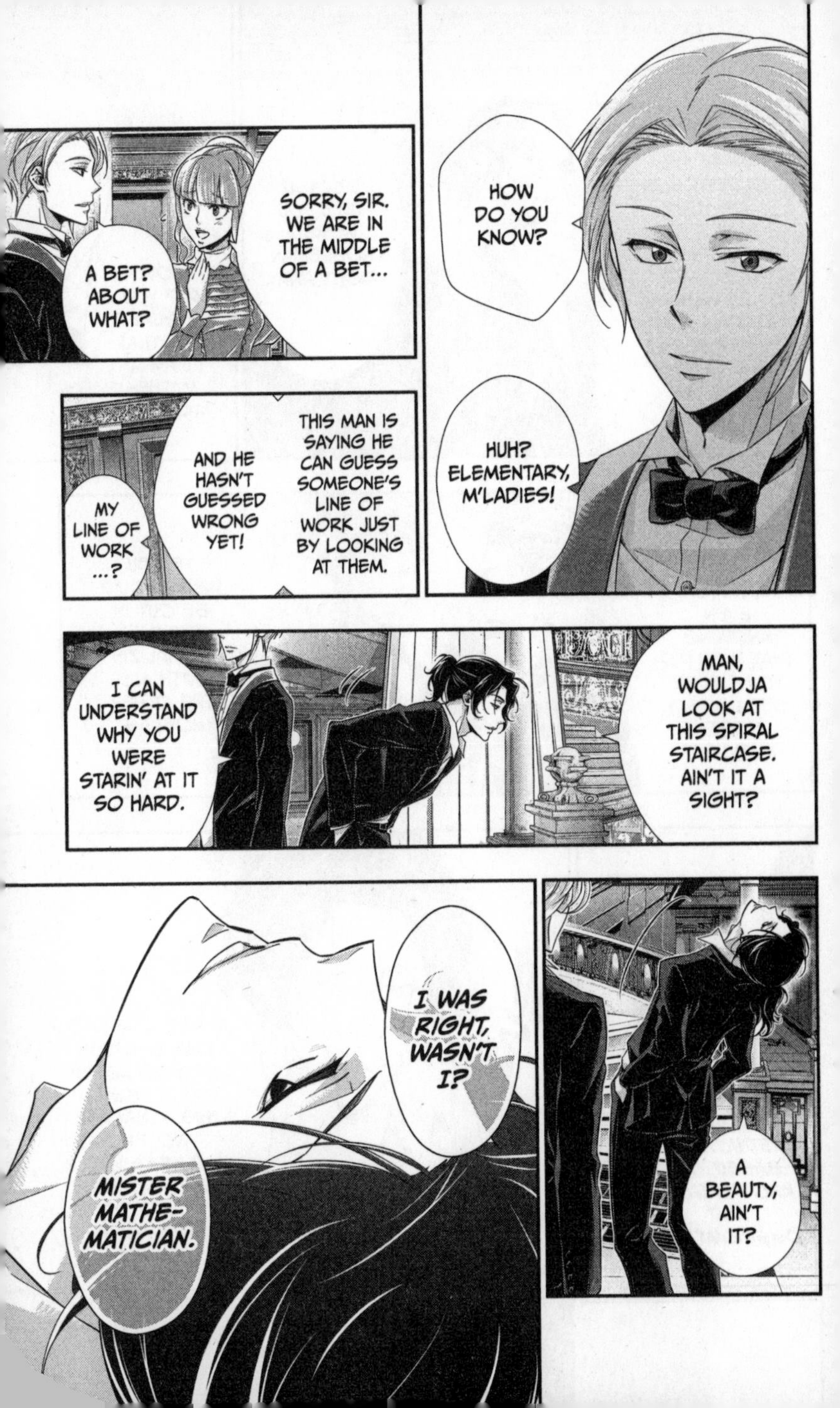
HOW DO YOU KNOW?
HUH? ELEMENTARY, M'LADIES!
SORRY, SIR. WE ARE IN THE MIDDLE OF A BET...
A BET? ABOUT WHAT?
THIS MAN IS SAYING HE CAN GUESS SOMEONE'S LINE OF WORK JUST BY LOOKING AT THEM.
AND HE HASN'T GUESSED WRONG YET!
MY LINE OF WORK ...?
MAN, WOULDJA LOOK AT THIS SPIRAL STAIRCASE. AIN'T IT A SIGHT?
I CAN UNDERSTAND WHY YOU WERE STARIN' AT IT SO HARD.
A BEAUTY, AIN'T IT?
I WAS RIGHT, WASN'T I?
MISTER MATHE-MATICIAN.

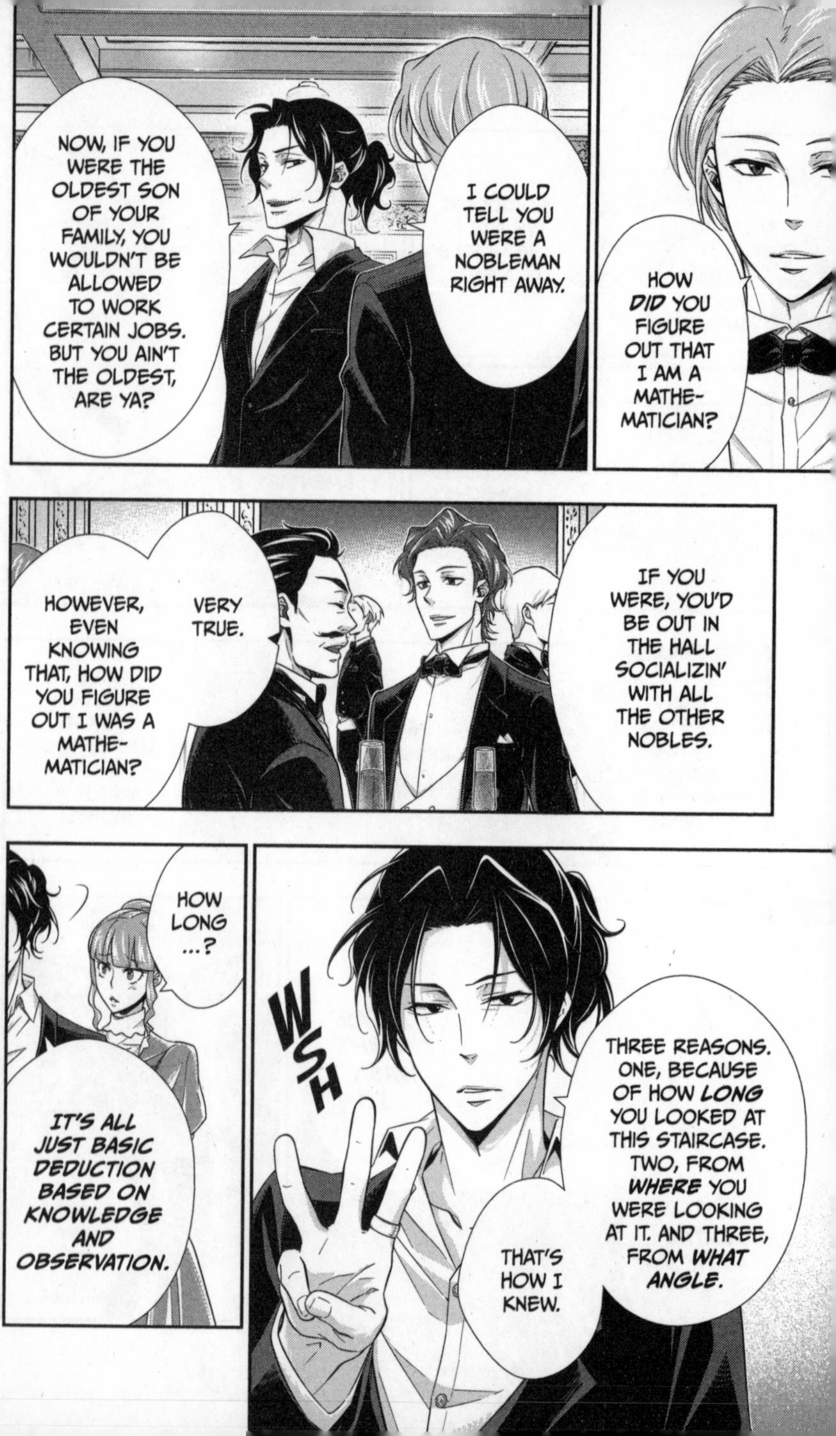
HOW *DID* YOU FIGURE OUT THAT I AM A MATHE-MATICIAN?
I COULD TELL YOU WERE A NOBLEMAN RIGHT AWAY.
NOW, IF YOU WERE THE OLDEST SON OF YOUR FAMILY, YOU WOULDN'T BE ALLOWED TO WORK CERTAIN JOBS. BUT YOU AIN'T THE OLDEST, ARE YA?
IF YOU WERE, YOU'D BE OUT IN THE HALL SOCIALIZIN' WITH ALL THE OTHER NOBLES.
VERY TRUE.
HOWEVER, EVEN KNOWING THAT, HOW DID YOU FIGURE OUT I WAS A MATHE-MATICIAN?
WSH
THREE REASONS. ONE, BECAUSE OF HOW *LONG* YOU LOOKED AT THIS STAIRCASE. TWO, FROM *WHERE* YOU WERE LOOKING AT IT. AND THREE, FROM *WHAT ANGLE*.
THAT'S HOW I KNEW.
HOW LONG ...?
IT'S ALL JUST BASIC DEDUCTION BASED ON KNOWLEDGE AND OBSERVATION.

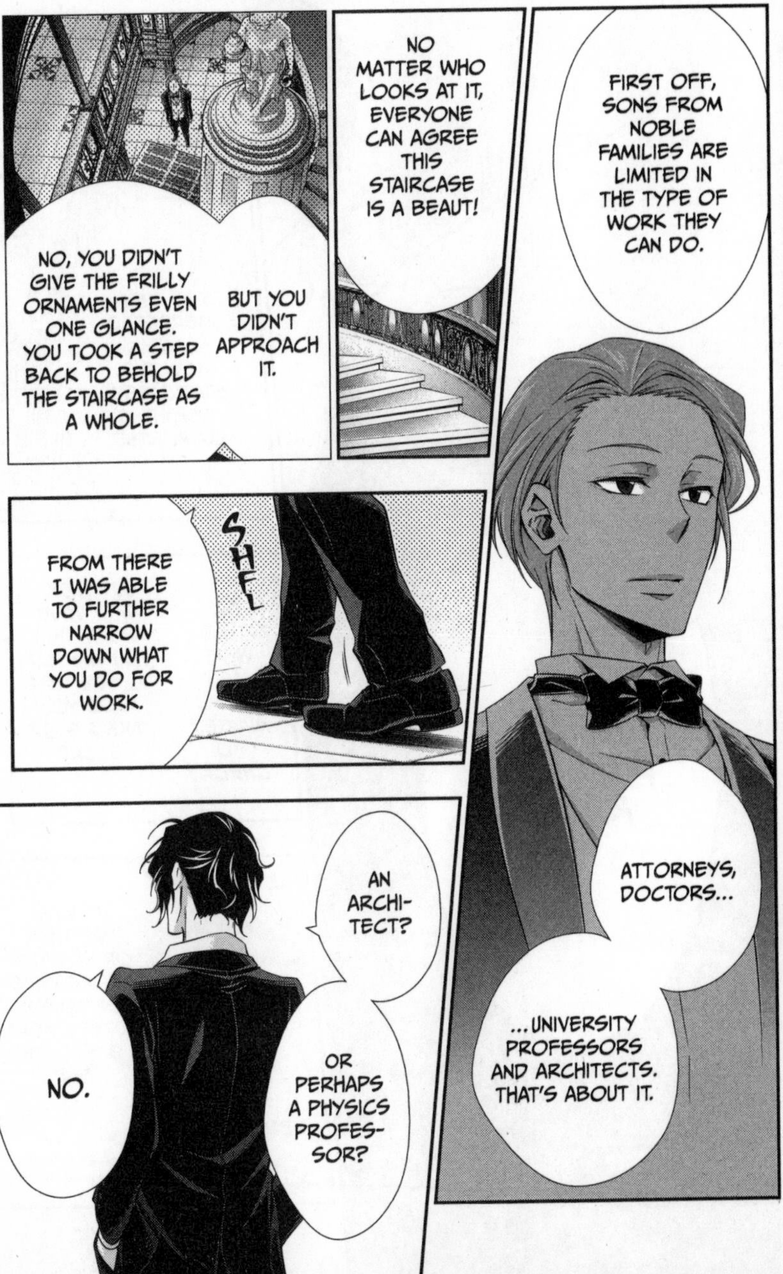
FIRST OFF, SONS FROM NOBLE FAMILIES ARE LIMITED IN THE TYPE OF WORK THEY CAN DO.
ATTORNEYS, DOCTORS...
...UNIVERSITY PROFESSORS AND ARCHITECTS. THAT'S ABOUT IT.
NO MATTER WHO LOOKS AT IT, EVERYONE CAN AGREE THIS STAIRCASE IS A BEAUT!
BUT YOU DIDN'T APPROACH IT.
NO, YOU DIDN'T GIVE THE FRILLY ORNAMENTS EVEN ONE GLANCE. YOU TOOK A STEP BACK TO BEHOLD THE STAIRCASE AS A WHOLE.
SHFL
FROM THERE I WAS ABLE TO FURTHER NARROW DOWN WHAT YOU DO FOR WORK.
AN ARCHI-TECT?
OR PERHAPS A PHYSICS PROFES-SOR?
NO.

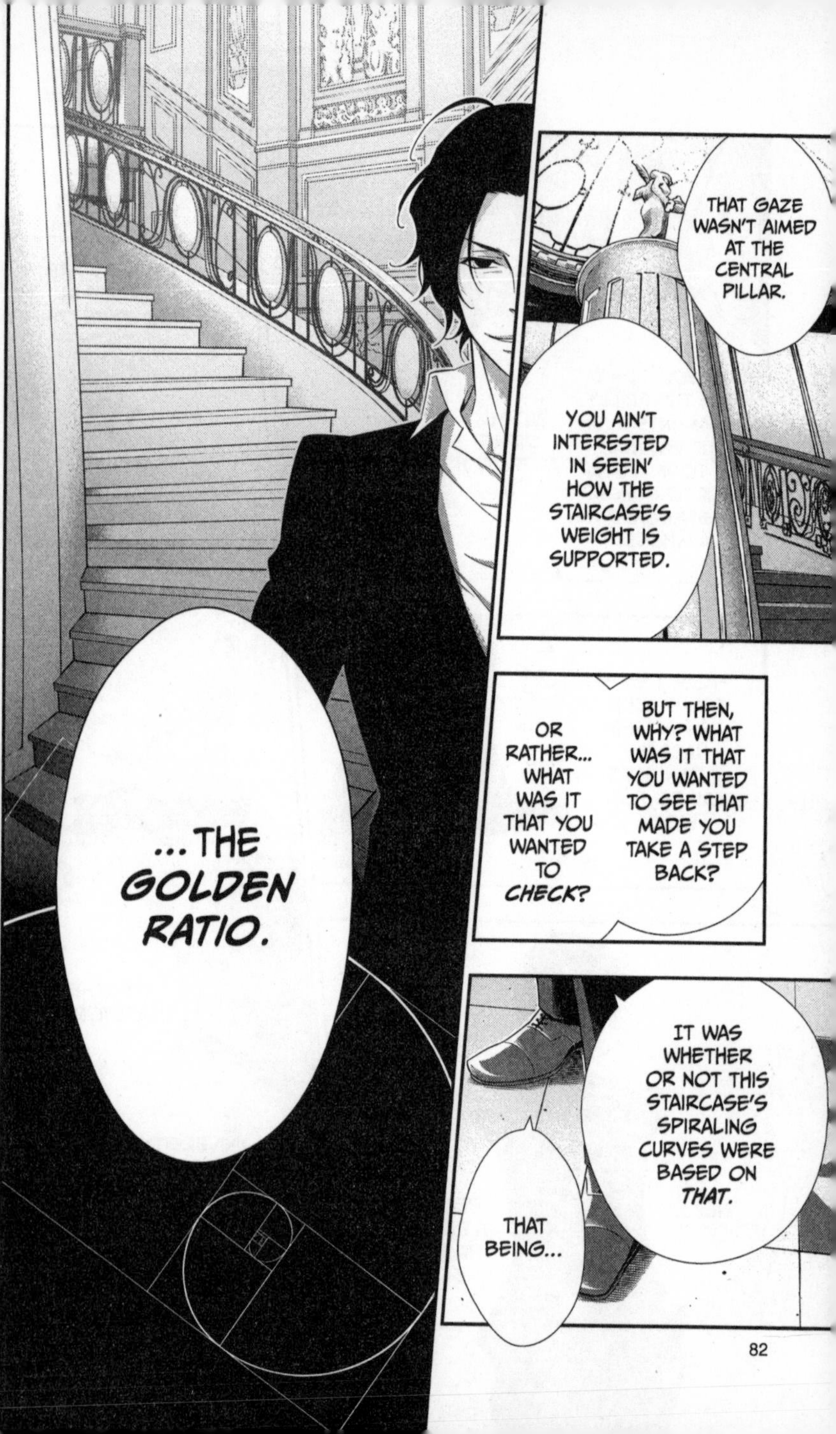
THAT GAZE WASN'T AIMED AT THE CENTRAL PILLAR.
YOU AIN'T INTERESTED IN SEEIN' HOW THE STAIRCASE'S WEIGHT IS SUPPORTED.
BUT THEN, WHY? WHAT WAS IT THAT YOU WANTED TO SEE THAT MADE YOU TAKE A STEP BACK?
OR RATHER... WHAT WAS IT THAT YOU WANTED TO *CHECK?*
IT WAS WHETHER OR NOT THIS STAIRCASE'S SPIRALING CURVES WERE BASED ON *THAT.*
THAT BEING...
...THE *GOLDEN RATIO.*

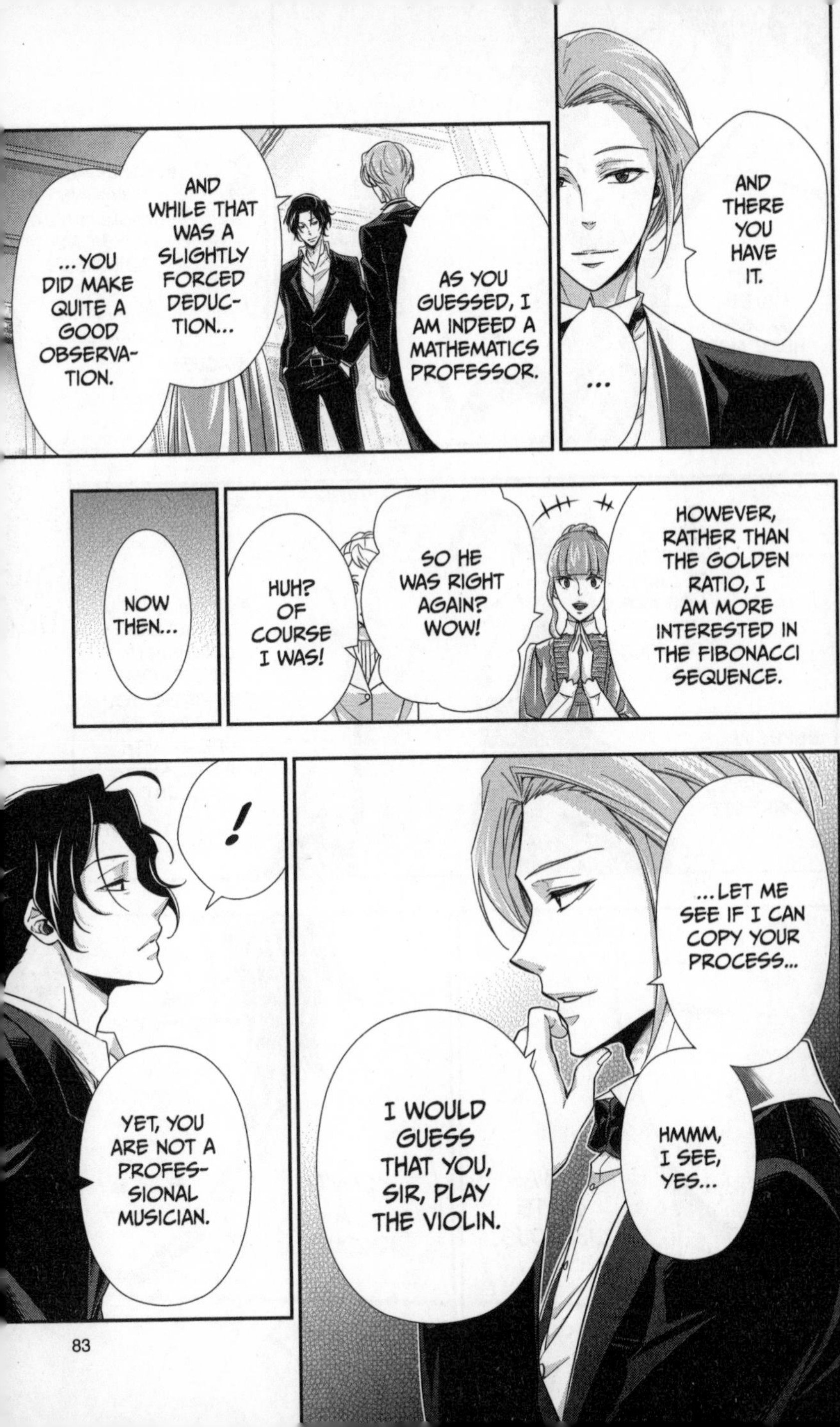
AND THERE YOU HAVE IT.
...
AS YOU GUESSED, I AM INDEED A MATHEMATICS PROFESSOR.
AND WHILE THAT WAS A SLIGHTLY FORCED DEDUC-TION...
...YOU DID MAKE QUITE A GOOD OBSERVA-TION.
HOWEVER, RATHER THAN THE GOLDEN RATIO, I AM MORE INTERESTED IN THE FIBONACCI SEQUENCE.
SO HE WAS RIGHT AGAIN? WOW!
HUH? OF COURSE I WAS!
NOW THEN...
...LET ME SEE IF I CAN COPY YOUR PROCESS...
HMMM, I SEE, YES...
I WOULD GUESS THAT YOU, SIR, PLAY THE VIOLIN.
!
YET, YOU ARE NOT A PROFES-SIONAL MUSICIAN.

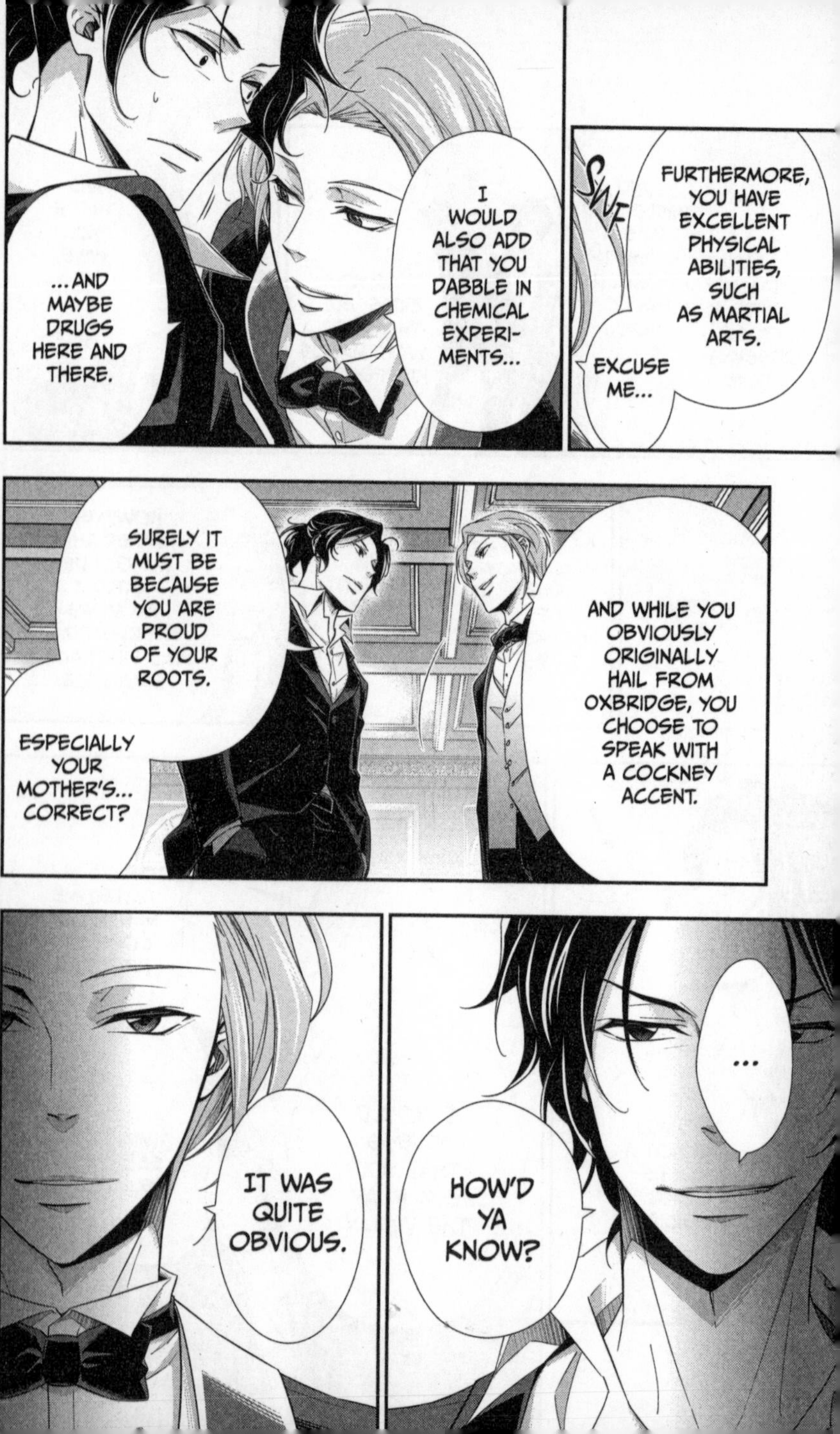
FURTHERMORE, YOU HAVE EXCELLENT PHYSICAL ABILITIES, SUCH AS MARTIAL ARTS.
SWF
EXCUSE ME...
I WOULD ALSO ADD THAT YOU DABBLE IN CHEMICAL EXPERI-MENTS...
...AND MAYBE DRUGS HERE AND THERE.
AND WHILE YOU OBVIOUSLY ORIGINALLY HAIL FROM OXBRIDGE, YOU CHOOSE TO SPEAK WITH A COCKNEY ACCENT.
SURELY IT MUST BE BECAUSE YOU ARE PROUD OF YOUR ROOTS.
ESPECIALLY YOUR MOTHER'S... CORRECT?
...
HOW'D YA KNOW?
IT WAS QUITE OBVIOUS.

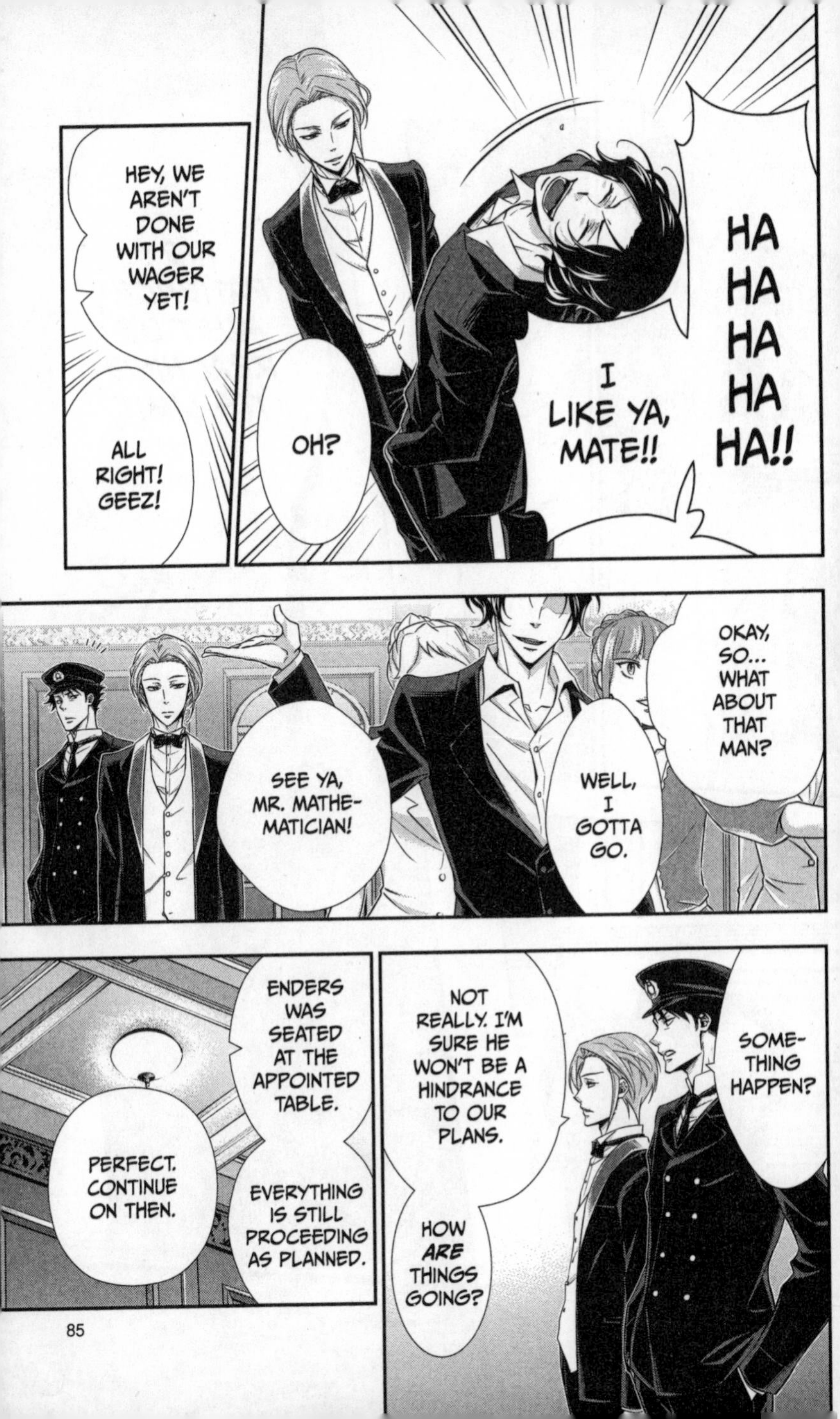
HA HA HA HA HA!!
I LIKE YA, MATE!!
OH?
HEY, WE AREN'T DONE WITH OUR WAGER YET!
ALL RIGHT! GEEZ!
OKAY, SO... WHAT ABOUT THAT MAN?
WELL, I GOTTA GO.
SEE YA, MR. MATHEMATICIAN!
SOMETHING HAPPEN?
NOT REALLY. I'M SURE HE WON'T BE A HINDRANCE TO OUR PLANS.
HOW *ARE* THINGS GOING?
ENDERS WAS SEATED AT THE APPOINTED TABLE.
EVERYTHING IS STILL PROCEEDING AS PLANNED.
PERFECT. CONTINUE ON THEN.

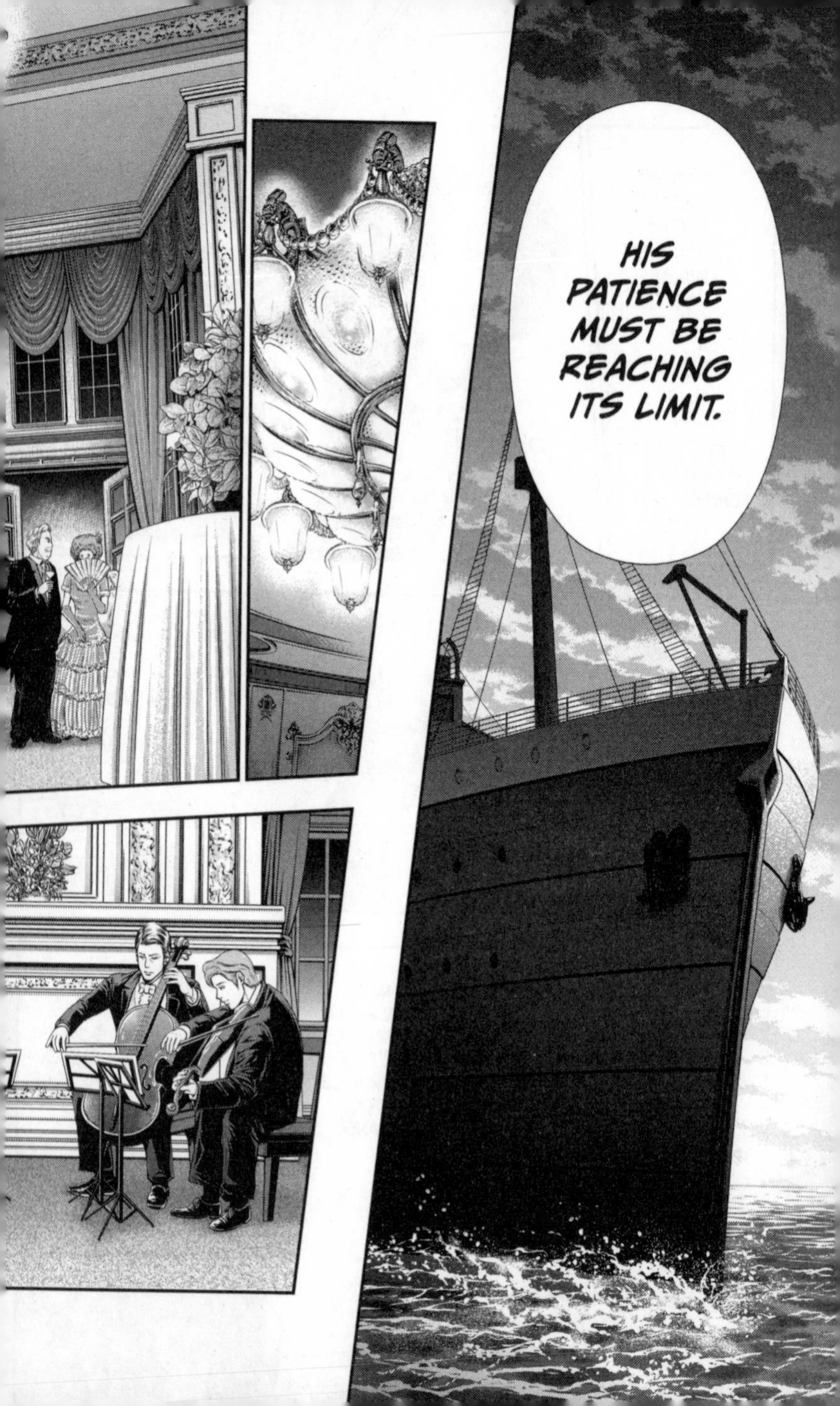
HIS PATIENCE MUST BE REACHING ITS LIMIT.

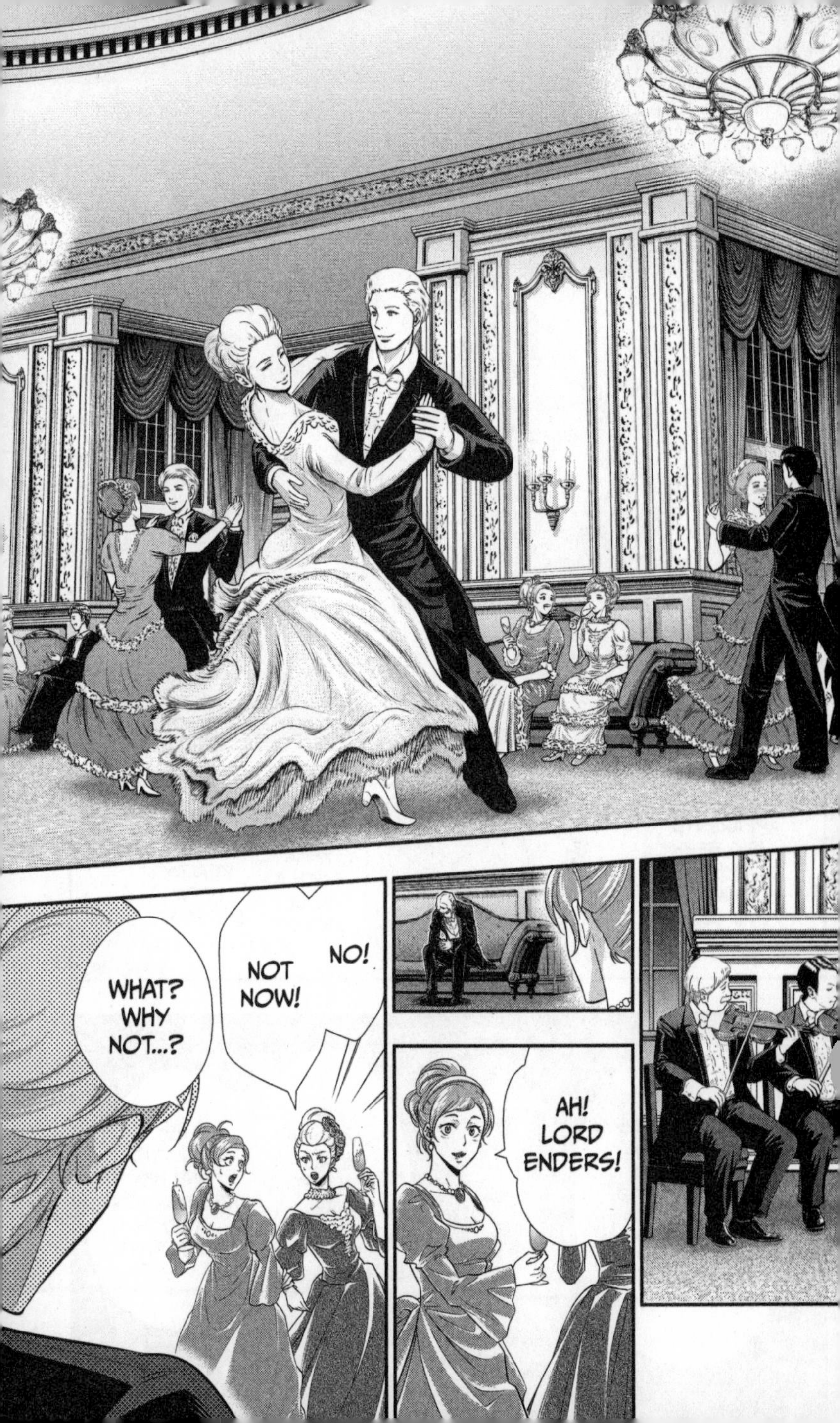
AH! LORD ENDERS!
NOT NOW! NO!
WHAT? WHY NOT...?

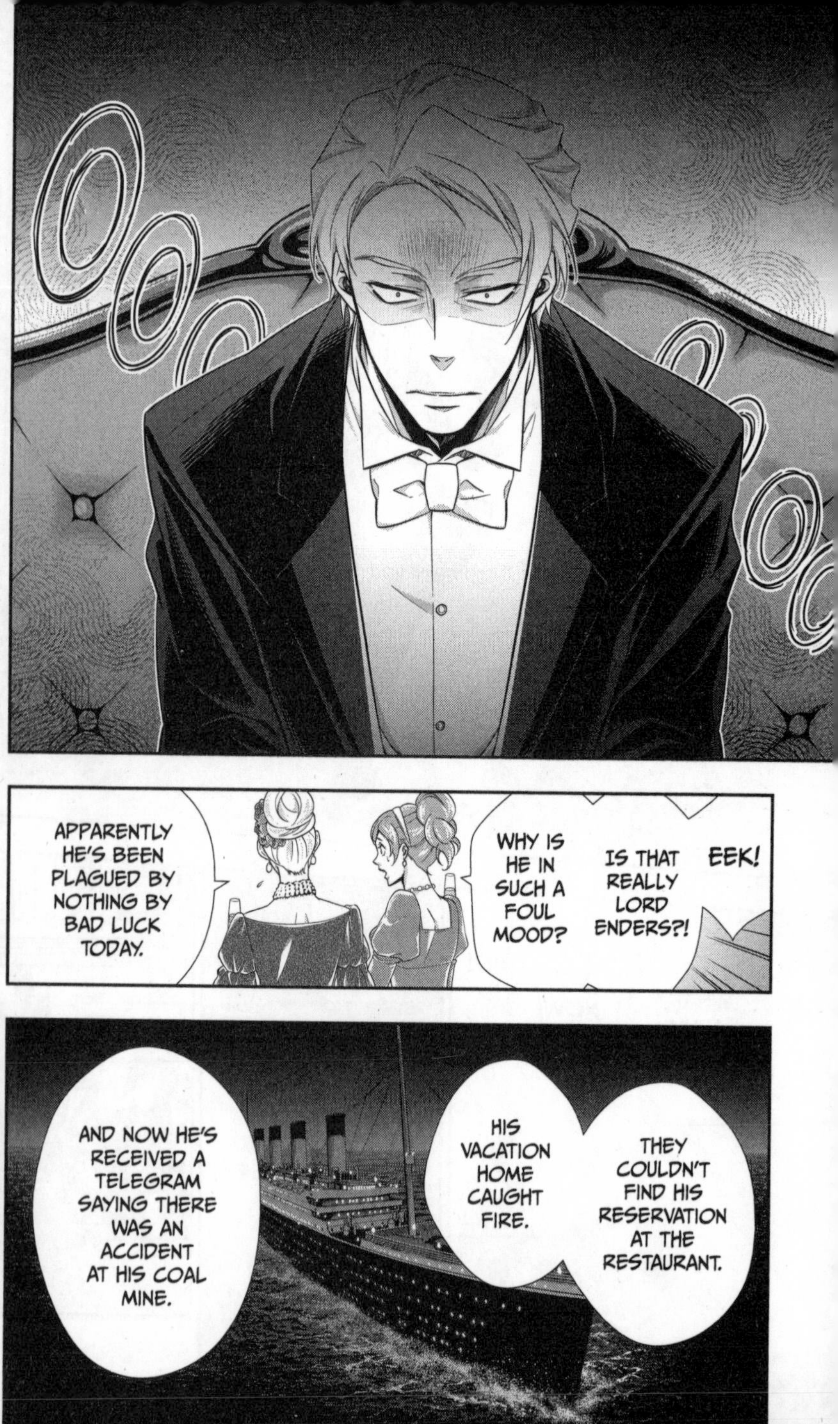
EEK!
IS THAT REALLY LORD ENDERS?!
WHY IS HE IN SUCH A FOUL MOOD?
APPARENTLY HE'S BEEN PLAGUED BY NOTHING BY BAD LUCK TODAY.
THEY COULDN'T FIND HIS RESERVATION AT THE RESTAURANT.
HIS VACATION HOME CAUGHT FIRE.
AND NOW HE'S RECEIVED A TELEGRAM SAYING THERE WAS AN ACCIDENT AT HIS COAL MINE.

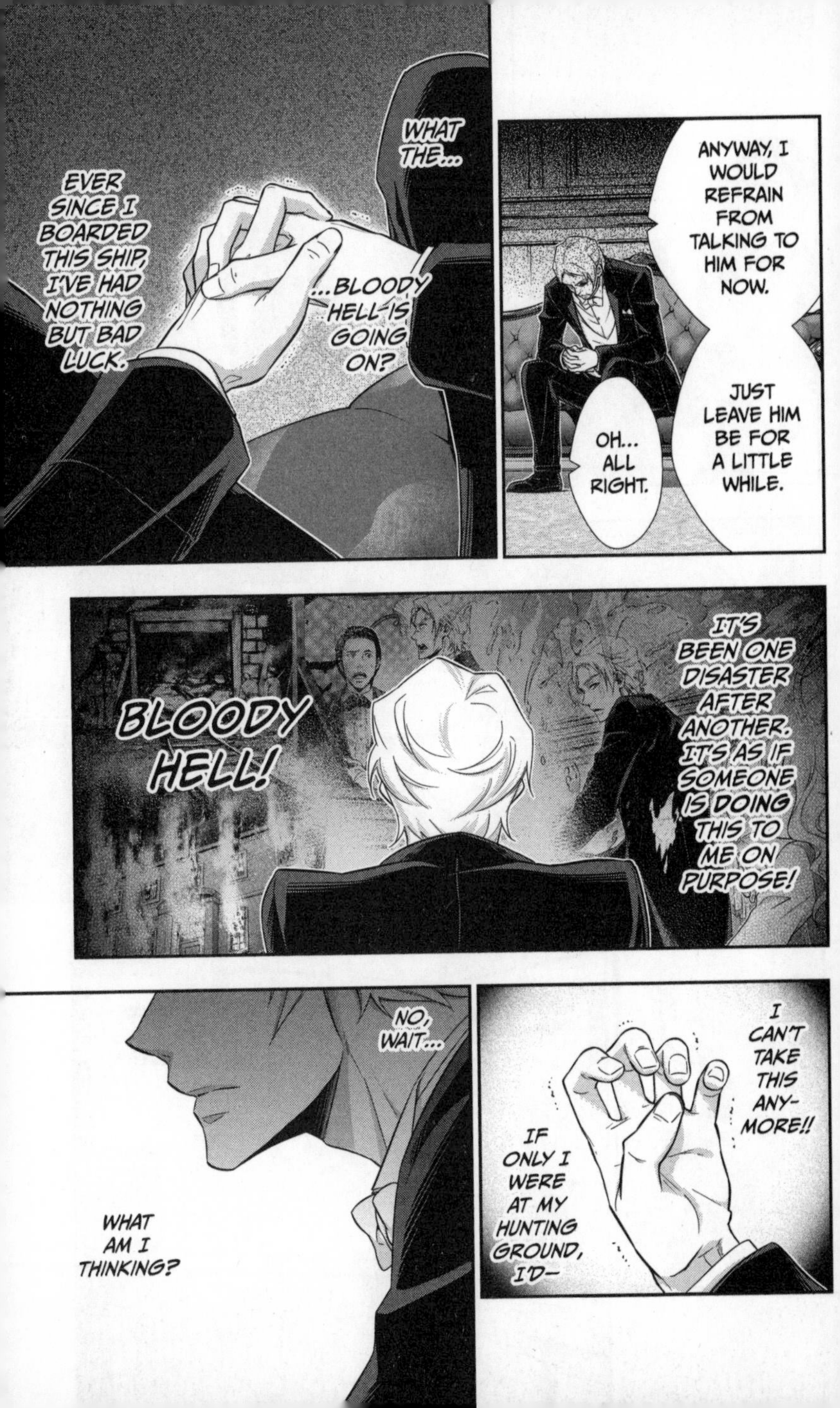
ANYWAY, I WOULD REFRAIN FROM TALKING TO HIM FOR NOW.
JUST LEAVE HIM BE FOR A LITTLE WHILE.
OH... ALL RIGHT.
WHAT THE...
...BLOODY HELL IS GOING ON?
EVER SINCE I BOARDED THIS SHIP, I'VE HAD NOTHING BUT BAD LUCK.
IT'S BEEN ONE DISASTER AFTER ANOTHER. IT'S AS IF SOMEONE IS DOING THIS TO ME ON PURPOSE!
BLOODY HELL!
I CAN'T TAKE THIS ANY-MORE!!
IF ONLY I WERE AT MY HUNTING GROUND, I'D—
NO, WAIT...
WHAT AM I THINKING?

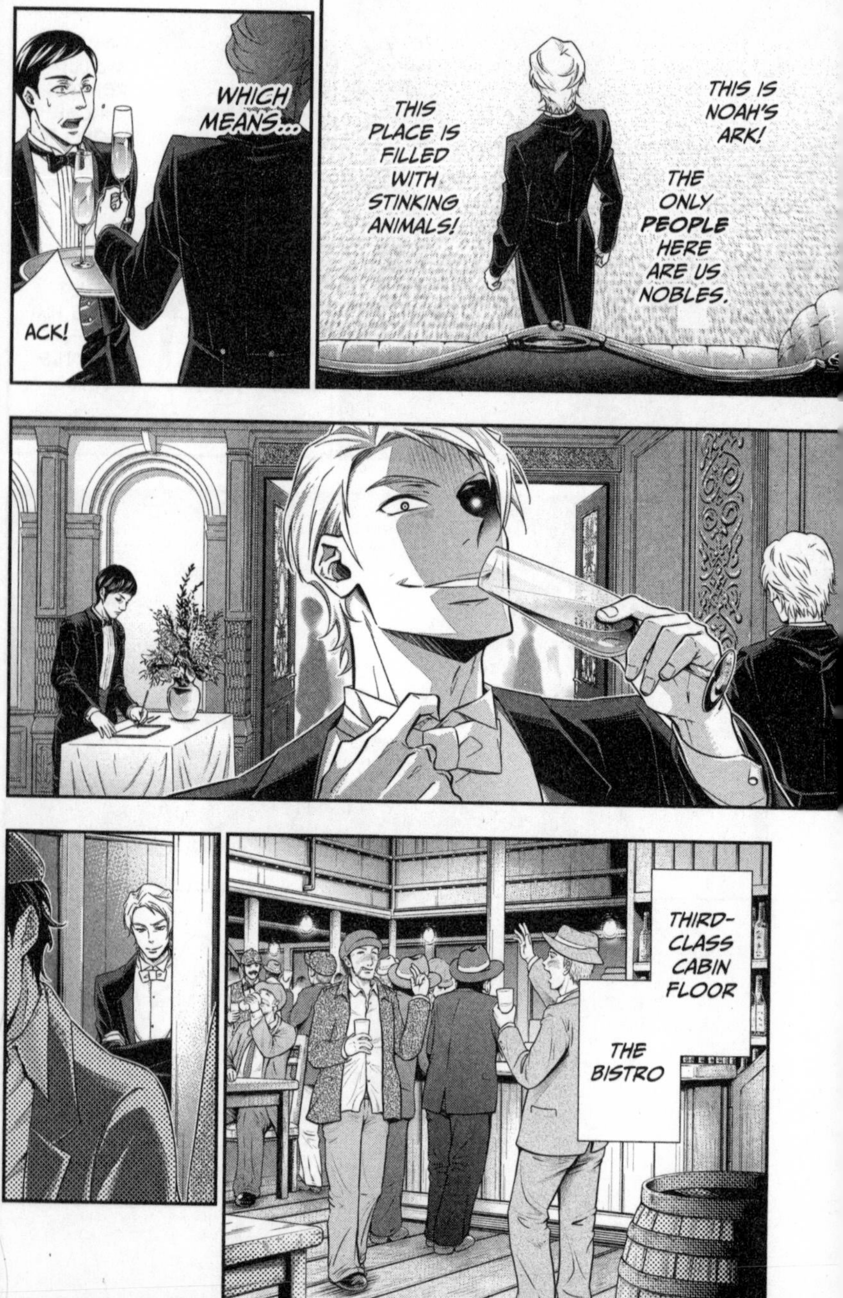
THIS IS NOAH'S ARK!
THE ONLY PEOPLE HERE ARE US NOBLES.
THIS PLACE IS FILLED WITH STINKING ANIMALS!
WHICH MEANS...
ACK!
THIRD-CLASS CABIN FLOOR
THE BISTRO

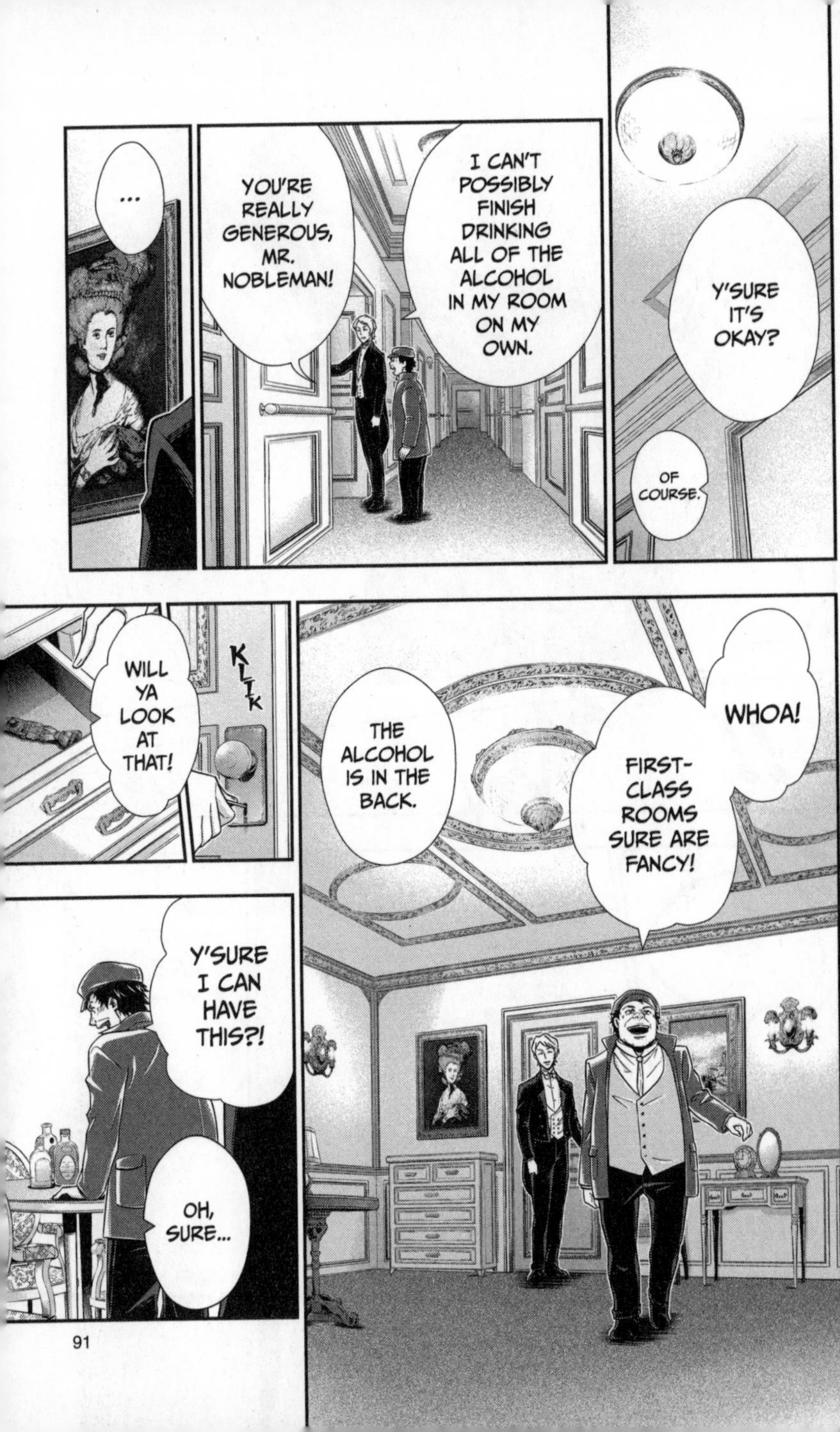
Y'SURE IT'S OKAY?
OF COURSE.
I CAN'T POSSIBLY FINISH DRINKING ALL OF THE ALCOHOL IN MY ROOM ON MY OWN.
YOU'RE REALLY GENEROUS, MR. NOBLEMAN!
...
WHOA!
FIRST-CLASS ROOMS SURE ARE FANCY!
THE ALCOHOL IS IN THE BACK.
KLIK
WILL YA LOOK AT THAT!
Y'SURE I CAN HAVE THIS?!
OH, SURE...

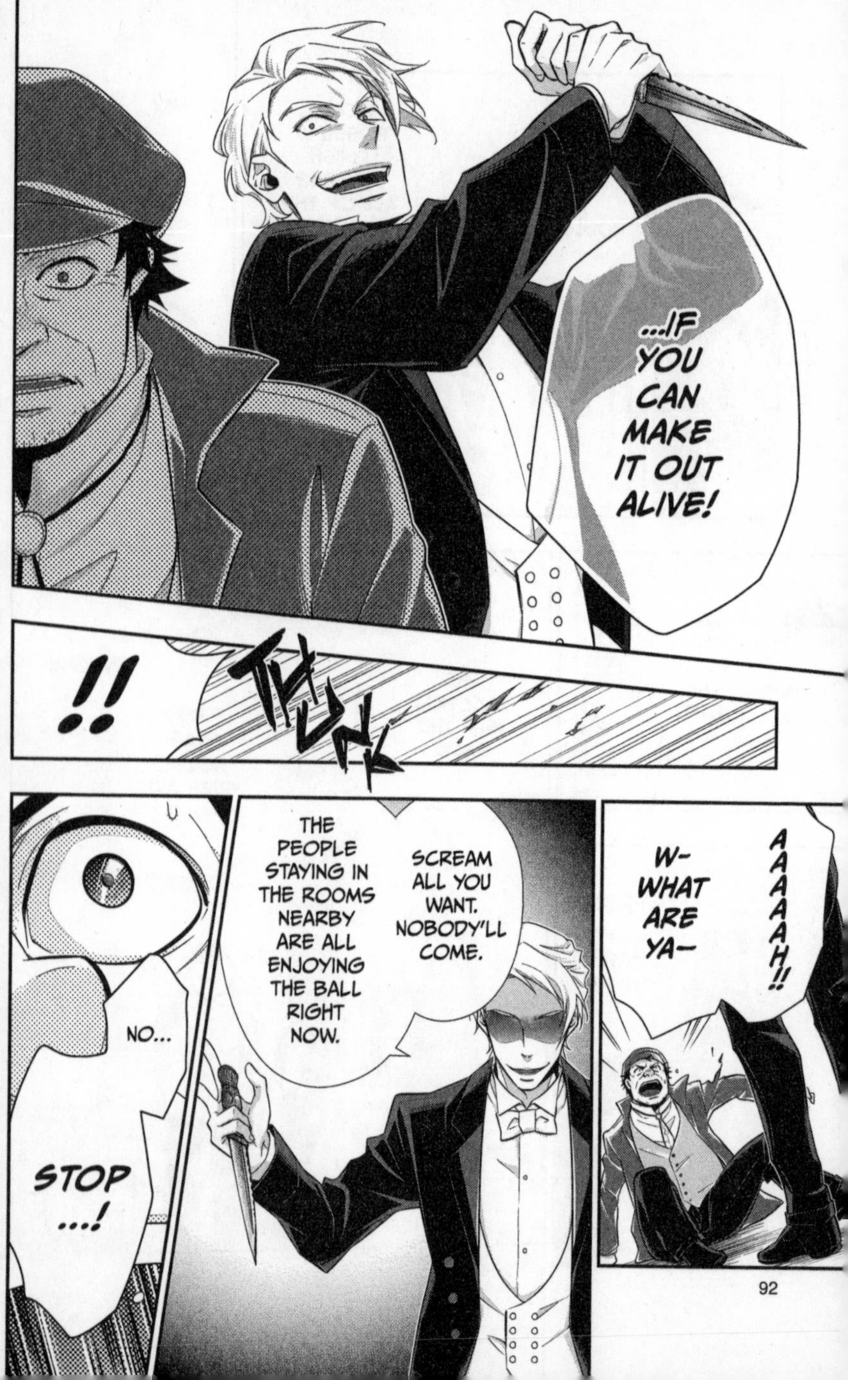
...IF YOU CAN MAKE IT OUT ALIVE!
THUNK
!!
AAAAAAH!!
W-WHAT ARE YA—
SCREAM ALL YOU WANT. NOBODY'LL COME.
THE PEOPLE STAYING IN THE ROOMS NEARBY ARE ALL ENJOYING THE BALL RIGHT NOW.
NO...
STOP...!

HA HA HA! YOU LOT REALLY ARE MERE ANIMALS!!

EVEN YOUR LAST SCREAMS SOUND JUST AS SAVAGE.

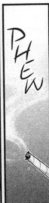

PHEW

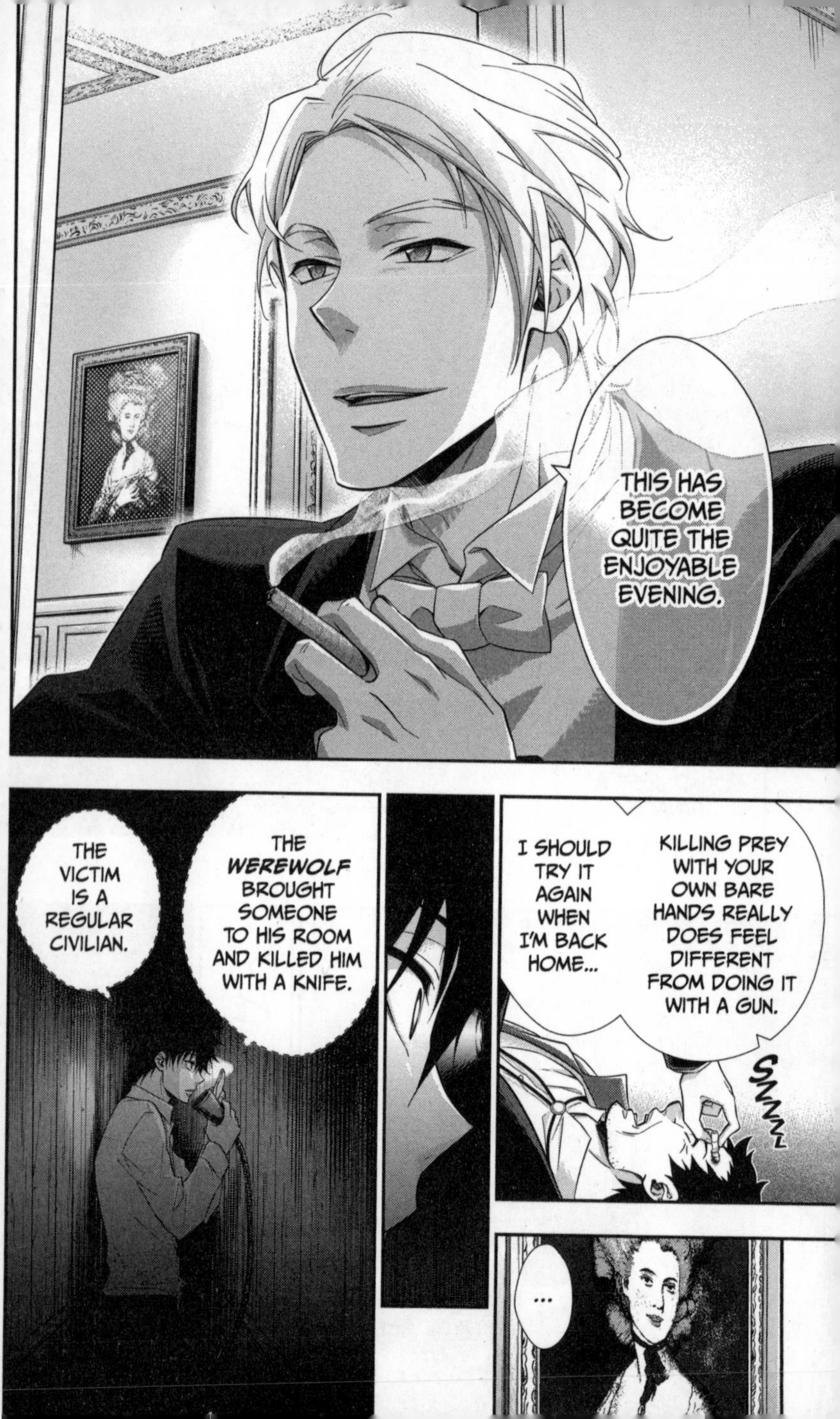
THIS HAS BECOME QUITE THE ENJOYABLE EVENING.
KILLING PREY WITH YOUR OWN BARE HANDS REALLY DOES FEEL DIFFERENT FROM DOING IT WITH A GUN.
I SHOULD TRY IT AGAIN WHEN I'M BACK HOME...
SZZZZ
...
THE *WEREWOLF* BROUGHT SOMEONE TO HIS ROOM AND KILLED HIM WITH A KNIFE.
THE VICTIM IS A REGULAR CIVILIAN.

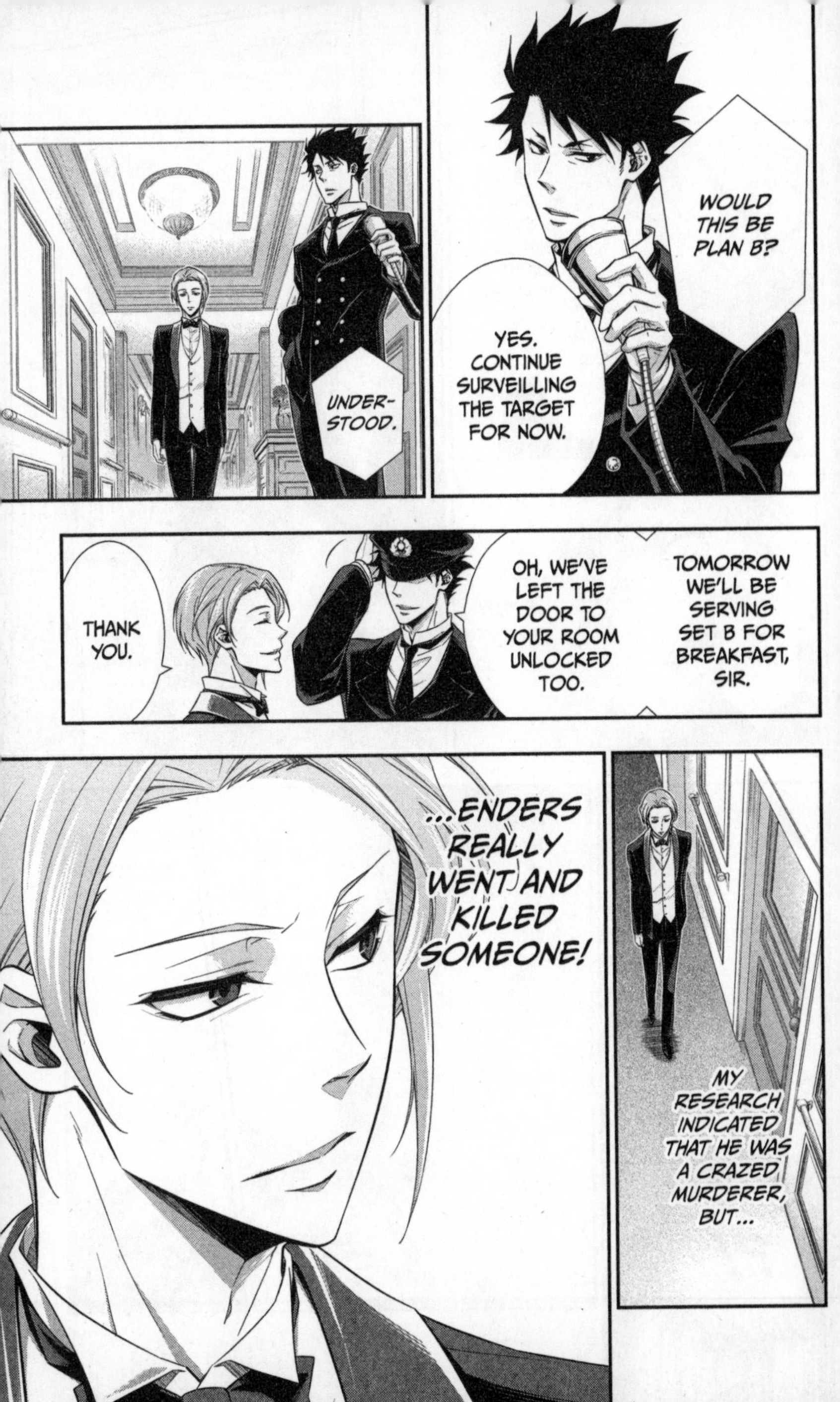
WOULD THIS BE PLAN B?
YES. CONTINUE SURVEILLING THE TARGET FOR NOW.
UNDER-STOOD.
TOMORROW WE'LL BE SERVING SET B FOR BREAKFAST, SIR.
OH, WE'VE LEFT THE DOOR TO YOUR ROOM UNLOCKED TOO.
THANK YOU.
MY RESEARCH INDICATED THAT HE WAS A CRAZED MURDERER, BUT...
...ENDERS REALLY WENT AND KILLED SOMEONE!

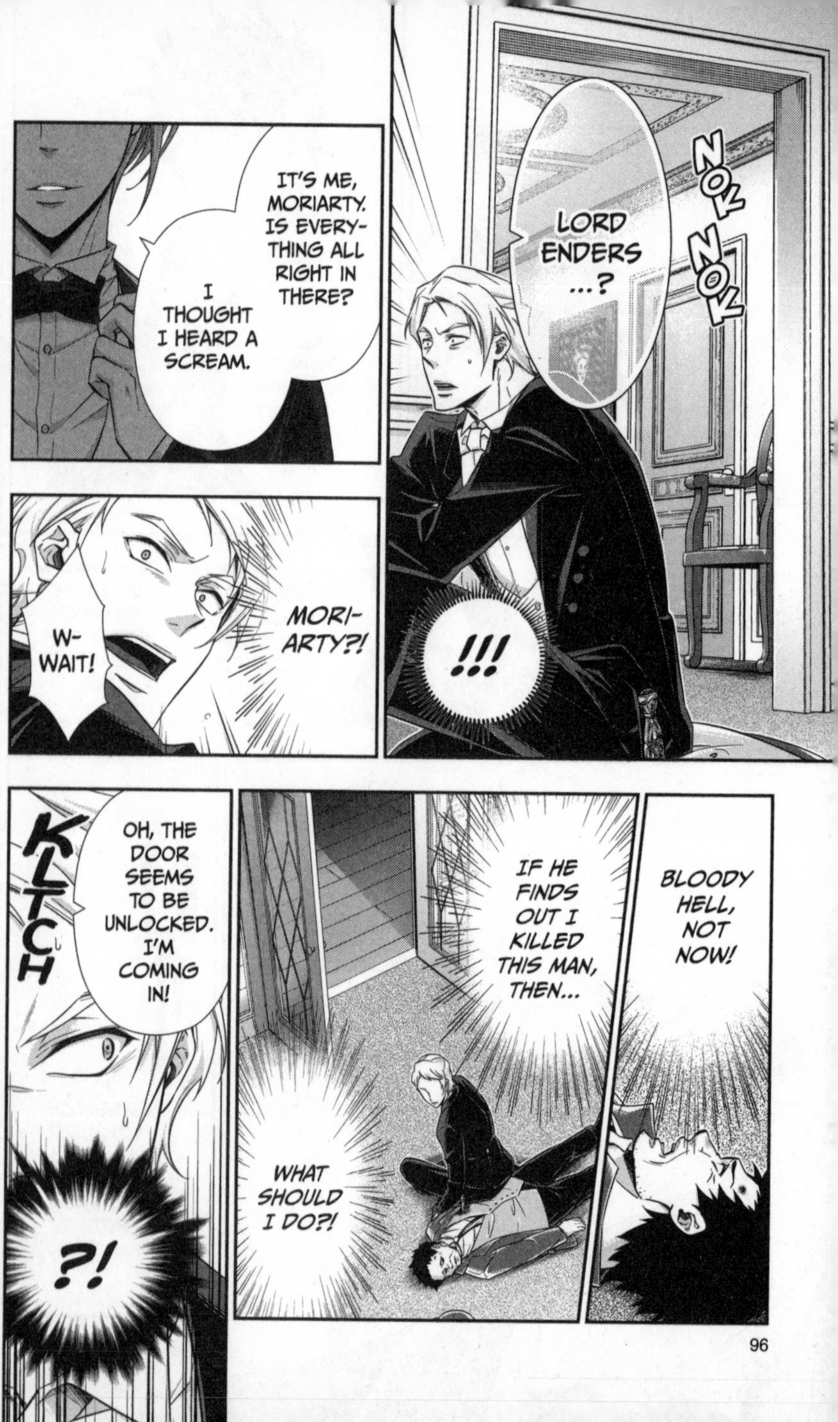

NOK NOK
LORD ENDERS ...?
!!!
IT'S ME, MORIARTY. IS EVERYTHING ALL RIGHT IN THERE?
I THOUGHT I HEARD A SCREAM.
MORI-ARTY?!
W-WAIT!
BLOODY HELL, NOT NOW!
IF HE FINDS OUT I KILLED THIS MAN, THEN...
WHAT SHOULD I DO?!
KLTCH
OH, THE DOOR SEEMS TO BE UNLOCKED. I'M COMING IN!
?!

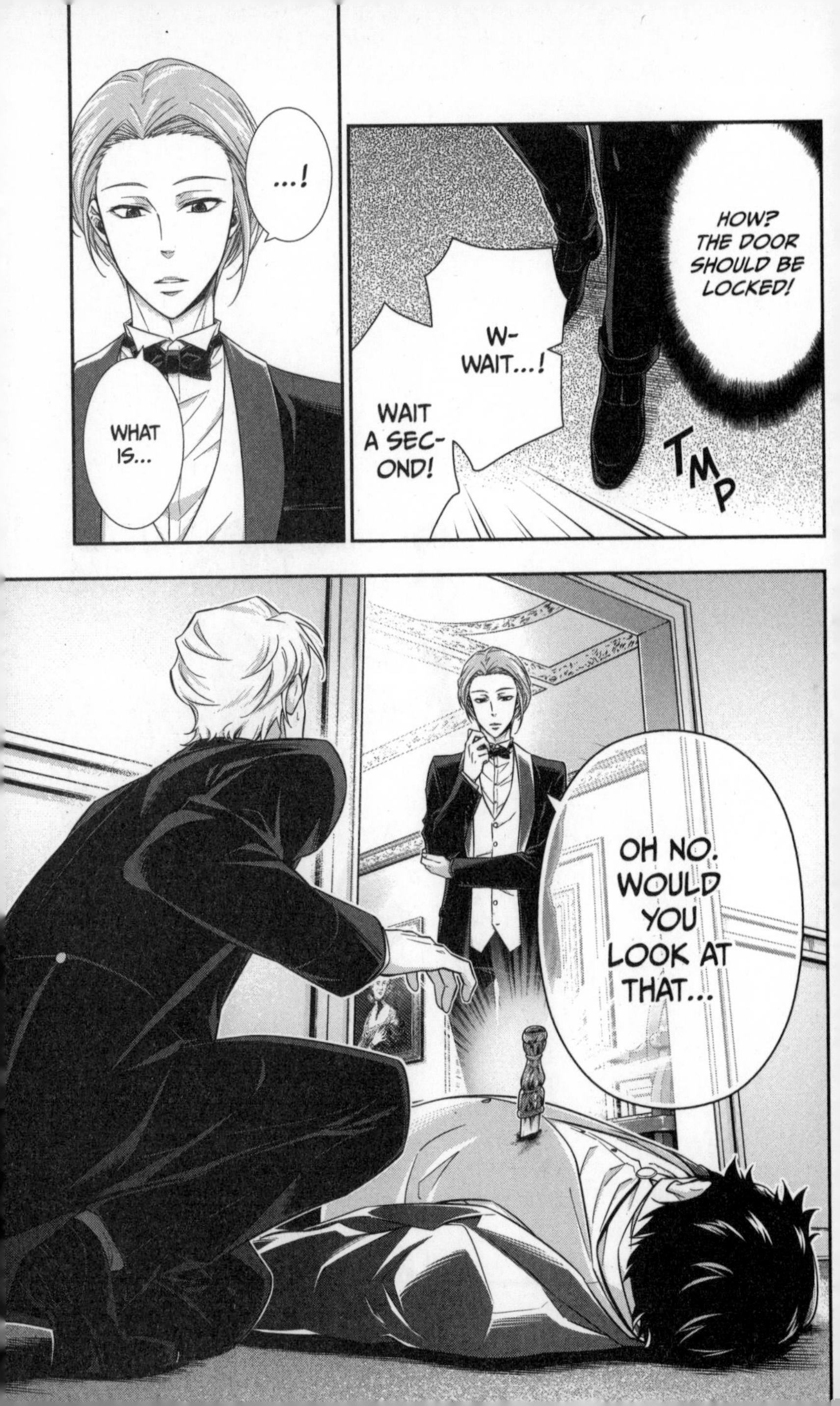
HOW? THE DOOR SHOULD BE LOCKED!
TMP
W- WAIT...!
WAIT A SEC-OND!
...!
WHAT IS...
OH NO. WOULD YOU LOOK AT THAT...

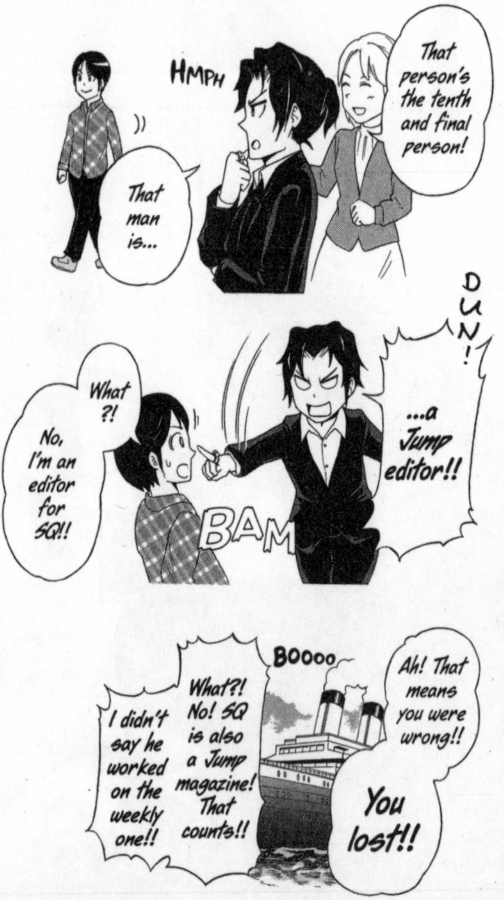
That person's the tenth and final person!
HMPH
That man is...
DUN!
...a Jump editor!!
BAM
What?!
No, I'm an editor for SQ!!
Ah! That means you were wrong!!
You lost!!
BOOOO
What?! No! SQ is also a Jump magazine! That counts!!
I didn't say he worked on the weekly one!!

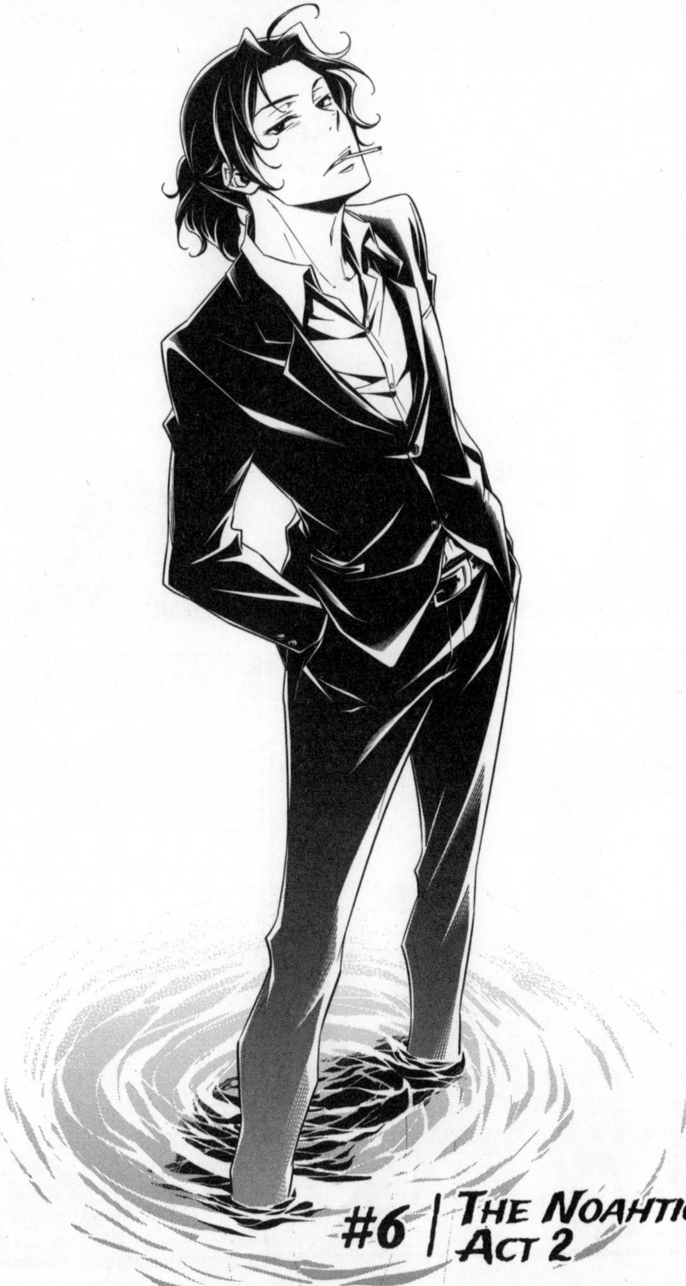

#6 | The Noahtic, Act 2

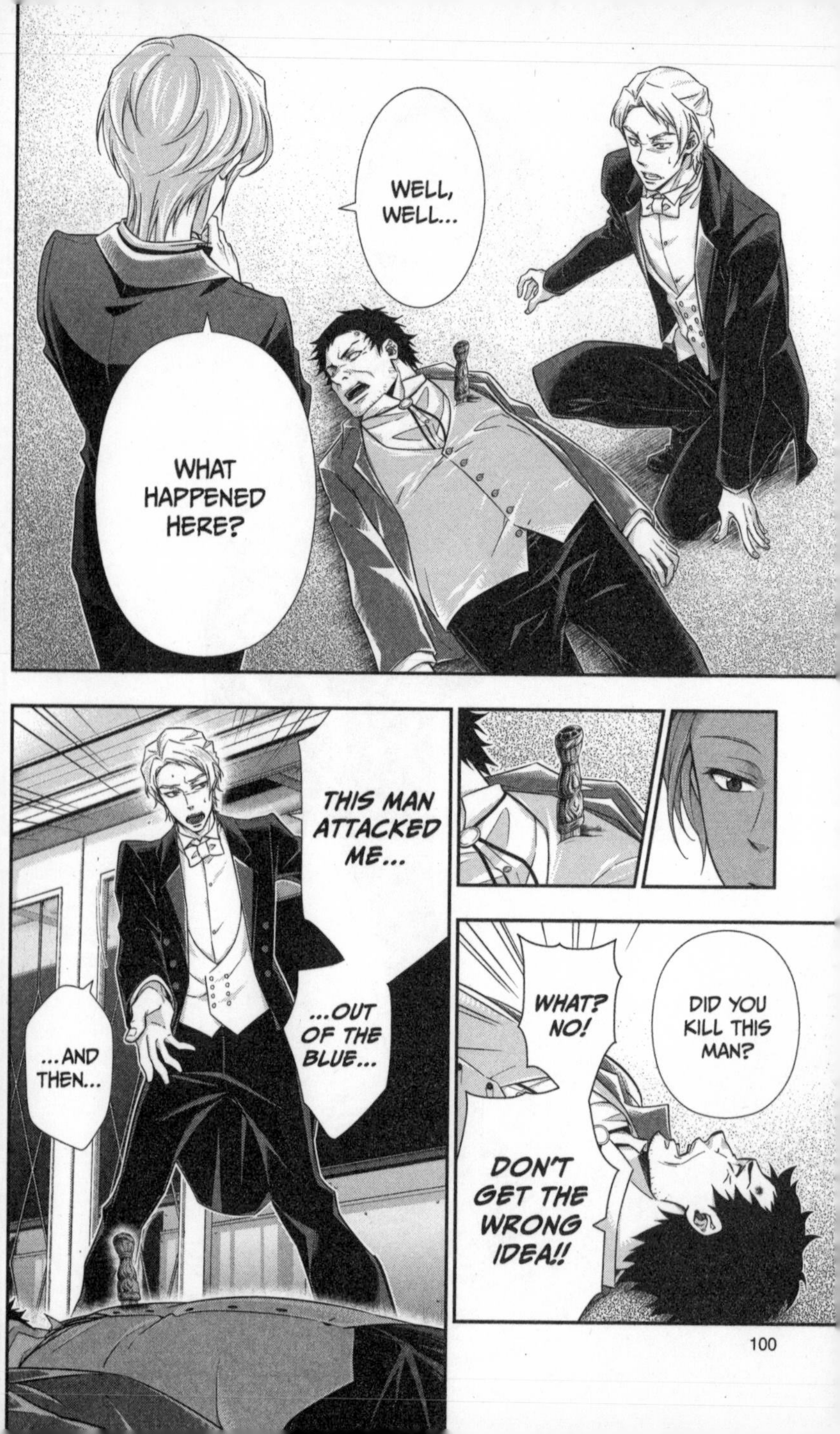

WELL, WELL...
WHAT HAPPENED HERE?
DID YOU KILL THIS MAN?
WHAT? NO!
DON'T GET THE WRONG IDEA!!
THIS MAN ATTACKED ME...
...OUT OF THE BLUE...
...AND THEN...

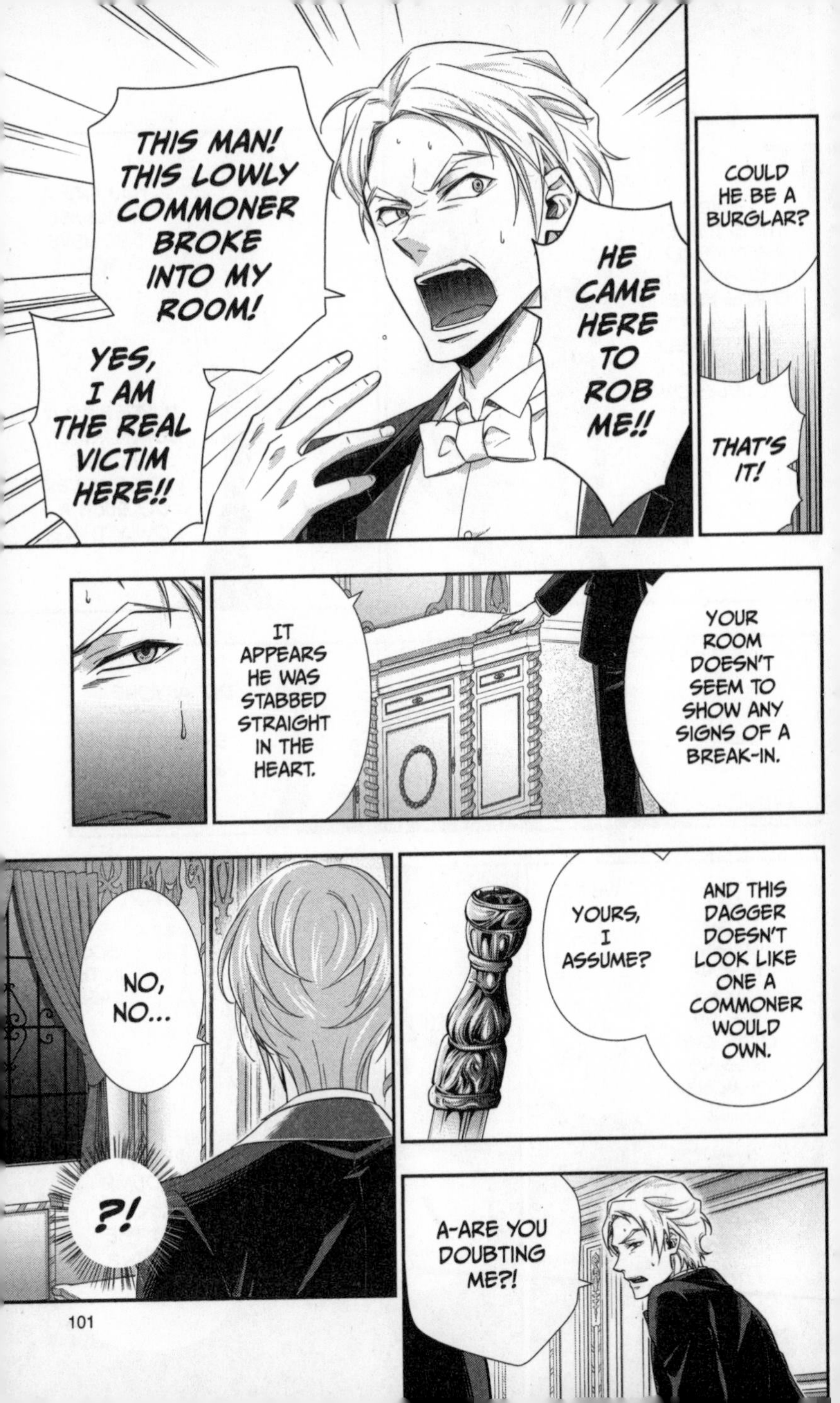

COULD HE BE A BURGLAR?
THAT'S IT!
HE CAME HERE TO ROB ME!!
THIS MAN! THIS LOWLY COMMONER BROKE INTO MY ROOM!
YES, I AM THE REAL VICTIM HERE!!
YOUR ROOM DOESN'T SEEM TO SHOW ANY SIGNS OF A BREAK-IN.
IT APPEARS HE WAS STABBED STRAIGHT IN THE HEART.
AND THIS DAGGER DOESN'T LOOK LIKE ONE A COMMONER WOULD OWN.
YOURS, I ASSUME?
A-ARE YOU DOUBTING ME?!
NO, NO...
?!

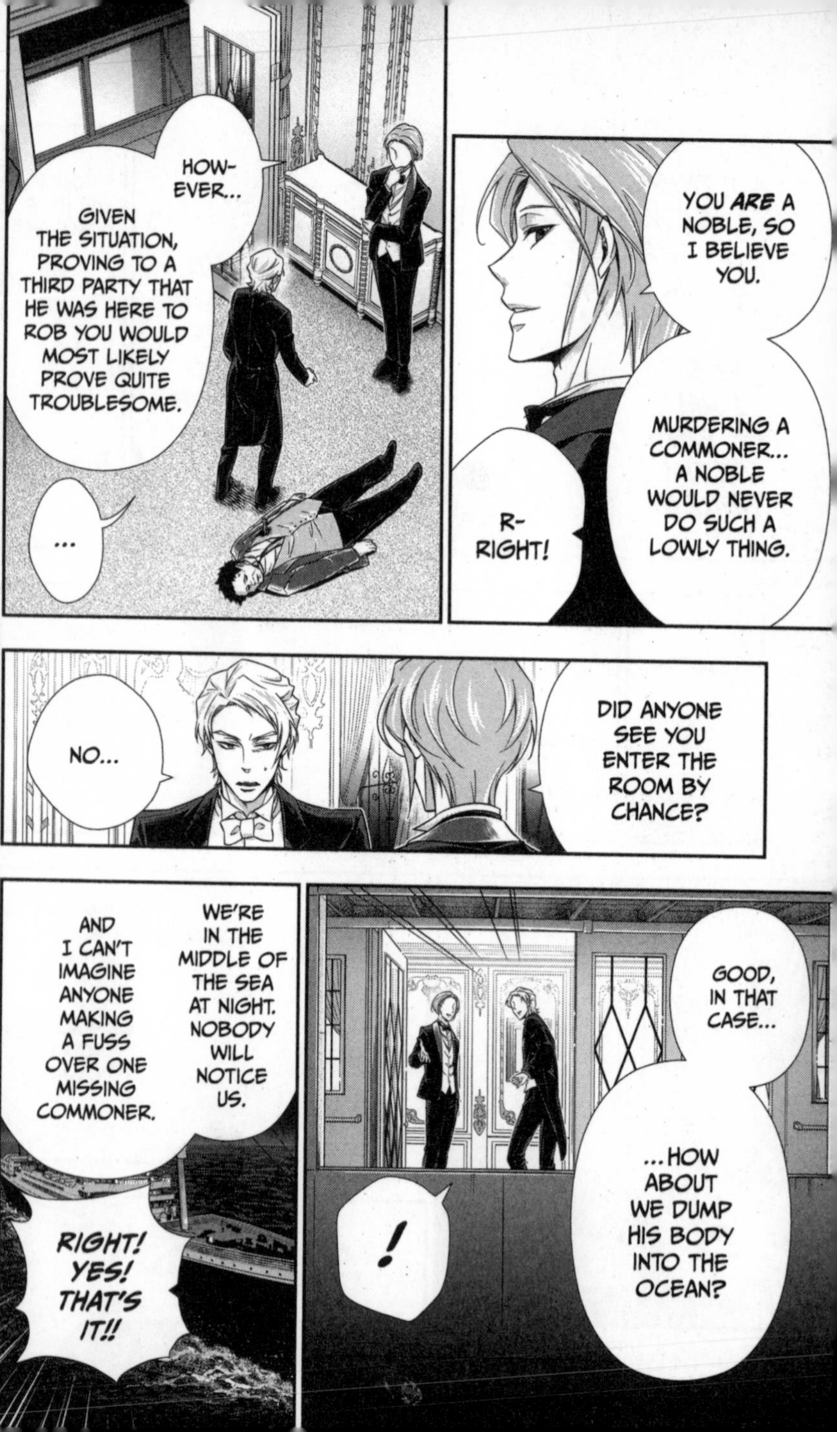
YOU *ARE* A NOBLE, SO I BELIEVE YOU.
MURDERING A COMMONER... A NOBLE WOULD NEVER DO SUCH A LOWLY THING.
R- RIGHT!
HOW- EVER...
GIVEN THE SITUATION, PROVING TO A THIRD PARTY THAT HE WAS HERE TO ROB YOU WOULD MOST LIKELY PROVE QUITE TROUBLESOME.
...
DID ANYONE SEE YOU ENTER THE ROOM BY CHANCE?
NO...
GOOD, IN THAT CASE...
...HOW ABOUT WE DUMP HIS BODY INTO THE OCEAN?
!
WE'RE IN THE MIDDLE OF THE SEA AT NIGHT. NOBODY WILL NOTICE US.
AND I CAN'T IMAGINE ANYONE MAKING A FUSS OVER ONE MISSING COMMONER.
RIGHT! YES! THAT'S IT!!

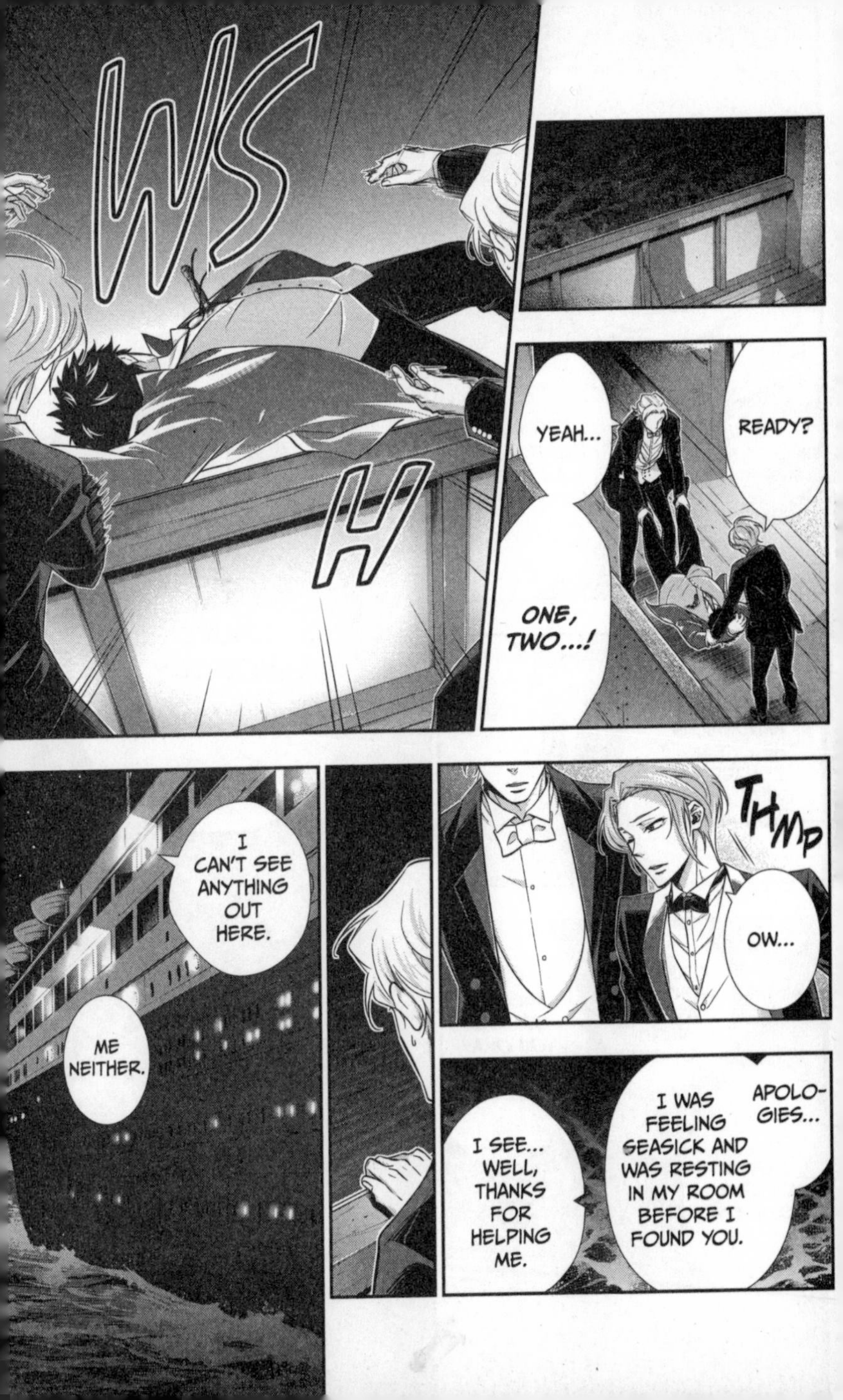
READY?
YEAH...
ONE, TWO...!
WS
H
THMP
OW...
APOLOGIES...
I WAS FEELING SEASICK AND WAS RESTING IN MY ROOM BEFORE I FOUND YOU.
I SEE... WELL, THANKS FOR HELPING ME.
I CAN'T SEE ANYTHING OUT HERE.
ME NEITHER.

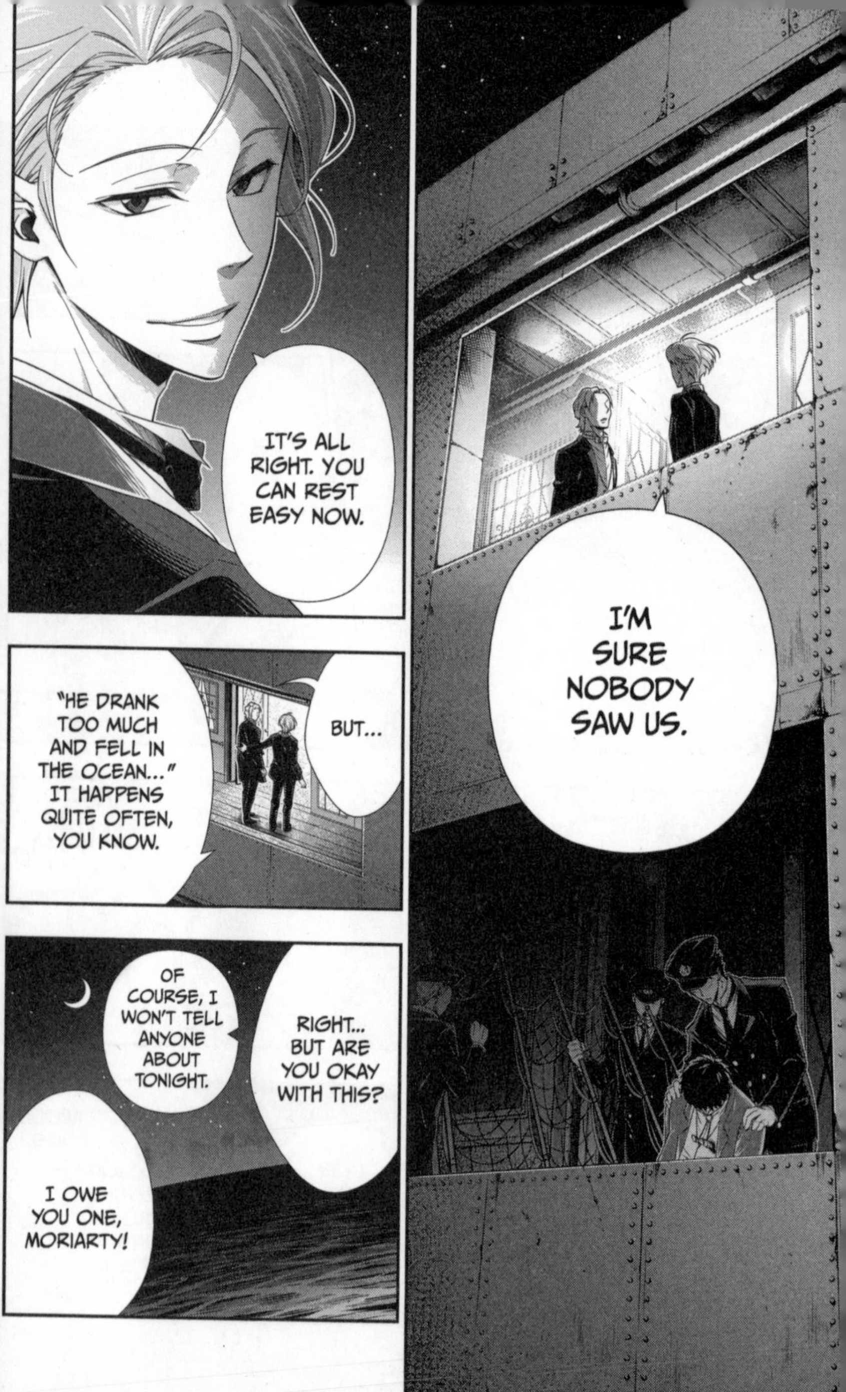
I'M SURE NOBODY SAW US.
IT'S ALL RIGHT. YOU CAN REST EASY NOW.
BUT...
"HE DRANK TOO MUCH AND FELL IN THE OCEAN..." IT HAPPENS QUITE OFTEN, YOU KNOW.
RIGHT... BUT ARE YOU OKAY WITH THIS?
OF COURSE, I WON'T TELL ANYONE ABOUT TONIGHT.
I OWE YOU ONE, MORIARTY!

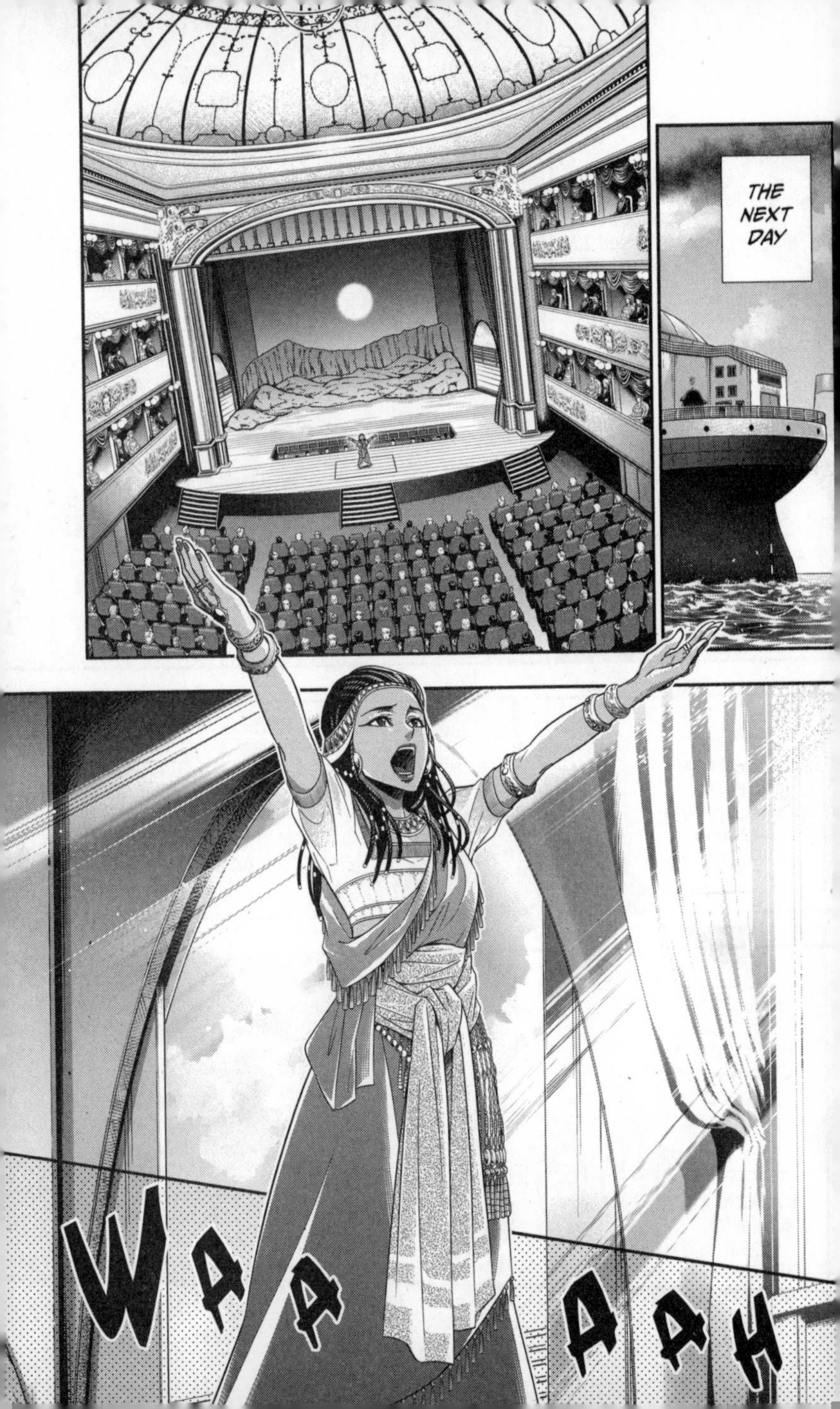
THE NEXT DAY
WAAAAH

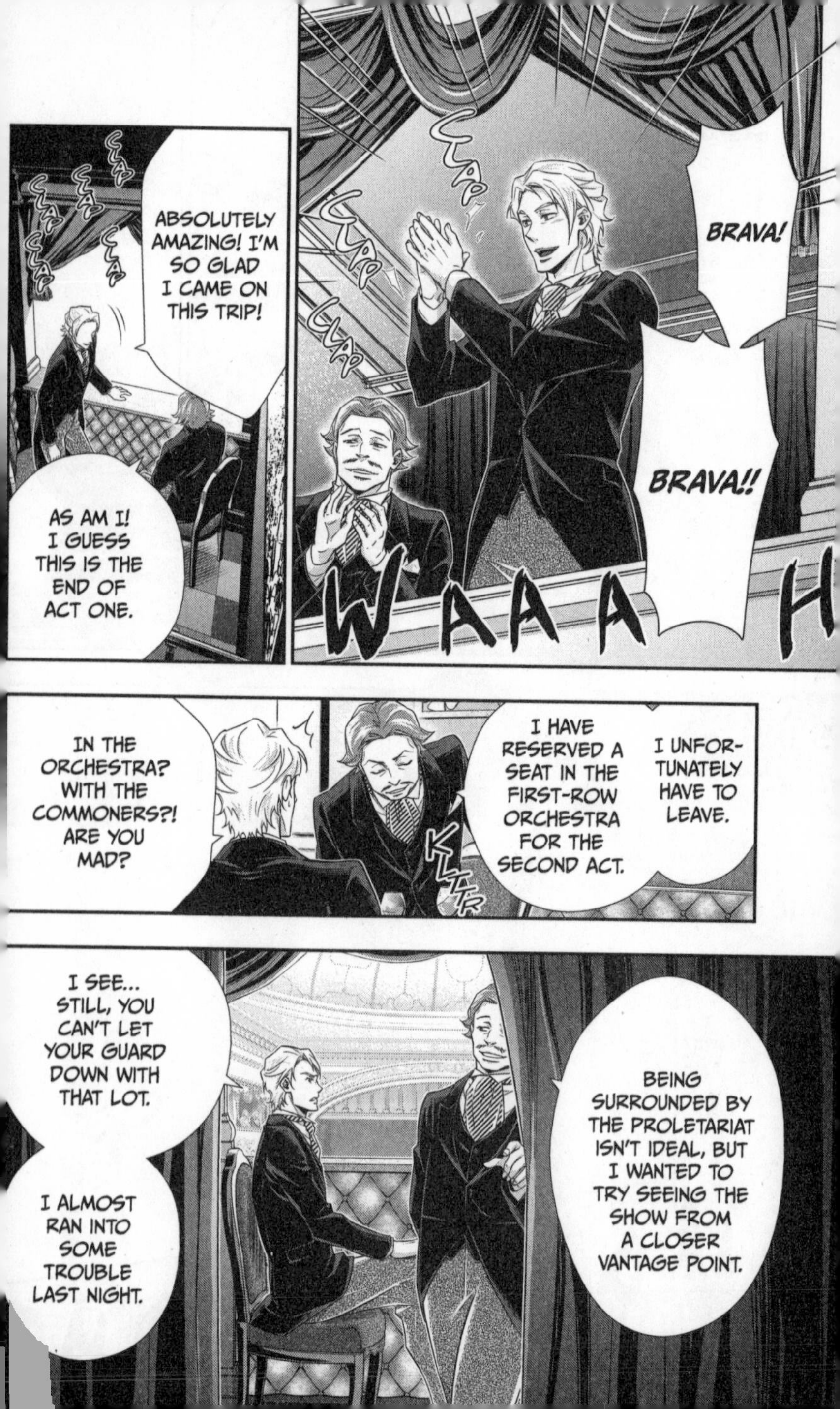
BRAVA!
BRAVA!!
CLAP CLAP CLAP
WAAAH
CLAP CLAP CLAP CLAP CLAP
ABSOLUTELY AMAZING! I'M SO GLAD I CAME ON THIS TRIP!
AS AM I! I GUESS THIS IS THE END OF ACT ONE.
I UNFOR-TUNATELY HAVE TO LEAVE.
I HAVE RESERVED A SEAT IN THE FIRST-ROW ORCHESTRA FOR THE SECOND ACT.
KLIIR
IN THE ORCHESTRA? WITH THE COMMONERS?! ARE YOU MAD?
BEING SURROUNDED BY THE PROLETARIAT ISN'T IDEAL, BUT I WANTED TO TRY SEEING THE SHOW FROM A CLOSER VANTAGE POINT.
I SEE... STILL, YOU CAN'T LET YOUR GUARD DOWN WITH THAT LOT.
I ALMOST RAN INTO SOME TROUBLE LAST NIGHT.

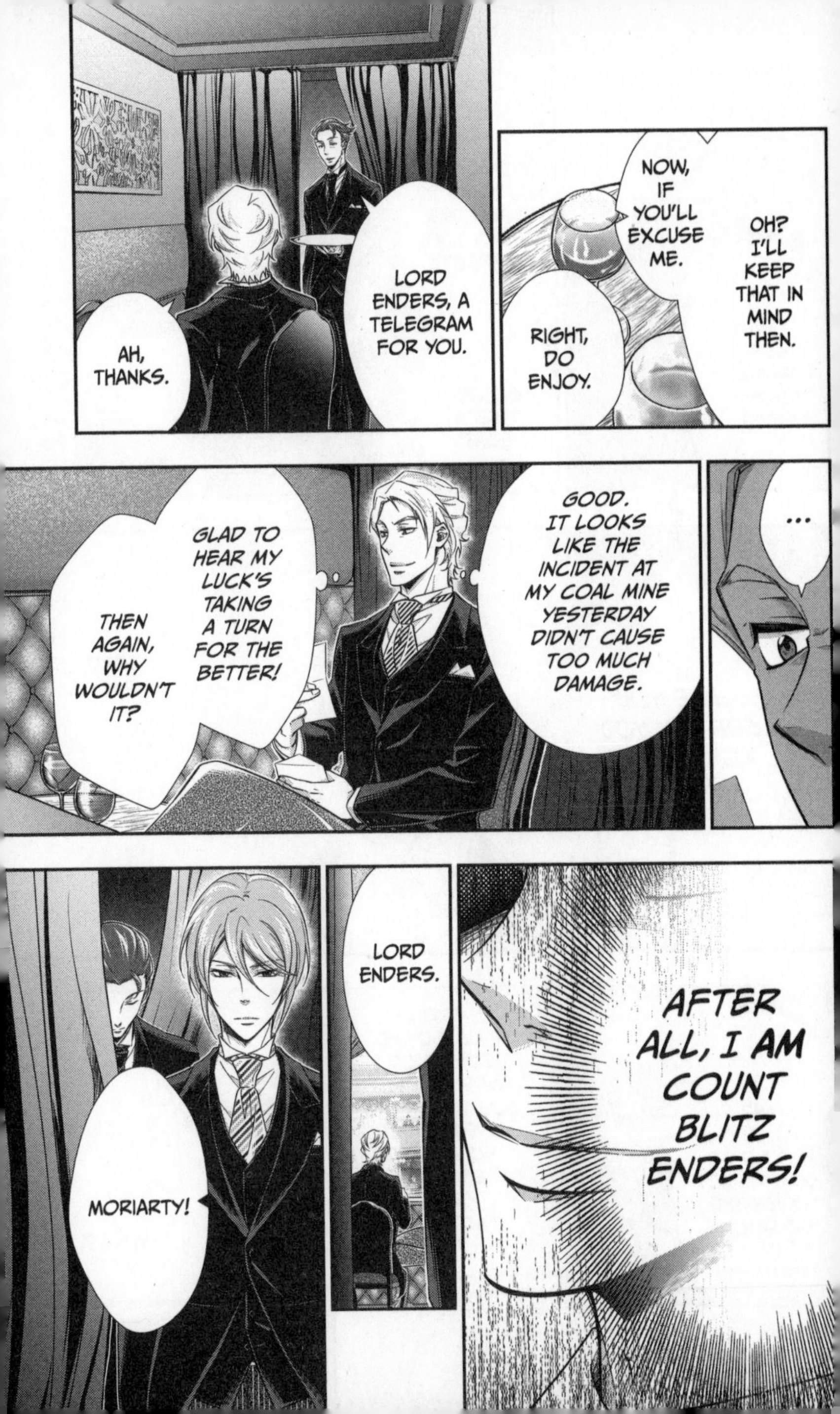
OH? I'LL KEEP THAT IN MIND THEN.
NOW, IF YOU'LL EXCUSE ME.
RIGHT, DO ENJOY.
LORD ENDERS, A TELEGRAM FOR YOU.
AH, THANKS.
...
GOOD. IT LOOKS LIKE THE INCIDENT AT MY COAL MINE YESTERDAY DIDN'T CAUSE TOO MUCH DAMAGE.
GLAD TO HEAR MY LUCK'S TAKING A TURN FOR THE BETTER!
THEN AGAIN, WHY WOULDN'T IT?
AFTER ALL, I AM COUNT BLITZ ENDERS!
LORD ENDERS.
MORIARTY!

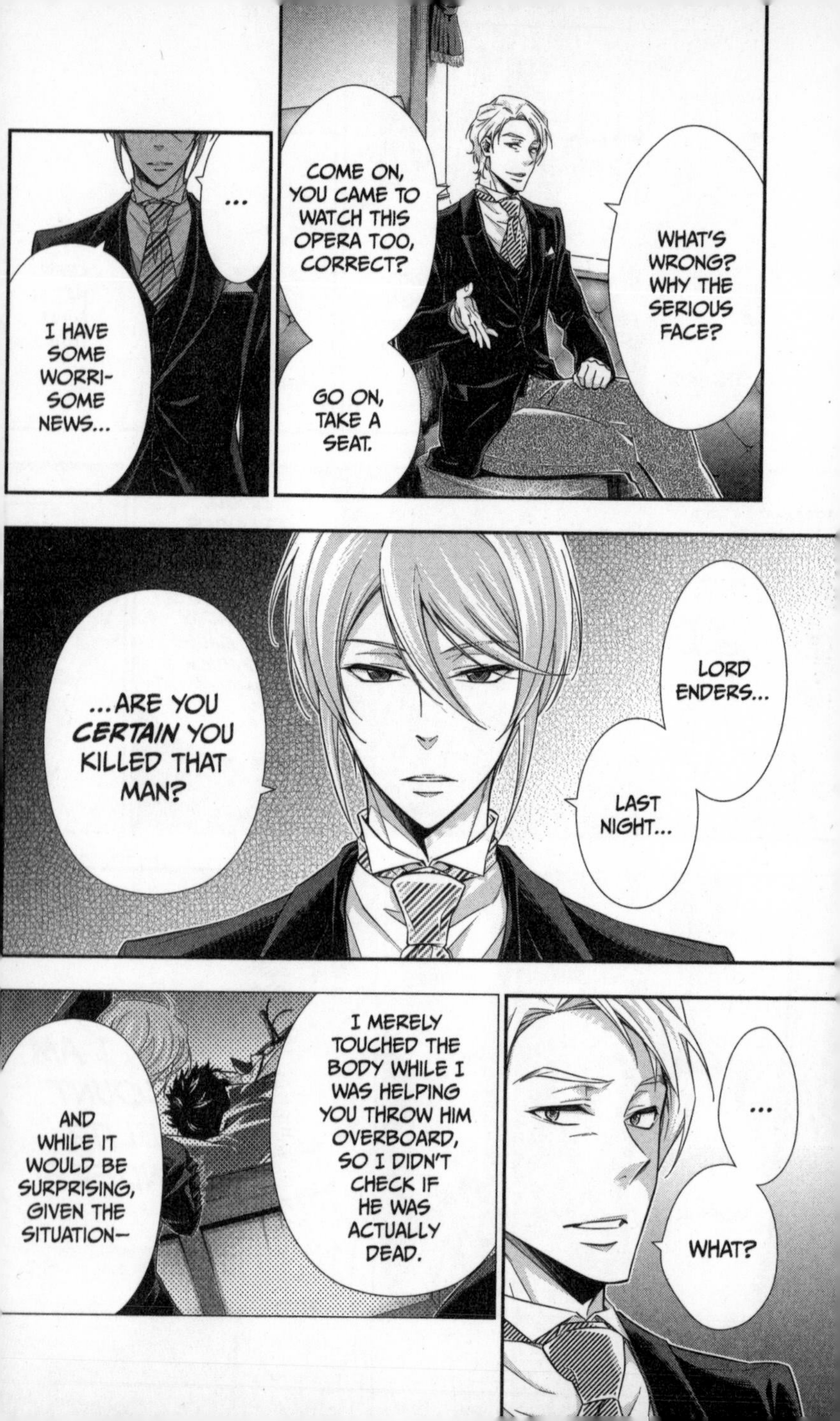
WHAT'S WRONG? WHY THE SERIOUS FACE?
COME ON, YOU CAME TO WATCH THIS OPERA TOO, CORRECT?
GO ON, TAKE A SEAT.
...
I HAVE SOME WORRI-SOME NEWS...
LORD ENDERS...
LAST NIGHT...
...ARE YOU *CERTAIN* YOU KILLED THAT MAN?
...
WHAT?
I MERELY TOUCHED THE BODY WHILE I WAS HELPING YOU THROW HIM OVERBOARD, SO I DIDN'T CHECK IF HE WAS ACTUALLY DEAD.
AND WHILE IT WOULD BE SURPRISING, GIVEN THE SITUATION—

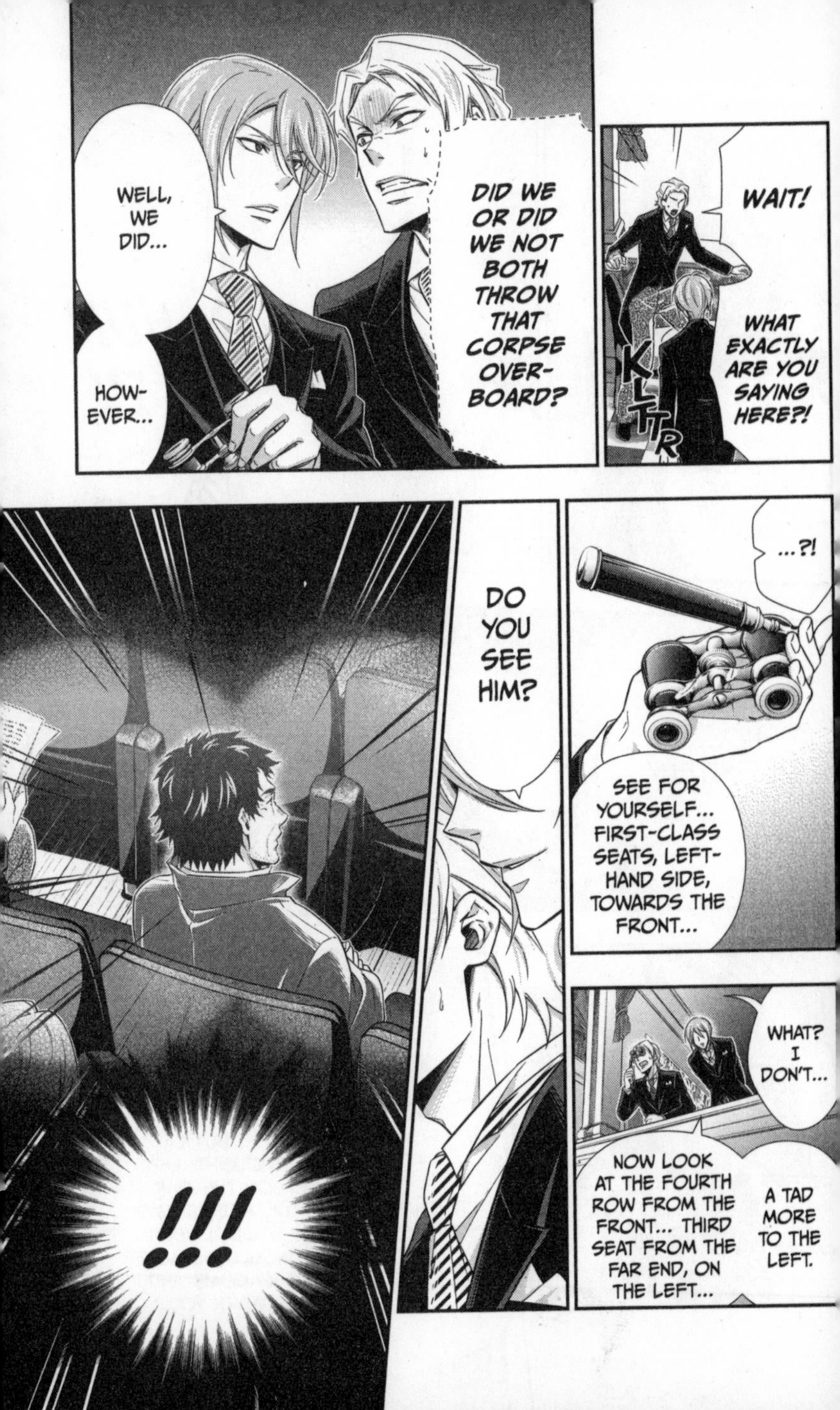
WAIT!
WHAT EXACTLY ARE YOU SAYING HERE?!
KLTTR
DID WE OR DID WE NOT BOTH THROW THAT CORPSE OVER-BOARD?
WELL, WE DID...
HOW-EVER...
...?!
SEE FOR YOURSELF... FIRST-CLASS SEATS, LEFT-HAND SIDE, TOWARDS THE FRONT...
WHAT? I DON'T...
A TAD MORE TO THE LEFT.
NOW LOOK AT THE FOURTH ROW FROM THE FRONT... THIRD SEAT FROM THE FAR END, ON THE LEFT...
DO YOU SEE HIM?
!!!

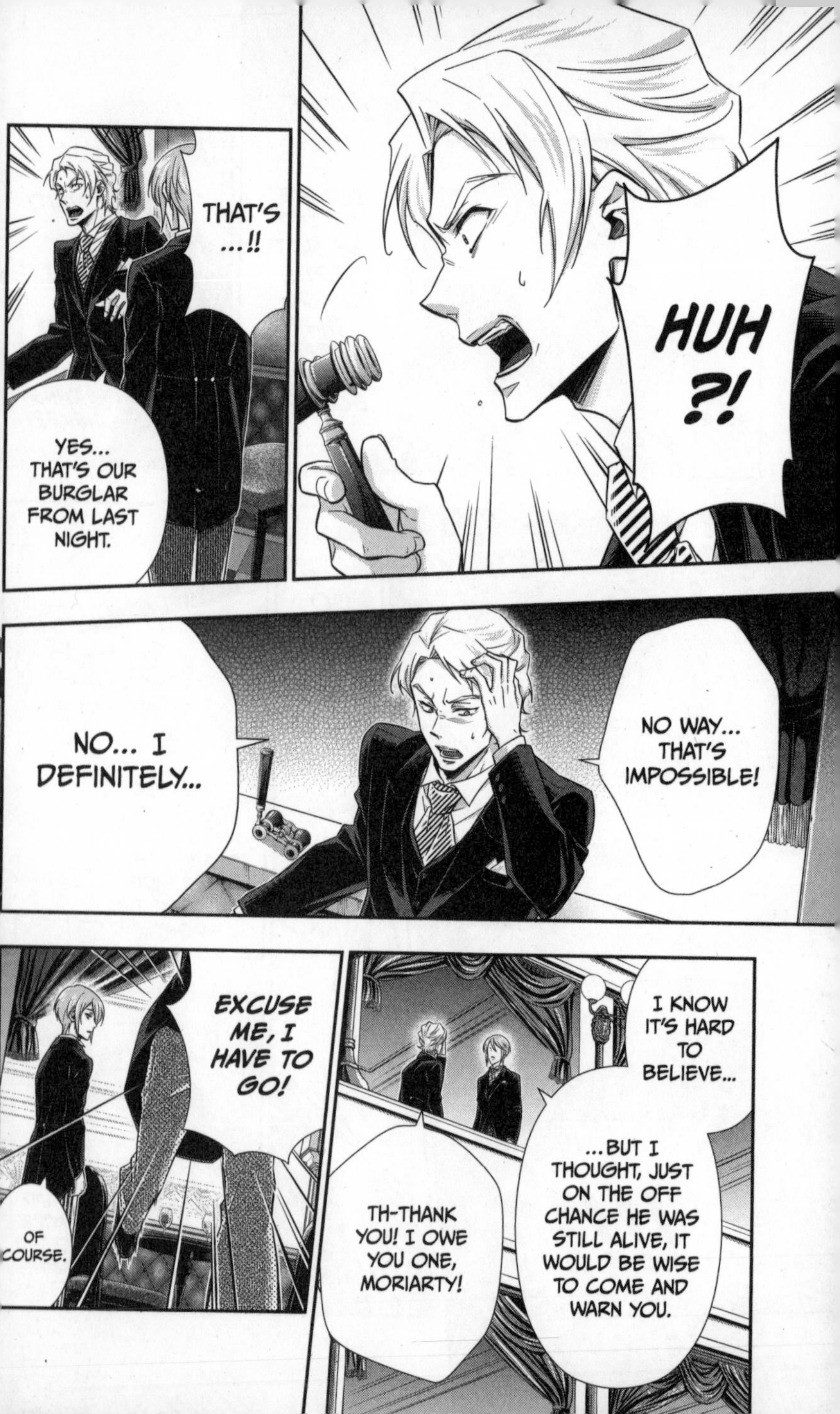
HUH ?!
THAT'S ...!!
YES... THAT'S OUR BURGLAR FROM LAST NIGHT.
NO WAY... THAT'S IMPOSSIBLE!
NO... I DEFINITELY...
I KNOW IT'S HARD TO BELIEVE...
...BUT I THOUGHT, JUST ON THE OFF CHANCE HE WAS STILL ALIVE, IT WOULD BE WISE TO COME AND WARN YOU.
TH-THANK YOU! I OWE YOU ONE, MORIARTY!
EXCUSE ME, I HAVE TO GO!
OF COURSE.

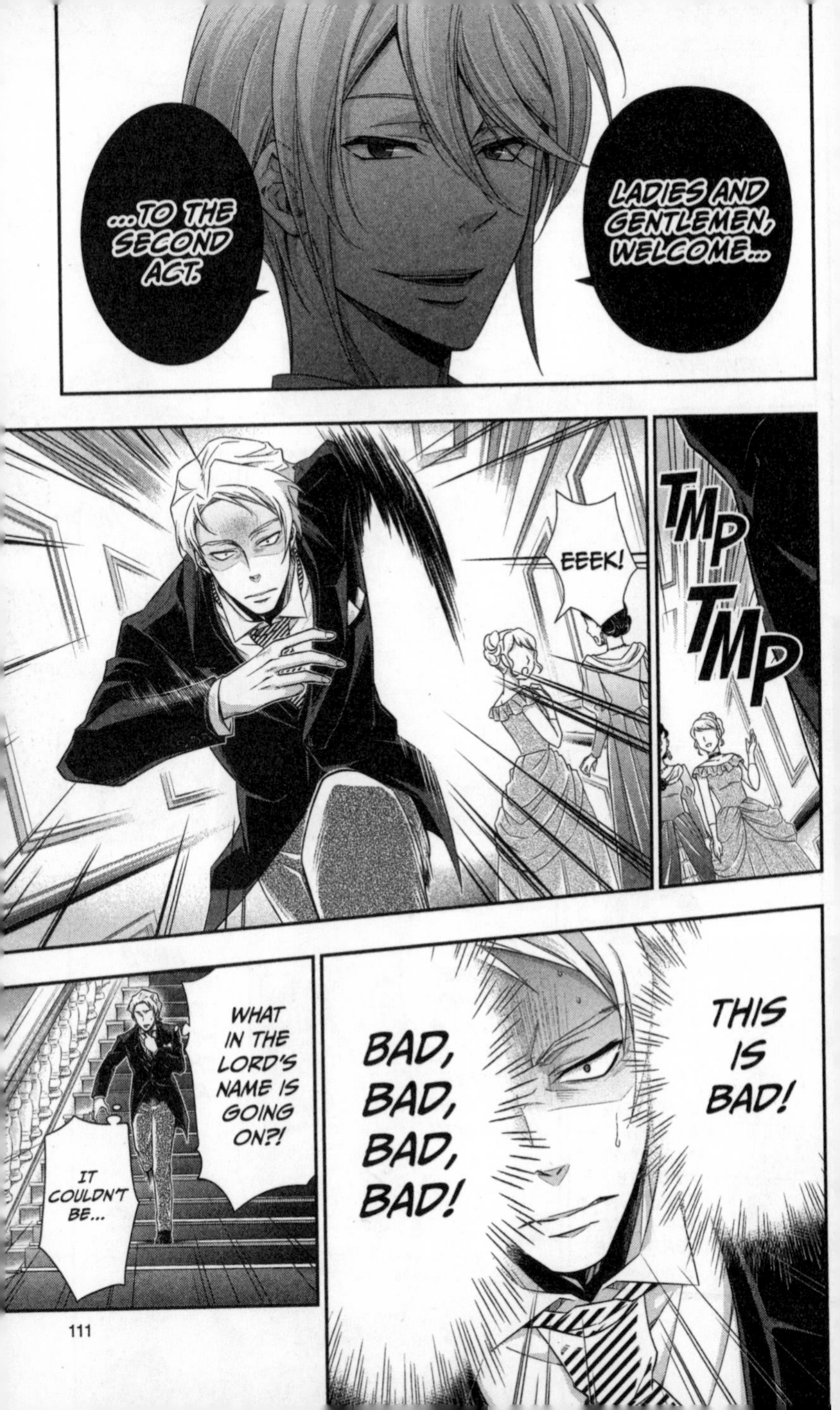
LADIES AND GENTLEMEN, WELCOME...
...TO THE SECOND ACT.
TMP TMP TMP
EEEK!
THIS IS BAD!
BAD, BAD, BAD, BAD!
WHAT IN THE LORD'S NAME IS GOING ON?!
IT COULDN'T BE...

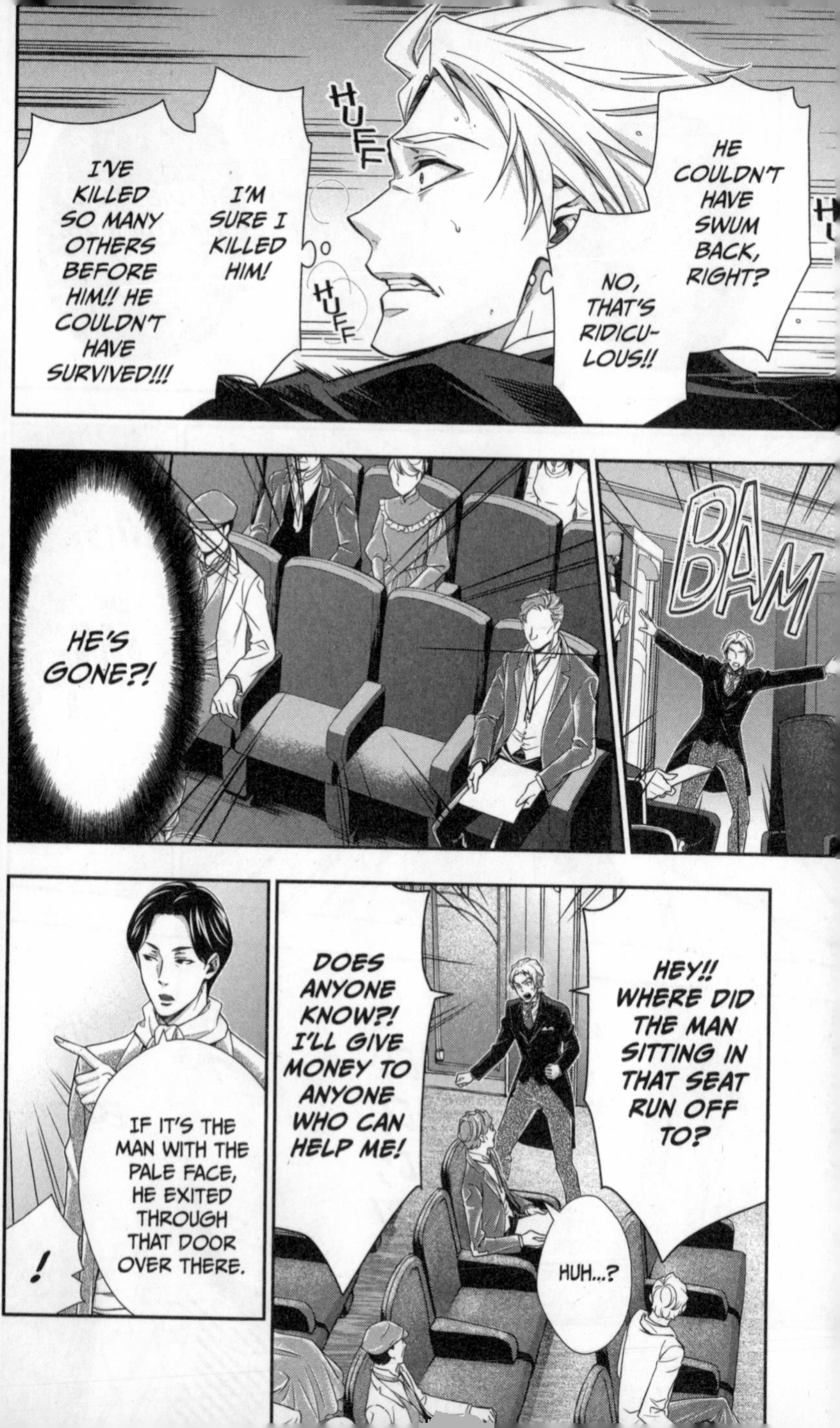
HE COULDN'T HAVE SWUM BACK, RIGHT?
NO, THAT'S RIDICU-LOUS!!
HUFF
HUFF
I'M SURE I KILLED HIM!
I'VE KILLED SO MANY OTHERS BEFORE HIM!! HE COULDN'T HAVE SURVIVED!!!
BAM
HE'S GONE?!
HEY!! WHERE DID THE MAN SITTING IN THAT SEAT RUN OFF TO?
DOES ANYONE KNOW?! I'LL GIVE MONEY TO ANYONE WHO CAN HELP ME!
HUH...?
IF IT'S THE MAN WITH THE PALE FACE, HE EXITED THROUGH THAT DOOR OVER THERE.
!

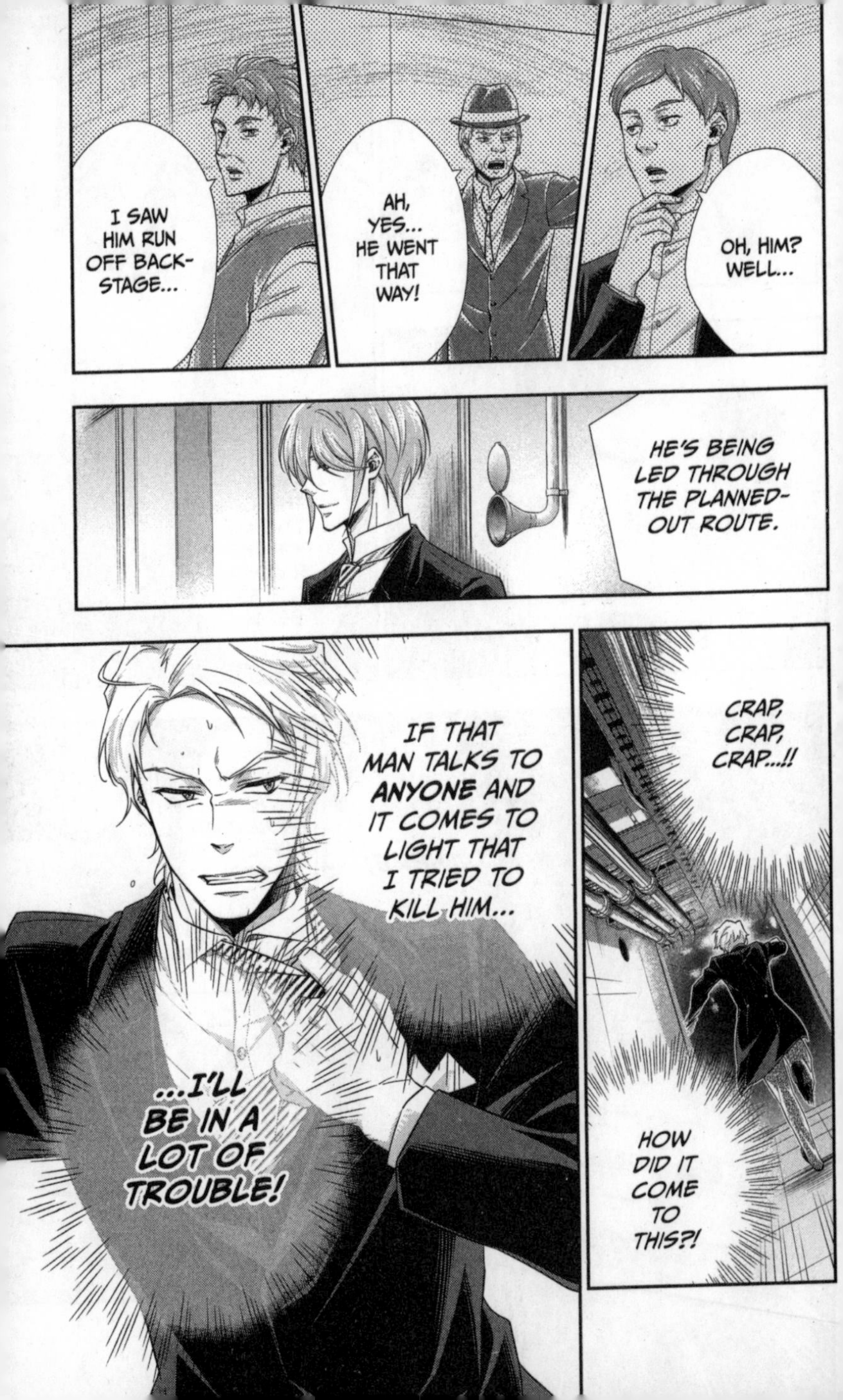
OH, HIM? WELL...
AH, YES... HE WENT THAT WAY!
I SAW HIM RUN OFF BACK-STAGE...
HE'S BEING LED THROUGH THE PLANNED-OUT ROUTE.
CRAP, CRAP, CRAP...!!
HOW DID IT COME TO THIS?!
IF THAT MAN TALKS TO ANYONE AND IT COMES TO LIGHT THAT I TRIED TO KILL HIM...
...I'LL BE IN A LOT OF TROUBLE!

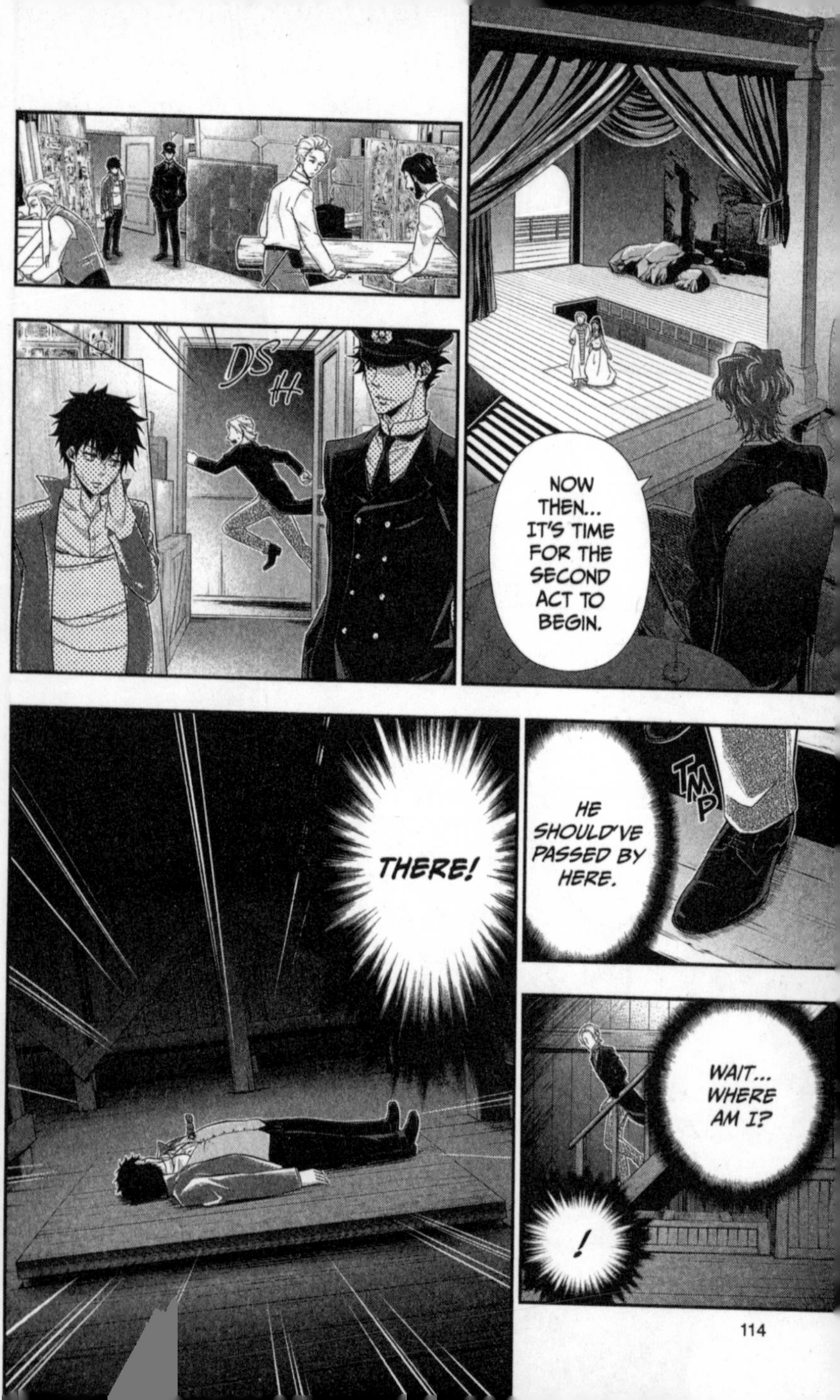
NOW THEN... IT'S TIME FOR THE SECOND ACT TO BEGIN.
DSH
TMP
HE SHOULD'VE PASSED BY HERE.
THERE!
WAIT... WHERE AM I?
!

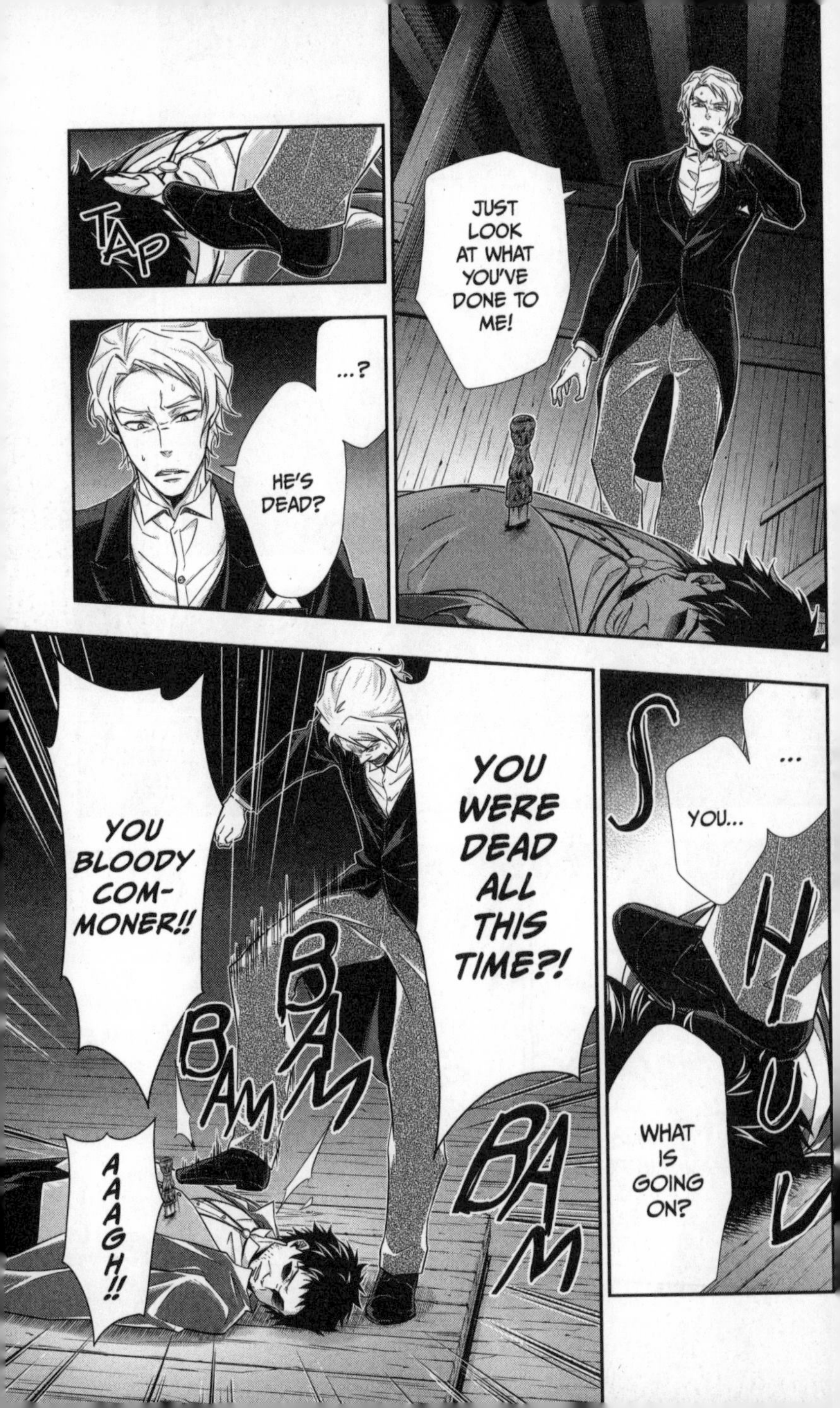
JUST LOOK AT WHAT YOU'VE DONE TO ME!
TAP
...?
HE'S DEAD?
SHUL
...
YOU...
WHAT IS GOING ON?
YOU WERE DEAD ALL THIS TIME?!
YOU BLOODY COM-MONER!!
BAM
BAM
BAM
BAM
AAAAGH!!

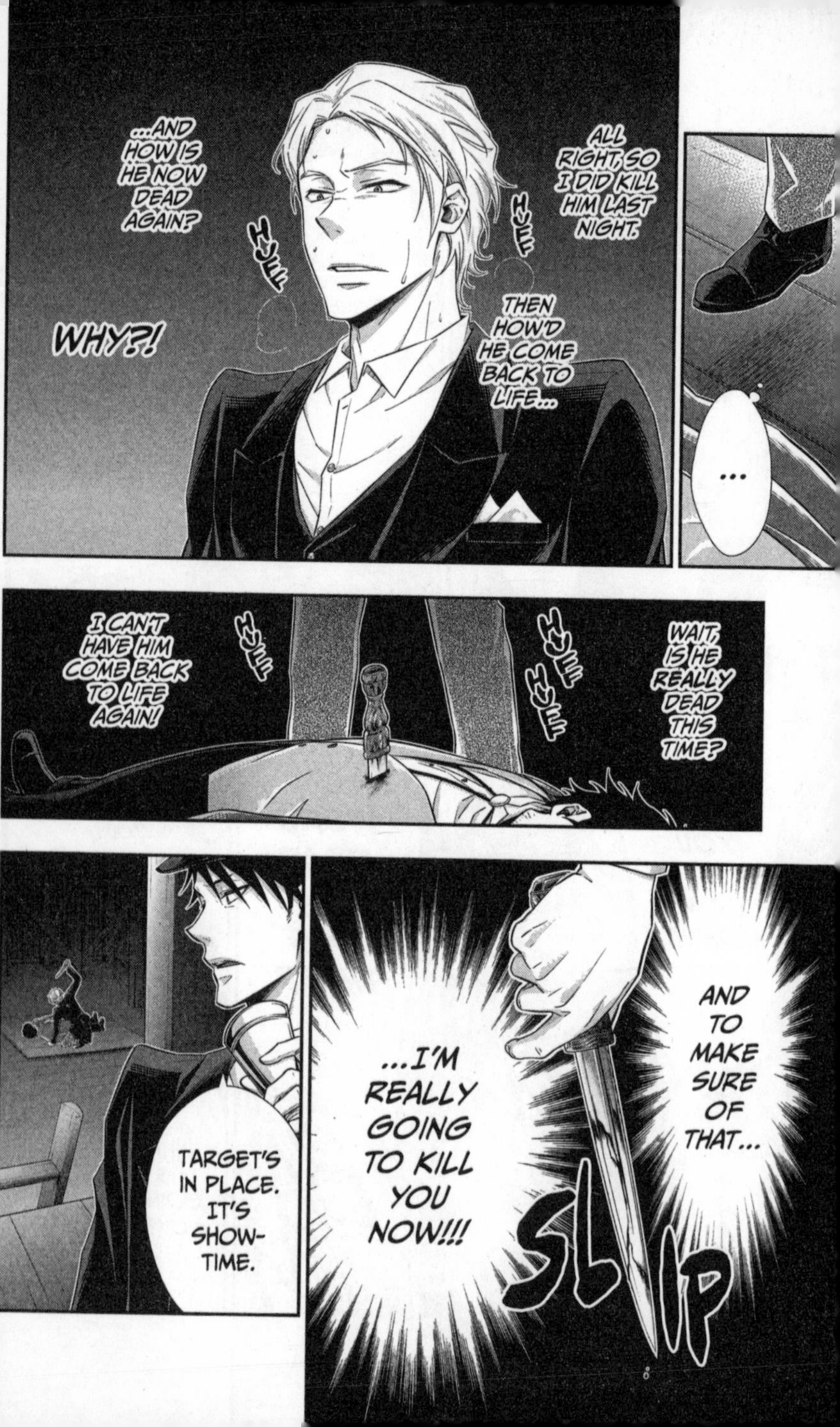
...
ALL RIGHT, SO I DID KILL HIM LAST NIGHT.
HJEF
THEN HOW'D HE COME BACK TO LIFE...
...AND HOW IS HE NOW DEAD AGAIN?
HJEF
WHY?!
WAIT, IS HE REALLY DEAD THIS TIME?
HJEF HJEF
HJEF
I CAN'T HAVE HIM COME BACK TO LIFE AGAIN!
AND TO MAKE SURE OF THAT...
...I'M REALLY GOING TO KILL YOU NOW!!!
SLIP
TARGET'S IN PLACE. IT'S SHOW-TIME.

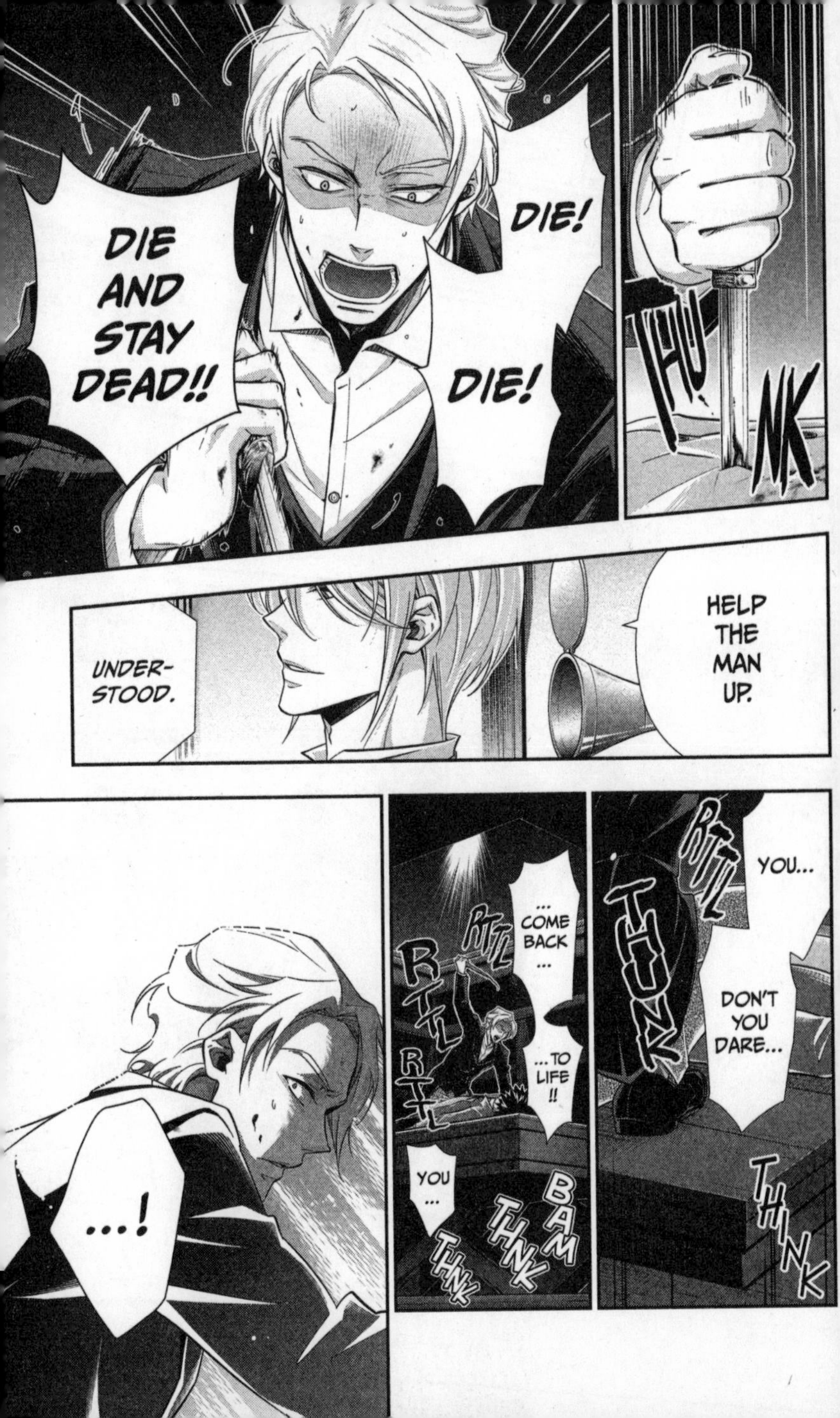
THUNK
DIE!
DIE!
DIE AND STAY DEAD!!
HELP THE MAN UP.
UNDER-STOOD.
RTTL
THUNK
YOU...
DON'T YOU DARE...
THINK
...COME BACK...
RTTL
RTTL
RTTL
...TO LIFE!!
YOU...
BAM
THNK
THNK
...!

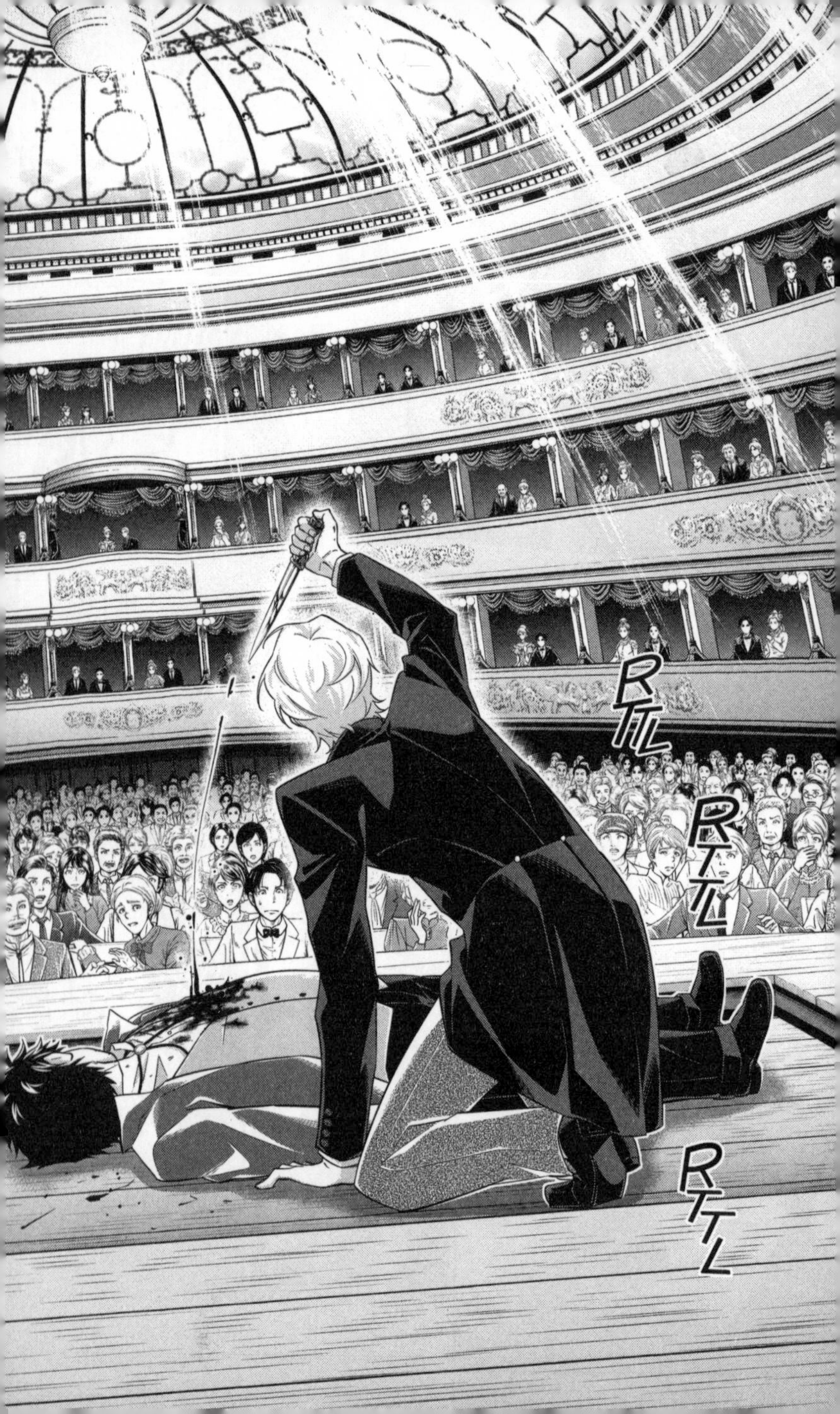
RTTL
RTTL
RTTL

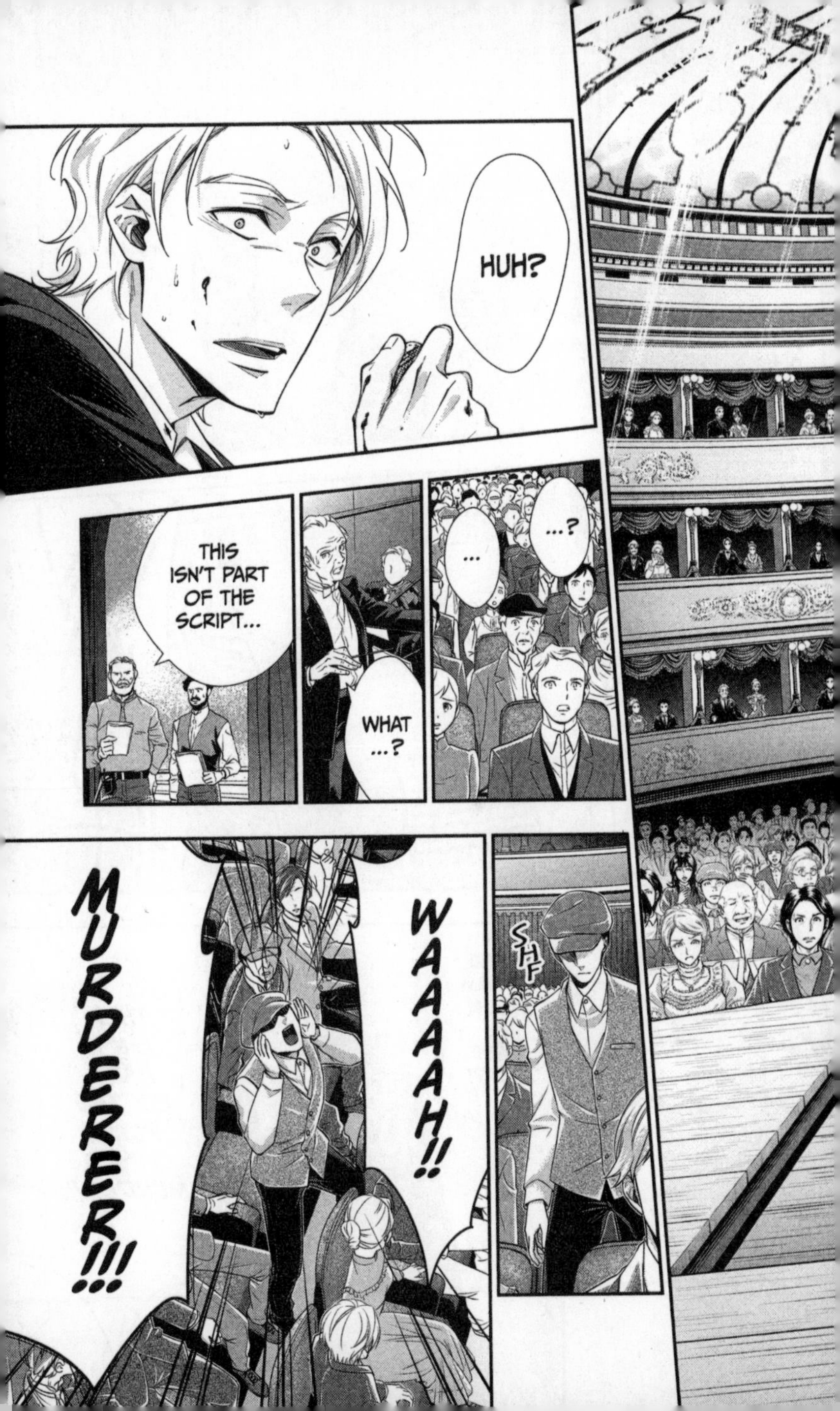
HUH?
...?
...
WHAT ...?
THIS ISN'T PART OF THE SCRIPT...
SHF
WAAAAH!!
MURDERER!!!

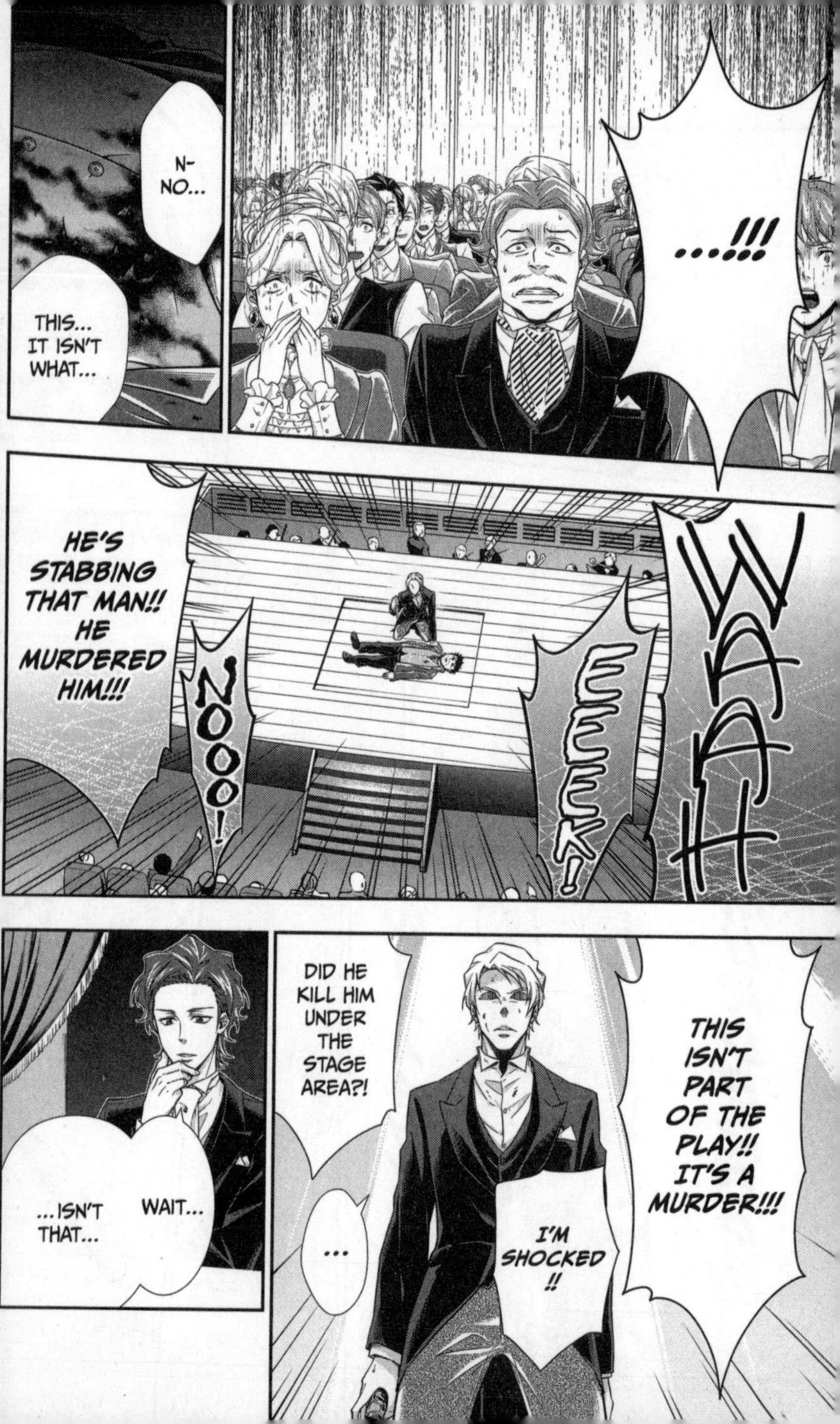

...!!!
N- NO...
THIS... IT ISN'T WHAT...
WAAH
EEEEEK!
NOOO!
HE'S STABBING THAT MAN!! HE MURDERED HIM!!!
THIS ISN'T PART OF THE PLAY!! IT'S A MURDER!!!
DID HE KILL HIM UNDER THE STAGE AREA?!
I'M SHOCKED !!
...
WAIT...
...ISN'T THAT...

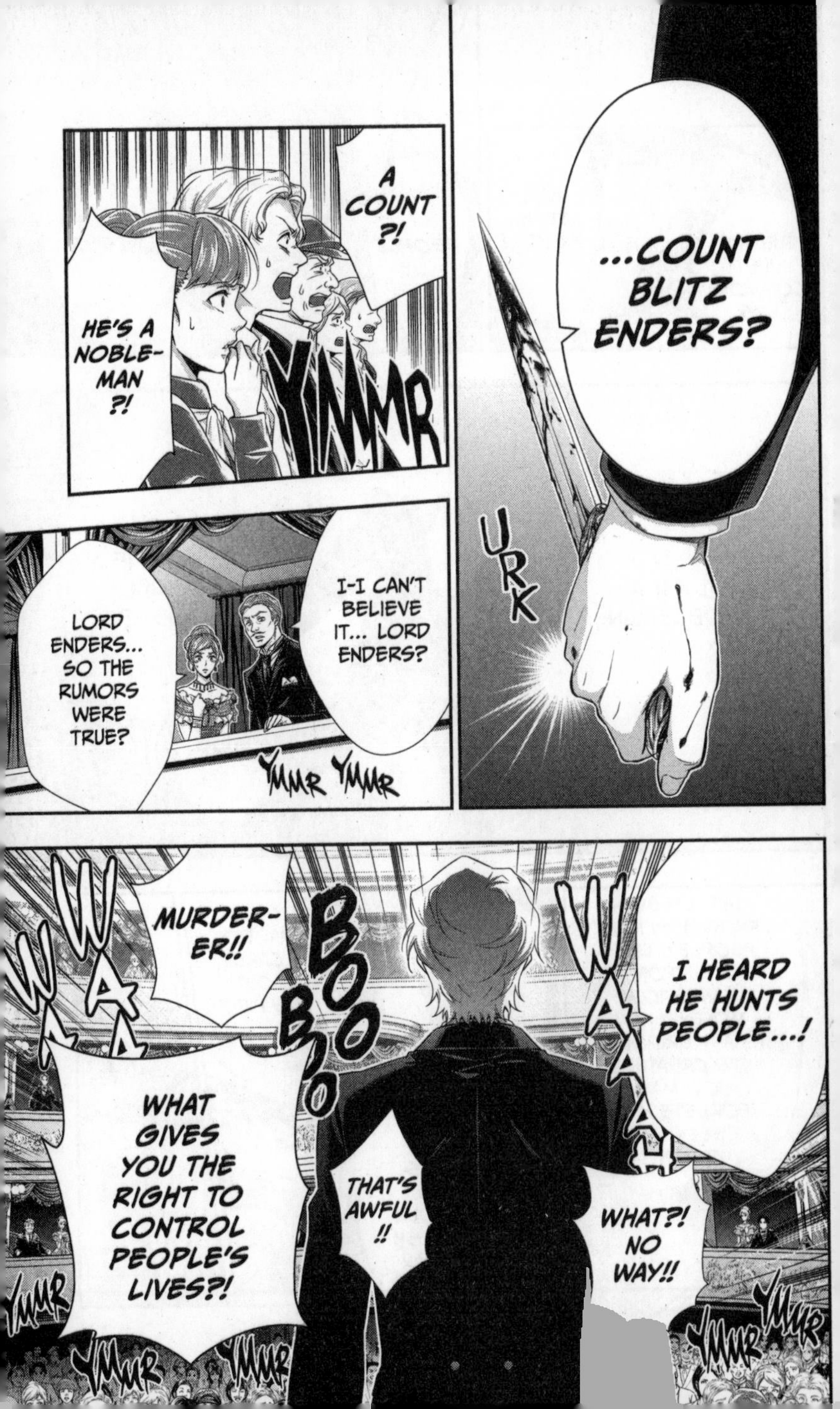
...COUNT BLITZ ENDERS?
URK
A COUNT ?!
HE'S A NOBLEMAN ?!
YMMMR
I-I CAN'T BELIEVE IT... LORD ENDERS?
LORD ENDERS... SO THE RUMORS WERE TRUE?
YMMR YMMR
I HEARD HE HUNTS PEOPLE...!
WAAAAH
BOO BOO
MURDERER!!
WAAA
WHAT?! NO WAY!!
THAT'S AWFUL !!
WHAT GIVES YOU THE RIGHT TO CONTROL PEOPLE'S LIVES?!
YMMR YMMR YMMR YMMR YMMR

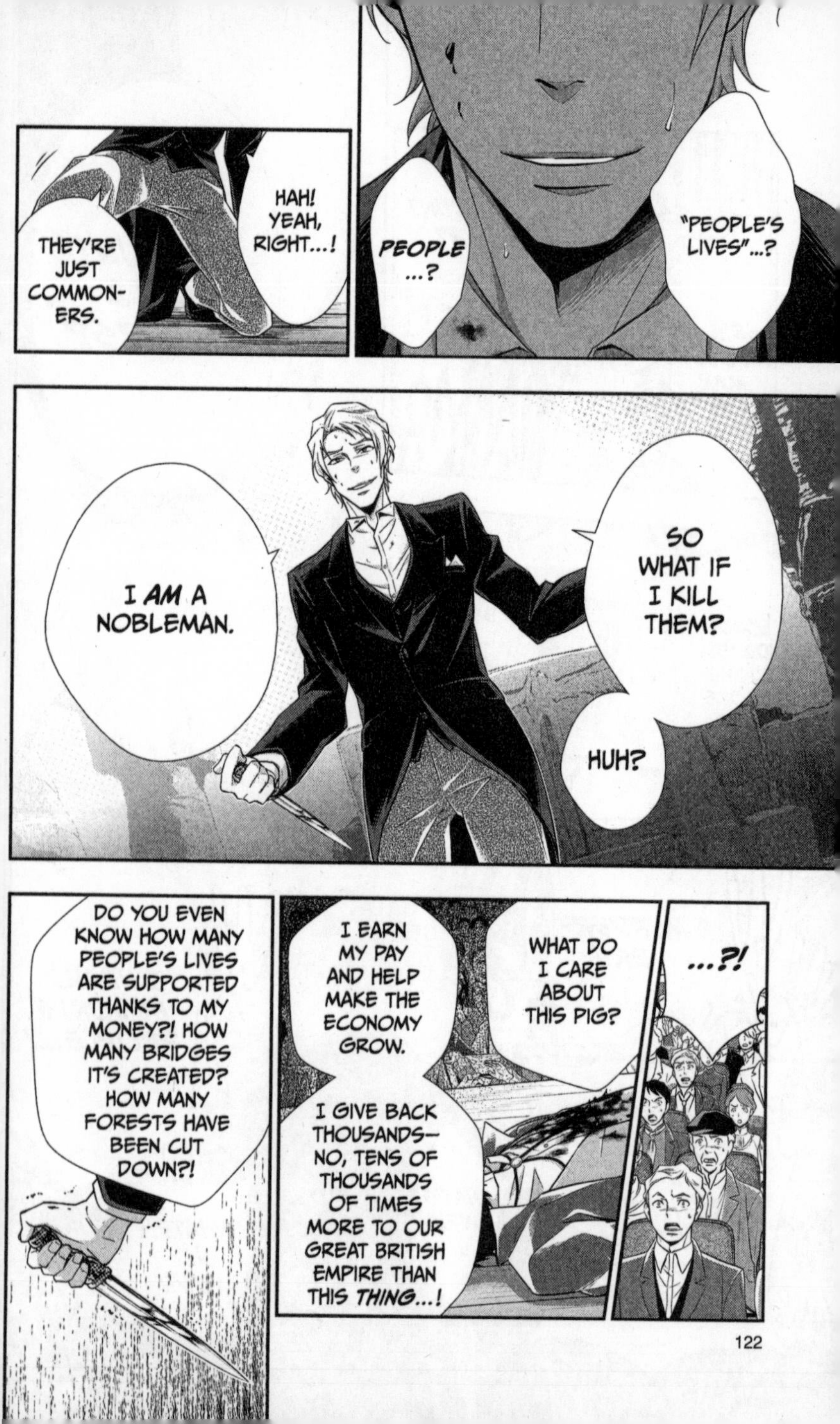

"PEOPLE'S LIVES"...?
PEOPLE ...?
HAH! YEAH, RIGHT...!
THEY'RE JUST COMMONERS.
SO WHAT IF I KILL THEM?
HUH?
I *AM* A NOBLEMAN.
...?!
WHAT DO I CARE ABOUT THIS PIG?
I EARN MY PAY AND HELP MAKE THE ECONOMY GROW.
I GIVE BACK THOUSANDS— NO, TENS OF THOUSANDS OF TIMES MORE TO OUR GREAT BRITISH EMPIRE THAN THIS *THING*...!
DO YOU EVEN KNOW HOW MANY PEOPLE'S LIVES ARE SUPPORTED THANKS TO MY MONEY?! HOW MANY BRIDGES IT'S CREATED? HOW MANY FORESTS HAVE BEEN CUT DOWN?!

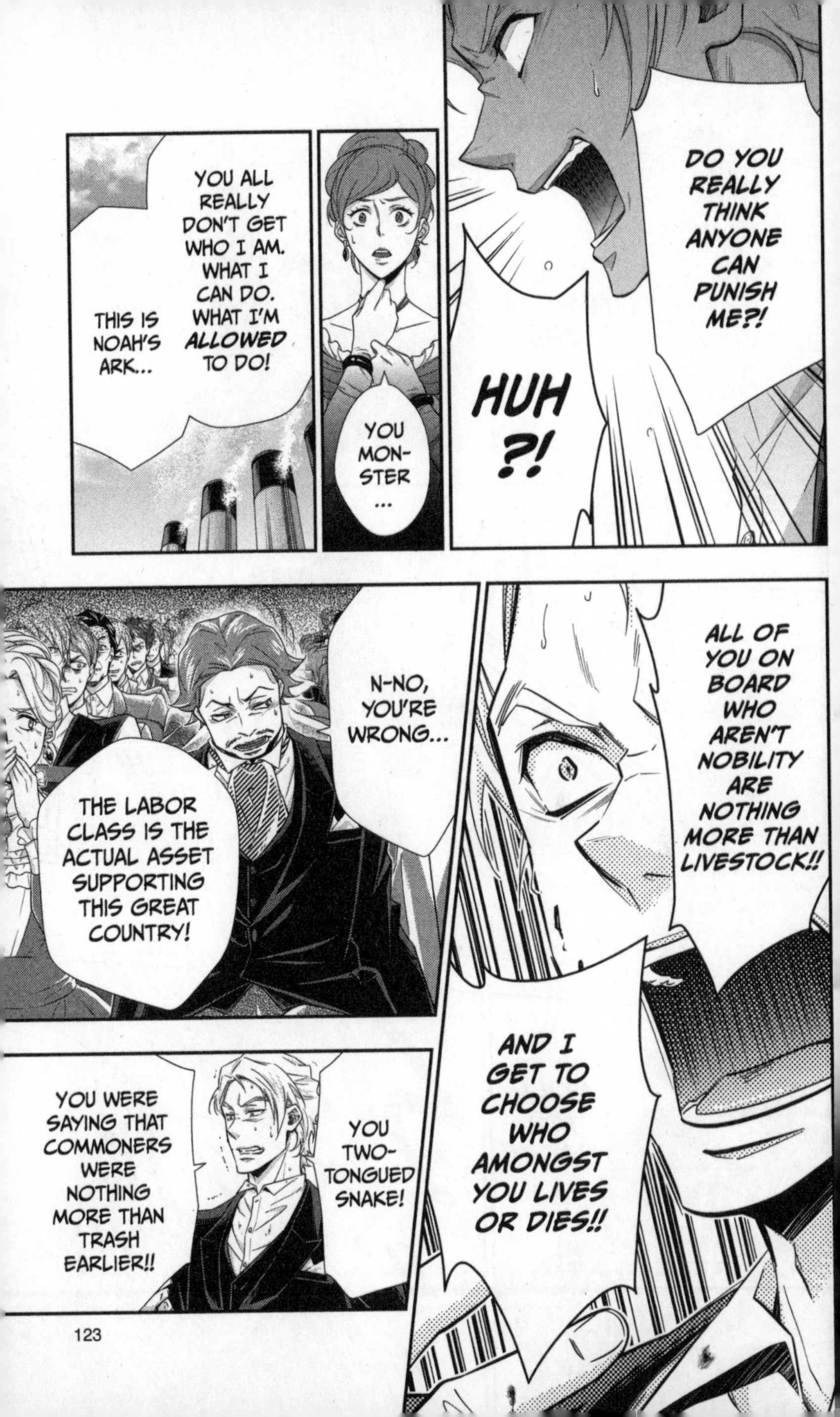
DO YOU REALLY THINK ANYONE CAN PUNISH ME?!
HUH ?!
YOU MON-STER ...
YOU ALL REALLY DON'T GET WHO I AM. WHAT I CAN DO. WHAT I'M *ALLOWED* TO DO!
THIS IS NOAH'S ARK...
ALL OF YOU ON BOARD WHO AREN'T NOBILITY ARE NOTHING MORE THAN LIVESTOCK!!
AND I GET TO CHOOSE WHO AMONGST YOU LIVES OR DIES!!
N-NO, YOU'RE WRONG...
THE LABOR CLASS IS THE ACTUAL ASSET SUPPORTING THIS GREAT COUNTRY!
YOU TWO-TONGUED SNAKE!
YOU WERE SAYING THAT COMMONERS WERE NOTHING MORE THAN TRASH EARLIER!!

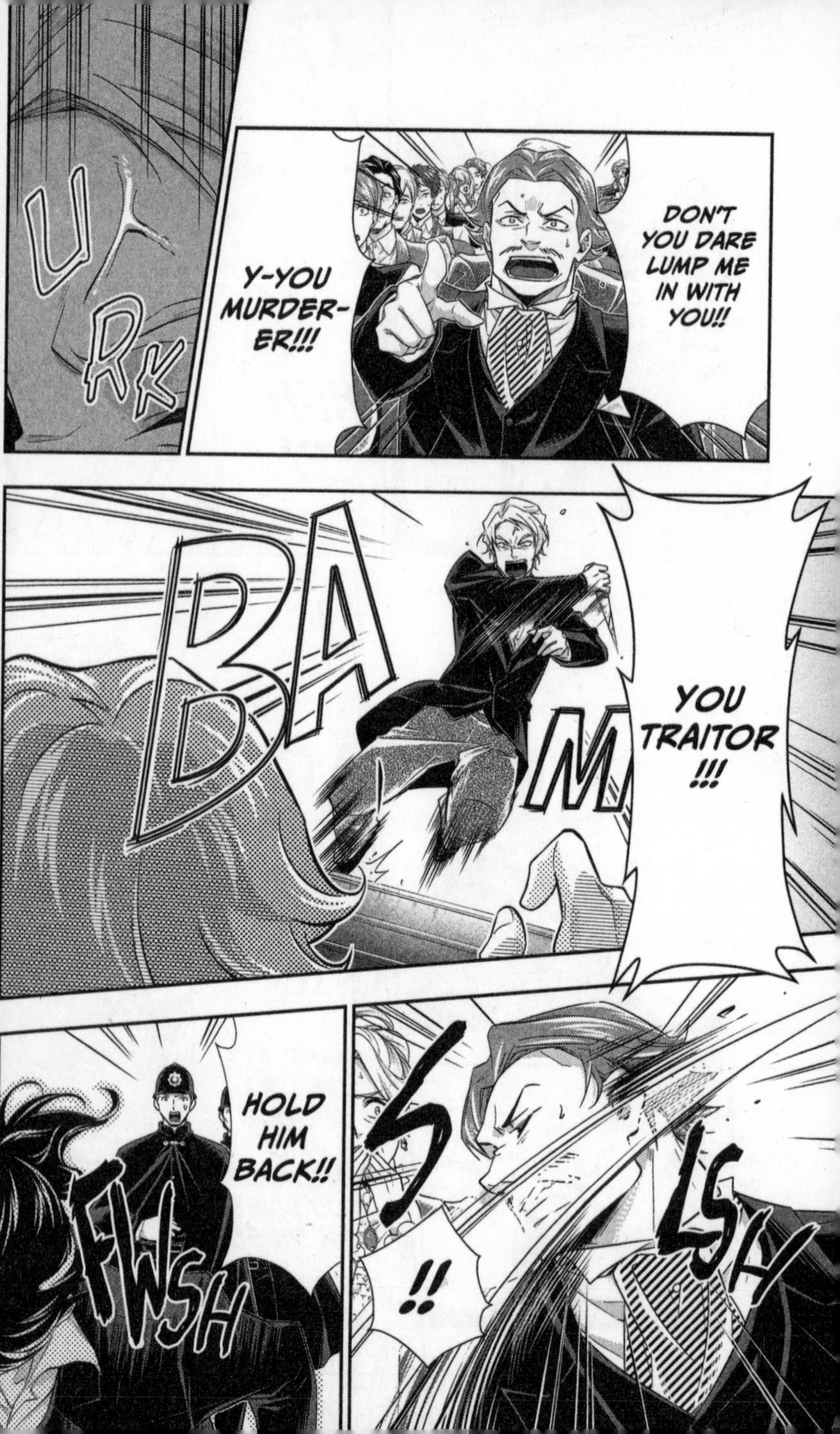
DON'T YOU DARE LUMP ME IN WITH YOU!!
Y-YOU MURDER-ER!!!
URK
YOU TRAITOR!!!
BAM
SLSH
!!
HOLD HIM BACK!!
FWSH

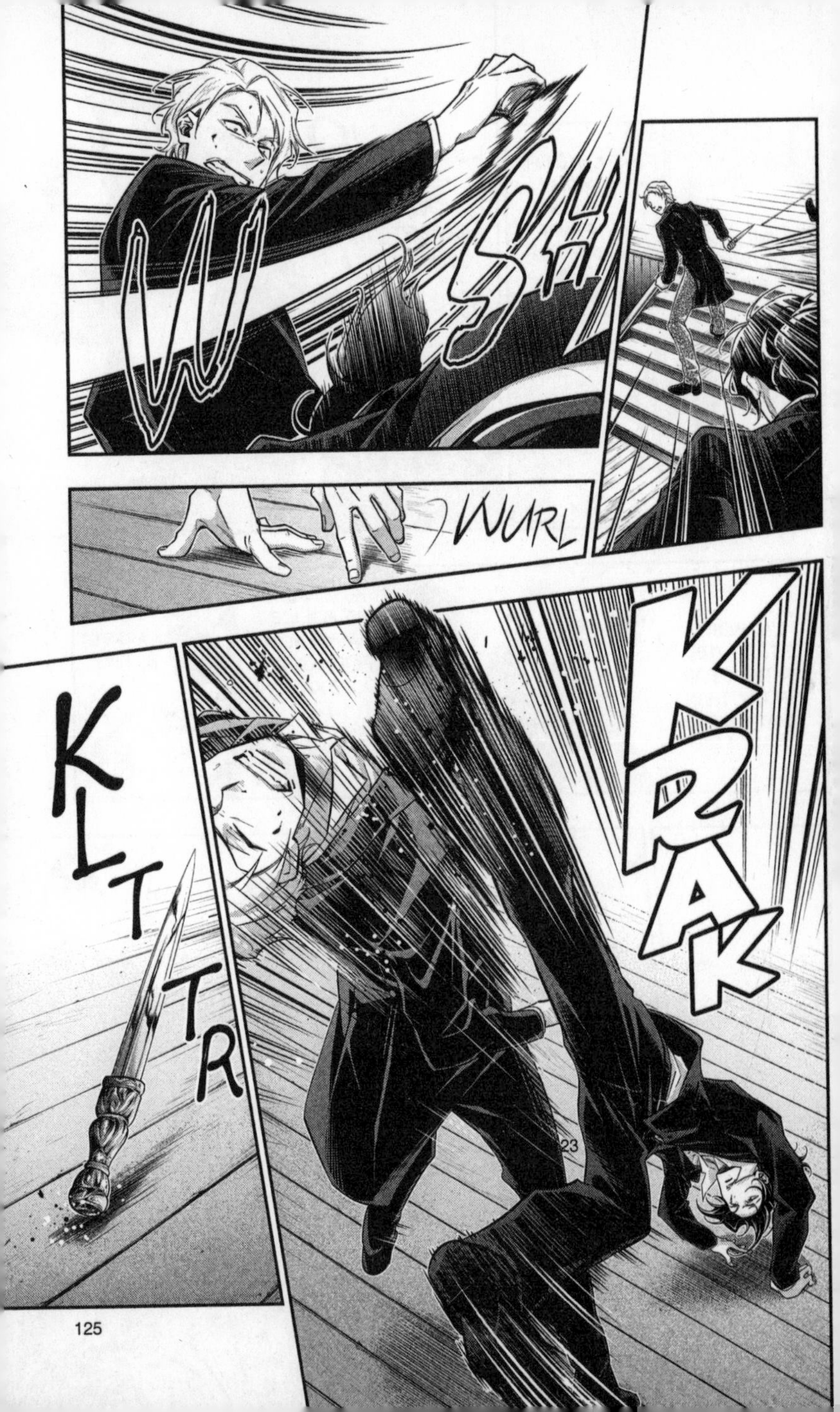
WSH
WURL
KRAK
KLTTR

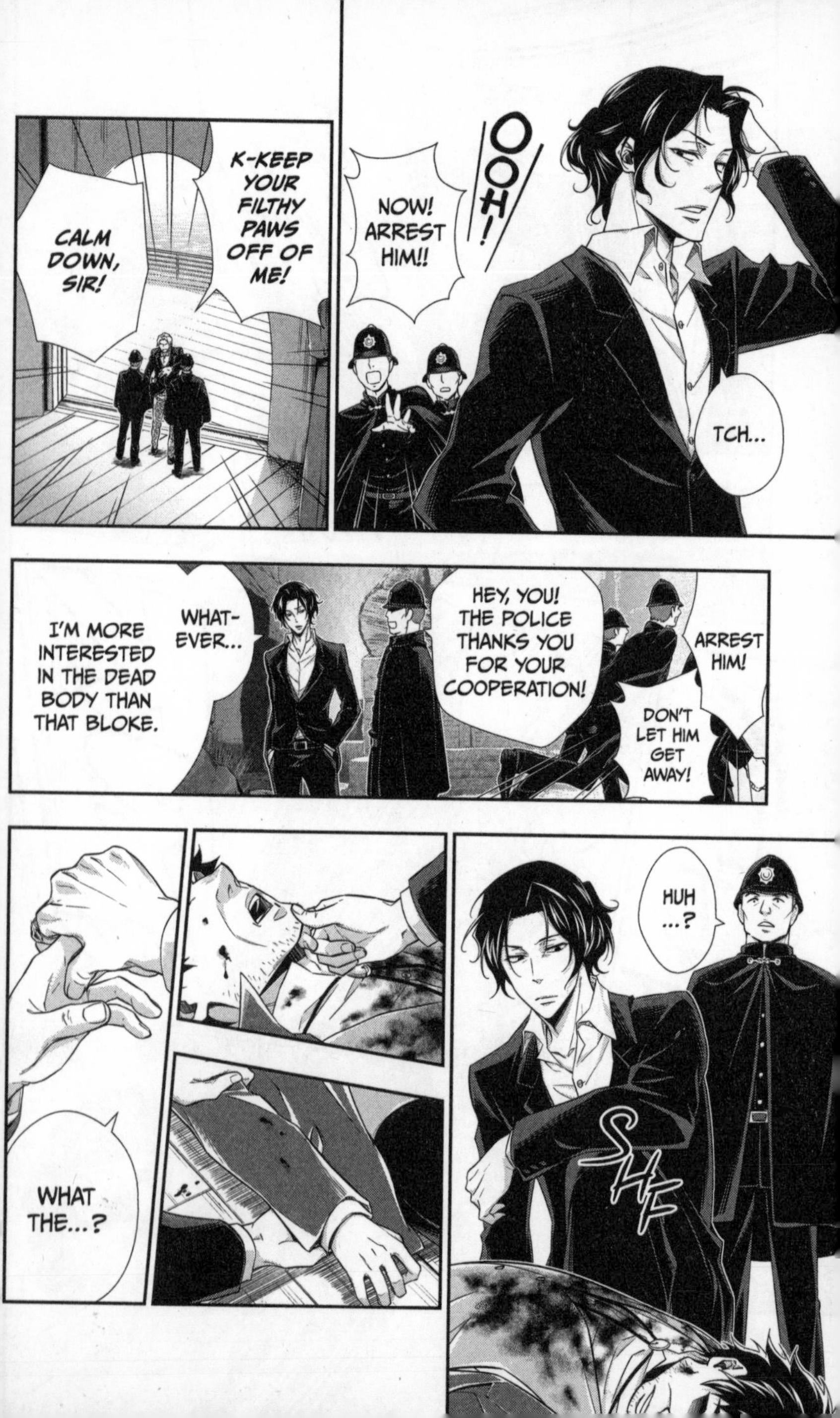
OOH!
NOW! ARREST HIM!!
TCH...
K-KEEP YOUR FILTHY PAWS OFF OF ME!
CALM DOWN, SIR!
ARREST HIM!
DON'T LET HIM GET AWAY!
HEY, YOU! THE POLICE THANKS YOU FOR YOUR COOPERATION!
WHAT-EVER...
I'M MORE INTERESTED IN THE DEAD BODY THAN THAT BLOKE.
HUH ...?
SHF
WHAT THE...?

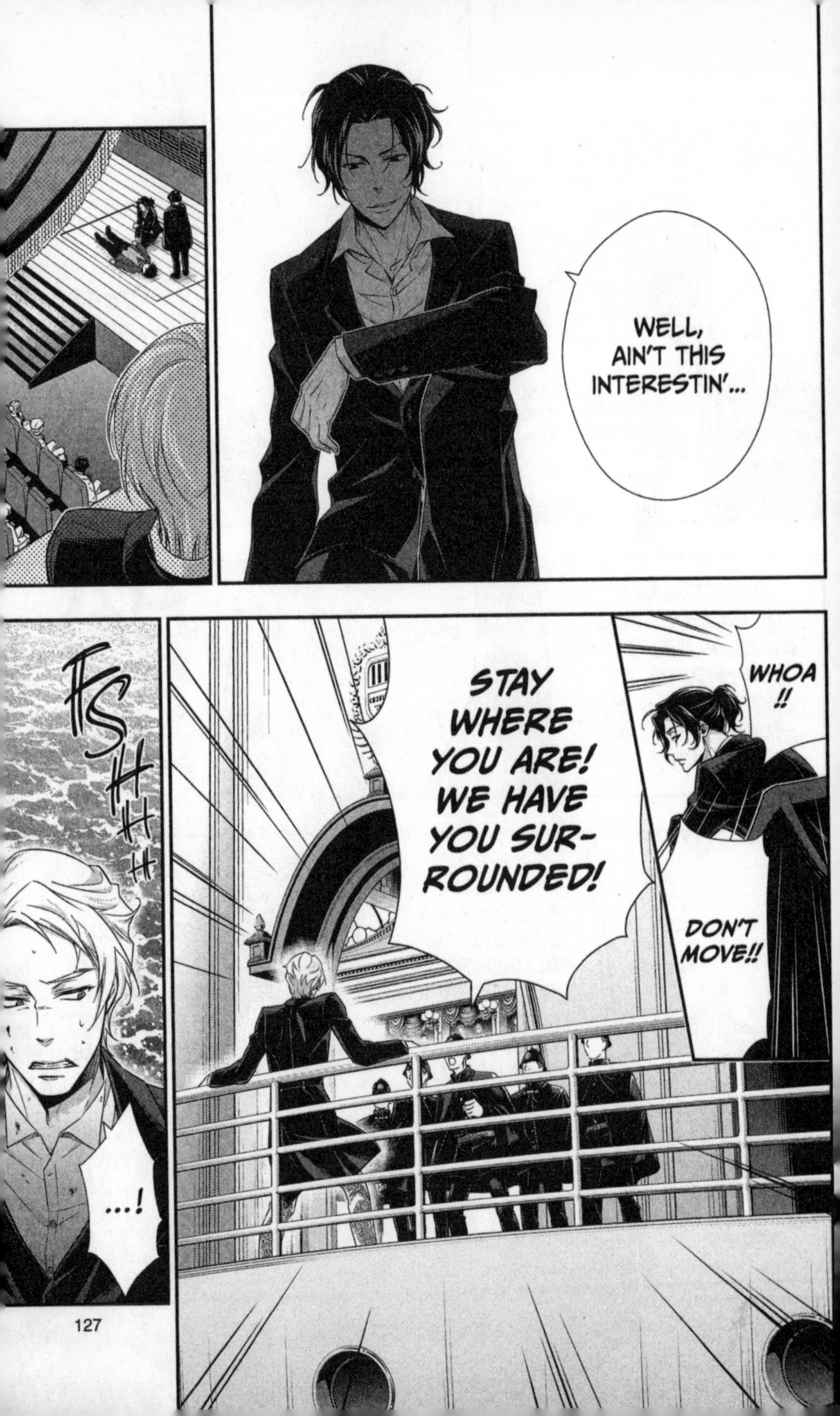
WELL, AIN'T THIS INTERESTIN'...
WHOA!!
DON'T MOVE!!
STAY WHERE YOU ARE! WE HAVE YOU SUR-ROUNDED!
FSHHH
...!

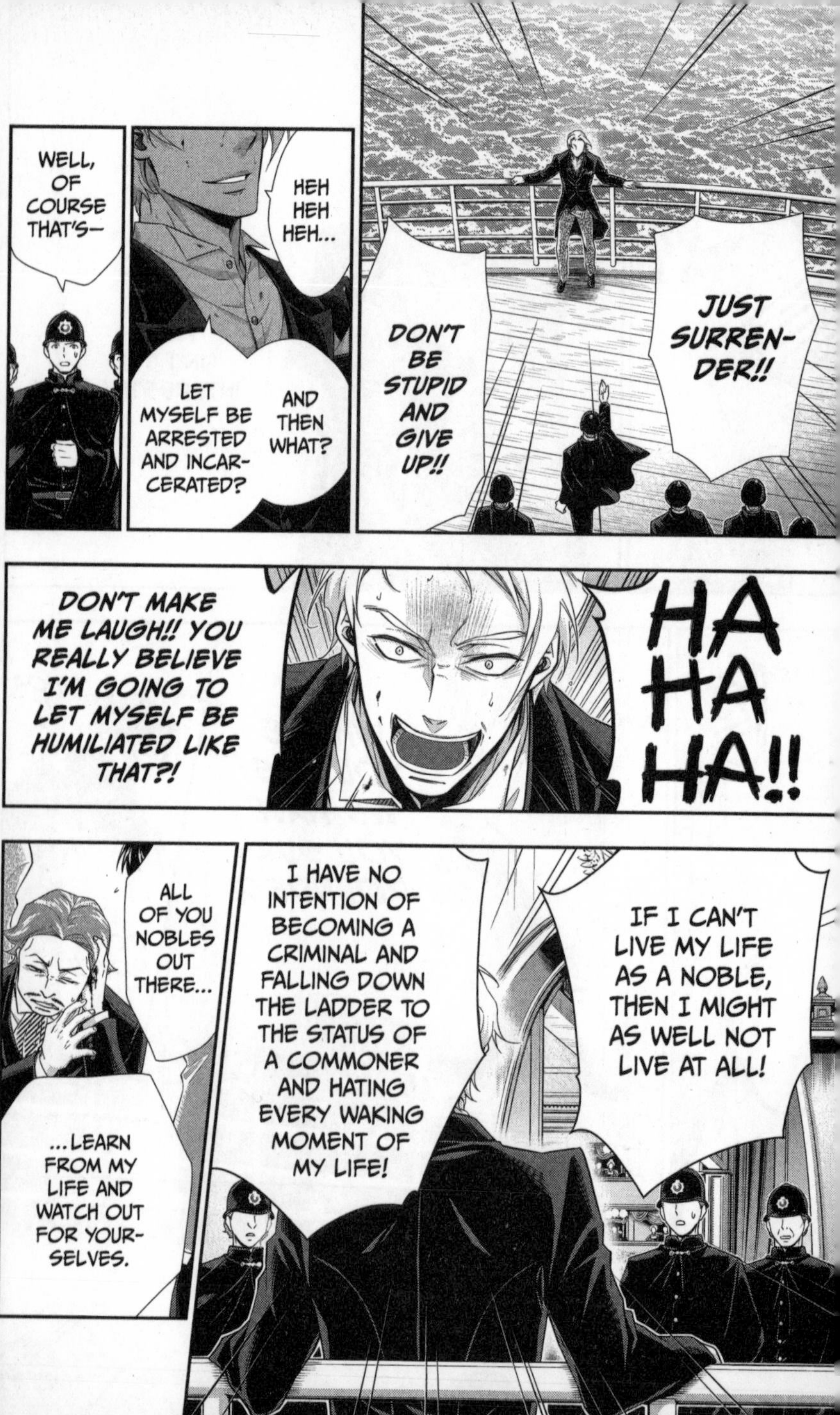
JUST SURREN-DER!!
DON'T BE STUPID AND GIVE UP!!
HEH HEH HEH...
AND THEN WHAT?
LET MYSELF BE ARRESTED AND INCAR-CERATED?
WELL, OF COURSE THAT'S—
HA HA HA!!
DON'T MAKE ME LAUGH!! YOU REALLY BELIEVE I'M GOING TO LET MYSELF BE HUMILIATED LIKE THAT?!
IF I CAN'T LIVE MY LIFE AS A NOBLE, THEN I MIGHT AS WELL NOT LIVE AT ALL!
I HAVE NO INTENTION OF BECOMING A CRIMINAL AND FALLING DOWN THE LADDER TO THE STATUS OF A COMMONER AND HATING EVERY WAKING MOMENT OF MY LIFE!
ALL OF YOU NOBLES OUT THERE...
...LEARN FROM MY LIFE AND WATCH OUT FOR YOUR-SELVES.

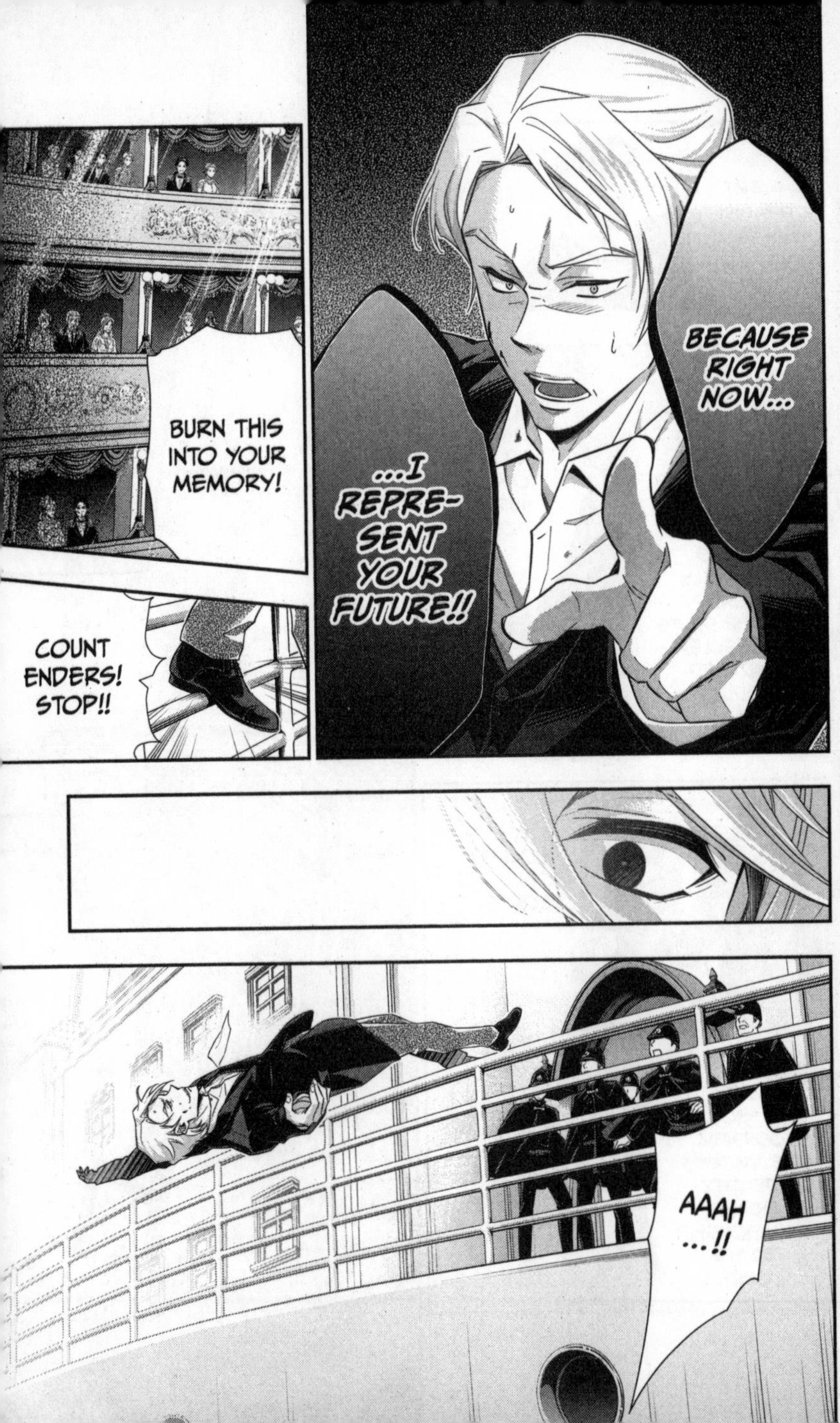
BECAUSE RIGHT NOW...
...I REPRE-SENT YOUR FUTURE!!
BURN THIS INTO YOUR MEMORY!
COUNT ENDERS! STOP!!
AAAH ...!!

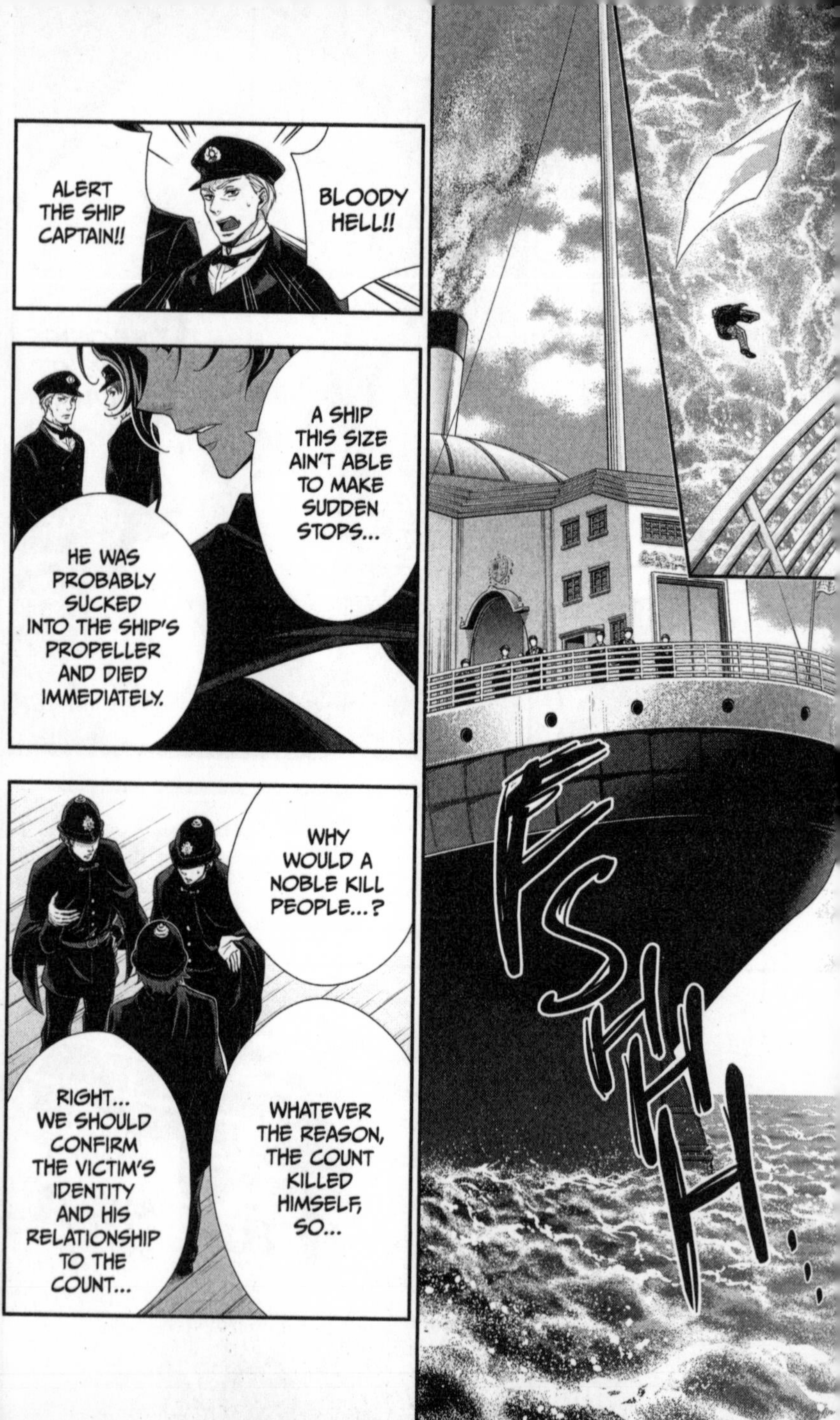
FSHHH...
BLOODY HELL!!
ALERT THE SHIP CAPTAIN!!
A SHIP THIS SIZE AIN'T ABLE TO MAKE SUDDEN STOPS...
HE WAS PROBABLY SUCKED INTO THE SHIP'S PROPELLER AND DIED IMMEDIATELY.
WHY WOULD A NOBLE KILL PEOPLE...?
WHATEVER THE REASON, THE COUNT KILLED HIMSELF, SO...
RIGHT... WE SHOULD CONFIRM THE VICTIM'S IDENTITY AND HIS RELATIONSHIP TO THE COUNT...

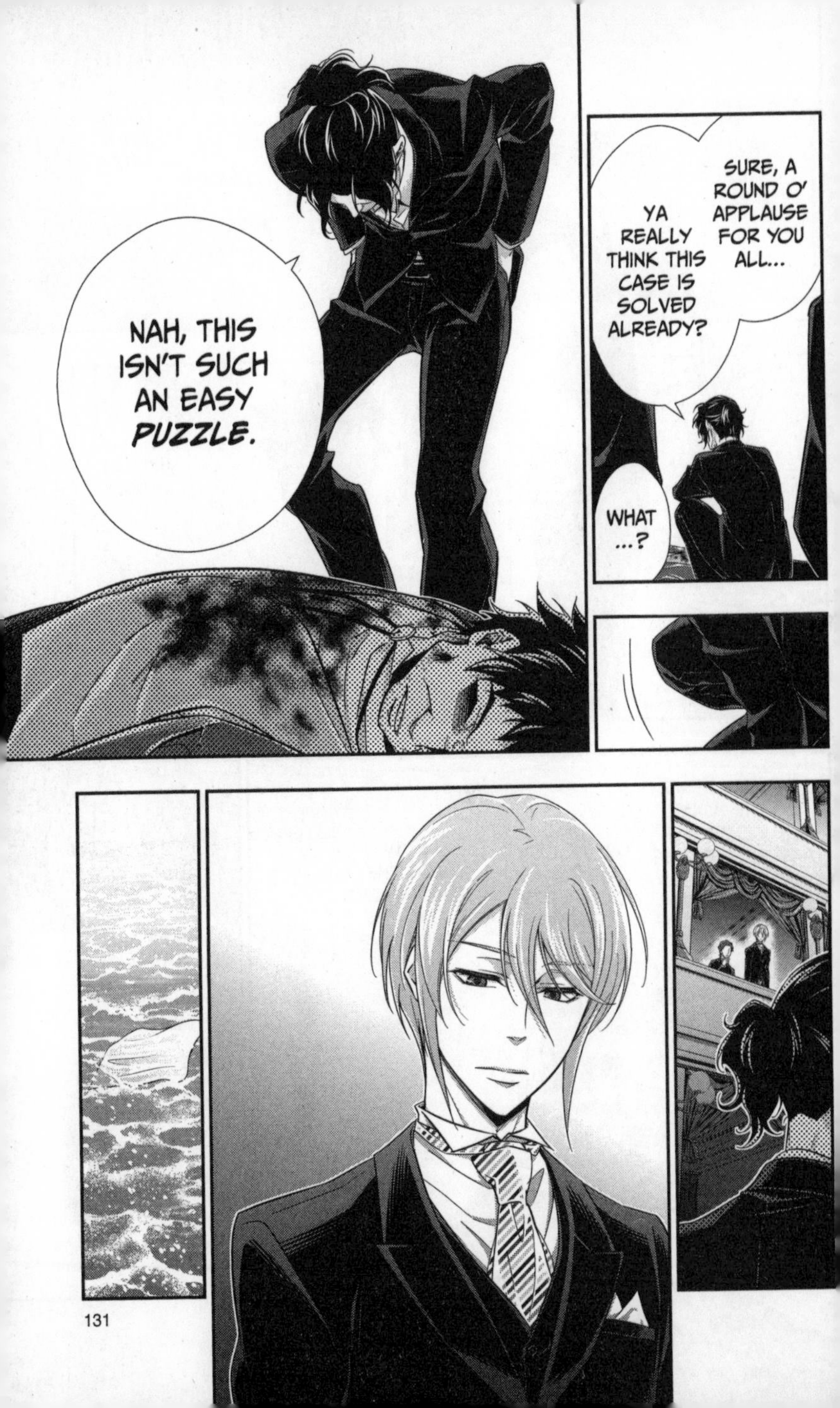
SURE, A ROUND O' APPLAUSE FOR YOU ALL...
YA REALLY THINK THIS CASE IS SOLVED ALREADY?
WHAT ...?
NAH, THIS ISN'T SUCH AN EASY *PUZZLE*.

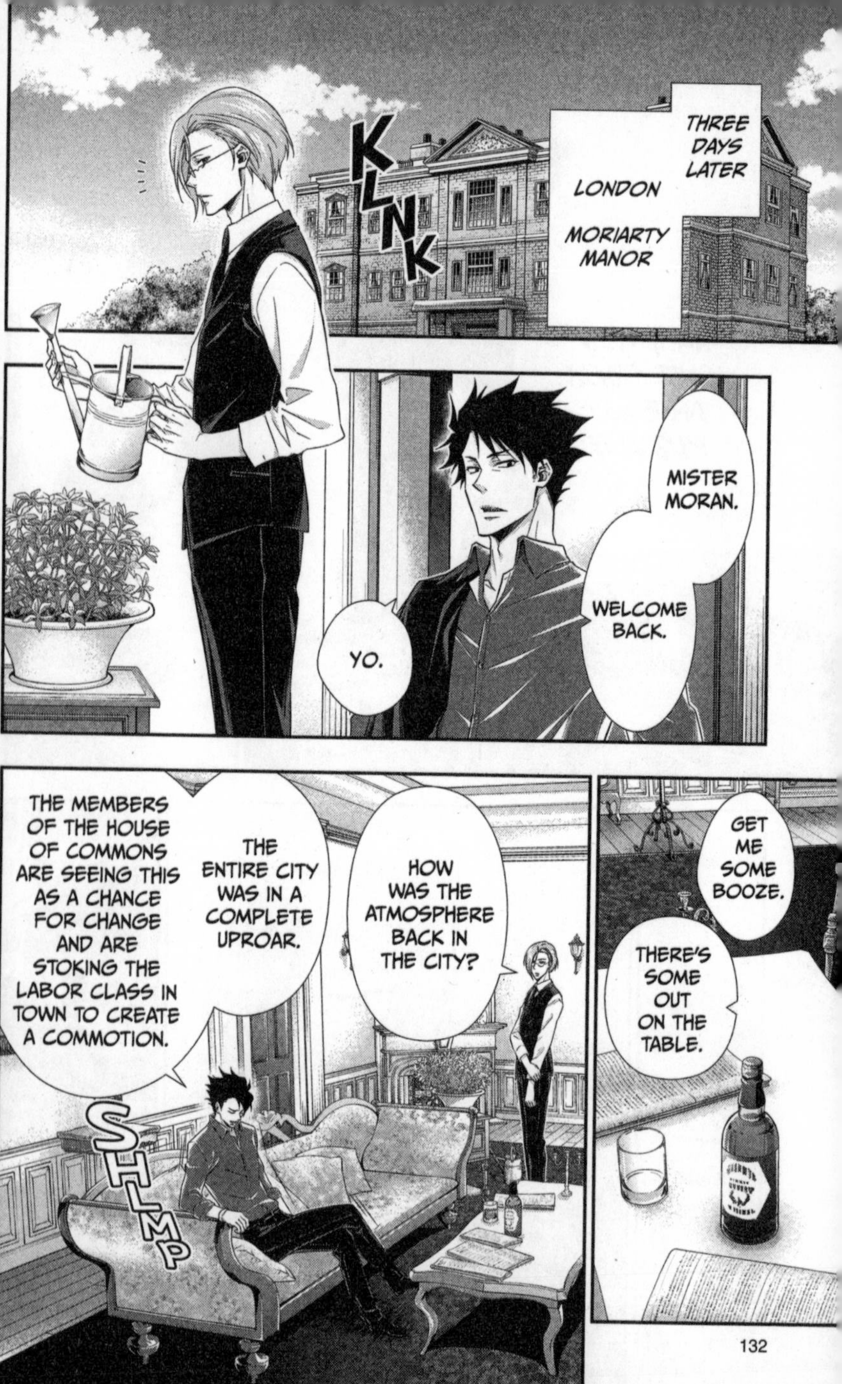
THREE DAYS LATER
LONDON
MORIARTY MANOR
KLNK
MISTER MORAN.
WELCOME BACK.
YO.
GET ME SOME BOOZE.
THERE'S SOME OUT ON THE TABLE.
HOW WAS THE ATMOSPHERE BACK IN THE CITY?
THE ENTIRE CITY WAS IN A COMPLETE UPROAR.
THE MEMBERS OF THE HOUSE OF COMMONS ARE SEEING THIS AS A CHANCE FOR CHANGE AND ARE STOKING THE LABOR CLASS IN TOWN TO CREATE A COMMOTION.
SHLMP

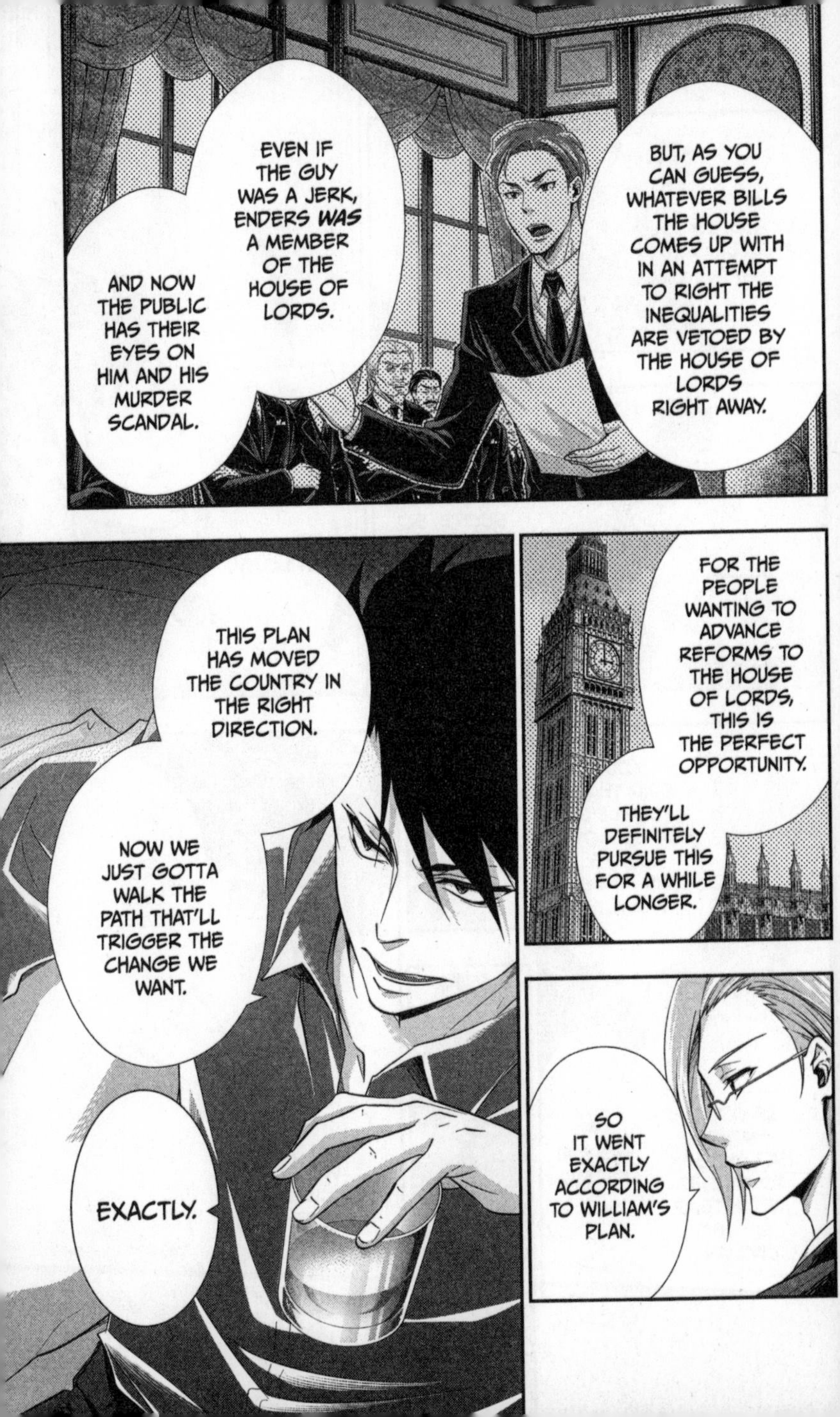
BUT, AS YOU CAN GUESS, WHATEVER BILLS THE HOUSE COMES UP WITH IN AN ATTEMPT TO RIGHT THE INEQUALITIES ARE VETOED BY THE HOUSE OF LORDS RIGHT AWAY.
EVEN IF THE GUY WAS A JERK, ENDERS *WAS* A MEMBER OF THE HOUSE OF LORDS.
AND NOW THE PUBLIC HAS THEIR EYES ON HIM AND HIS MURDER SCANDAL.
FOR THE PEOPLE WANTING TO ADVANCE REFORMS TO THE HOUSE OF LORDS, THIS IS THE PERFECT OPPORTUNITY.
THEY'LL DEFINITELY PURSUE THIS FOR A WHILE LONGER.
SO IT WENT EXACTLY ACCORDING TO WILLIAM'S PLAN.
THIS PLAN HAS MOVED THE COUNTRY IN THE RIGHT DIRECTION.
NOW WE JUST GOTTA WALK THE PATH THAT'LL TRIGGER THE CHANGE WE WANT.
EXACTLY.

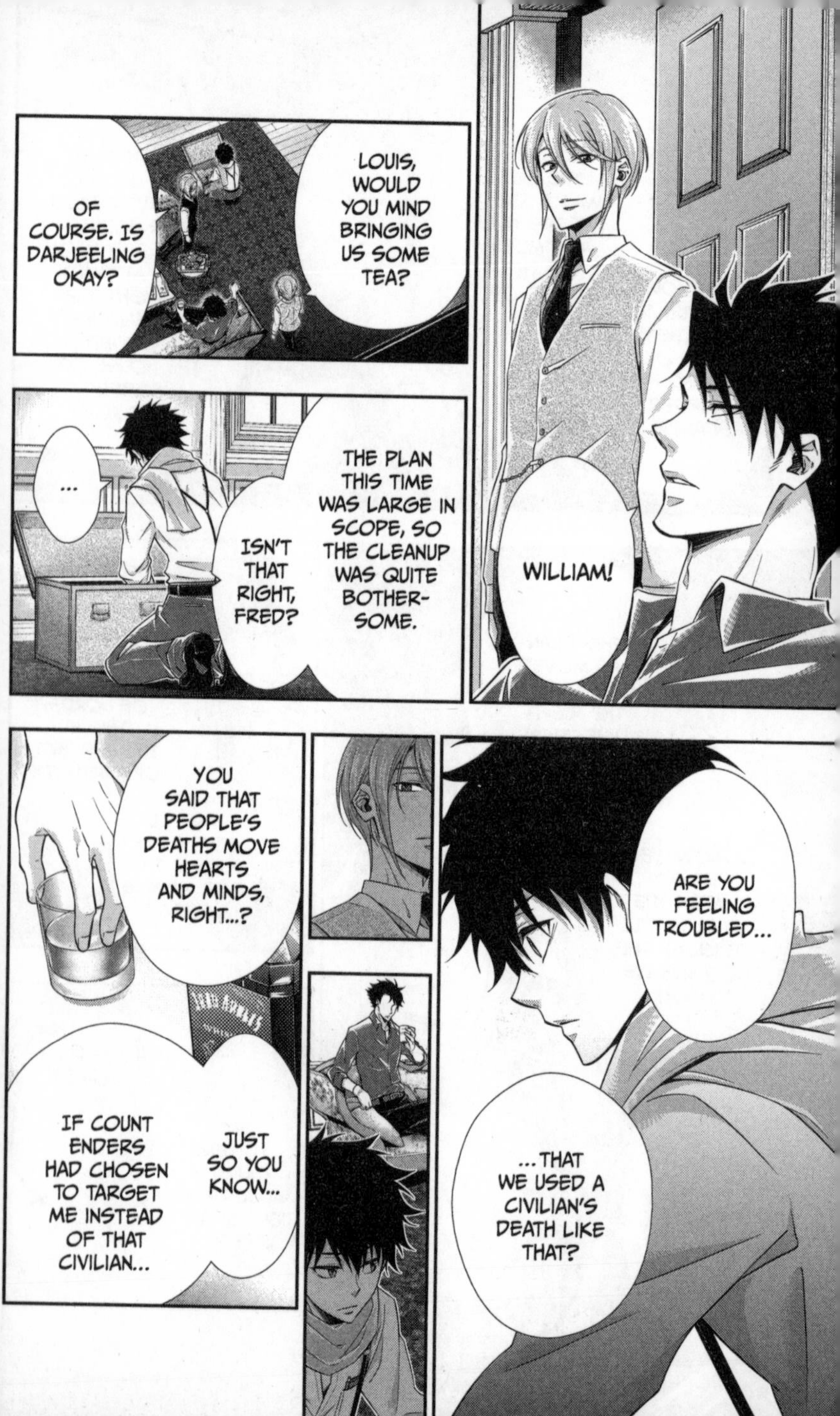
WILLIAM!
LOUIS, WOULD YOU MIND BRINGING US SOME TEA?
OF COURSE. IS DARJEELING OKAY?
THE PLAN THIS TIME WAS LARGE IN SCOPE, SO THE CLEANUP WAS QUITE BOTHER-SOME.
ISN'T THAT RIGHT, FRED?
...
ARE YOU FEELING TROUBLED...
...THAT WE USED A CIVILIAN'S DEATH LIKE THAT?
YOU SAID THAT PEOPLE'S DEATHS MOVE HEARTS AND MINDS, RIGHT...?
JUST SO YOU KNOW...
IF COUNT ENDERS HAD CHOSEN TO TARGET ME INSTEAD OF THAT CIVILIAN...

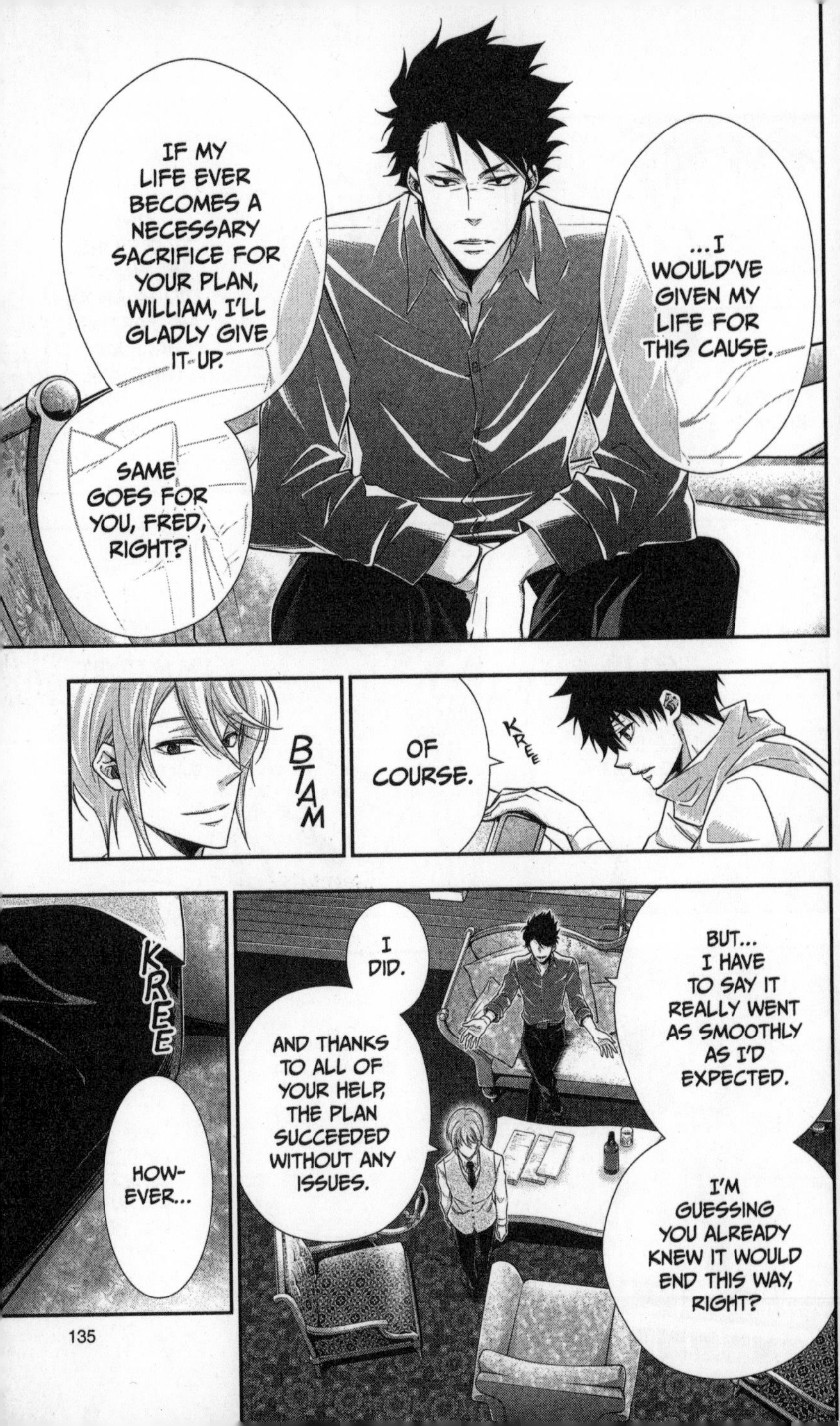
...I WOULD'VE GIVEN MY LIFE FOR THIS CAUSE.
IF MY LIFE EVER BECOMES A NECESSARY SACRIFICE FOR YOUR PLAN, WILLIAM, I'LL GLADLY GIVE IT UP.
SAME GOES FOR YOU, FRED, RIGHT?
KREE
OF COURSE.
BTAM
BUT... I HAVE TO SAY IT REALLY WENT AS SMOOTHLY AS I'D EXPECTED.
I'M GUESSING YOU ALREADY KNEW IT WOULD END THIS WAY, RIGHT?
I DID.
AND THANKS TO ALL OF YOUR HELP, THE PLAN SUCCEEDED WITHOUT ANY ISSUES.
KREE
HOW-EVER...

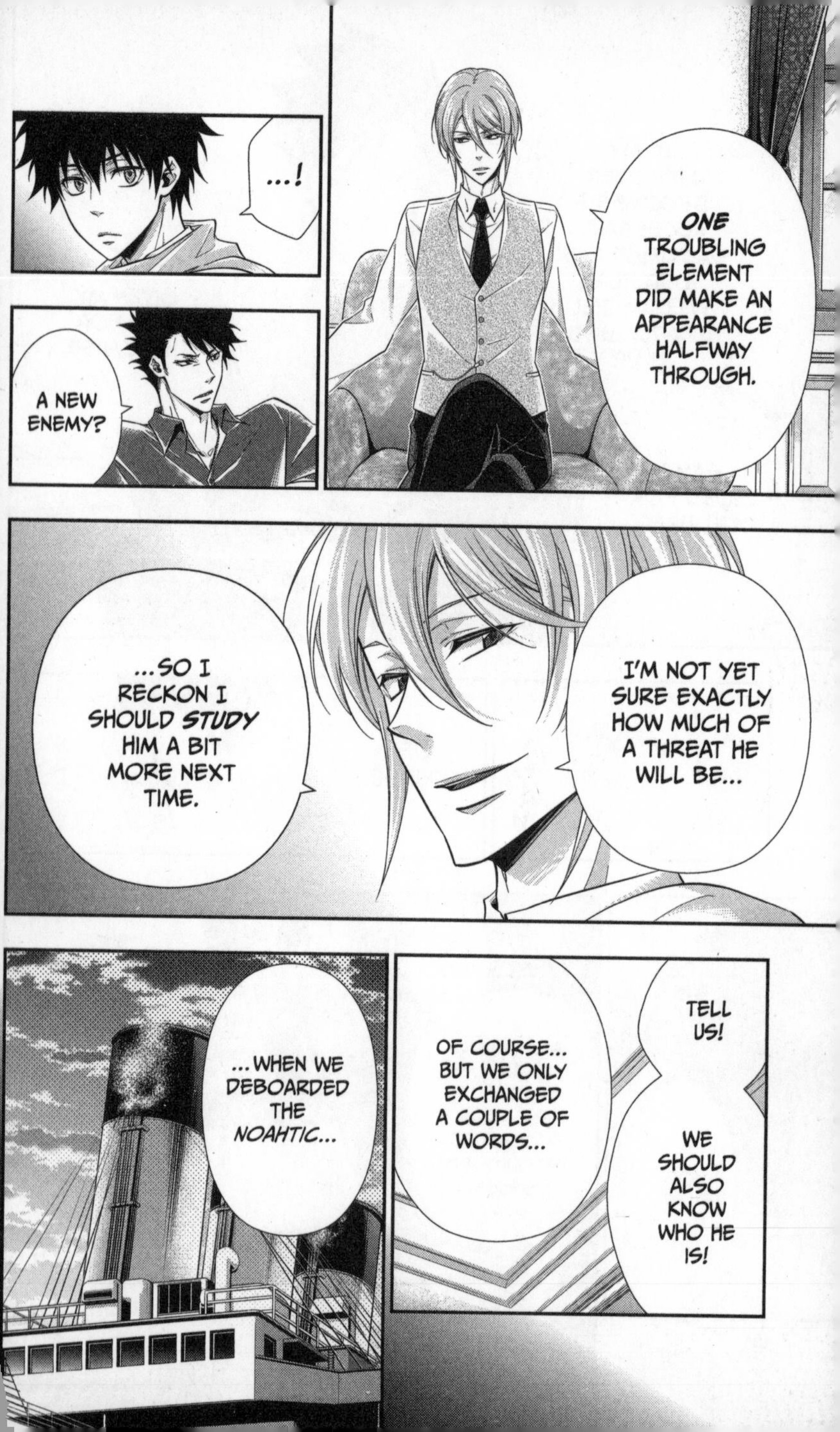
ONE TROUBLING ELEMENT DID MAKE AN APPEARANCE HALFWAY THROUGH.
...!
A NEW ENEMY?
I'M NOT YET SURE EXACTLY HOW MUCH OF A THREAT HE WILL BE...
...SO I RECKON I SHOULD STUDY HIM A BIT MORE NEXT TIME.
TELL US!
WE SHOULD ALSO KNOW WHO HE IS!
OF COURSE... BUT WE ONLY EXCHANGED A COUPLE OF WORDS...
...WHEN WE DEBOARDED THE NOAHTIC...

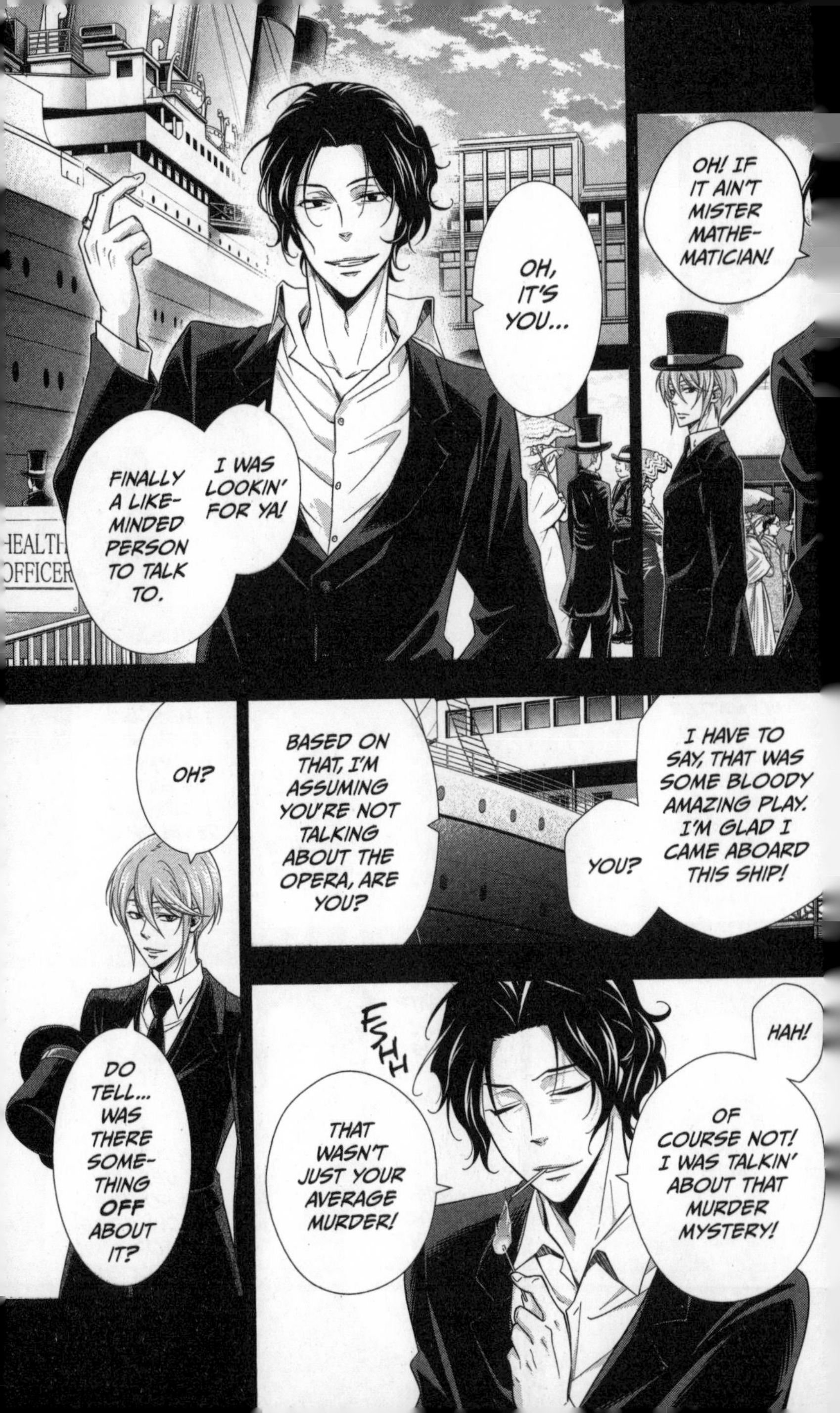
OH! IF IT AIN'T MISTER MATHE-MATICIAN!
OH, IT'S YOU...
I WAS LOOKIN' FOR YA!
FINALLY A LIKE-MINDED PERSON TO TALK TO.
I HAVE TO SAY, THAT WAS SOME BLOODY AMAZING PLAY. I'M GLAD I CAME ABOARD THIS SHIP!
YOU?
BASED ON THAT, I'M ASSUMING YOU'RE NOT TALKING ABOUT THE OPERA, ARE YOU?
HAH!
OF COURSE NOT! I WAS TALKIN' ABOUT THAT MURDER MYSTERY!
FSHH
THAT WASN'T JUST YOUR AVERAGE MURDER!
OH?
DO TELL... WAS THERE SOME-THING OFF ABOUT IT?

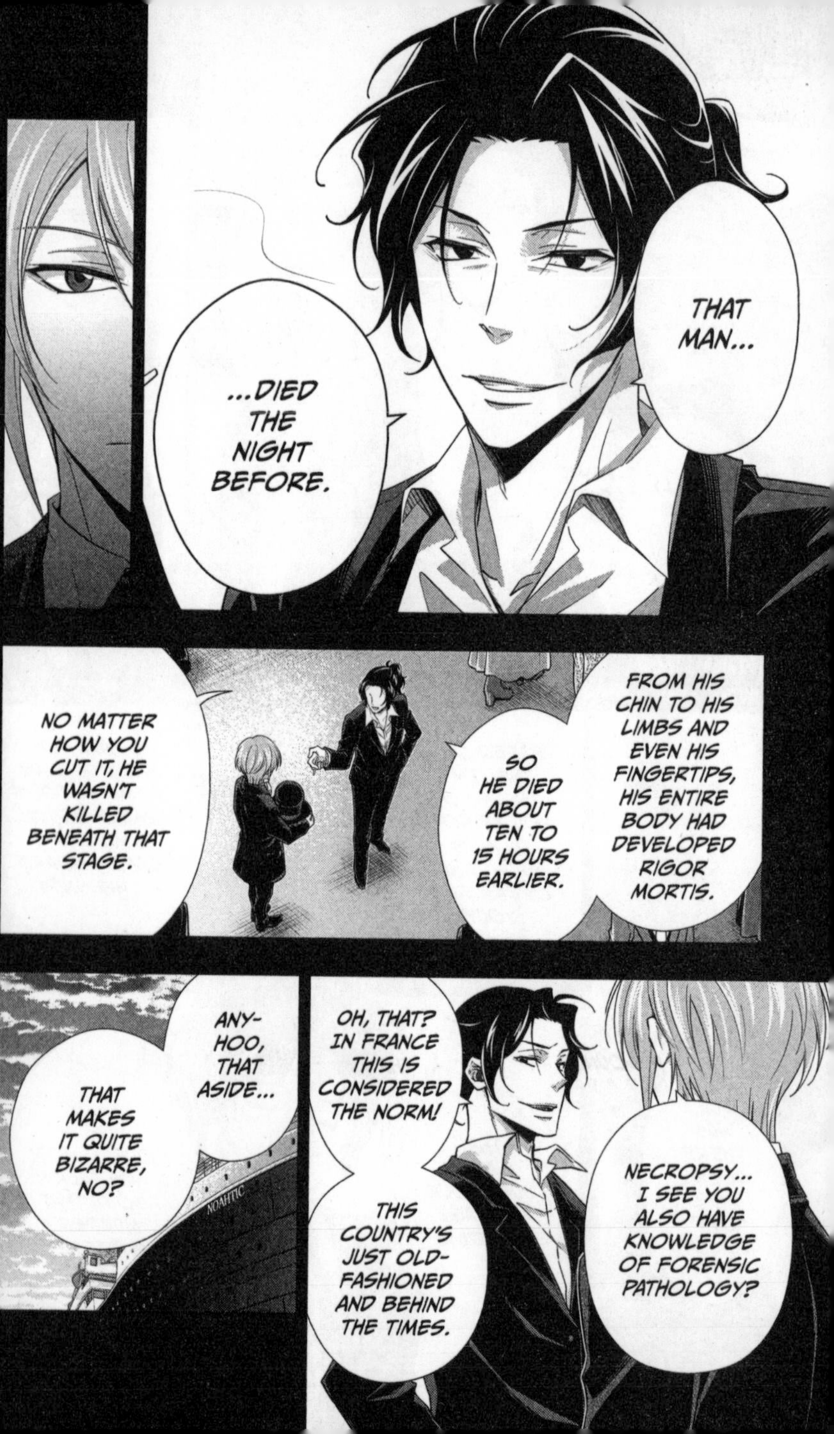
THAT MAN...
...DIED THE NIGHT BEFORE.
FROM HIS CHIN TO HIS LIMBS AND EVEN HIS FINGERTIPS, HIS ENTIRE BODY HAD DEVELOPED RIGOR MORTIS.
SO HE DIED ABOUT TEN TO 15 HOURS EARLIER.
NO MATTER HOW YOU CUT IT, HE WASN'T KILLED BENEATH THAT STAGE.
NECROPSY... I SEE YOU ALSO HAVE KNOWLEDGE OF FORENSIC PATHOLOGY?
OH, THAT? IN FRANCE THIS IS CONSIDERED THE NORM!
THIS COUNTRY'S JUST OLD-FASHIONED AND BEHIND THE TIMES.
ANY-HOO, THAT ASIDE...
THAT MAKES IT QUITE BIZARRE, NO?
NOAHTIC

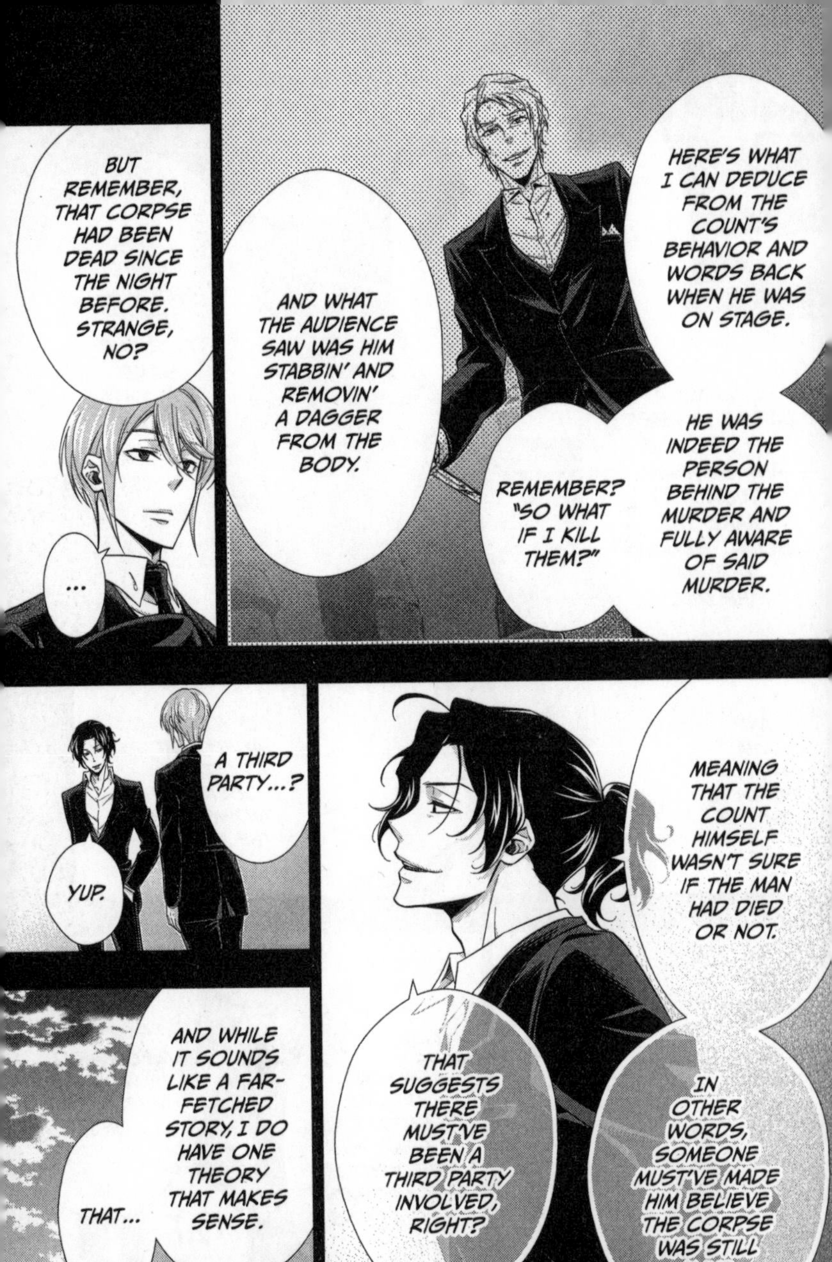
HERE'S WHAT I CAN DEDUCE FROM THE COUNT'S BEHAVIOR AND WORDS BACK WHEN HE WAS ON STAGE.
HE WAS INDEED THE PERSON BEHIND THE MURDER AND FULLY AWARE OF SAID MURDER.
REMEMBER? "SO WHAT IF I KILL THEM?"
AND WHAT THE AUDIENCE SAW WAS HIM STABBIN' AND REMOVIN' A DAGGER FROM THE BODY.
BUT REMEMBER, THAT CORPSE HAD BEEN DEAD SINCE THE NIGHT BEFORE. STRANGE, NO?
...
MEANING THAT THE COUNT HIMSELF WASN'T SURE IF THE MAN HAD DIED OR NOT.
IN OTHER WORDS, SOMEONE MUST'VE MADE HIM BELIEVE THE CORPSE WAS STILL ALIVE.
THAT SUGGESTS THERE MUST'VE BEEN A THIRD PARTY INVOLVED, RIGHT?
A THIRD PARTY...?
YUP.
AND WHILE IT SOUNDS LIKE A FAR-FETCHED STORY, I DO HAVE ONE THEORY THAT MAKES SENSE.
THAT...

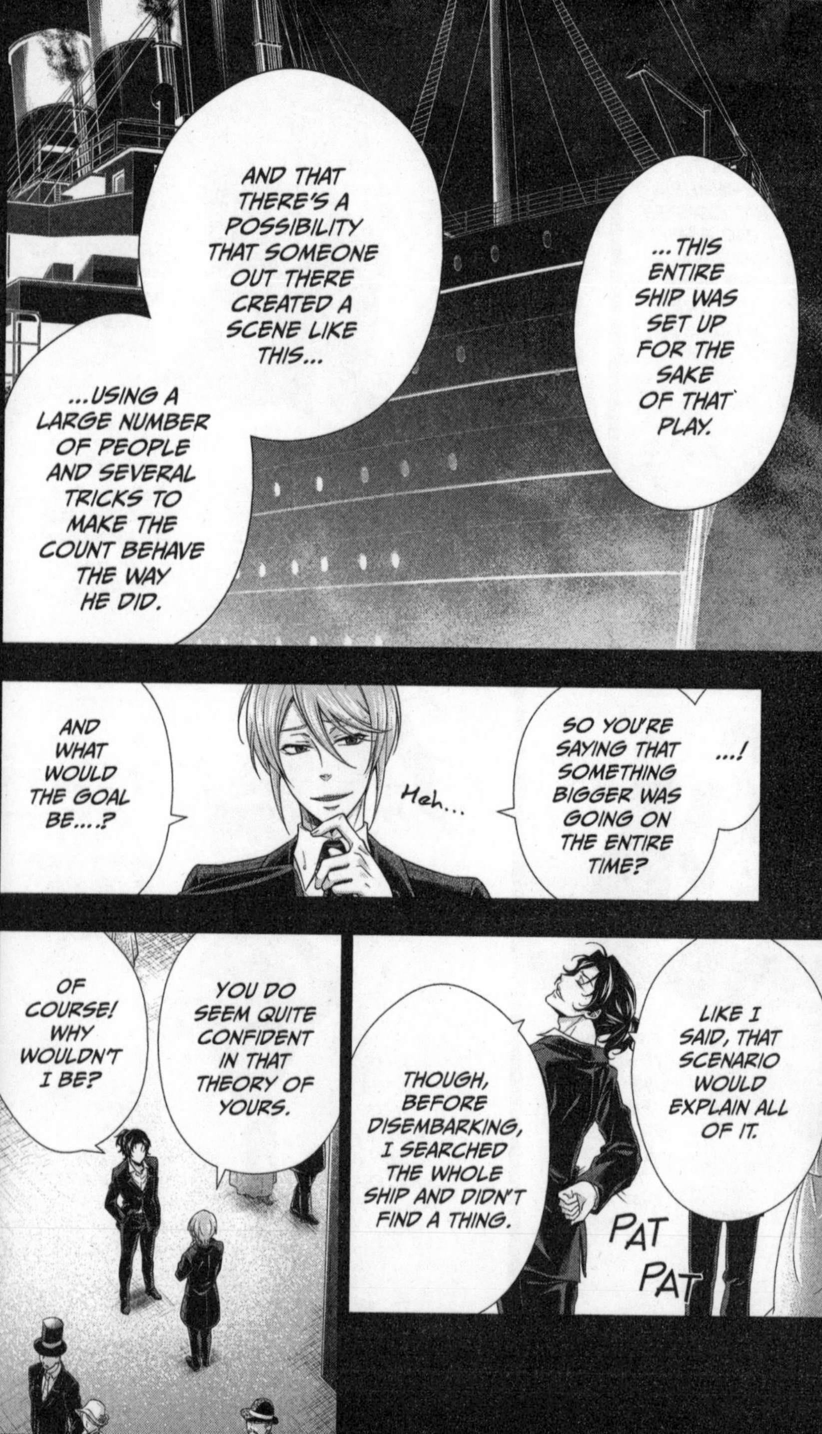
...THIS ENTIRE SHIP WAS SET UP FOR THE SAKE OF THAT PLAY.
AND THAT THERE'S A POSSIBILITY THAT SOMEONE OUT THERE CREATED A SCENE LIKE THIS...
...USING A LARGE NUMBER OF PEOPLE AND SEVERAL TRICKS TO MAKE THE COUNT BEHAVE THE WAY HE DID.
...!
SO YOU'RE SAYING THAT SOMETHING BIGGER WAS GOING ON THE ENTIRE TIME?
Heh...
AND WHAT WOULD THE GOAL BE....?
LIKE I SAID, THAT SCENARIO WOULD EXPLAIN ALL OF IT.
PAT PAT
THOUGH, BEFORE DISEMBARKING, I SEARCHED THE WHOLE SHIP AND DIDN'T FIND A THING.
YOU DO SEEM QUITE CONFIDENT IN THAT THEORY OF YOURS.
OF COURSE! WHY WOULDN'T I BE?

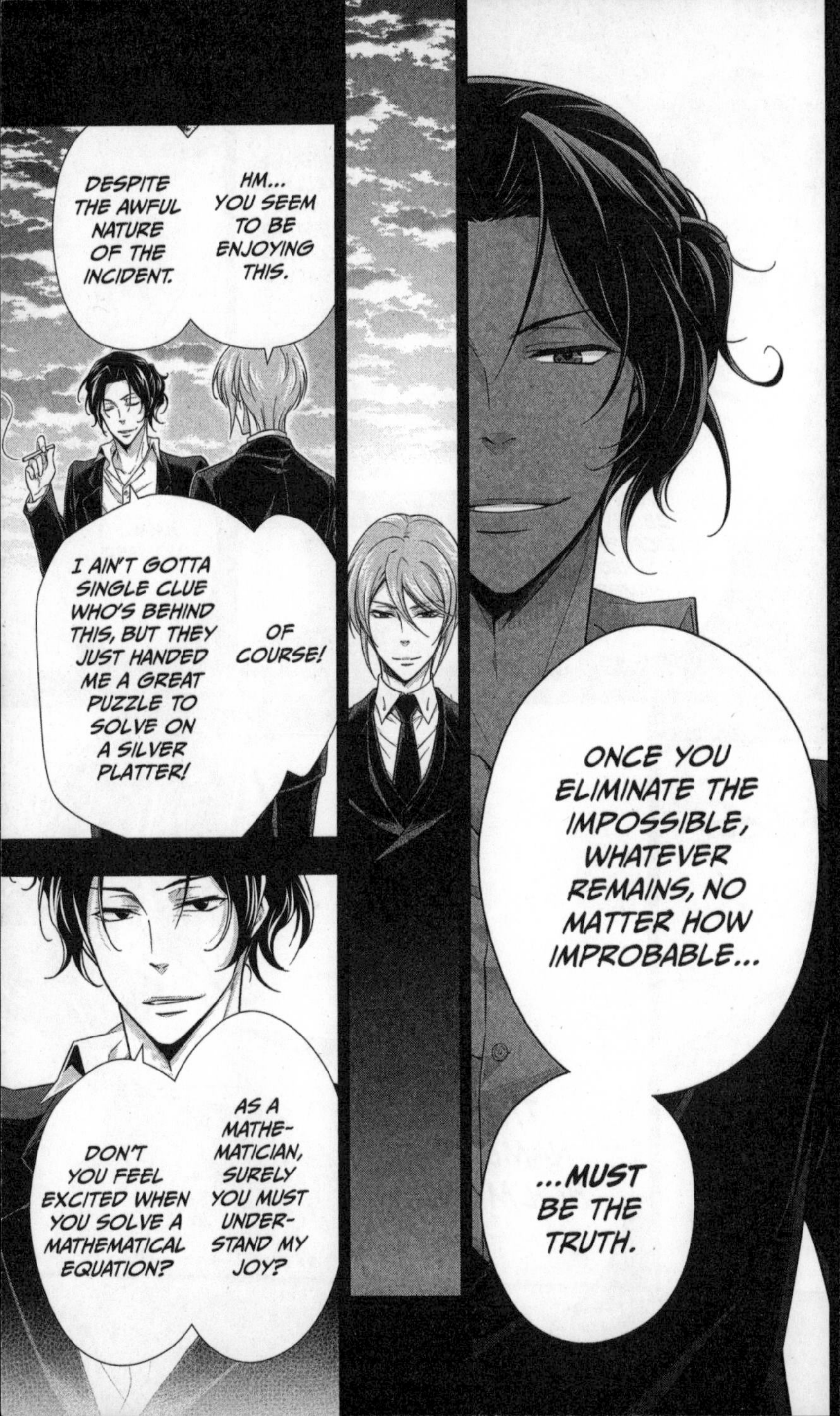
ONCE YOU ELIMINATE THE IMPOSSIBLE, WHATEVER REMAINS, NO MATTER HOW IMPROBABLE...
...MUST BE THE TRUTH.
HM... YOU SEEM TO BE ENJOYING THIS.
DESPITE THE AWFUL NATURE OF THE INCIDENT.
OF COURSE!
I AIN'T GOTTA SINGLE CLUE WHO'S BEHIND THIS, BUT THEY JUST HANDED ME A GREAT PUZZLE TO SOLVE ON A SILVER PLATTER!
AS A MATHE-MATICIAN, SURELY YOU MUST UNDER-STAND MY JOY?
DON'T YOU FEEL EXCITED WHEN YOU SOLVE A MATHEMATICAL EQUATION?

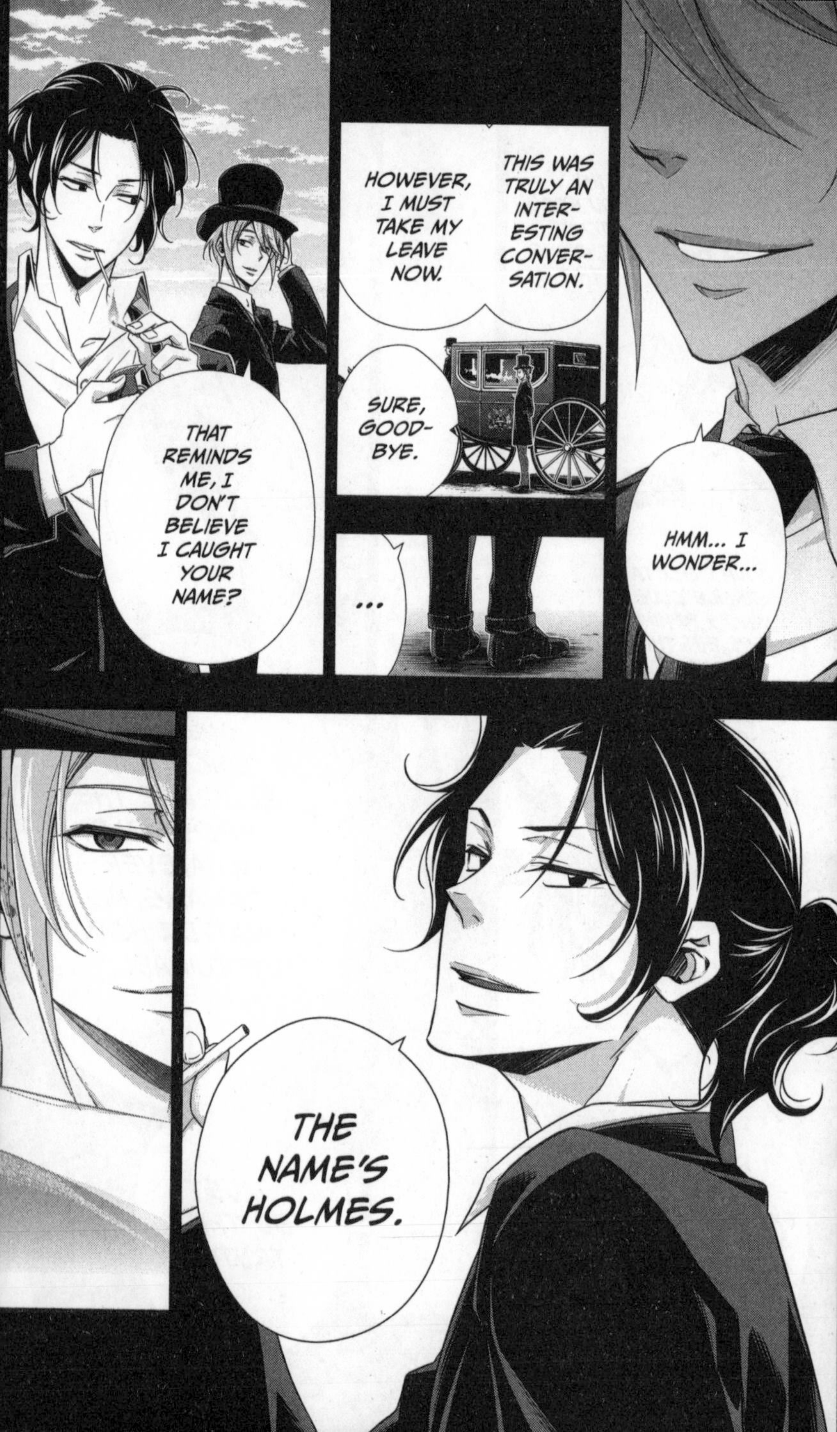
HMM... I WONDER...
THIS WAS TRULY AN INTERESTING CONVERSATION.
HOWEVER, I MUST TAKE MY LEAVE NOW.
SURE, GOODBYE.
...
THAT REMINDS ME, I DON'T BELIEVE I CAUGHT YOUR NAME?
THE NAME'S HOLMES.

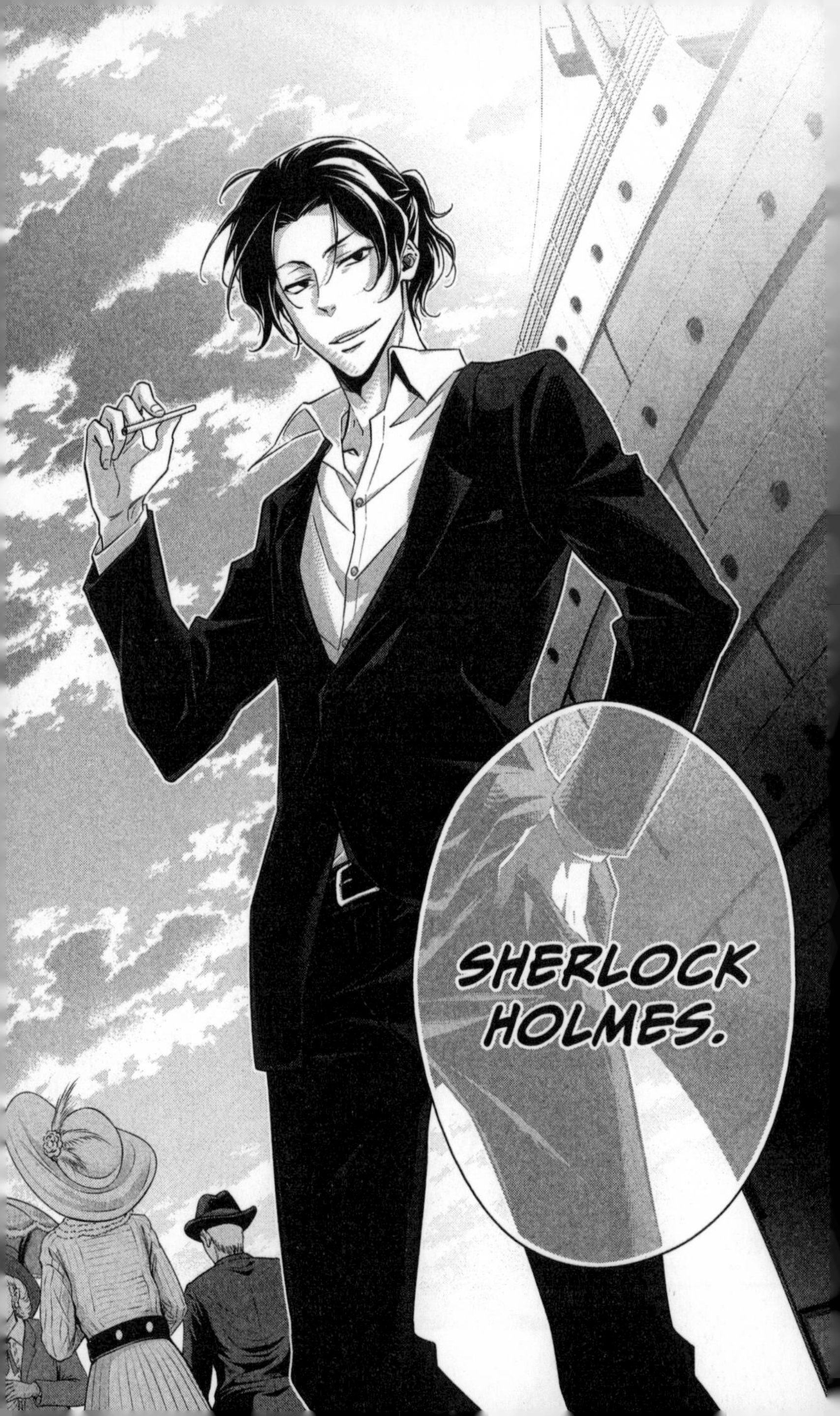
SHERLOCK HOLMES.

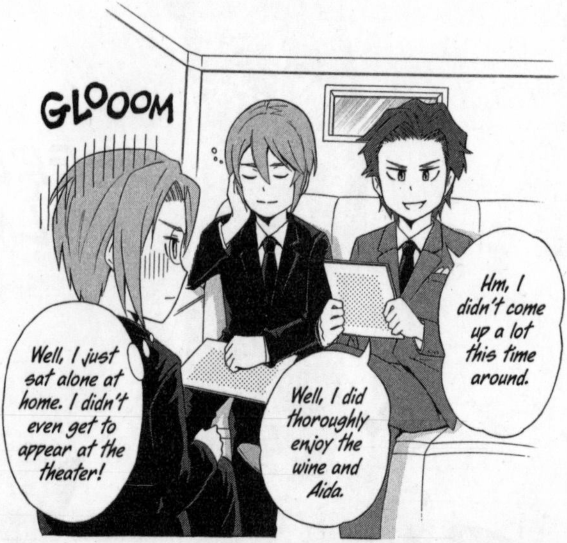
Hm, I didn't come up a lot this time around.
Well, I did thoroughly enjoy the wine and Aida.
GLOOOM
Well, I just sat alone at home. I didn't even get to appear at the theater!

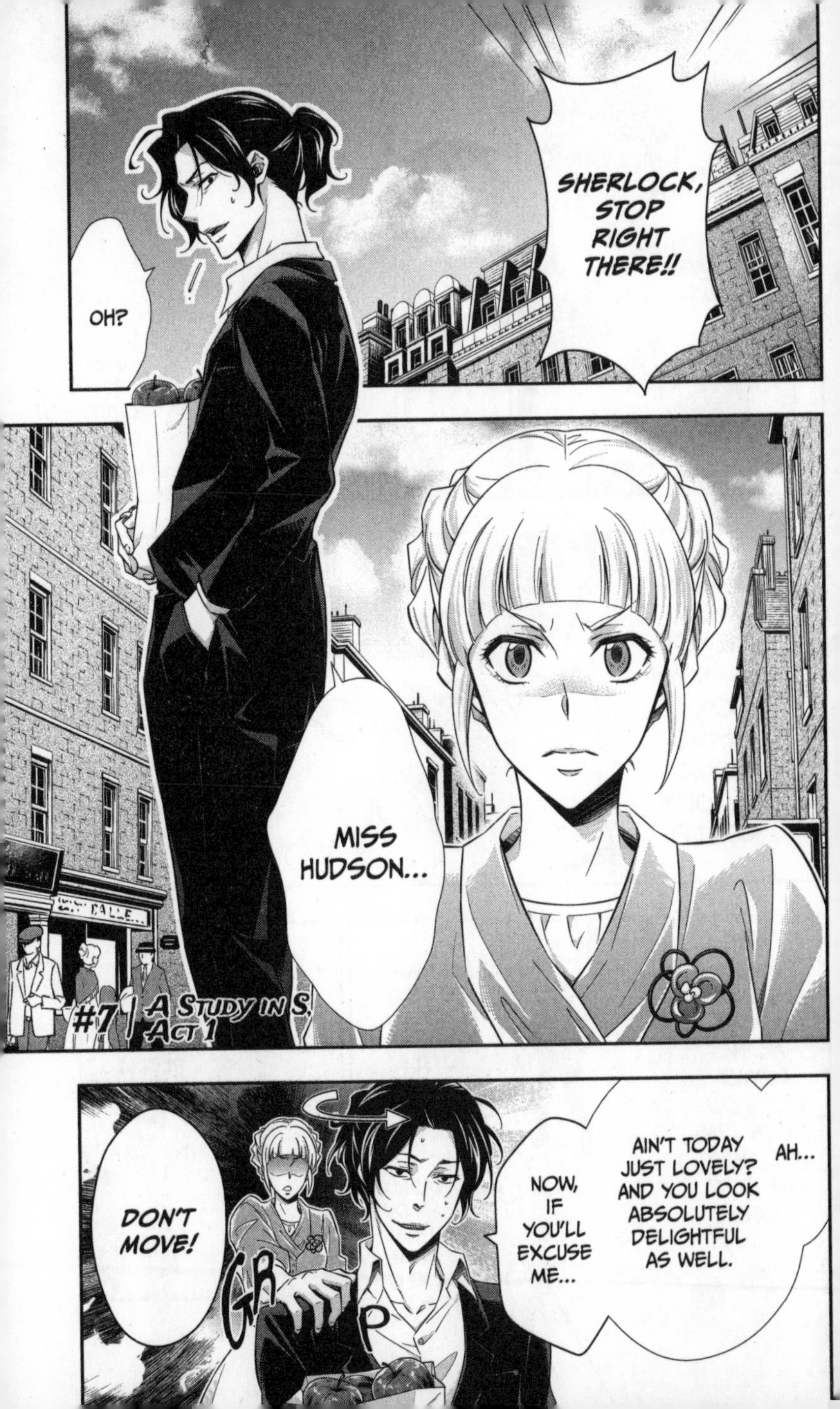
SHERLOCK, STOP RIGHT THERE!!
!
OH?
MISS HUDSON...
#7 A Study in S, Act 1
AH...
AIN'T TODAY JUST LOVELY? AND YOU LOOK ABSOLUTELY DELIGHTFUL AS WELL.
NOW, IF YOU'LL EXCUSE ME...
GRIP
DON'T MOVE!

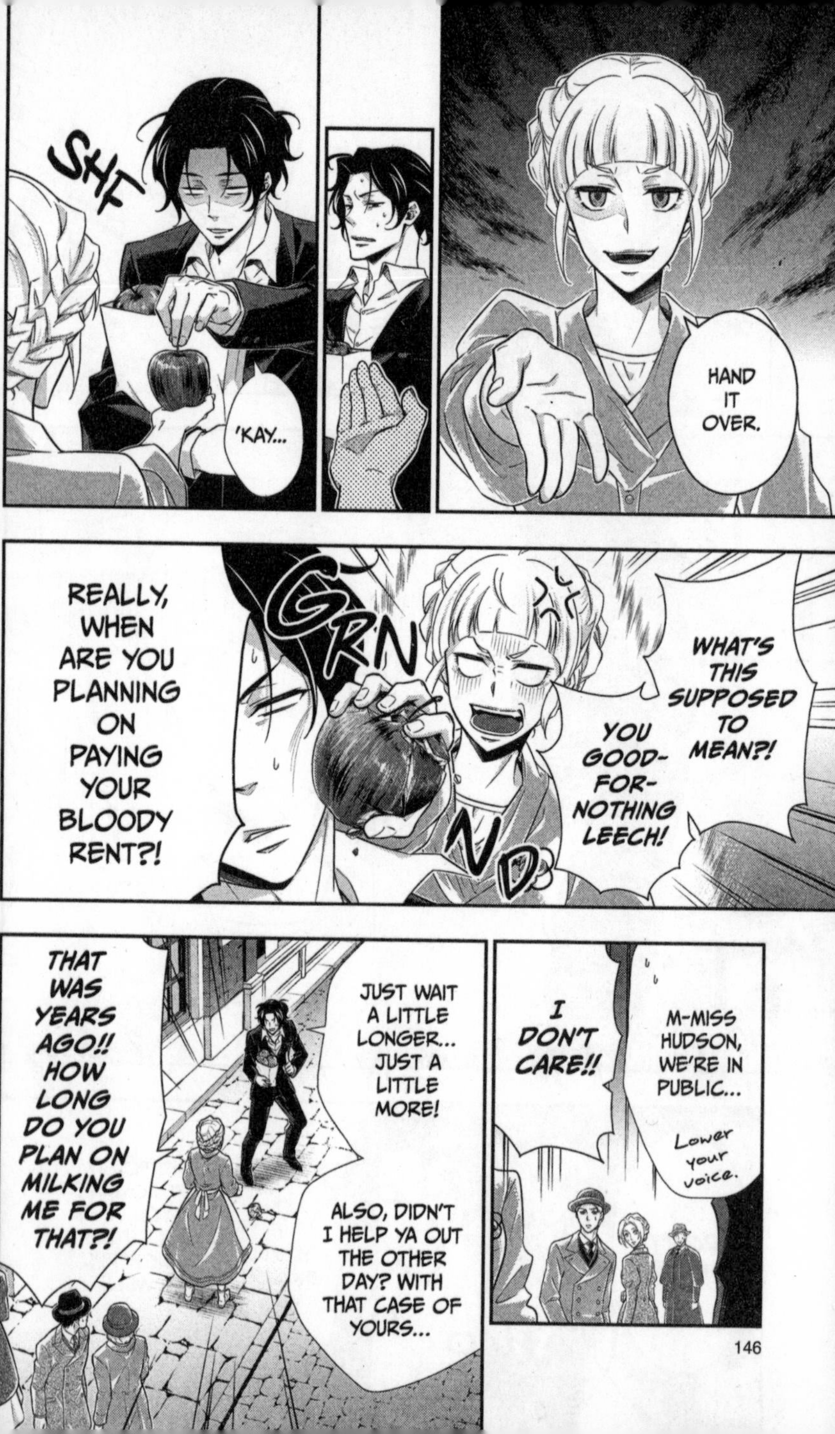
HAND IT OVER.
SHF
'KAY...
WHAT'S THIS SUPPOSED TO MEAN?!
YOU GOOD-FOR-NOTHING LEECH!
GRNND
REALLY, WHEN ARE YOU PLANNING ON PAYING YOUR BLOODY RENT?!
M-MISS HUDSON, WE'RE IN PUBLIC...
Lower your voice.
I DON'T CARE!!
JUST WAIT A LITTLE LONGER... JUST A LITTLE MORE!
ALSO, DIDN'T I HELP YA OUT THE OTHER DAY? WITH THAT CASE OF YOURS...
THAT WAS YEARS AGO!! HOW LONG DO YOU PLAN ON MILKING ME FOR THAT?!

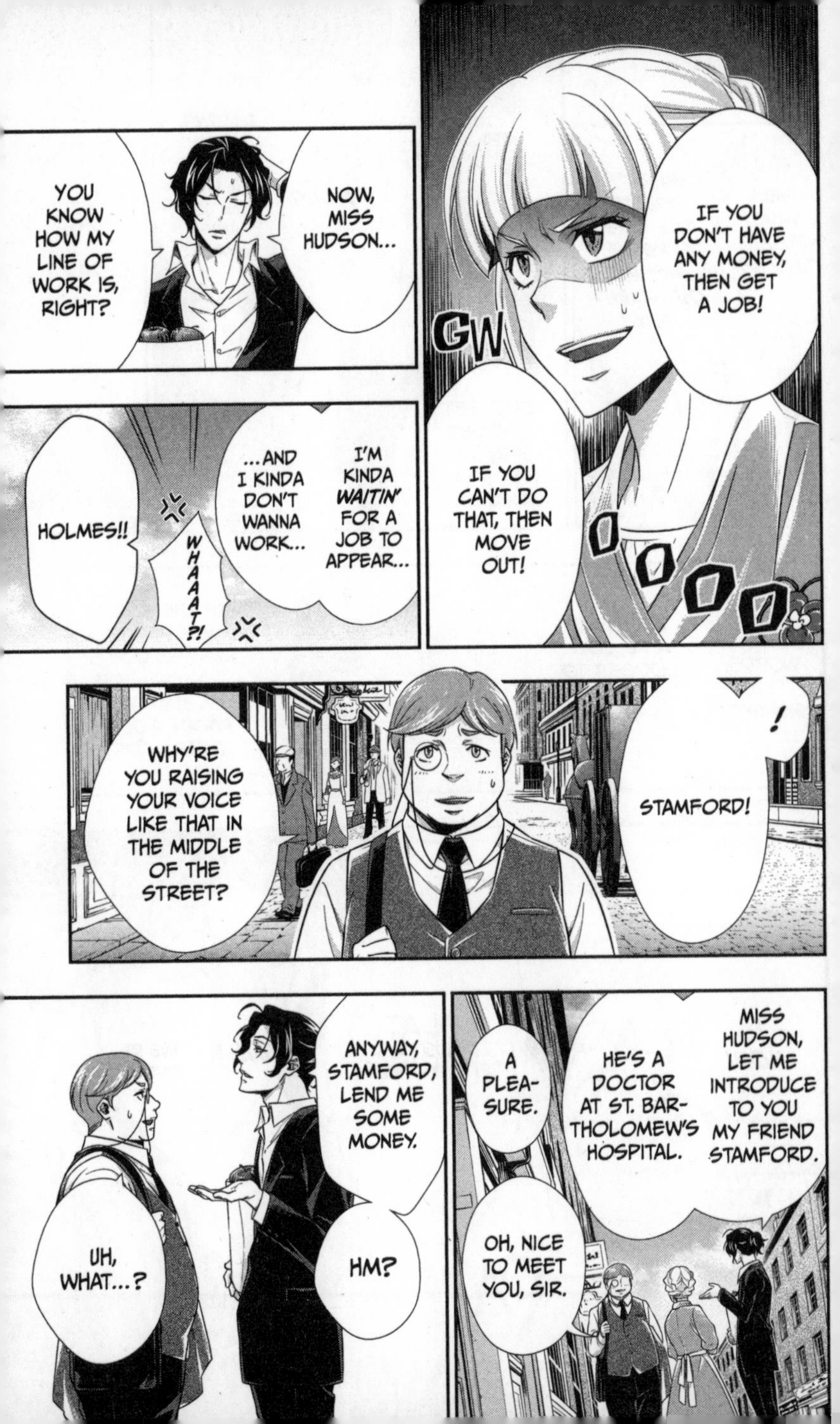
IF YOU DON'T HAVE ANY MONEY, THEN GET A JOB!
GW
IF YOU CAN'T DO THAT, THEN MOVE OUT!
NOW, MISS HUDSON...
YOU KNOW HOW MY LINE OF WORK IS, RIGHT?
I'M KINDA *WAITIN'* FOR A JOB TO APPEAR...
...AND I KINDA DON'T WANNA WORK...
WHAAAAT?!
HOLMES!!
!
STAMFORD!
WHY'RE YOU RAISING YOUR VOICE LIKE THAT IN THE MIDDLE OF THE STREET?
MISS HUDSON, LET ME INTRODUCE TO YOU MY FRIEND STAMFORD.
HE'S A DOCTOR AT ST. BARTHOLOMEW'S HOSPITAL.
A PLEASURE.
OH, NICE TO MEET YOU, SIR.
ANYWAY, STAMFORD, LEND ME SOME MONEY.
HM?
UH, WHAT...?

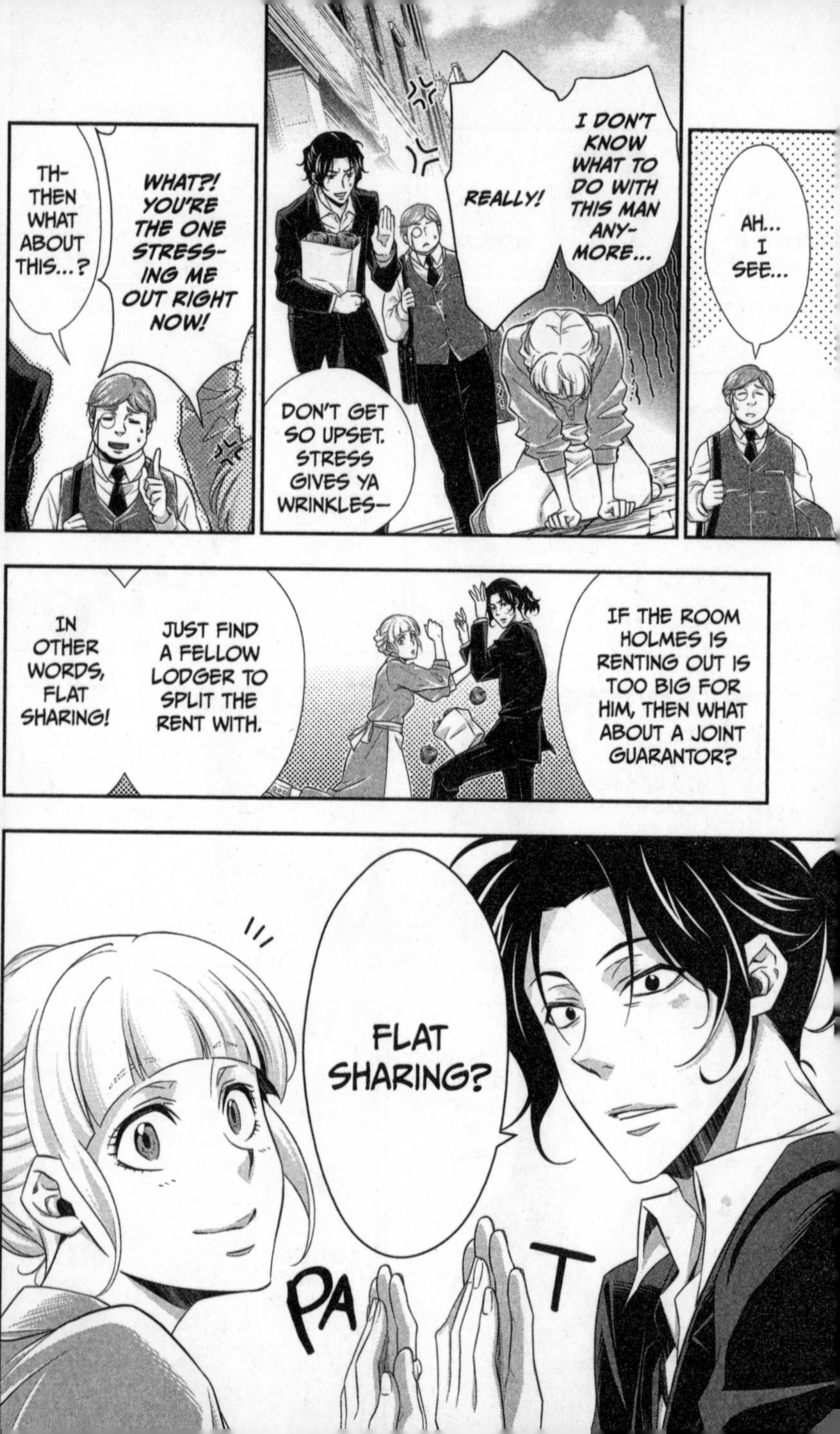
AH... I SEE...
I DON'T KNOW WHAT TO DO WITH THIS MAN ANYMORE...
REALLY!
DON'T GET SO UPSET. STRESS GIVES YA WRINKLES—
WHAT?! YOU'RE THE ONE STRESSING ME OUT RIGHT NOW!
TH-THEN WHAT ABOUT THIS...?
IF THE ROOM HOLMES IS RENTING OUT IS TOO BIG FOR HIM, THEN WHAT ABOUT A JOINT GUARANTOR?
JUST FIND A FELLOW LODGER TO SPLIT THE RENT WITH.
IN OTHER WORDS, FLAT SHARING!
FLAT SHARING?
PAT

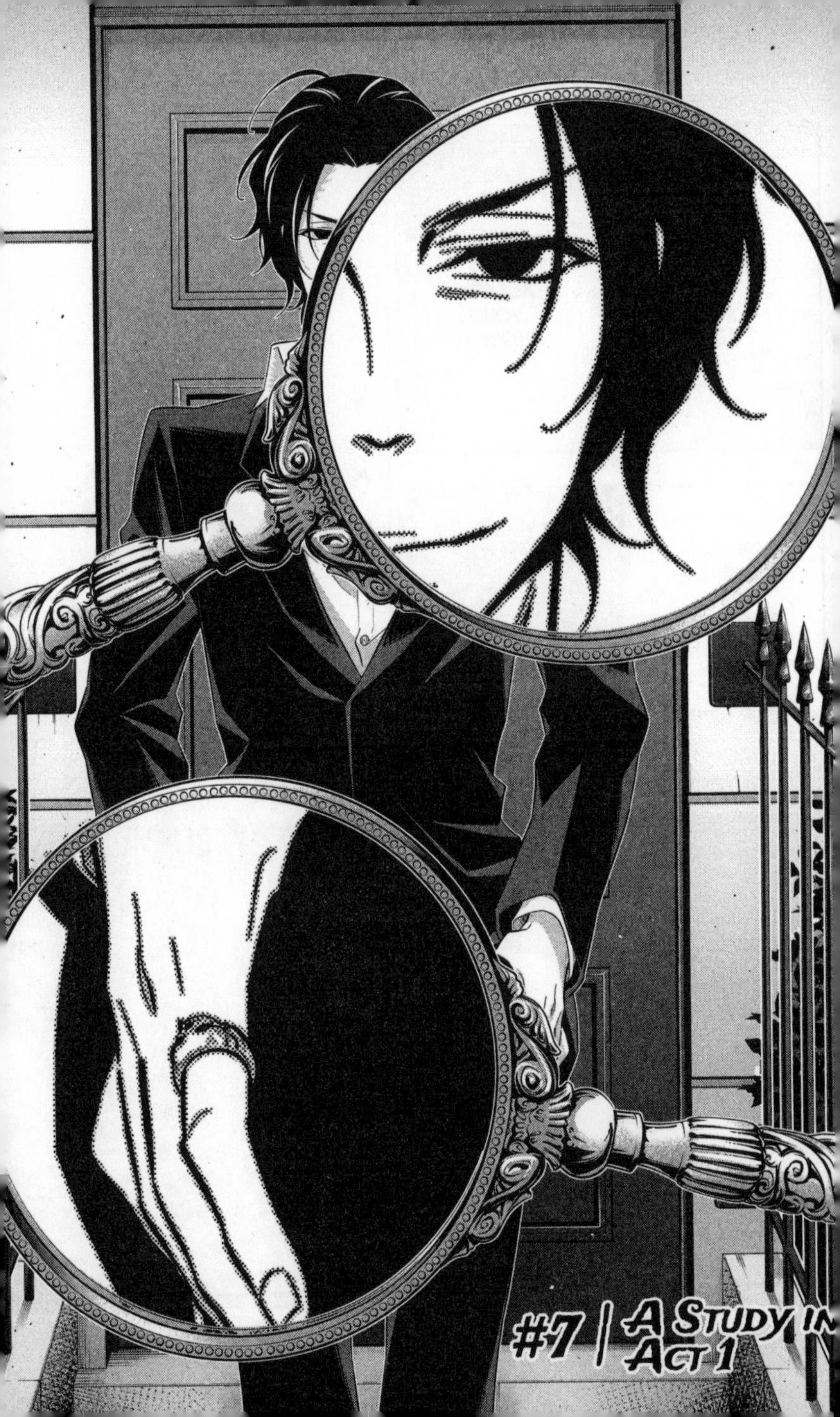
#7 | A Study in
Act 1

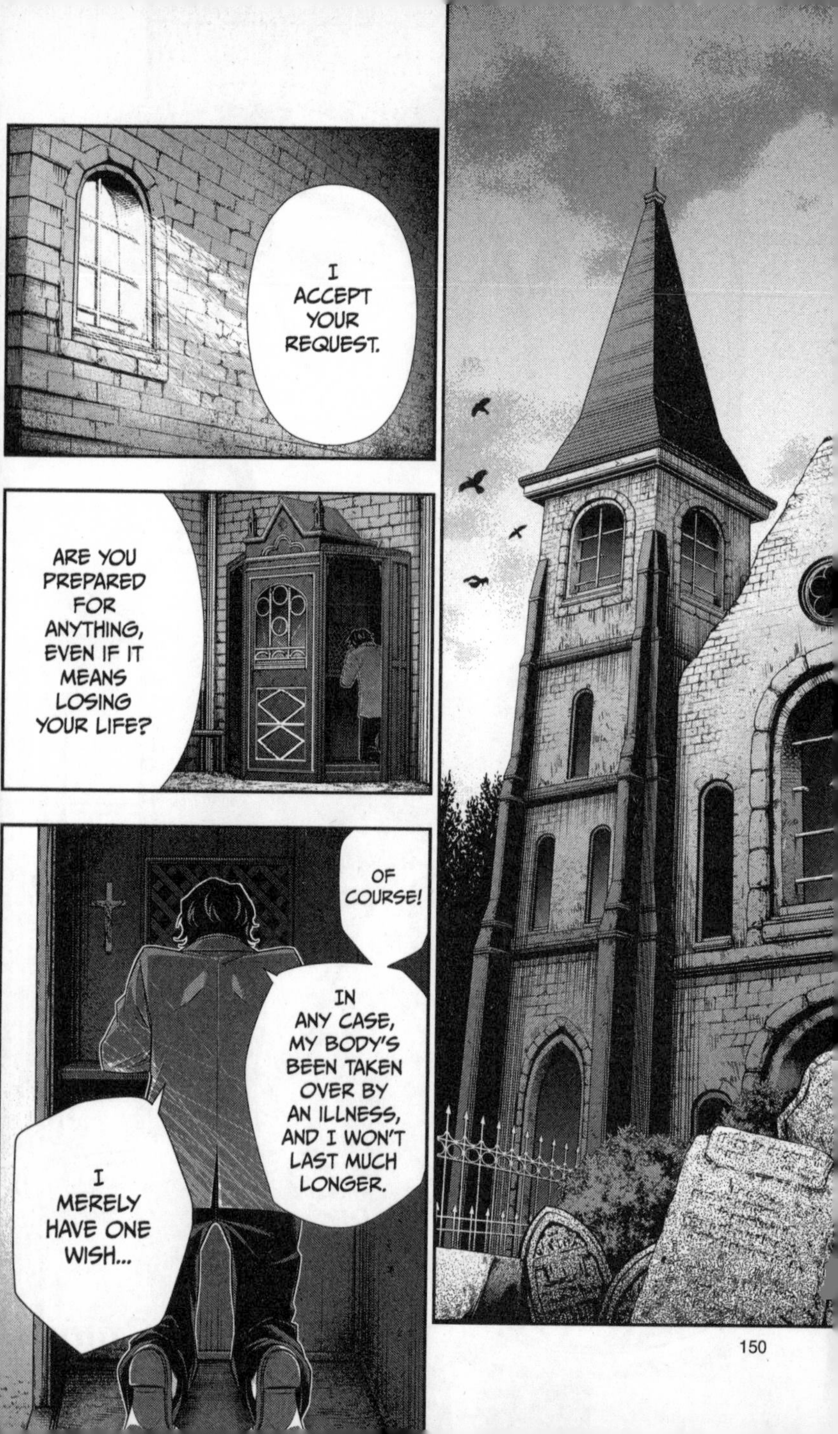
I ACCEPT YOUR REQUEST.
ARE YOU PREPARED FOR ANYTHING, EVEN IF IT MEANS LOSING YOUR LIFE?
OF COURSE!
IN ANY CASE, MY BODY'S BEEN TAKEN OVER BY AN ILLNESS, AND I WON'T LAST MUCH LONGER.
I MERELY HAVE ONE WISH...

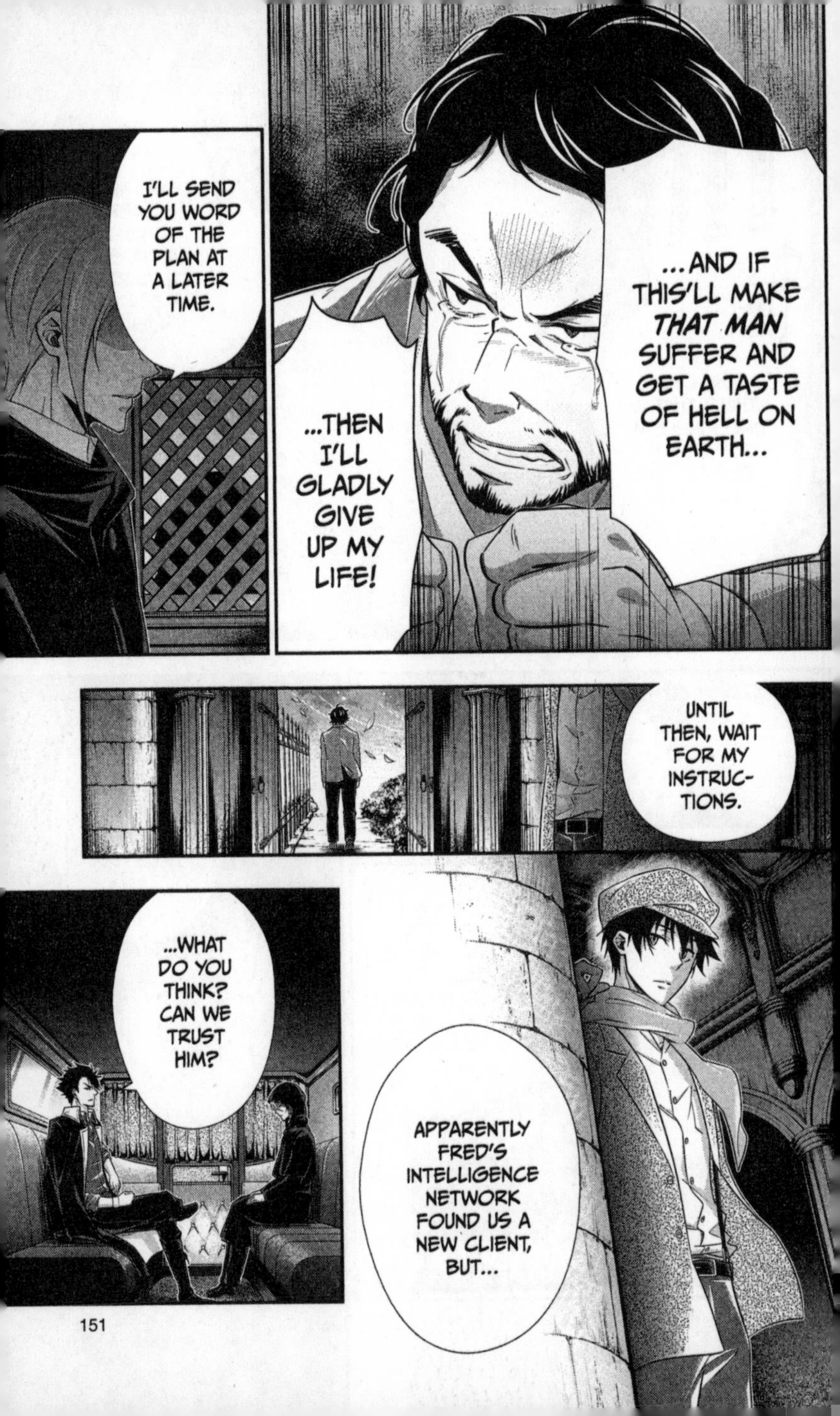
...AND IF THIS'LL MAKE *THAT MAN* SUFFER AND GET A TASTE OF HELL ON EARTH...
...THEN I'LL GLADLY GIVE UP MY LIFE!
I'LL SEND YOU WORD OF THE PLAN AT A LATER TIME.
UNTIL THEN, WAIT FOR MY INSTRUCTIONS.
APPARENTLY FRED'S INTELLIGENCE NETWORK FOUND US A NEW CLIENT, BUT...
...WHAT DO YOU THINK? CAN WE TRUST HIM?

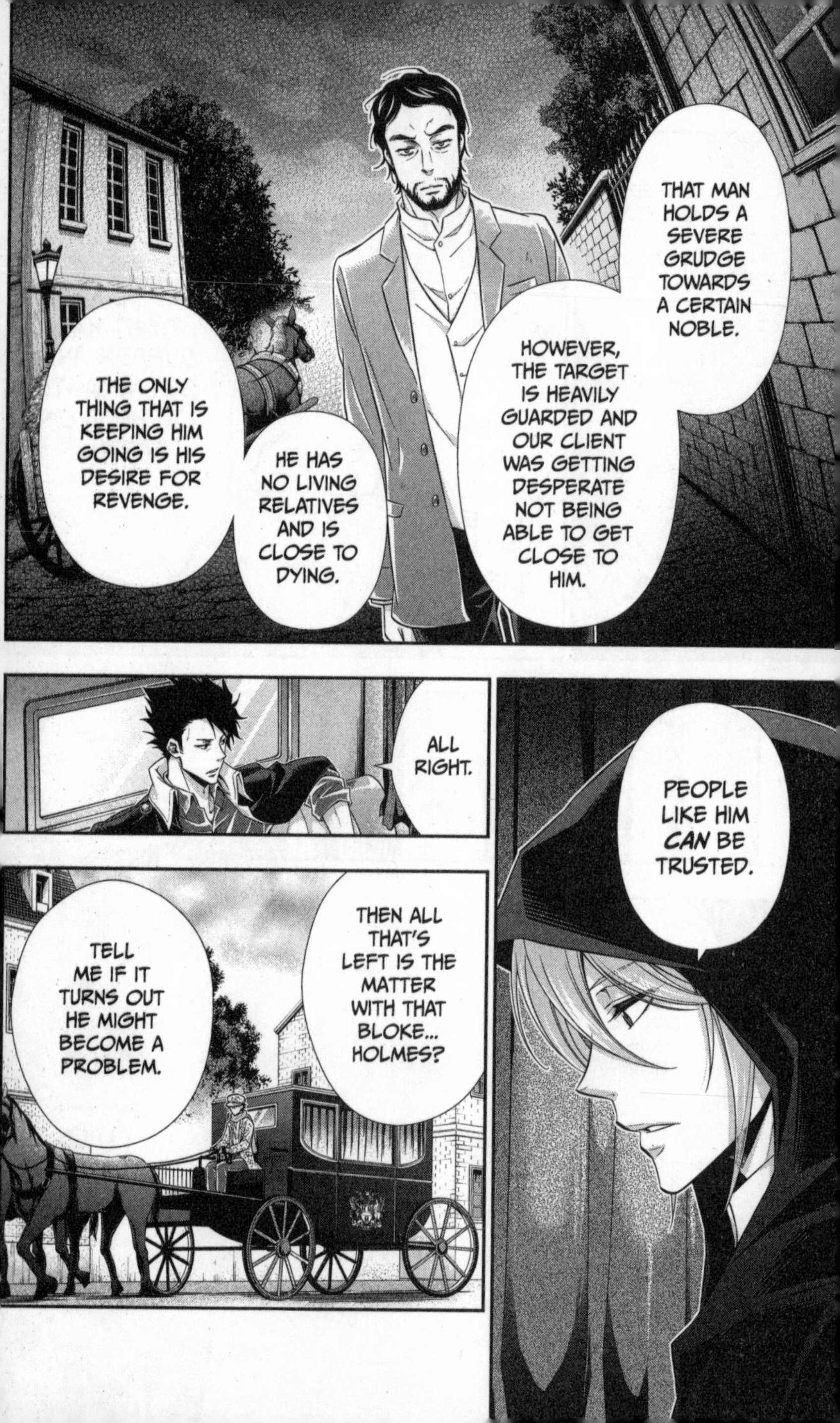
THAT MAN HOLDS A SEVERE GRUDGE TOWARDS A CERTAIN NOBLE.
HOWEVER, THE TARGET IS HEAVILY GUARDED AND OUR CLIENT WAS GETTING DESPERATE NOT BEING ABLE TO GET CLOSE TO HIM.
HE HAS NO LIVING RELATIVES AND IS CLOSE TO DYING.
THE ONLY THING THAT IS KEEPING HIM GOING IS HIS DESIRE FOR REVENGE.
PEOPLE LIKE HIM *CAN* BE TRUSTED.
ALL RIGHT.
THEN ALL THAT'S LEFT IS THE MATTER WITH THAT BLOKE... HOLMES?
TELL ME IF IT TURNS OUT HE MIGHT BECOME A PROBLEM.

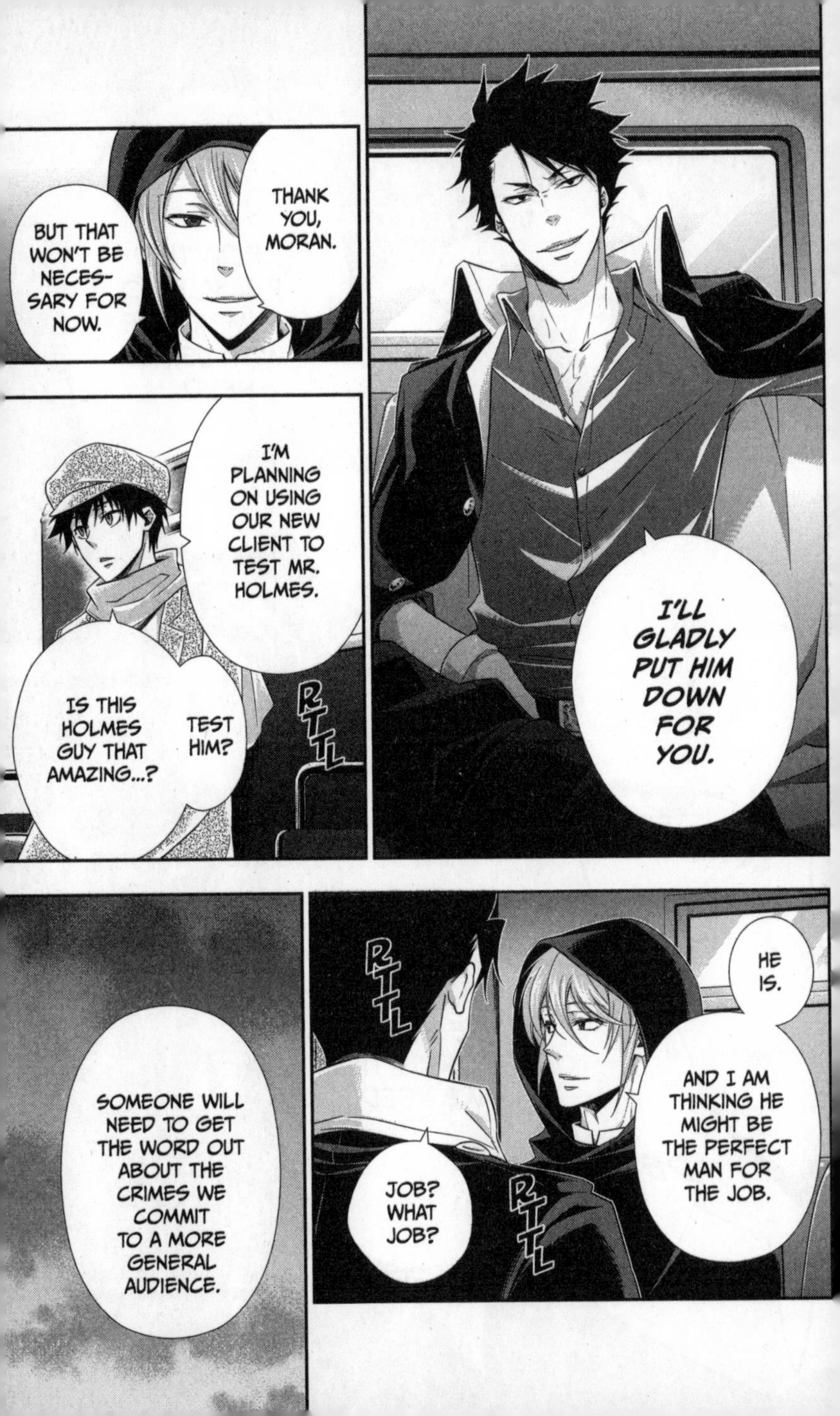
I'LL GLADLY PUT HIM DOWN FOR YOU.
THANK YOU, MORAN.
BUT THAT WON'T BE NECES-SARY FOR NOW.
I'M PLANNING ON USING OUR NEW CLIENT TO TEST MR. HOLMES.
RTTL
TEST HIM?
IS THIS HOLMES GUY THAT AMAZING...?
HE IS.
AND I AM THINKING HE MIGHT BE THE PERFECT MAN FOR THE JOB.
RTTL
RTTL
JOB? WHAT JOB?
SOMEONE WILL NEED TO GET THE WORD OUT ABOUT THE CRIMES WE COMMIT TO A MORE GENERAL AUDIENCE.

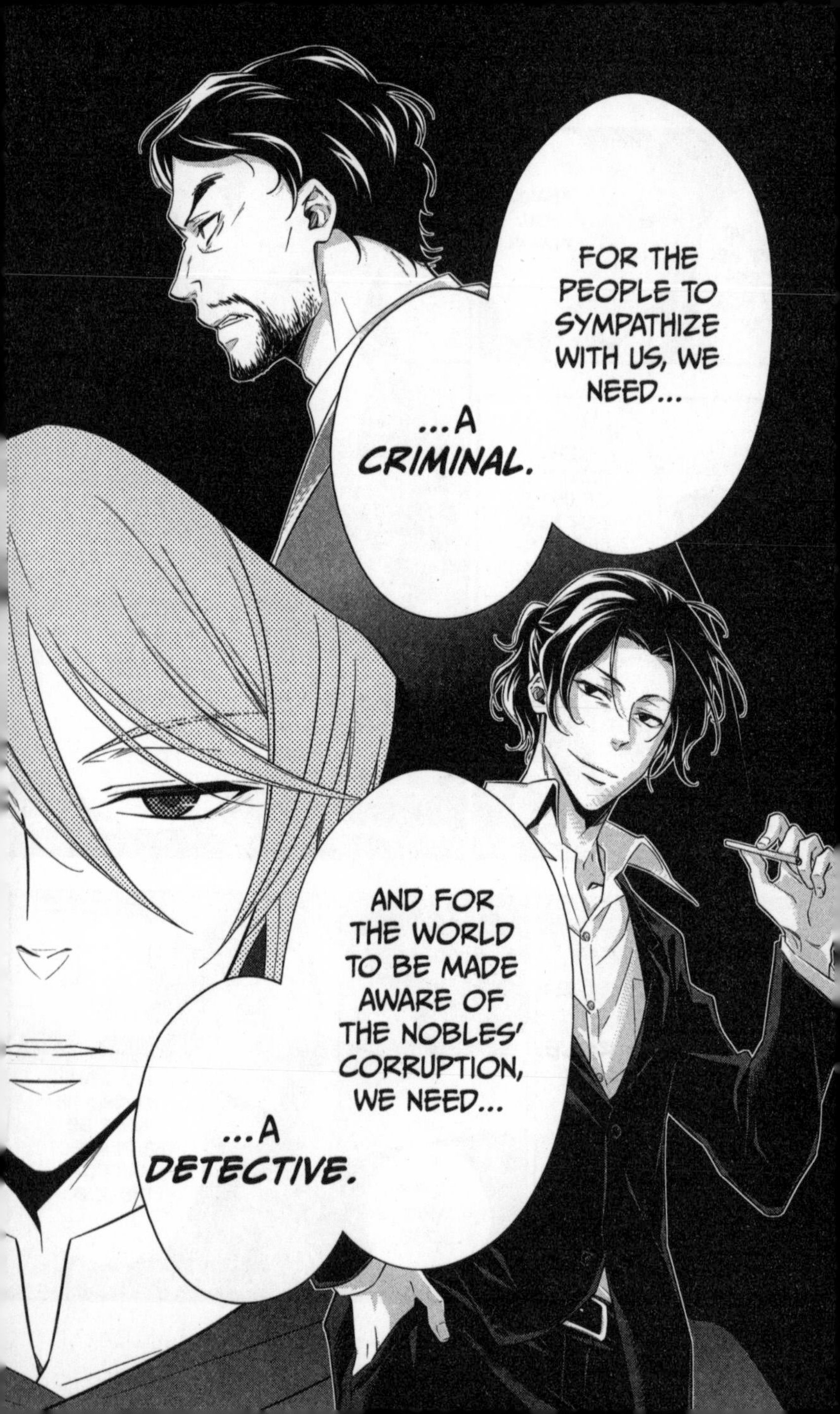
FOR THE PEOPLE TO SYMPATHIZE WITH US, WE NEED...
...A CRIMINAL.
AND FOR THE WORLD TO BE MADE AWARE OF THE NOBLES' CORRUPTION, WE NEED...
...A DETECTIVE.

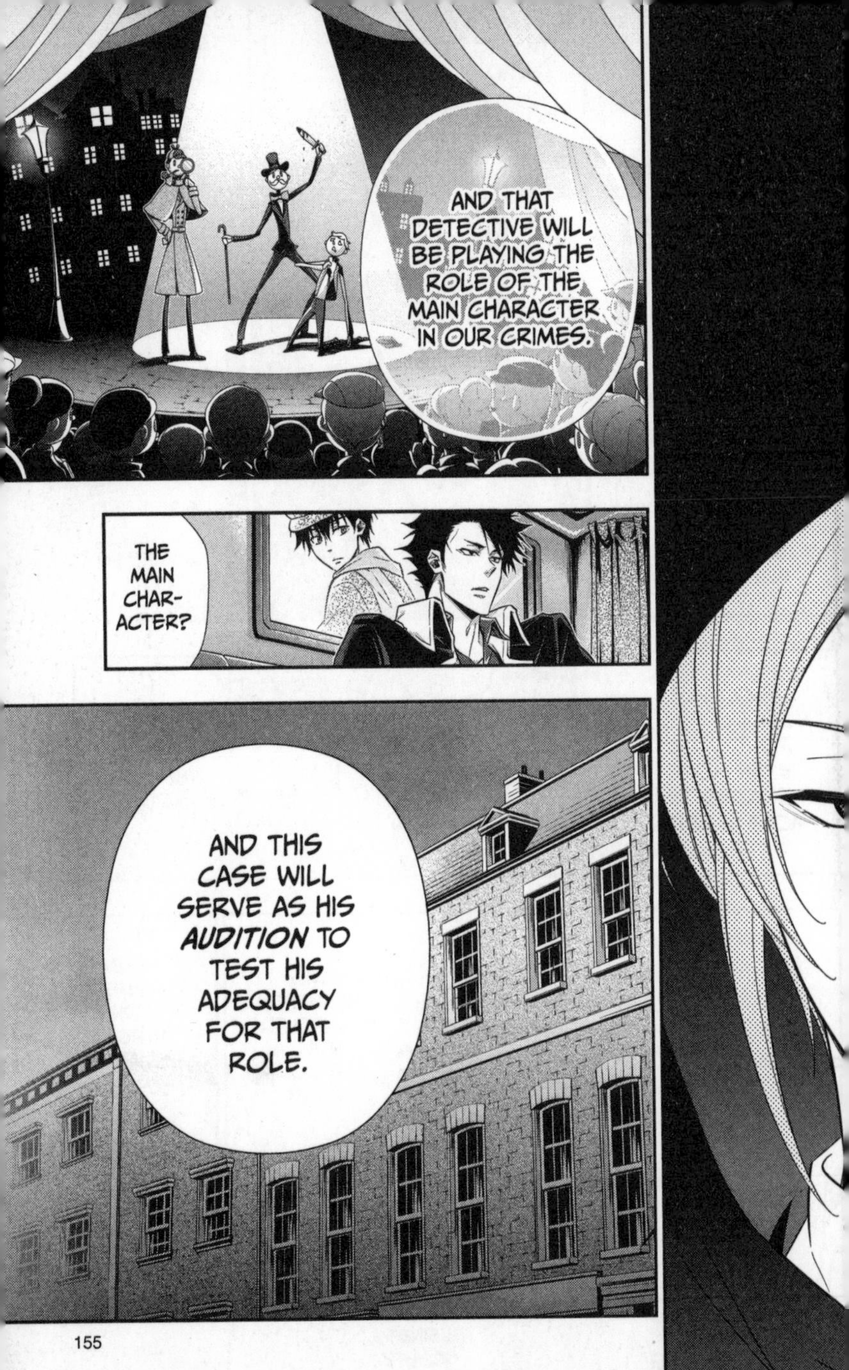
AND THAT DETECTIVE WILL BE PLAYING THE ROLE OF THE MAIN CHARACTER IN OUR CRIMES.
THE MAIN CHAR-ACTER?
AND THIS CASE WILL SERVE AS HIS *AUDITION* TO TEST HIS ADEQUACY FOR THAT ROLE.

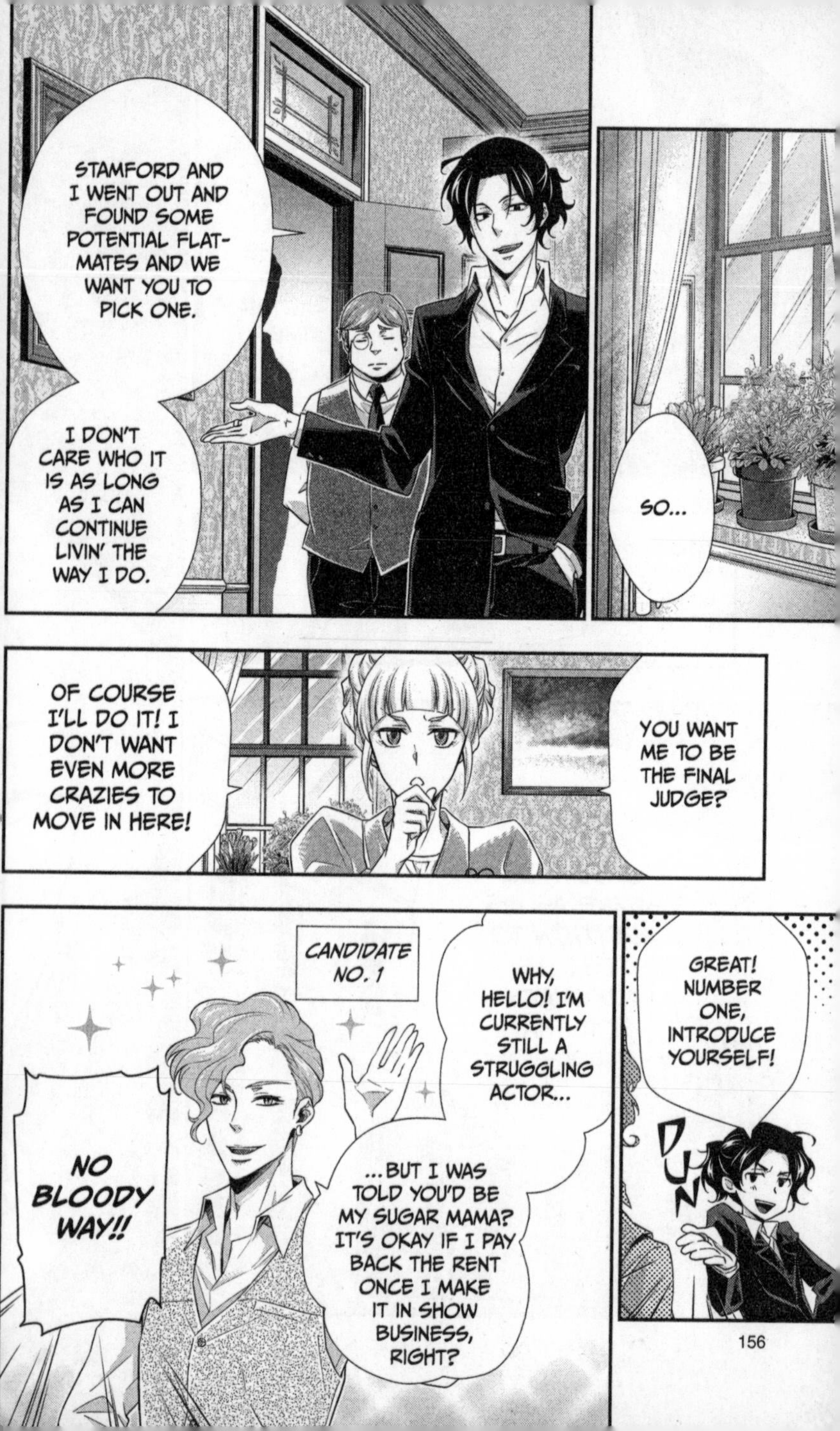
SO...
STAMFORD AND I WENT OUT AND FOUND SOME POTENTIAL FLAT-MATES AND WE WANT YOU TO PICK ONE.
I DON'T CARE WHO IT IS AS LONG AS I CAN CONTINUE LIVIN' THE WAY I DO.
YOU WANT ME TO BE THE FINAL JUDGE?
OF COURSE I'LL DO IT! I DON'T WANT EVEN MORE CRAZIES TO MOVE IN HERE!
GREAT! NUMBER ONE, INTRODUCE YOURSELF!
DUN
CANDIDATE NO. 1
WHY, HELLO! I'M CURRENTLY STILL A STRUGGLING ACTOR...
...BUT I WAS TOLD YOU'D BE MY SUGAR MAMA? IT'S OKAY IF I PAY BACK THE RENT ONCE I MAKE IT IN SHOW BUSINESS, RIGHT?
NO BLOODY WAY!!

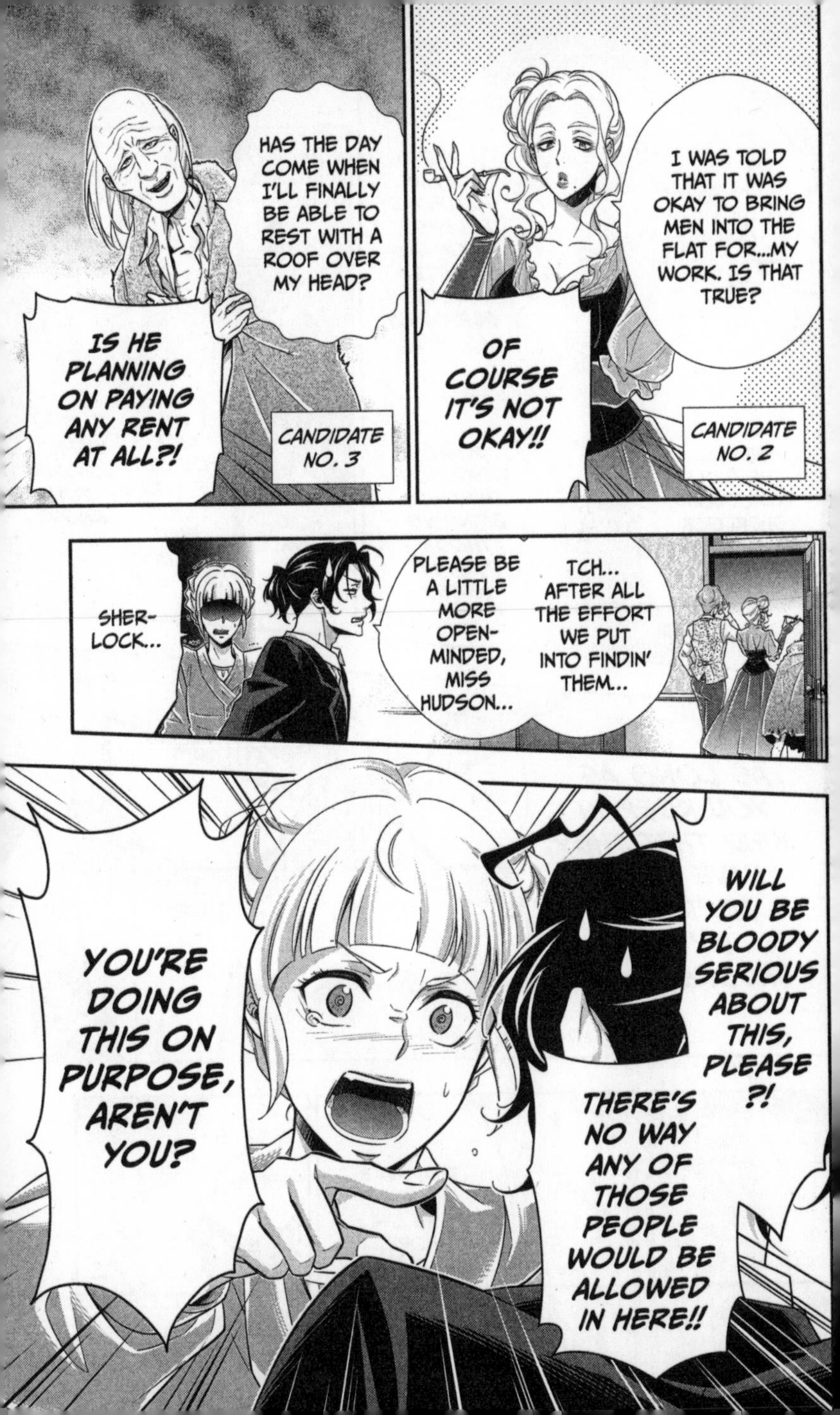
I WAS TOLD THAT IT WAS OKAY TO BRING MEN INTO THE FLAT FOR...MY WORK. IS THAT TRUE?
CANDIDATE NO. 2
OF COURSE IT'S NOT OKAY!!
HAS THE DAY COME WHEN I'LL FINALLY BE ABLE TO REST WITH A ROOF OVER MY HEAD?
CANDIDATE NO. 3
IS HE PLANNING ON PAYING ANY RENT AT ALL?!
TCH... AFTER ALL THE EFFORT WE PUT INTO FINDIN' THEM...
PLEASE BE A LITTLE MORE OPEN-MINDED, MISS HUDSON...
SHER-LOCK...
WILL YOU BE BLOODY SERIOUS ABOUT THIS, PLEASE?!
THERE'S NO WAY ANY OF THOSE PEOPLE WOULD BE ALLOWED IN HERE!!
YOU'RE DOING THIS ON PURPOSE, AREN'T YOU?

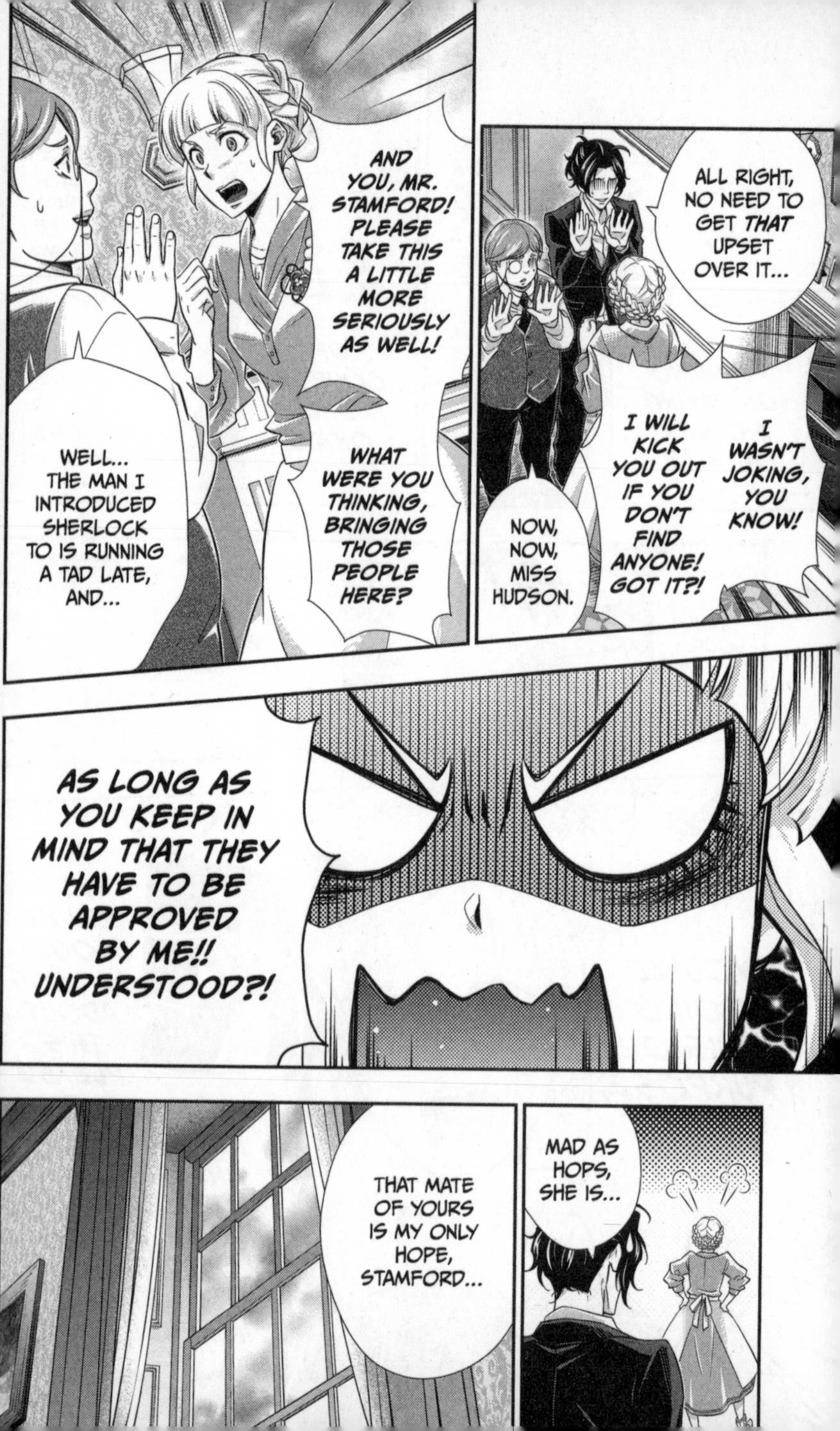
ALL RIGHT, NO NEED TO GET THAT UPSET OVER IT...
I WASN'T JOKING, YOU KNOW!
I WILL KICK YOU OUT IF YOU DON'T FIND ANYONE! GOT IT?!
NOW, NOW, MISS HUDSON.
AND YOU, MR. STAMFORD! PLEASE TAKE THIS A LITTLE MORE SERIOUSLY AS WELL!
WHAT WERE YOU THINKING, BRINGING THOSE PEOPLE HERE?
WELL... THE MAN I INTRODUCED SHERLOCK TO IS RUNNING A TAD LATE, AND...
AS LONG AS YOU KEEP IN MIND THAT THEY HAVE TO BE APPROVED BY ME!! UNDERSTOOD?!
MAD AS HOPS, SHE IS...
THAT MATE OF YOURS IS MY ONLY HOPE, STAMFORD...

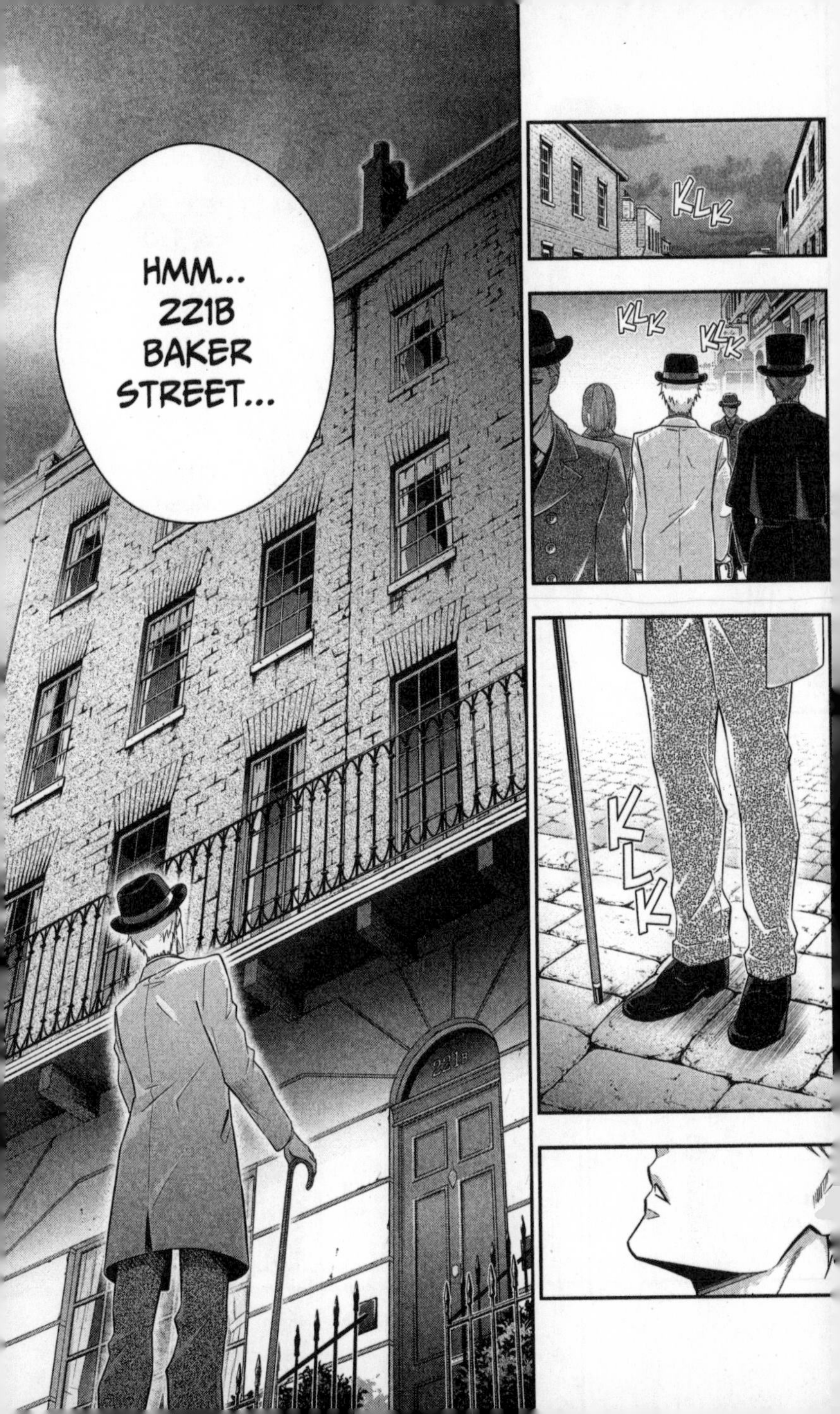
KLK
KLK
KLK
KLK
HMM... 221B BAKER STREET...

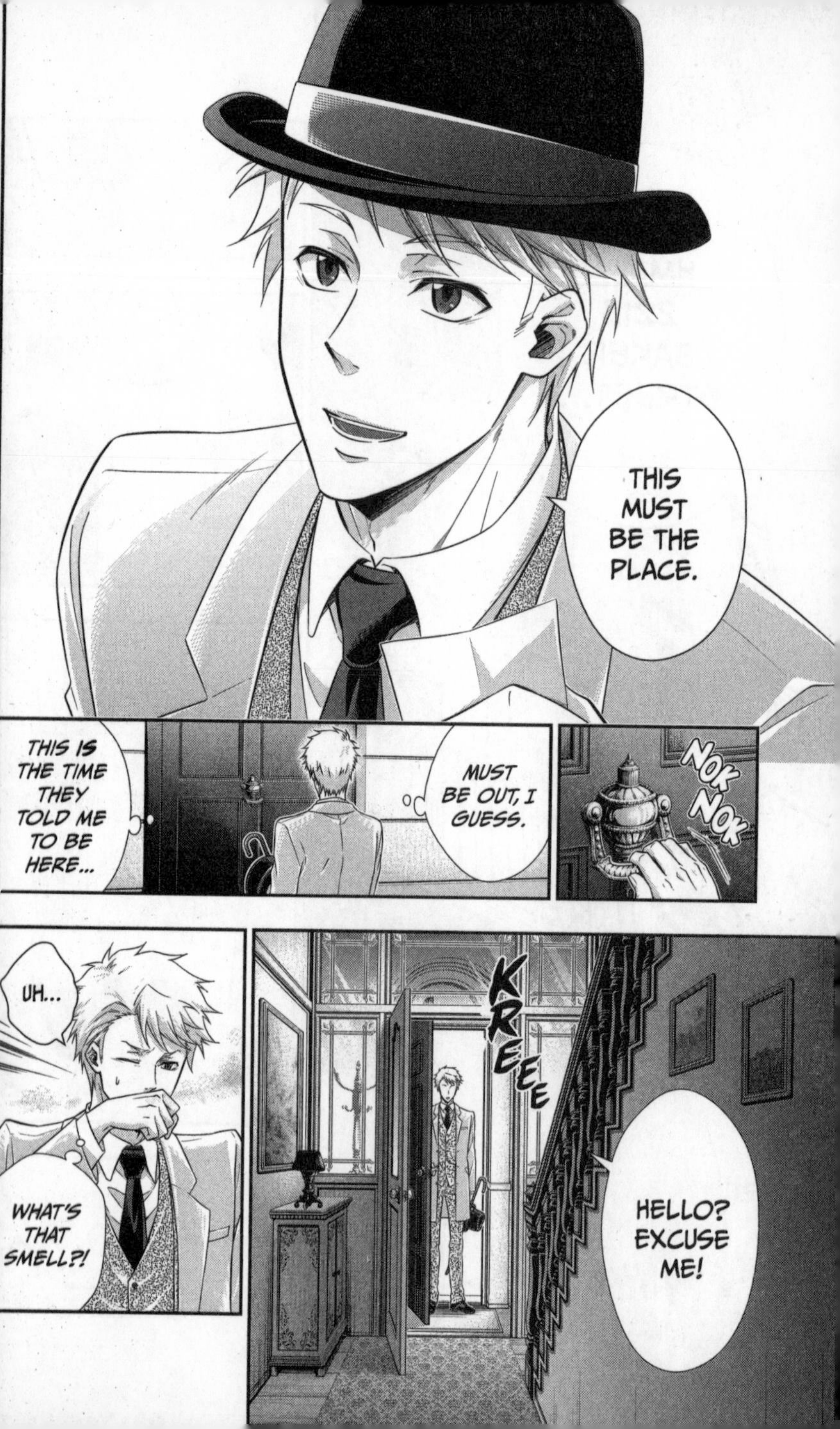
THIS MUST BE THE PLACE.
NOK NOK
THIS IS THE TIME THEY TOLD ME TO BE HERE...
MUST BE OUT, I GUESS.
KREEEE
HELLO? EXCUSE ME!
UH...
WHAT'S THAT SMELL?!

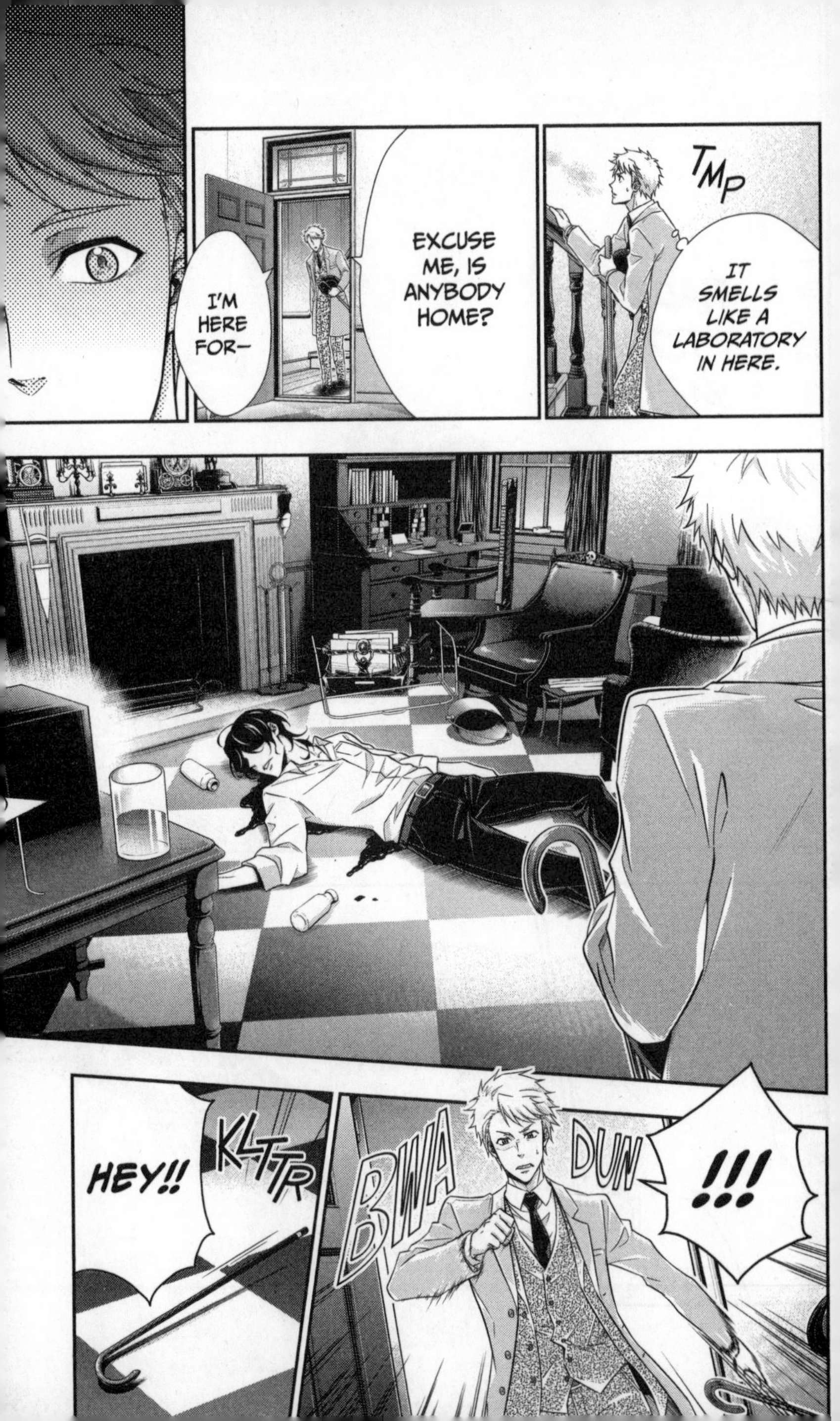
TMP
IT SMELLS LIKE A LABORATORY IN HERE.
EXCUSE ME, IS ANYBODY HOME?
I'M HERE FOR—
!!!
BWA DUN
HEY!!
KLTTR

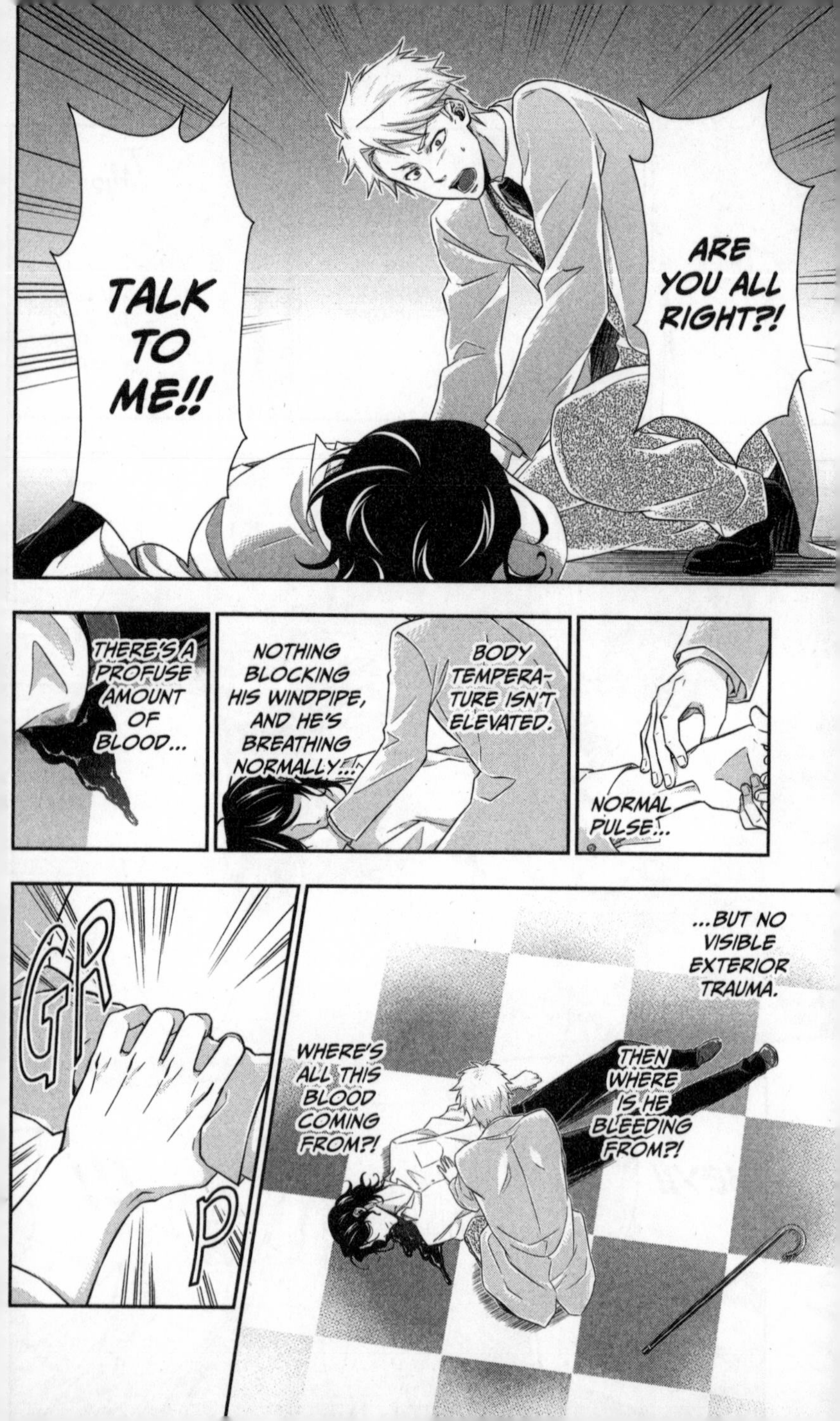
ARE YOU ALL RIGHT?!
TALK TO ME!!
NORMAL PULSE...
BODY TEMPERA-TURE ISN'T ELEVATED.
NOTHING BLOCKING HIS WINDPIPE, AND HE'S BREATHING NORMALLY...
THERE'S A PROFUSE AMOUNT OF BLOOD...
...BUT NO VISIBLE EXTERIOR TRAUMA.
THEN WHERE IS HE BLEEDING FROM?!
WHERE'S ALL THIS BLOOD COMING FROM?!
GRIP

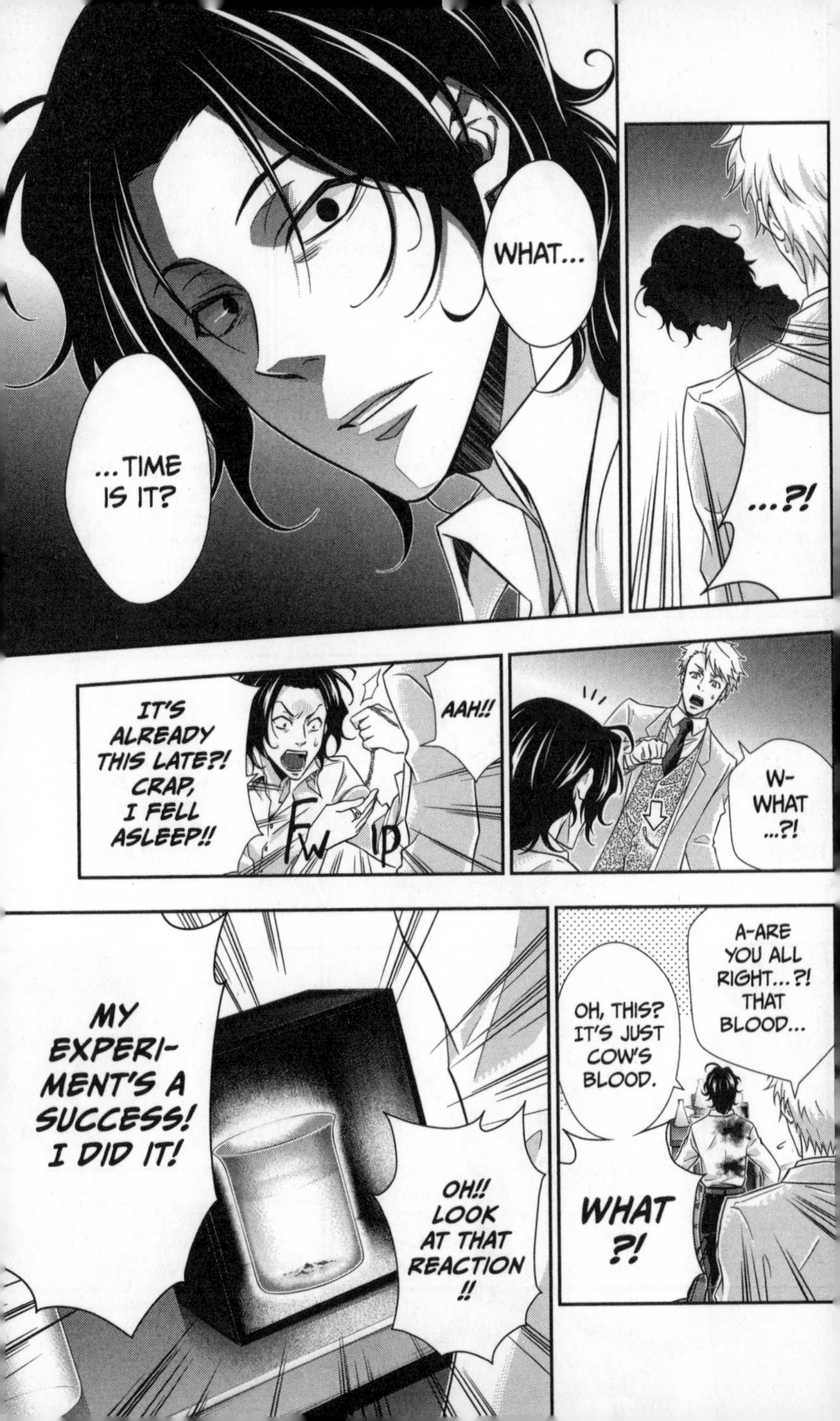
...?!
WHAT...
...TIME IS IT?
W-WHAT...?!
AAH!!
IT'S ALREADY THIS LATE?! CRAP, I FELL ASLEEP!!
FWIP
A-ARE YOU ALL RIGHT...?! THAT BLOOD...
OH, THIS? IT'S JUST COW'S BLOOD.
WHAT?!
OH!! LOOK AT THAT REACTION!!
MY EXPERIMENT'S A SUCCESS! I DID IT!

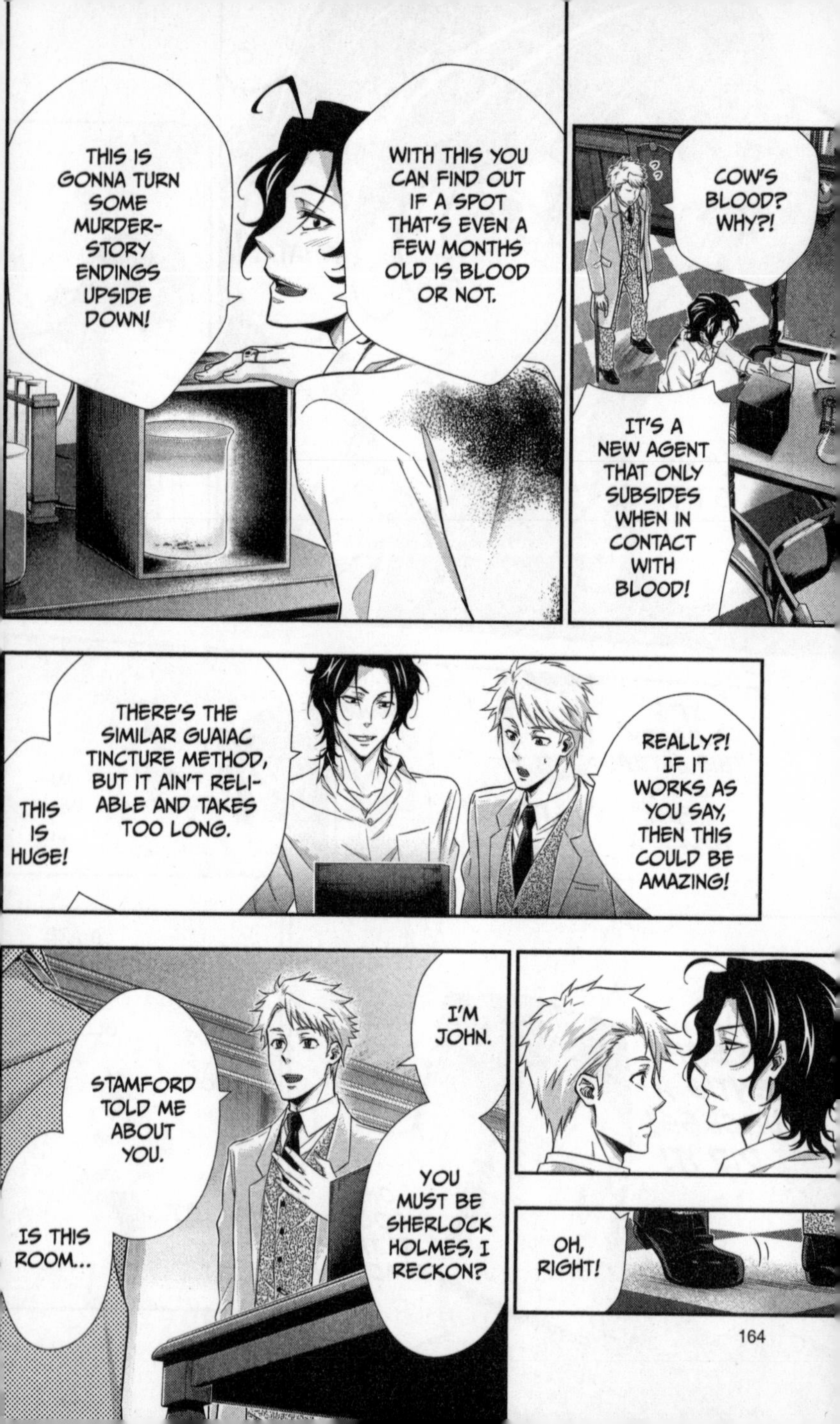
COW'S BLOOD? WHY?!
IT'S A NEW AGENT THAT ONLY SUBSIDES WHEN IN CONTACT WITH BLOOD!
WITH THIS YOU CAN FIND OUT IF A SPOT THAT'S EVEN A FEW MONTHS OLD IS BLOOD OR NOT.
THIS IS GONNA TURN SOME MURDER-STORY ENDINGS UPSIDE DOWN!
REALLY?! IF IT WORKS AS YOU SAY, THEN THIS COULD BE AMAZING!
THERE'S THE SIMILAR GUAIAC TINCTURE METHOD, BUT IT AIN'T RELI-ABLE AND TAKES TOO LONG.
THIS IS HUGE!
OH, RIGHT!
I'M JOHN.
YOU MUST BE SHERLOCK HOLMES, I RECKON?
STAMFORD TOLD ME ABOUT YOU.
IS THIS ROOM...

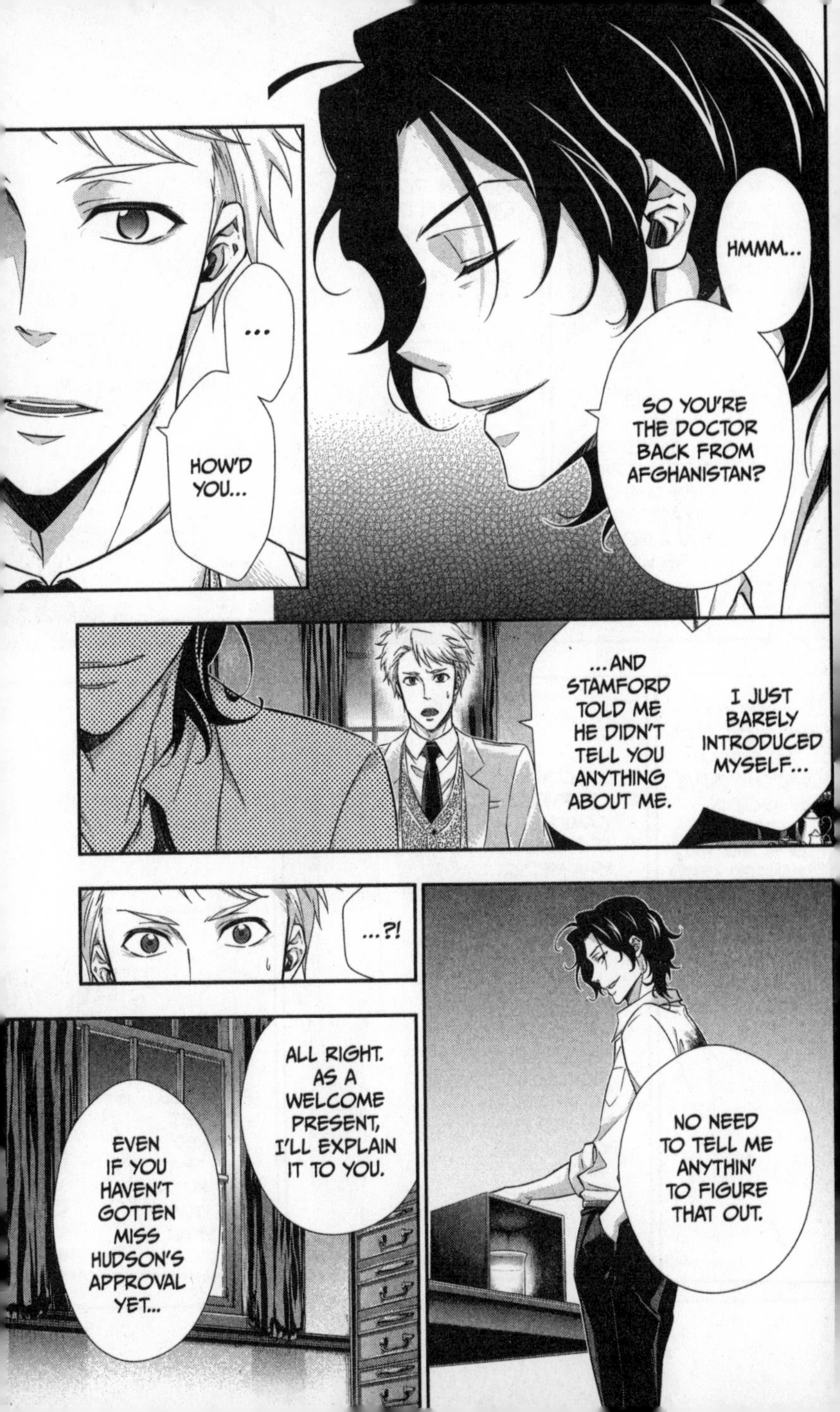
HMMM...
SO YOU'RE THE DOCTOR BACK FROM AFGHANISTAN?
...
HOW'D YOU...
I JUST BARELY INTRODUCED MYSELF...
...AND STAMFORD TOLD ME HE DIDN'T TELL YOU ANYTHING ABOUT ME.
NO NEED TO TELL ME ANYTHIN' TO FIGURE THAT OUT.
...?!
ALL RIGHT. AS A WELCOME PRESENT, I'LL EXPLAIN IT TO YOU.
EVEN IF YOU HAVEN'T GOTTEN MISS HUDSON'S APPROVAL YET...

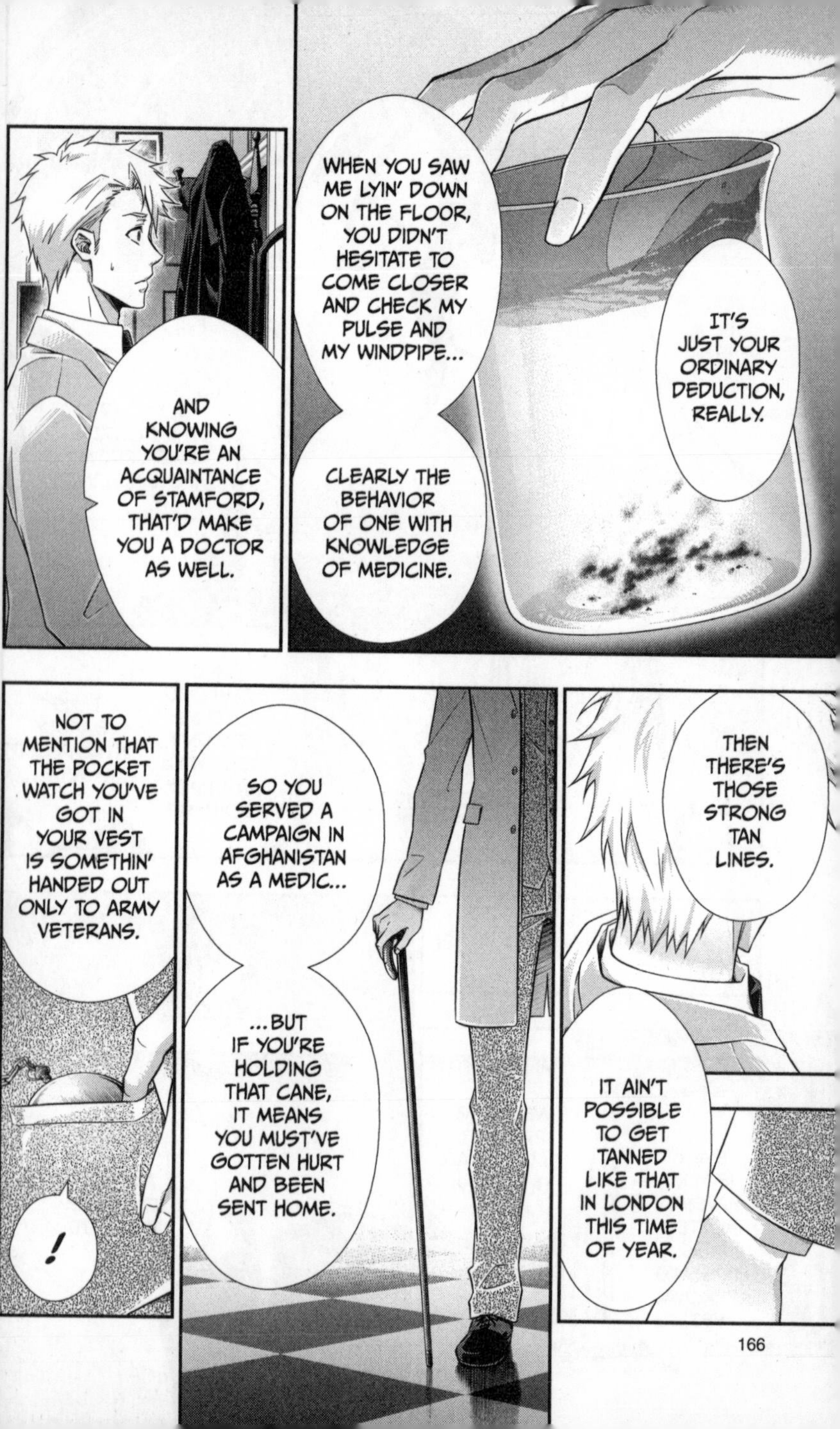
IT'S JUST YOUR ORDINARY DEDUCTION, REALLY.
WHEN YOU SAW ME LYIN' DOWN ON THE FLOOR, YOU DIDN'T HESITATE TO COME CLOSER AND CHECK MY PULSE AND MY WINDPIPE...
CLEARLY THE BEHAVIOR OF ONE WITH KNOWLEDGE OF MEDICINE.
AND KNOWING YOU'RE AN ACQUAINTANCE OF STAMFORD, THAT'D MAKE YOU A DOCTOR AS WELL.
THEN THERE'S THOSE STRONG TAN LINES.
IT AIN'T POSSIBLE TO GET TANNED LIKE THAT IN LONDON THIS TIME OF YEAR.
SO YOU SERVED A CAMPAIGN IN AFGHANISTAN AS A MEDIC...
...BUT IF YOU'RE HOLDING THAT CANE, IT MEANS YOU MUST'VE GOTTEN HURT AND BEEN SENT HOME.
NOT TO MENTION THAT THE POCKET WATCH YOU'VE GOT IN YOUR VEST IS SOMETHIN' HANDED OUT ONLY TO ARMY VETERANS.
!

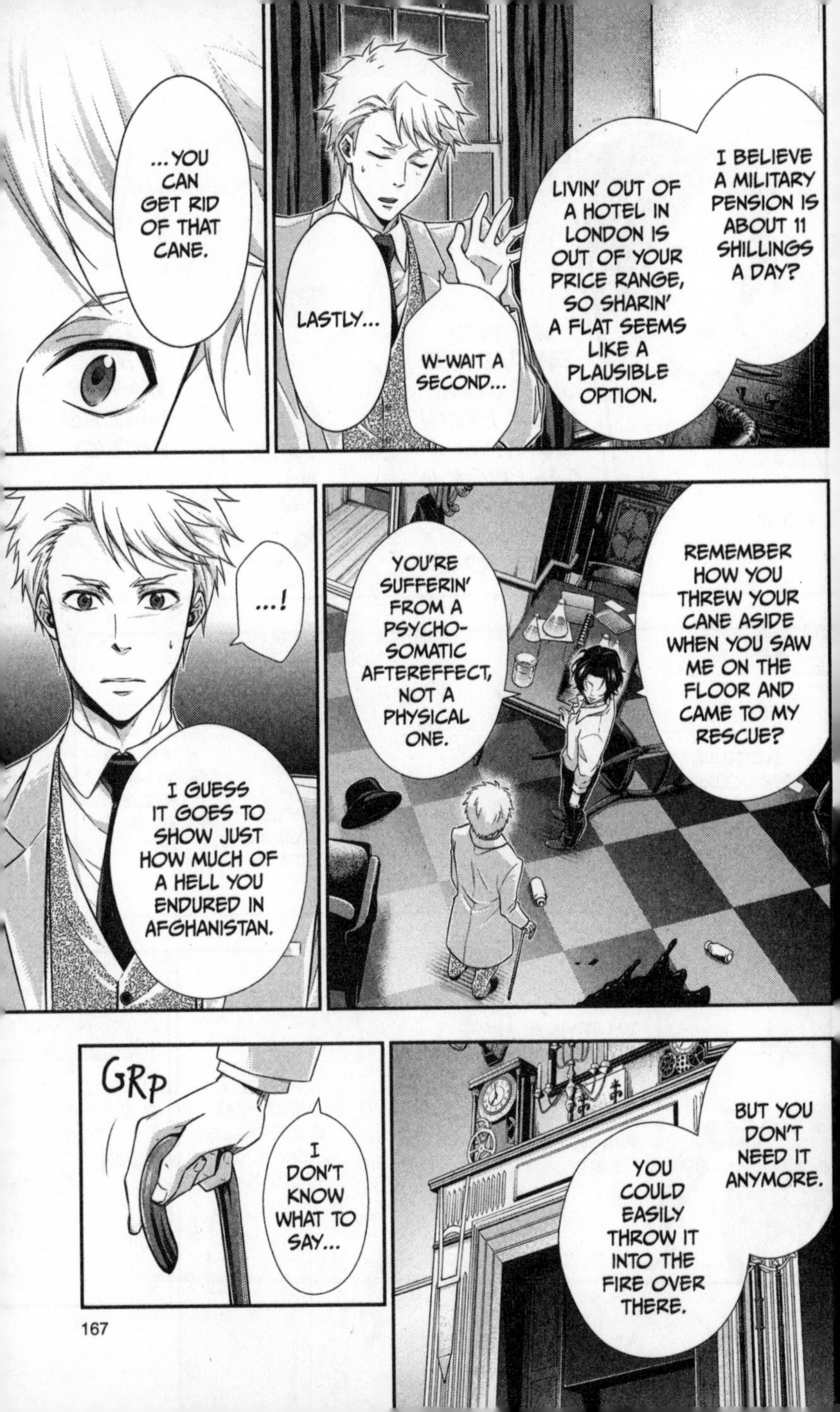
I BELIEVE A MILITARY PENSION IS ABOUT 11 SHILLINGS A DAY?
LIVIN' OUT OF A HOTEL IN LONDON IS OUT OF YOUR PRICE RANGE, SO SHARIN' A FLAT SEEMS LIKE A PLAUSIBLE OPTION.
W-WAIT A SECOND...
LASTLY...
...YOU CAN GET RID OF THAT CANE.
REMEMBER HOW YOU THREW YOUR CANE ASIDE WHEN YOU SAW ME ON THE FLOOR AND CAME TO MY RESCUE?
YOU'RE SUFFERIN' FROM A PSYCHO-SOMATIC AFTEREFFECT, NOT A PHYSICAL ONE.
...!
I GUESS IT GOES TO SHOW JUST HOW MUCH OF A HELL YOU ENDURED IN AFGHANISTAN.
BUT YOU DON'T NEED IT ANYMORE.
YOU COULD EASILY THROW IT INTO THE FIRE OVER THERE.
GRP
I DON'T KNOW WHAT TO SAY...

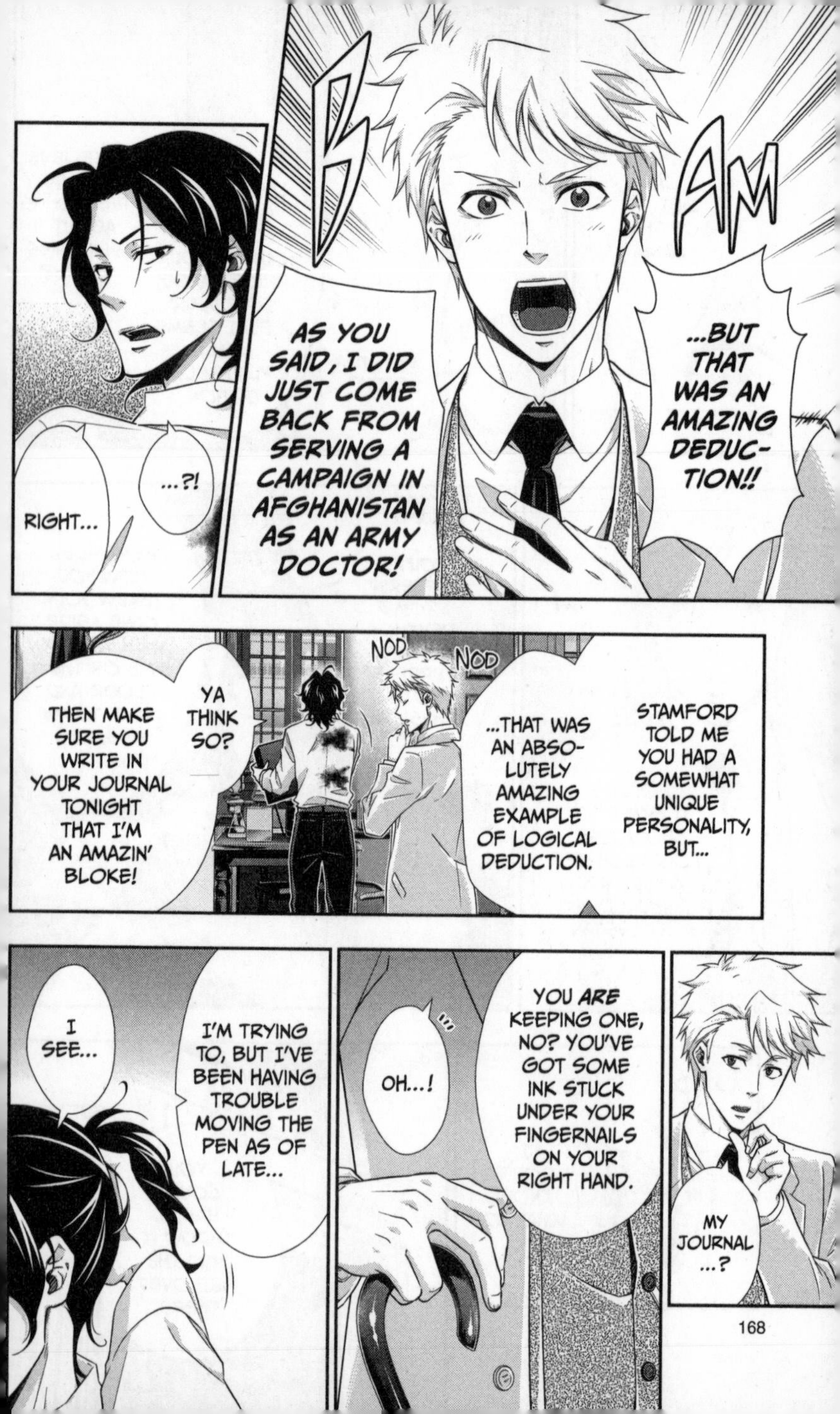
BAM
...BUT THAT WAS AN AMAZING DEDUCTION!!
AS YOU SAID, I DID JUST COME BACK FROM SERVING A CAMPAIGN IN AFGHANISTAN AS AN ARMY DOCTOR!
...?!
RIGHT...
NOD NOD
STAMFORD TOLD ME YOU HAD A SOMEWHAT UNIQUE PERSONALITY, BUT...
...THAT WAS AN ABSOLUTELY AMAZING EXAMPLE OF LOGICAL DEDUCTION.
YA THINK SO?
THEN MAKE SURE YOU WRITE IN YOUR JOURNAL TONIGHT THAT I'M AN AMAZIN' BLOKE!
MY JOURNAL...?
YOU ARE KEEPING ONE, NO? YOU'VE GOT SOME INK STUCK UNDER YOUR FINGERNAILS ON YOUR RIGHT HAND.
...
OH...!
I'M TRYING TO, BUT I'VE BEEN HAVING TROUBLE MOVING THE PEN AS OF LATE...
I SEE...

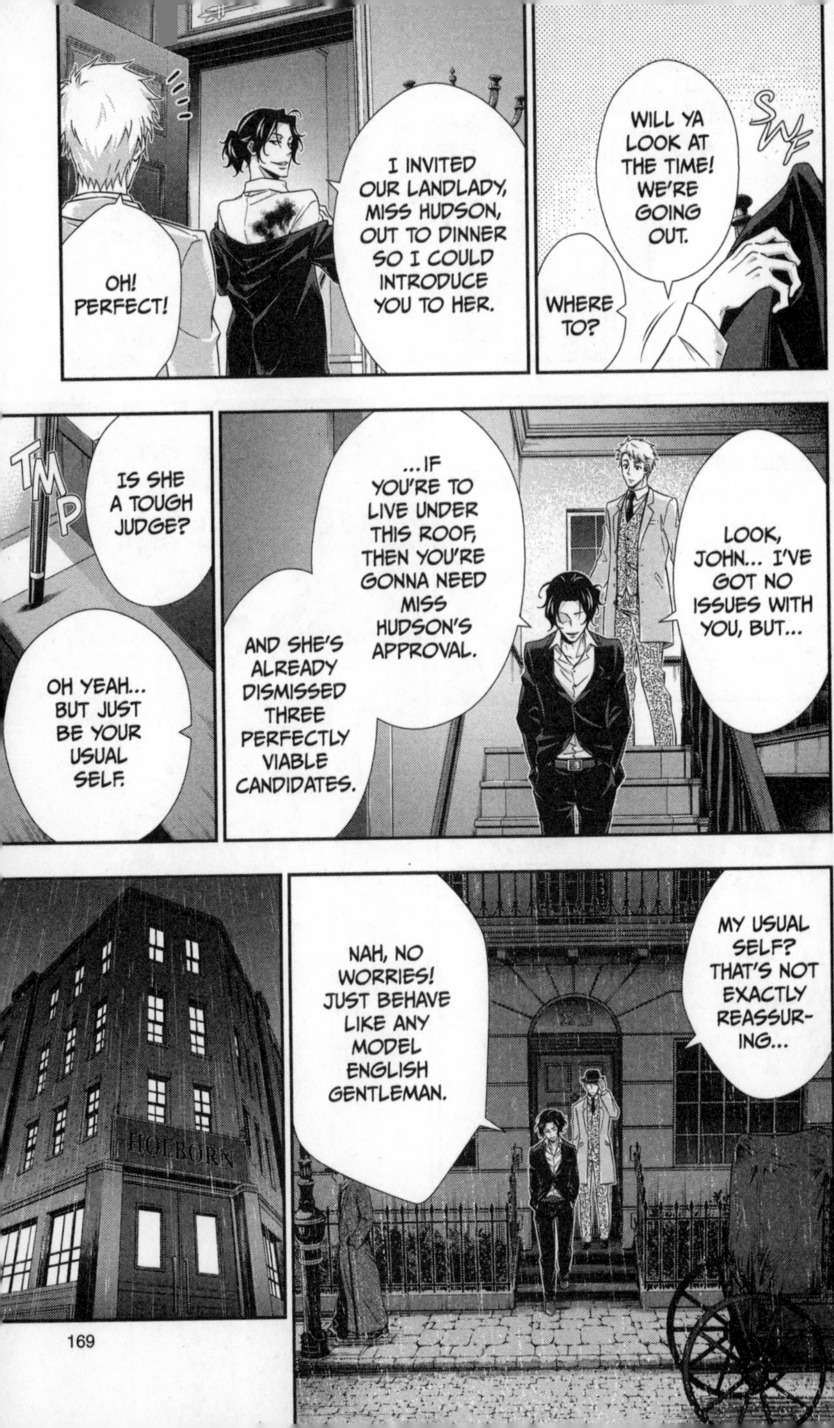
SWF
WILL YA LOOK AT THE TIME! WE'RE GOING OUT.
WHERE TO?
I INVITED OUR LANDLADY, MISS HUDSON, OUT TO DINNER SO I COULD INTRODUCE YOU TO HER.
OH! PERFECT!
LOOK, JOHN... I'VE GOT NO ISSUES WITH YOU, BUT...
...IF YOU'RE TO LIVE UNDER THIS ROOF, THEN YOU'RE GONNA NEED MISS HUDSON'S APPROVAL.
AND SHE'S ALREADY DISMISSED THREE PERFECTLY VIABLE CANDIDATES.
TMP
IS SHE A TOUGH JUDGE?
OH YEAH... BUT JUST BE YOUR USUAL SELF.
MY USUAL SELF? THAT'S NOT EXACTLY REASSURING...
NAH, NO WORRIES! JUST BEHAVE LIKE ANY MODEL ENGLISH GENTLEMAN.
HOLBORN

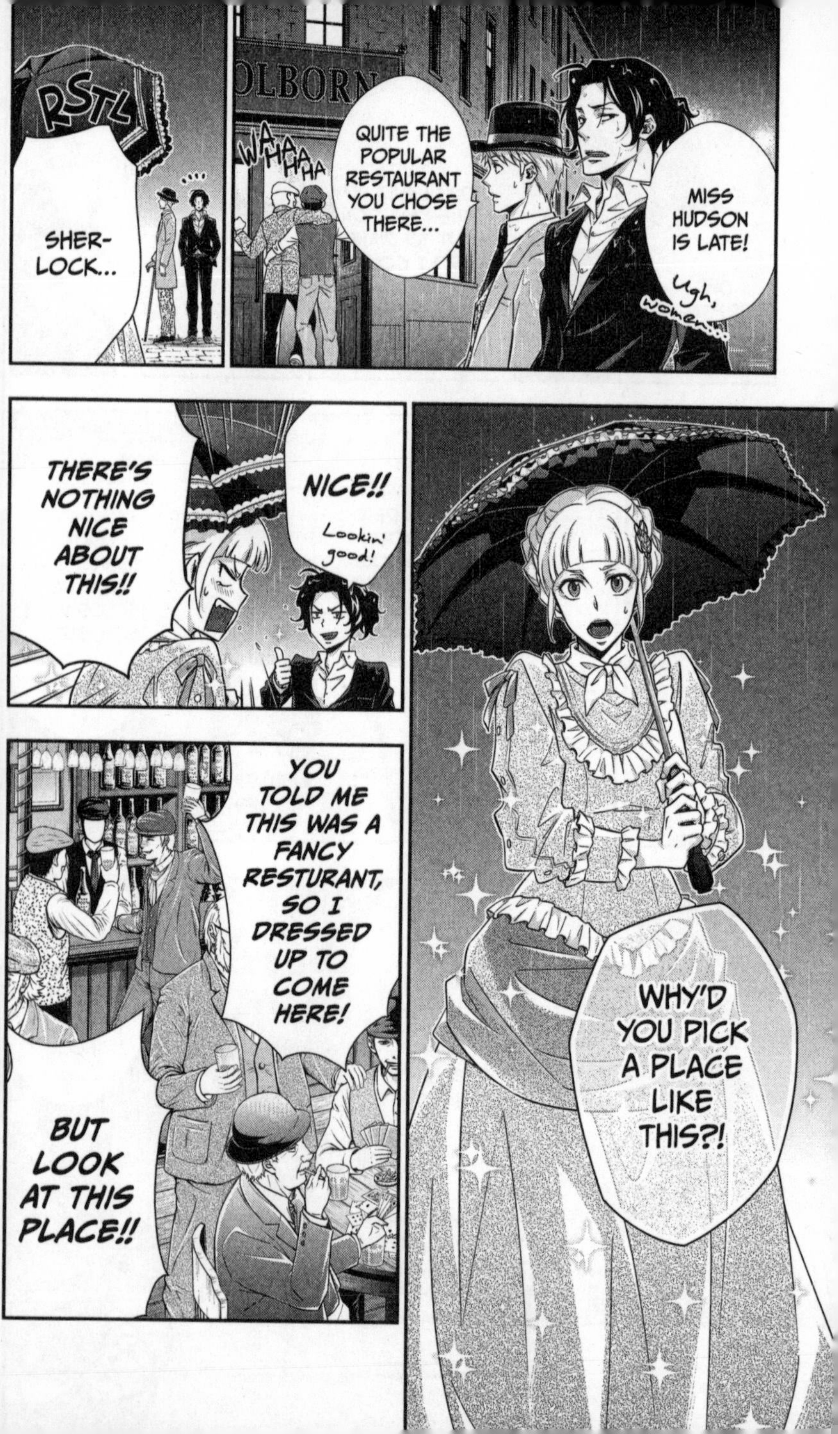
MISS HUDSON IS LATE!
Ugh, women...
OLBORN
QUITE THE POPULAR RESTAURANT YOU CHOSE THERE...
WAHAHAHA
RSTL
....
SHER-LOCK...
WHY'D YOU PICK A PLACE LIKE THIS?!
NICE!!
Lookin' good!
THERE'S NOTHING NICE ABOUT THIS!!
YOU TOLD ME THIS WAS A FANCY RESTURANT, SO I DRESSED UP TO COME HERE!
BUT LOOK AT THIS PLACE!!

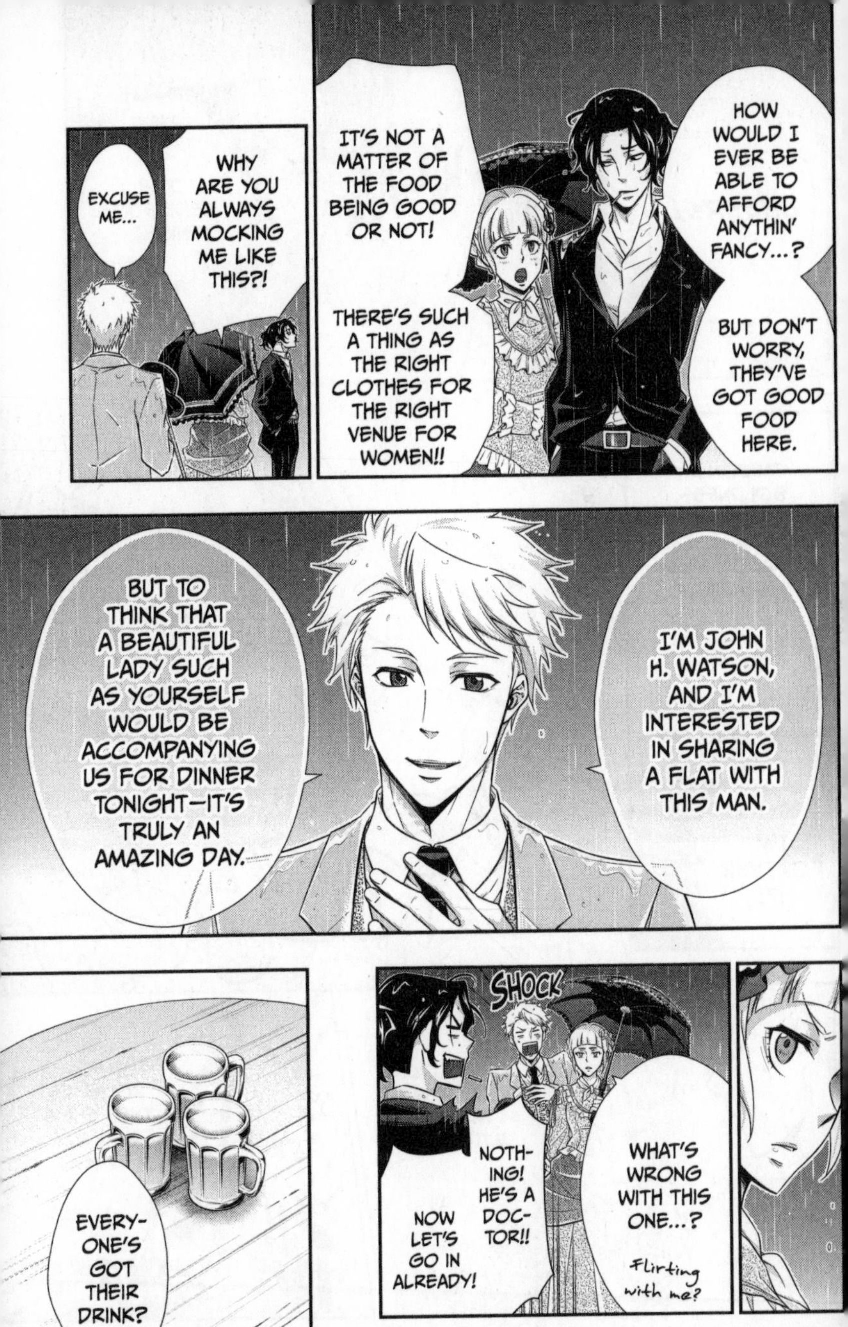
HOW WOULD I EVER BE ABLE TO AFFORD ANYTHIN' FANCY...?
BUT DON'T WORRY, THEY'VE GOT GOOD FOOD HERE.
IT'S NOT A MATTER OF THE FOOD BEING GOOD OR NOT!
THERE'S SUCH A THING AS THE RIGHT CLOTHES FOR THE RIGHT VENUE FOR WOMEN!!
WHY ARE YOU ALWAYS MOCKING ME LIKE THIS?!
EXCUSE ME...
I'M JOHN H. WATSON, AND I'M INTERESTED IN SHARING A FLAT WITH THIS MAN.
BUT TO THINK THAT A BEAUTIFUL LADY SUCH AS YOURSELF WOULD BE ACCOMPANYING US FOR DINNER TONIGHT—IT'S TRULY AN AMAZING DAY.
WHAT'S WRONG WITH THIS ONE...?
Flirting with me?
SHOCK
NOTH-ING! HE'S A DOC-TOR!!
NOW LET'S GO IN ALREADY!
EVERY-ONE'S GOT THEIR DRINK?

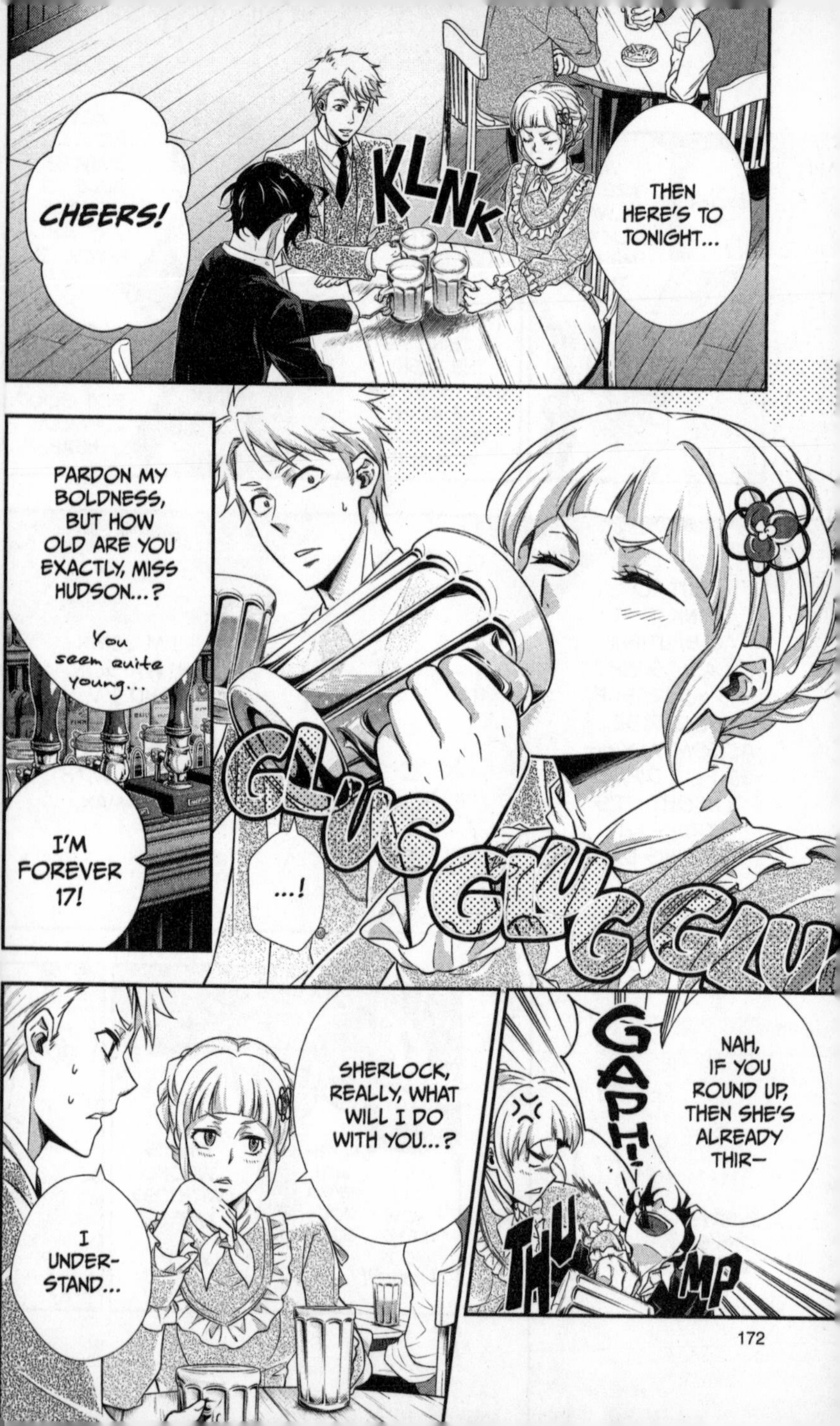
THEN HERE'S TO TONIGHT...
KLNK
CHEERS!
PARDON MY BOLDNESS, BUT HOW OLD ARE YOU EXACTLY, MISS HUDSON...?
You seem quite young...
GLUG GLUG GLU
I'M FOREVER 17!
...!
NAH, IF YOU ROUND UP, THEN SHE'S ALREADY THIR—
GAPH!
THUMP
SHERLOCK, REALLY, WHAT WILL I DO WITH YOU...?
I UNDER-STAND...

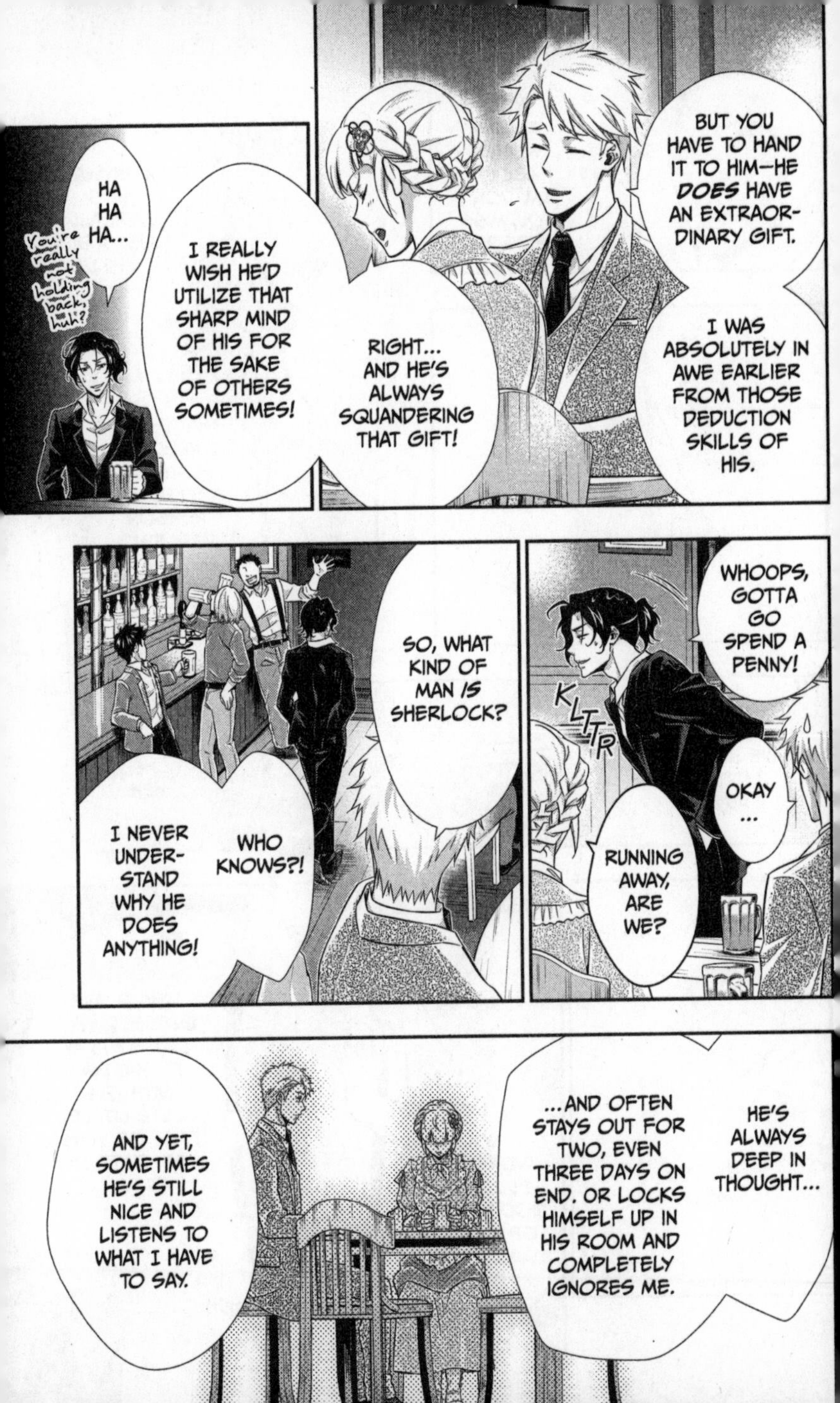
BUT YOU HAVE TO HAND IT TO HIM—HE *DOES* HAVE AN EXTRAOR-DINARY GIFT.
I WAS ABSOLUTELY IN AWE EARLIER FROM THOSE DEDUCTION SKILLS OF HIS.
RIGHT... AND HE'S ALWAYS SQUANDERING THAT GIFT!
I REALLY WISH HE'D UTILIZE THAT SHARP MIND OF HIS FOR THE SAKE OF OTHERS SOMETIMES!
HA HA HA...
You're really not holding back, huh?
WHOOPS, GOTTA GO SPEND A PENNY!
KLTTR
OKAY ...
RUNNING AWAY, ARE WE?
SO, WHAT KIND OF MAN *IS* SHERLOCK?
WHO KNOWS?!
I NEVER UNDER-STAND WHY HE DOES ANYTHING!
HE'S ALWAYS DEEP IN THOUGHT...
...AND OFTEN STAYS OUT FOR TWO, EVEN THREE DAYS ON END. OR LOCKS HIMSELF UP IN HIS ROOM AND COMPLETELY IGNORES ME.
AND YET, SOMETIMES HE'S STILL NICE AND LISTENS TO WHAT I HAVE TO SAY.

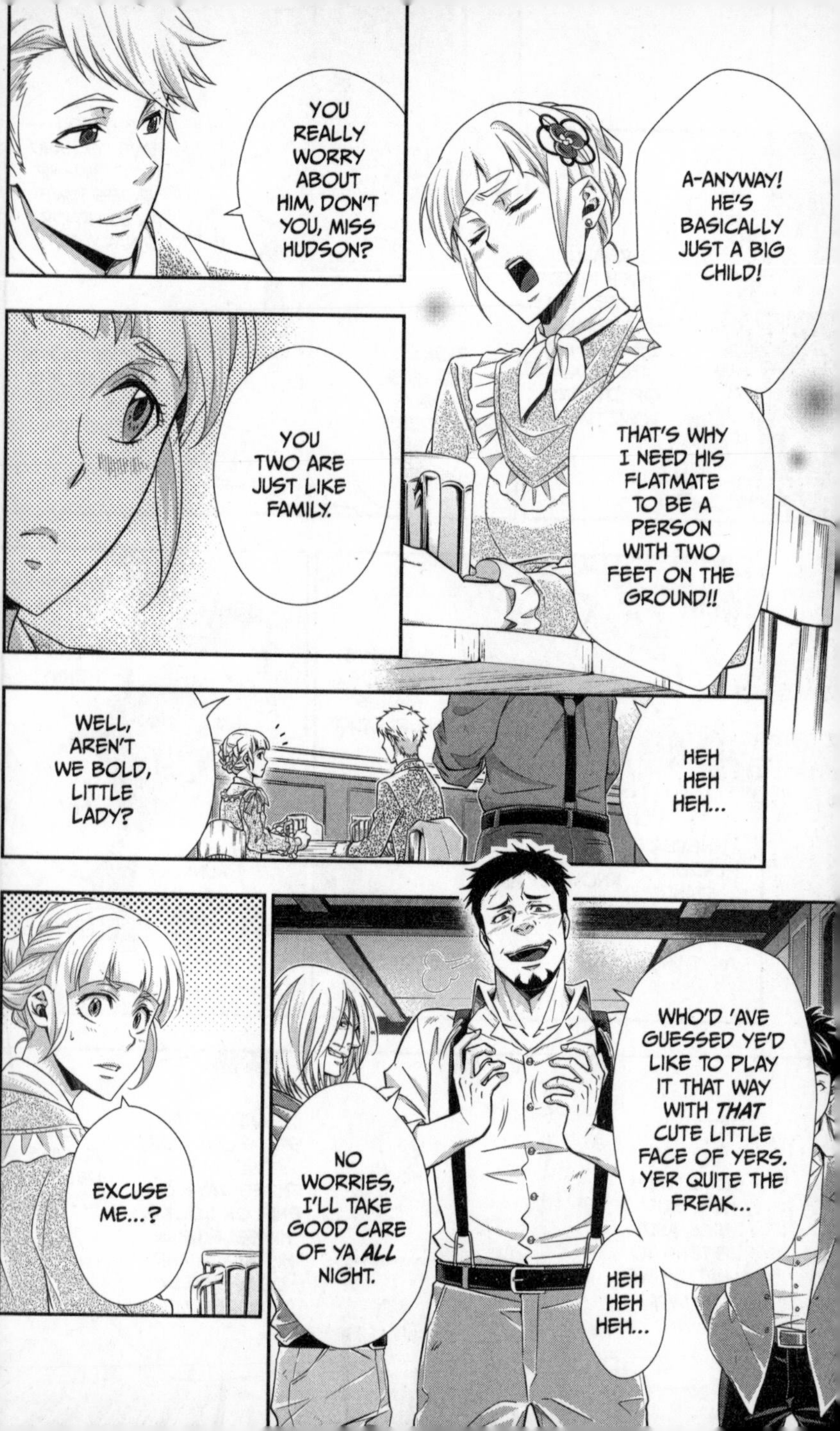
A-ANYWAY! HE'S BASICALLY JUST A BIG CHILD!
THAT'S WHY I NEED HIS FLATMATE TO BE A PERSON WITH TWO FEET ON THE GROUND!!
YOU REALLY WORRY ABOUT HIM, DON'T YOU, MISS HUDSON?
YOU TWO ARE JUST LIKE FAMILY.
HEH HEH HEH...
WELL, AREN'T WE BOLD, LITTLE LADY?
WHO'D 'AVE GUESSED YE'D LIKE TO PLAY IT THAT WAY WITH *THAT* CUTE LITTLE FACE OF YERS. YER QUITE THE FREAK...
HEH HEH HEH...
NO WORRIES, I'LL TAKE GOOD CARE OF YA *ALL* NIGHT.
EXCUSE ME...?

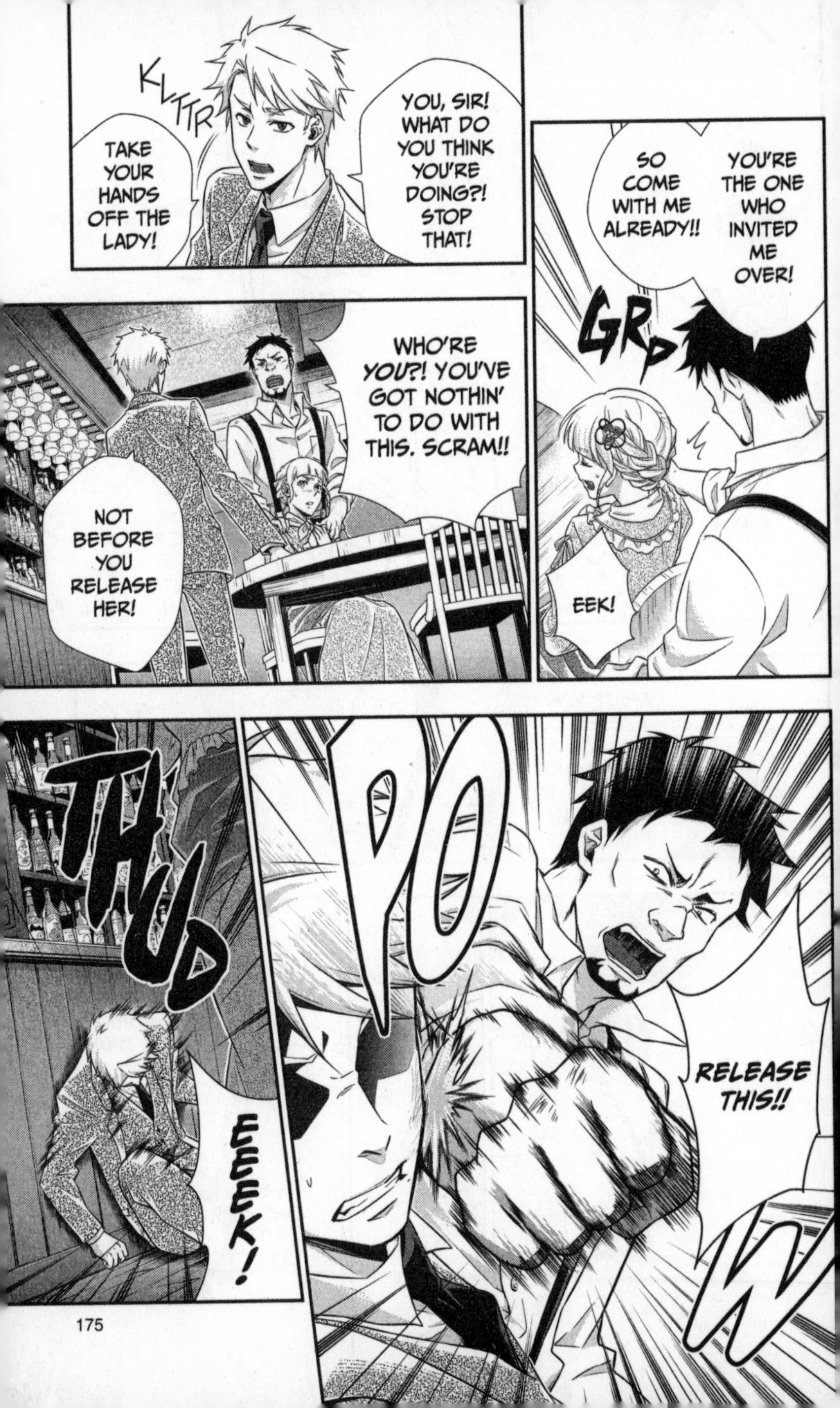
YOU'RE THE ONE WHO INVITED ME OVER!
SO COME WITH ME ALREADY!!
GRP
EEK!
YOU, SIR! WHAT DO YOU THINK YOU'RE DOING?! STOP THAT!
KLTTTR
TAKE YOUR HANDS OFF THE LADY!
WHO'RE *YOU*?! YOU'VE GOT NOTHIN' TO DO WITH THIS. SCRAM!!
NOT BEFORE YOU RELEASE HER!
RELEASE THIS!!
PO
W
THUD
EEEEK!

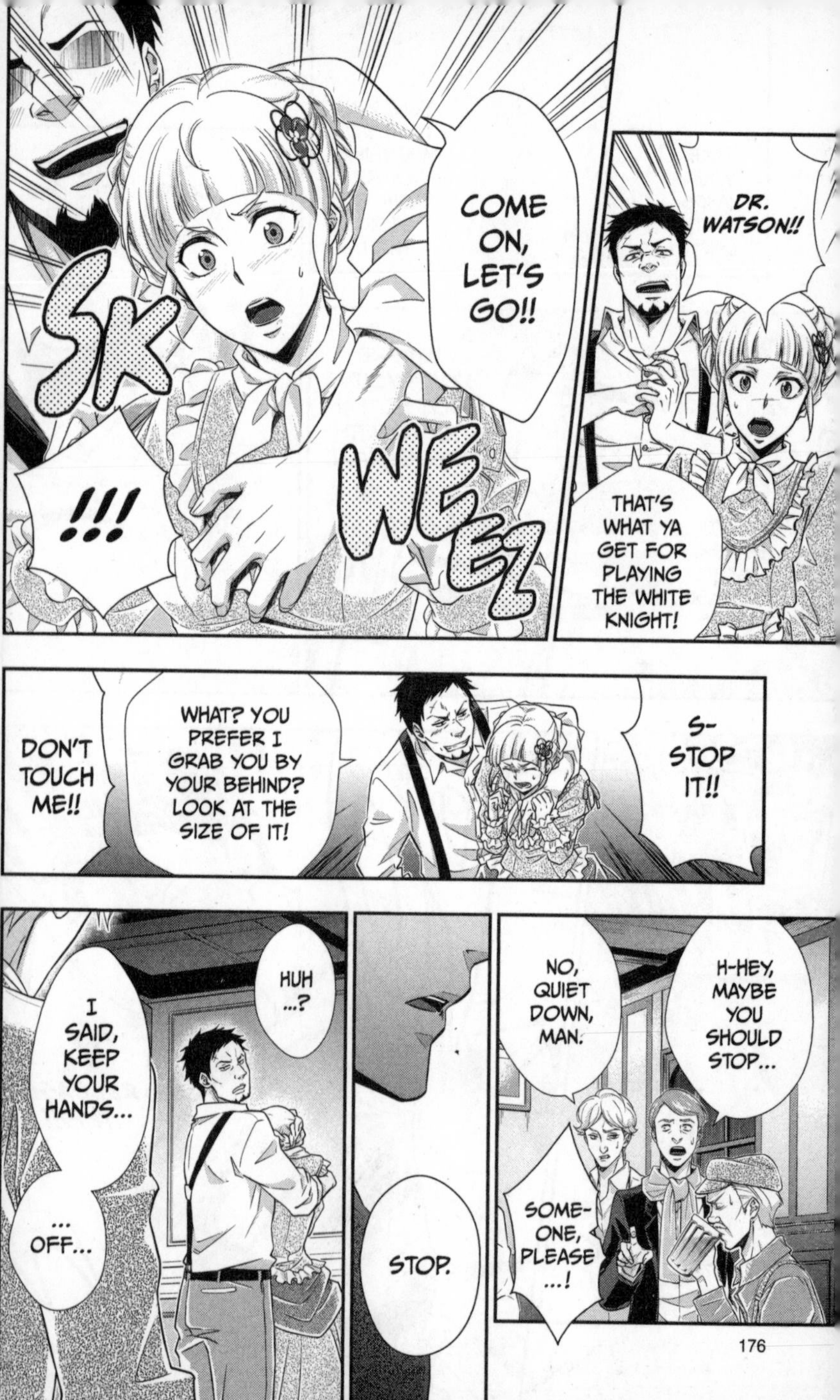
DR. WATSON!!
THAT'S WHAT YA GET FOR PLAYING THE WHITE KNIGHT!
COME ON, LET'S GO!!
SK WEEZ
!!!
S-STOP IT!!
WHAT? YOU PREFER I GRAB YOU BY YOUR BEHIND? LOOK AT THE SIZE OF IT!
DON'T TOUCH ME!!
H-HEY, MAYBE YOU SHOULD STOP...
NO, QUIET DOWN, MAN.
SOME-ONE, PLEASE ...!
STOP.
HUH ...?
I SAID, KEEP YOUR HANDS...
... OFF...

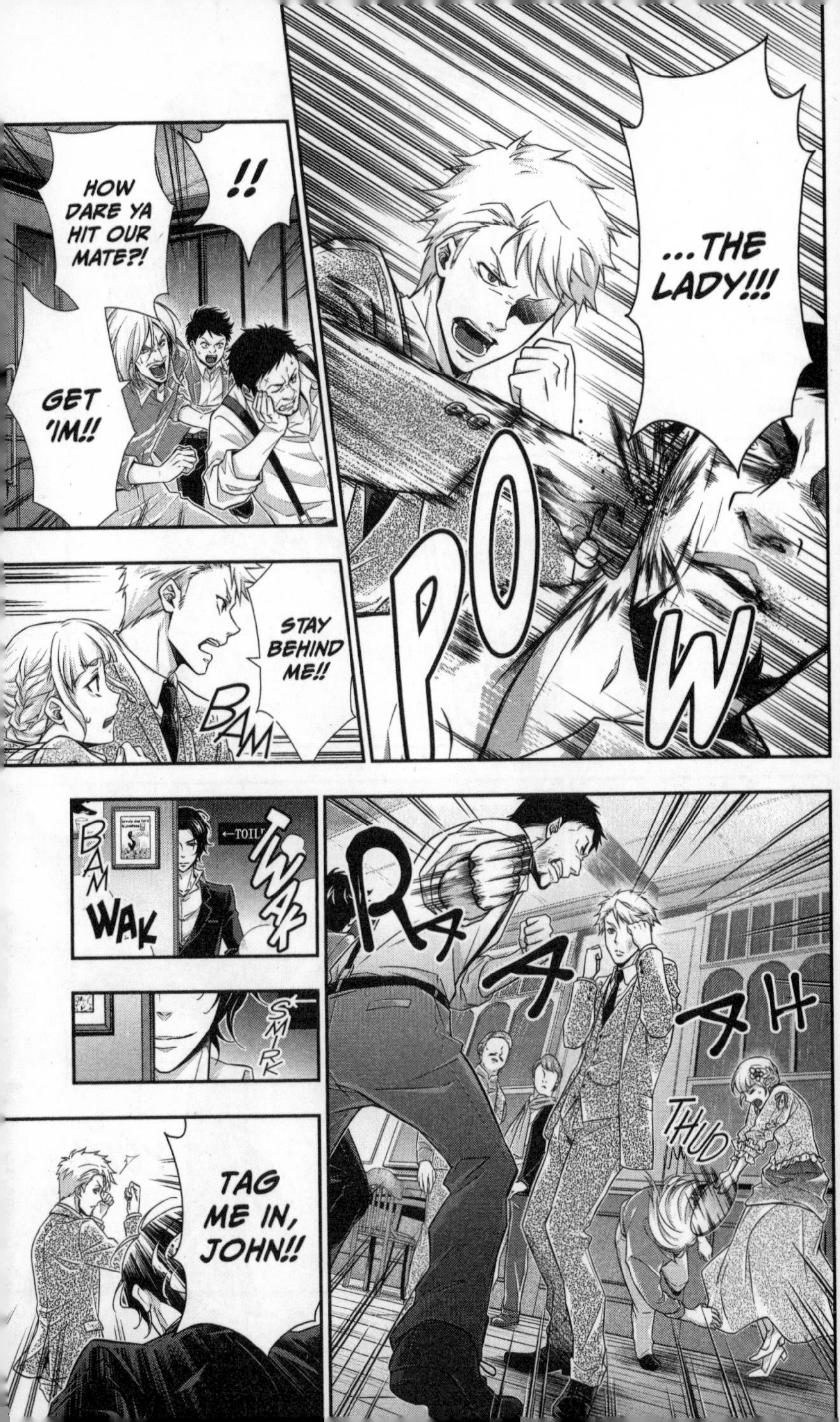
...THE LADY!!!
POW
!!
HOW DARE YA HIT OUR MATE?!
GET 'IM!!
STAY BEHIND ME!!
BAM
RAAAH
THUD
TWAK
←TOIL
BAM
WAK
SMIRK
TAG ME IN, JOHN!!

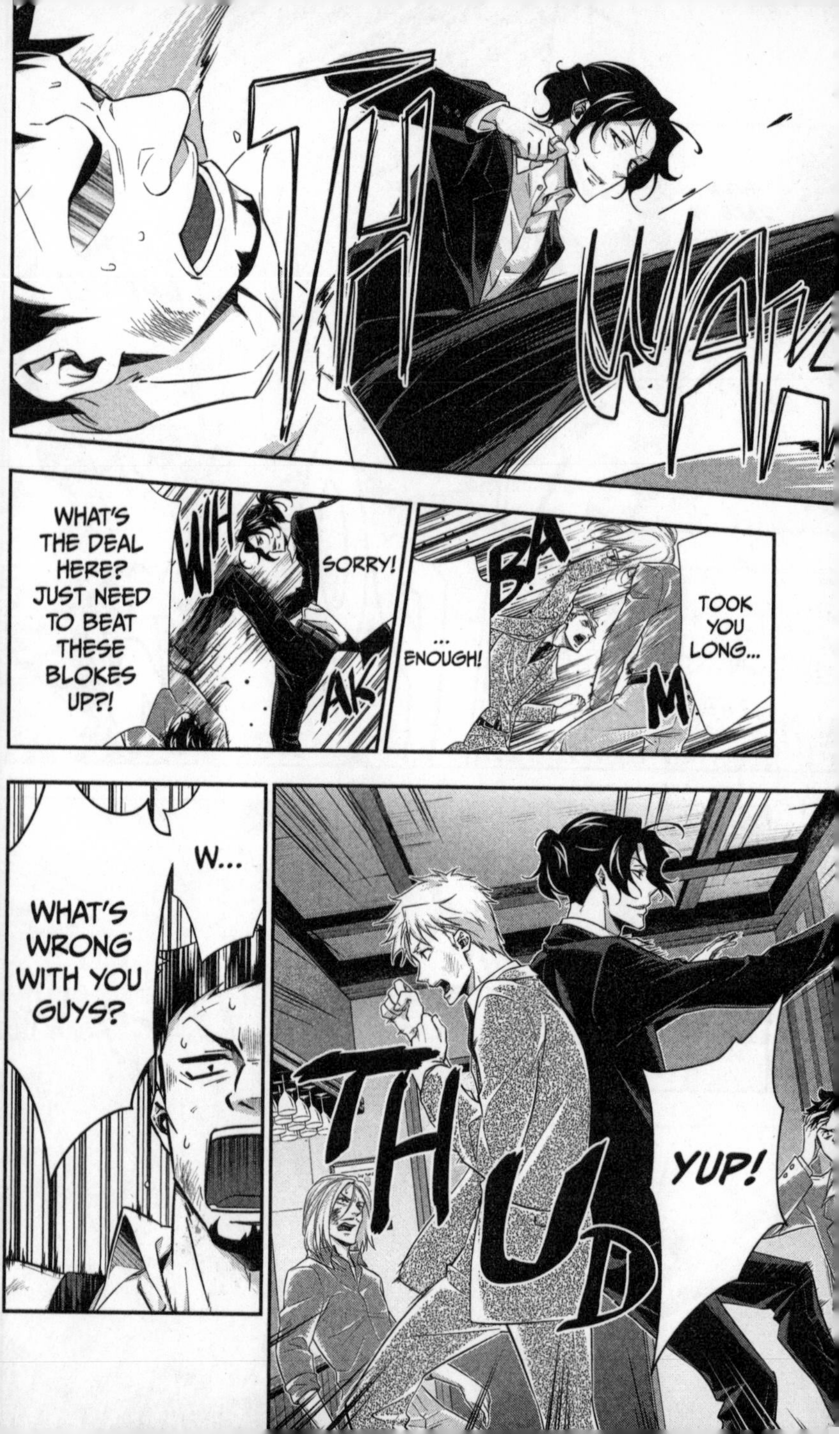
THWAK
TOOK YOU LONG...
BAM
...ENOUGH!
SORRY!
WHAK
WHAT'S THE DEAL HERE? JUST NEED TO BEAT THESE BLOKES UP?!
YUP!
THUD
W...
WHAT'S WRONG WITH YOU GUYS?

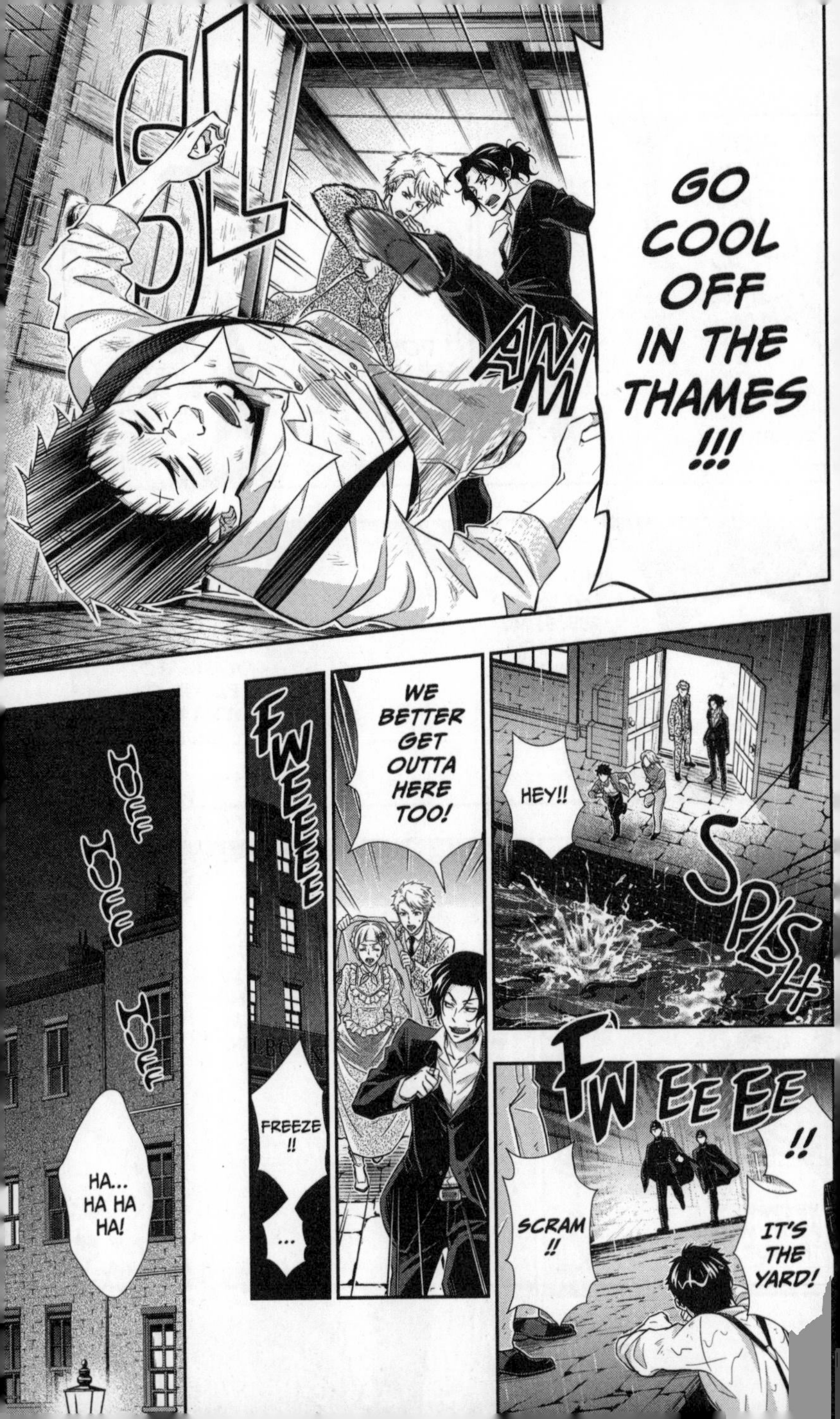
GO COOL OFF IN THE THAMES !!!
SLAM
HEY!!
SPLSH
FW EE EE
!!
IT'S THE YARD!
SCRAM !!
WE BETTER GET OUTTA HERE TOO!
FWEEEE
FREEZE !!
...
HUFF HUFF HUFF HUFF
HA... HA HA HA!

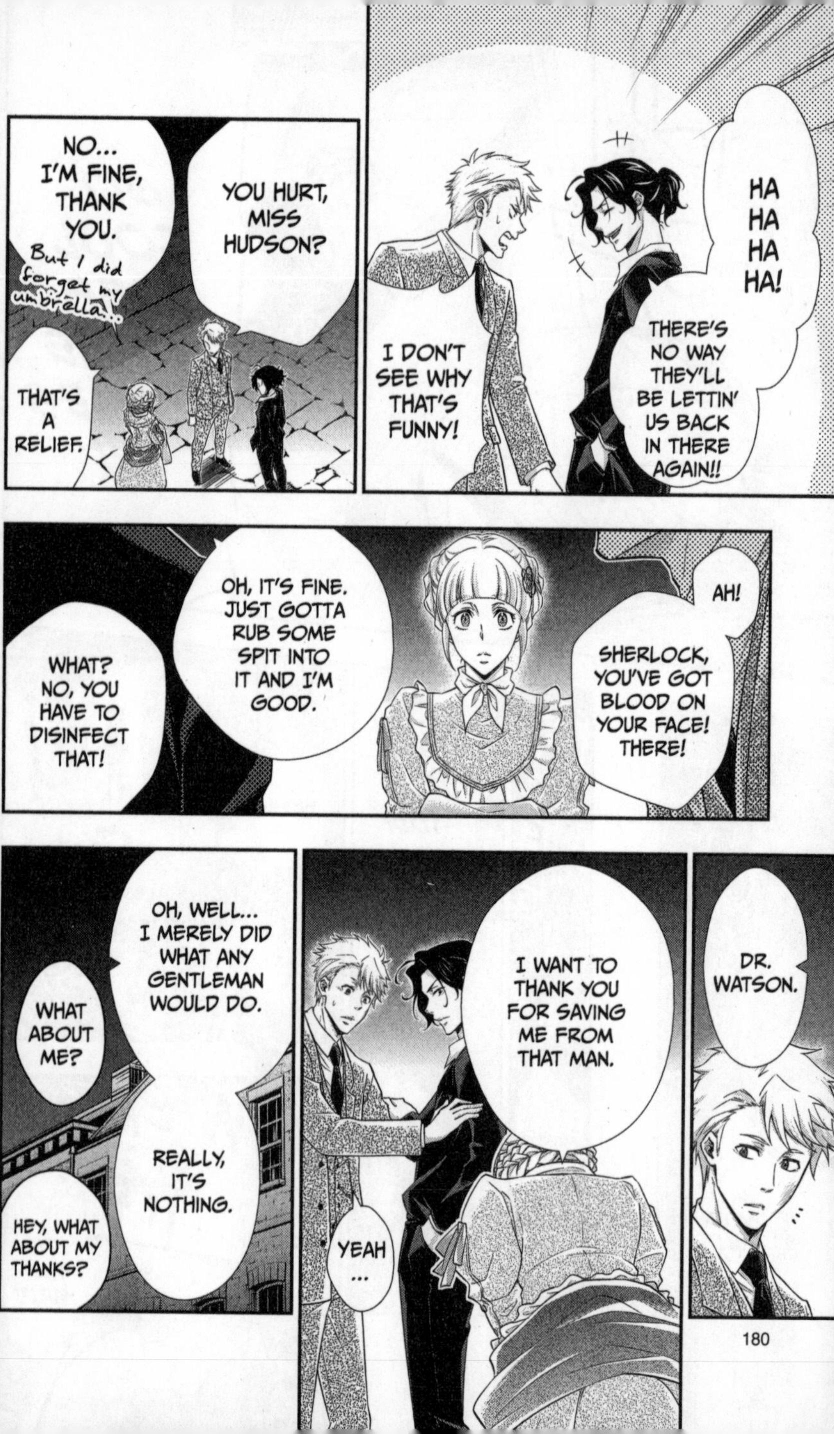
HA HA HA HA!
THERE'S NO WAY THEY'LL BE LETTIN' US BACK IN THERE AGAIN!!
I DON'T SEE WHY THAT'S FUNNY!
YOU HURT, MISS HUDSON?
NO... I'M FINE, THANK YOU.
But I did forget my umbrella...
THAT'S A RELIEF.
AH!
SHERLOCK, YOU'VE GOT BLOOD ON YOUR FACE! THERE!
OH, IT'S FINE. JUST GOTTA RUB SOME SPIT INTO IT AND I'M GOOD.
WHAT? NO, YOU HAVE TO DISINFECT THAT!
DR. WATSON.
...
I WANT TO THANK YOU FOR SAVING ME FROM THAT MAN.
YEAH...
OH, WELL... I MERELY DID WHAT ANY GENTLEMAN WOULD DO.
WHAT ABOUT ME?
REALLY, IT'S NOTHING.
HEY, WHAT ABOUT MY THANKS?

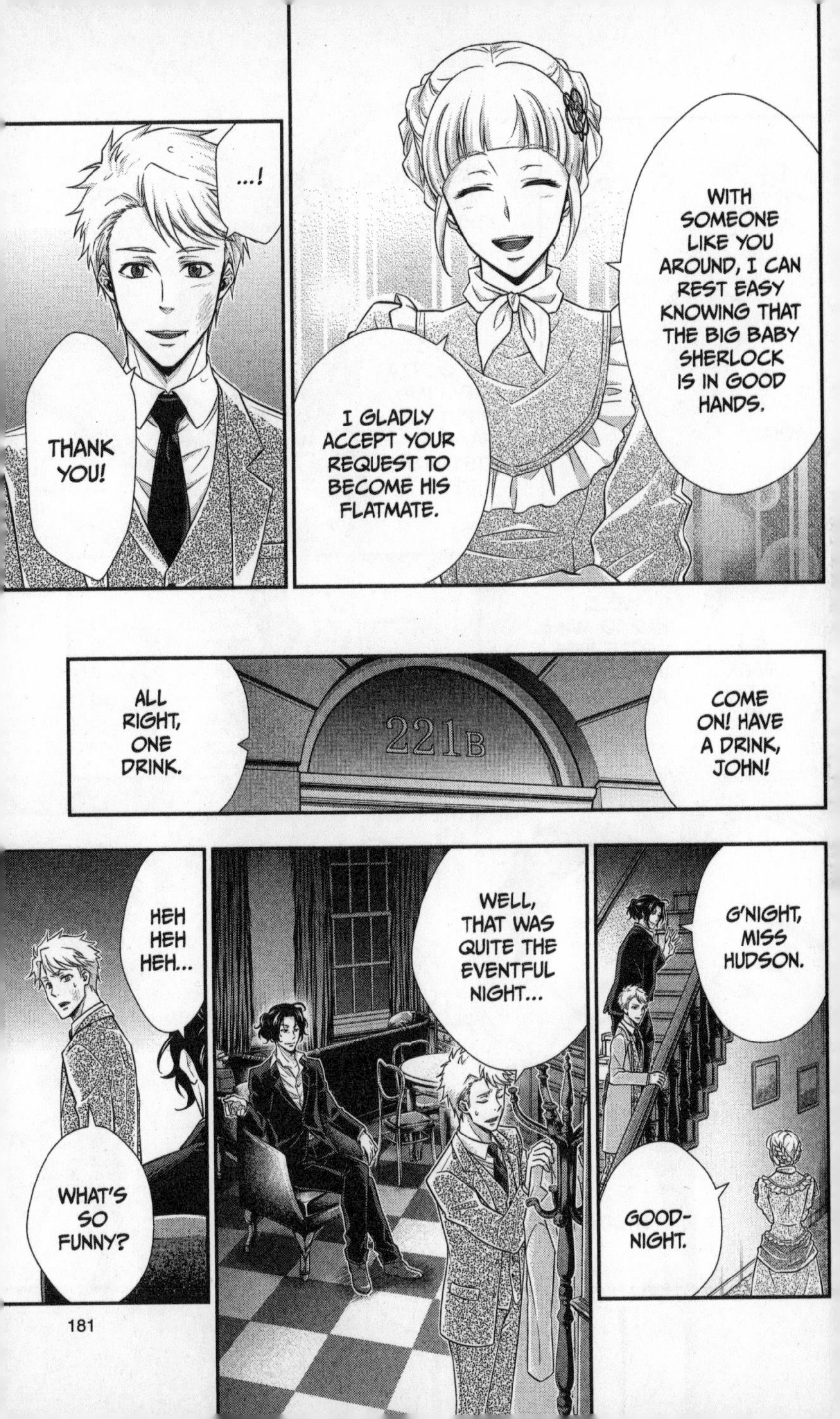
WITH SOMEONE LIKE YOU AROUND, I CAN REST EASY KNOWING THAT THE BIG BABY SHERLOCK IS IN GOOD HANDS.
I GLADLY ACCEPT YOUR REQUEST TO BECOME HIS FLATMATE.
...!
THANK YOU!
COME ON! HAVE A DRINK, JOHN!
221B
ALL RIGHT, ONE DRINK.
G'NIGHT, MISS HUDSON.
GOOD-NIGHT.
WELL, THAT WAS QUITE THE EVENTFUL NIGHT...
HEH HEH HEH...
WHAT'S SO FUNNY?

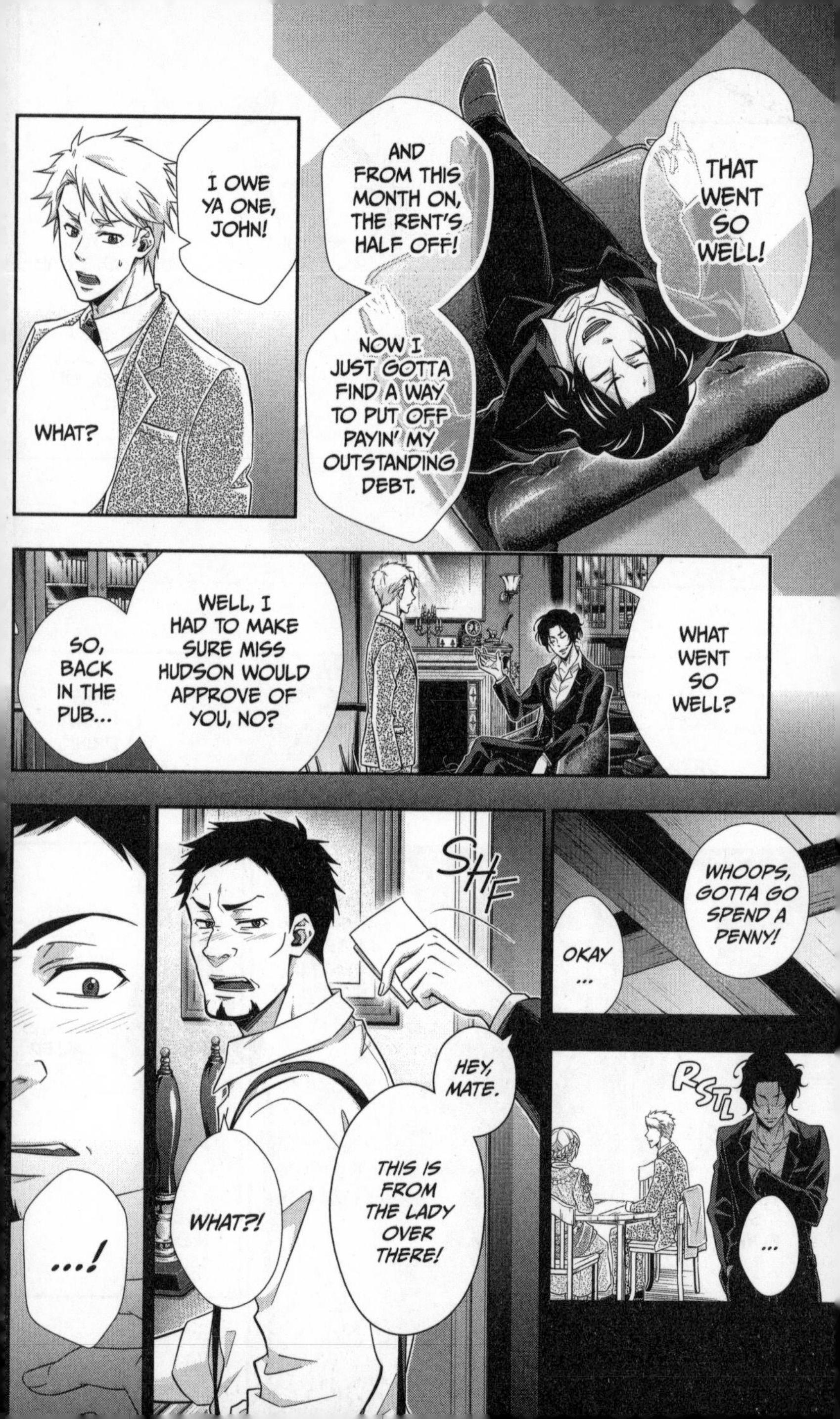
THAT WENT SO WELL!
AND FROM THIS MONTH ON, THE RENT'S HALF OFF!
NOW I JUST GOTTA FIND A WAY TO PUT OFF PAYIN' MY OUTSTANDING DEBT.
I OWE YA ONE, JOHN!
WHAT?
WHAT WENT SO WELL?
WELL, I HAD TO MAKE SURE MISS HUDSON WOULD APPROVE OF YOU, NO?
SO, BACK IN THE PUB...
WHOOPS, GOTTA GO SPEND A PENNY!
OKAY ...
RSTL
...
SHF
HEY, MATE.
THIS IS FROM THE LADY OVER THERE!
WHAT?!
...!

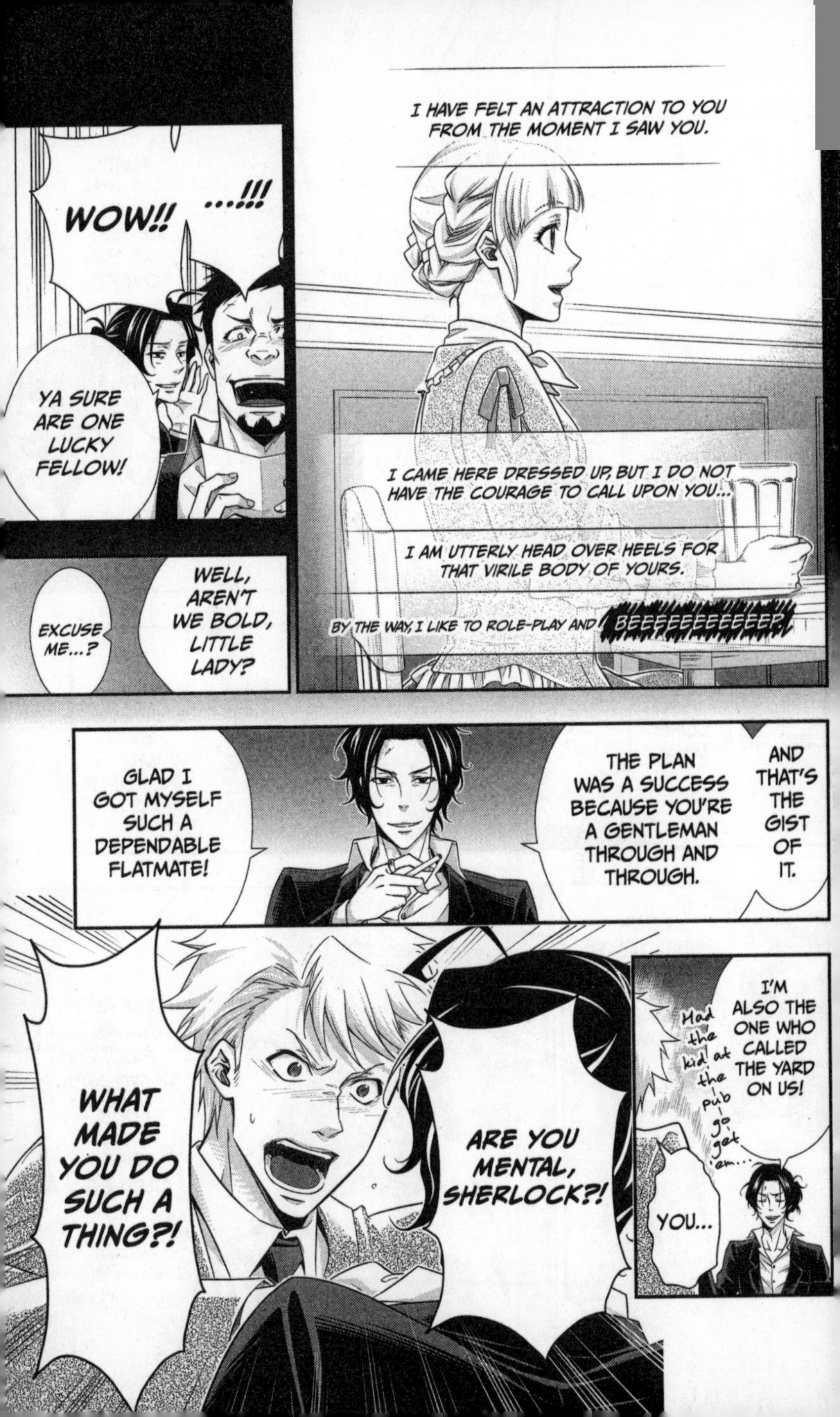

I HAVE FELT AN ATTRACTION TO YOU FROM THE MOMENT I SAW YOU.
I CAME HERE DRESSED UP, BUT I DO NOT HAVE THE COURAGE TO CALL UPON YOU...
I AM UTTERLY HEAD OVER HEELS FOR THAT VIRILE BODY OF YOURS.
BY THE WAY, I LIKE TO ROLE-PLAY AND BEEEEEEEEEEEEP.
...!!!
WOW!!
YA SURE ARE ONE LUCKY FELLOW!
WELL, AREN'T WE BOLD, LITTLE LADY?
EXCUSE ME...?
AND THAT'S THE GIST OF IT.
THE PLAN WAS A SUCCESS BECAUSE YOU'RE A GENTLEMAN THROUGH AND THROUGH.
GLAD I GOT MYSELF SUCH A DEPENDABLE FLATMATE!
I'M ALSO THE ONE WHO CALLED THE YARD ON US!
Had the kid at the pub go get 'em...
YOU...
ARE YOU MENTAL, SHERLOCK?!
WHAT MADE YOU DO SUCH A THING?!

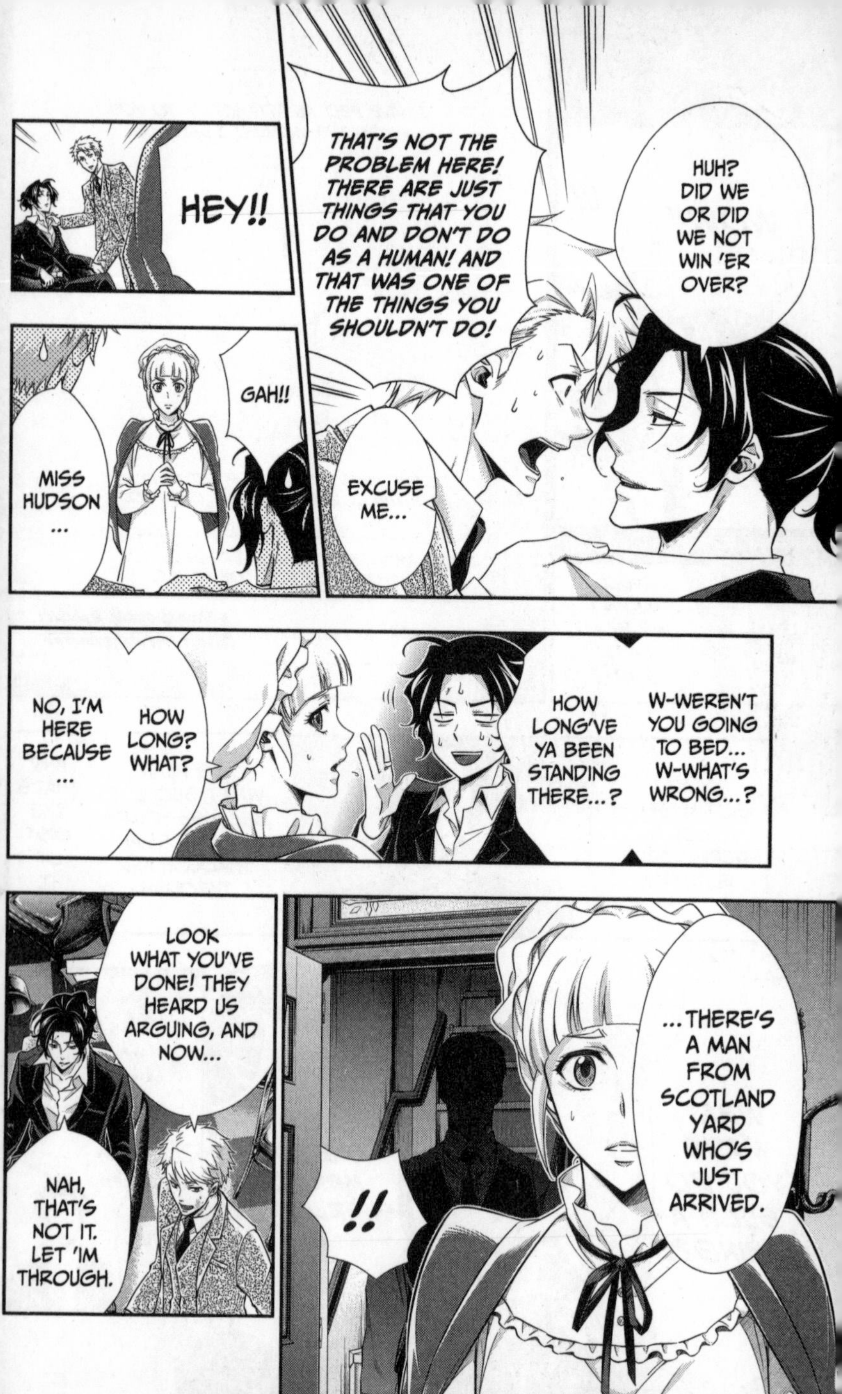
HUH? DID WE OR DID WE NOT WIN 'ER OVER?
THAT'S NOT THE PROBLEM HERE! THERE ARE JUST THINGS THAT YOU DO AND DON'T DO AS A HUMAN! AND THAT WAS ONE OF THE THINGS YOU SHOULDN'T DO!
EXCUSE ME...
HEY!!
GAH!!
MISS HUDSON ...
W-WEREN'T YOU GOING TO BED... W-WHAT'S WRONG...?
HOW LONG'VE YA BEEN STANDING THERE...?
HOW LONG? WHAT?
NO, I'M HERE BECAUSE ...
...THERE'S A MAN FROM SCOTLAND YARD WHO'S JUST ARRIVED.
!!
LOOK WHAT YOU'VE DONE! THEY HEARD US ARGUING, AND NOW...
NAH, THAT'S NOT IT. LET 'IM THROUGH.

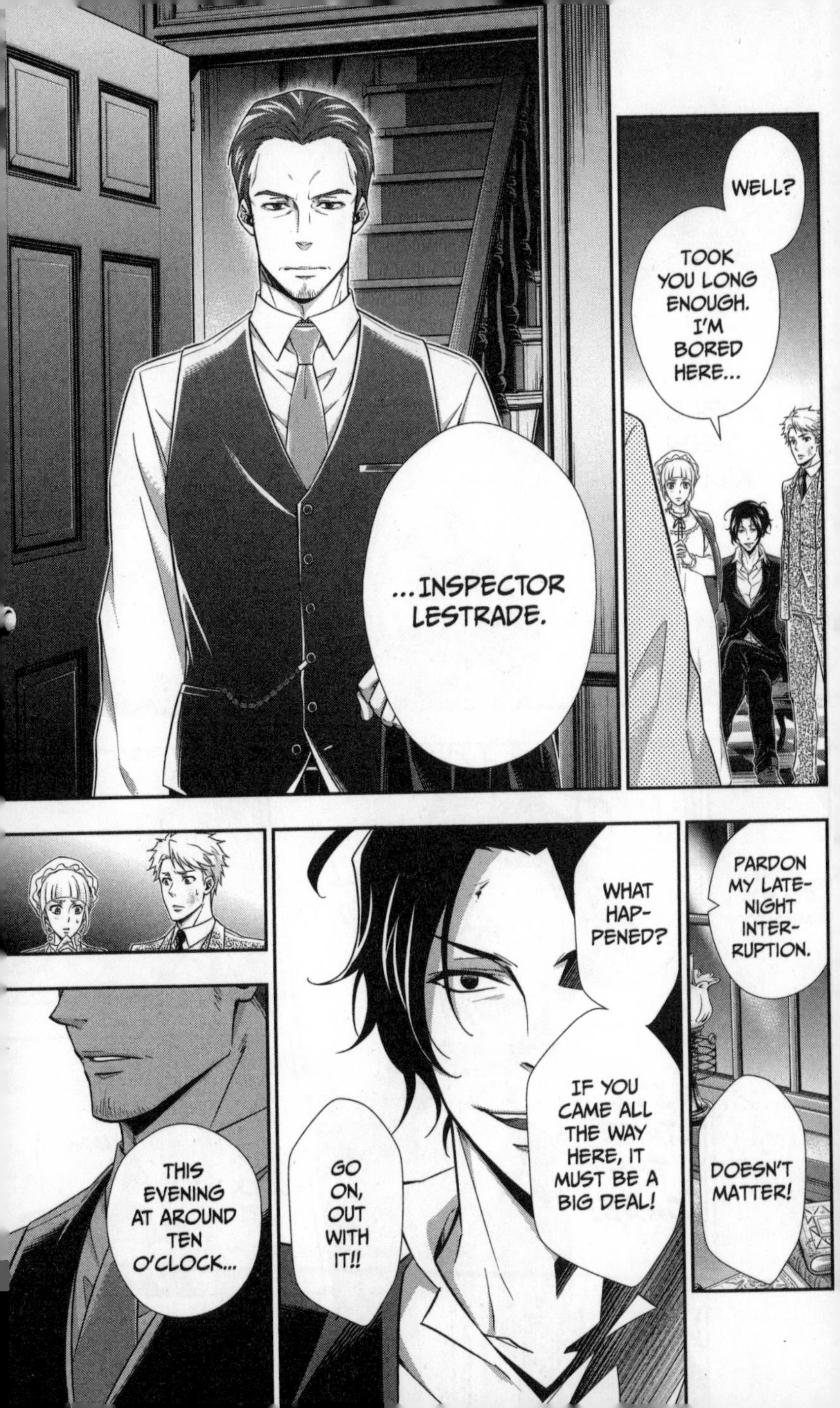
WELL?
TOOK YOU LONG ENOUGH. I'M BORED HERE...
...INSPECTOR LESTRADE.
PARDON MY LATE-NIGHT INTER-RUPTION.
DOESN'T MATTER!
WHAT HAP-PENED?
IF YOU CAME ALL THE WAY HERE, IT MUST BE A BIG DEAL!
GO ON, OUT WITH IT!!
THIS EVENING AT AROUND TEN O'CLOCK...

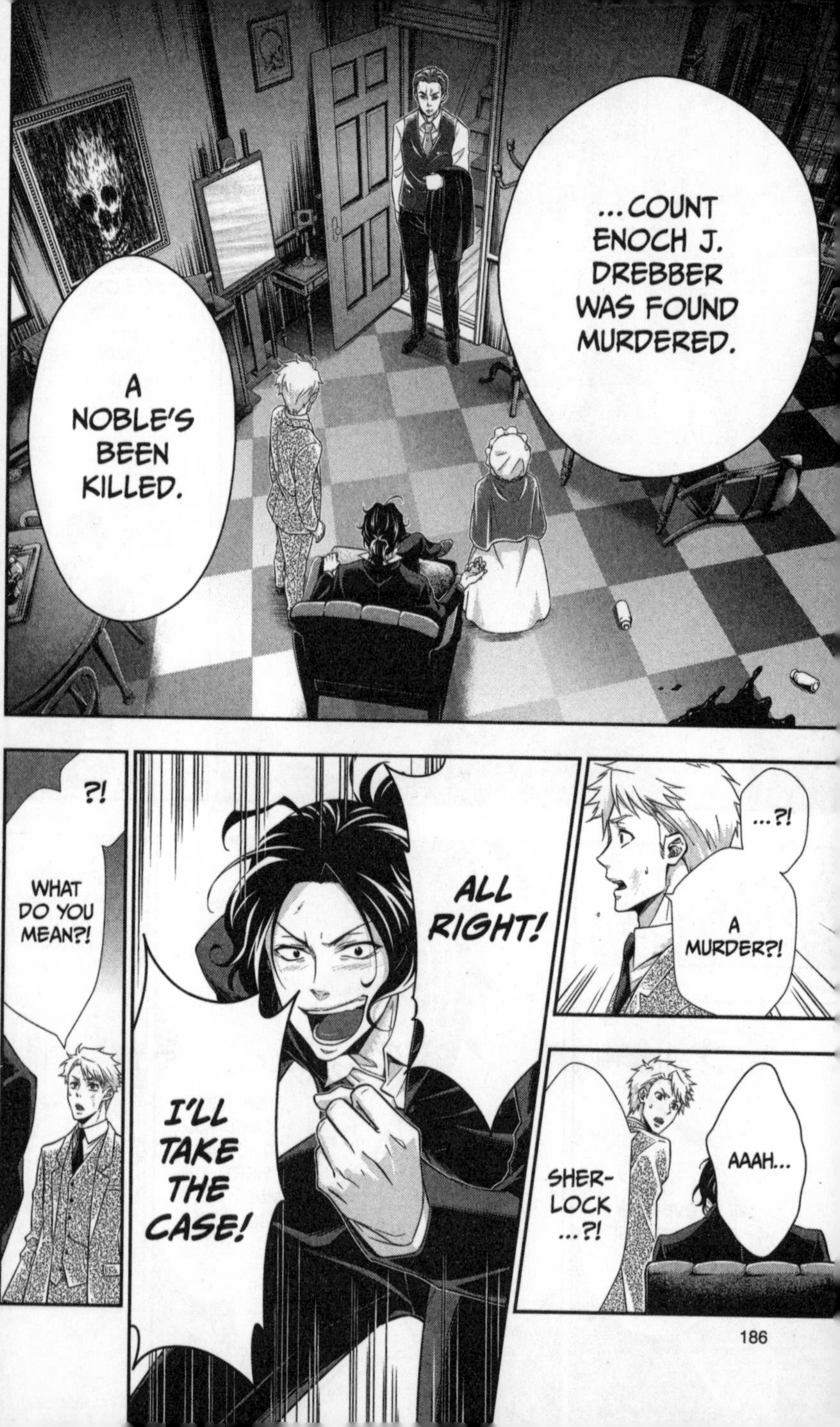
...COUNT ENOCH J. DREBBER WAS FOUND MURDERED.
A NOBLE'S BEEN KILLED.
...?!
A MURDER?!
AAAH...
SHER-LOCK ...?!
ALL RIGHT!
I'LL TAKE THE CASE!
?!
WHAT DO YOU MEAN?!

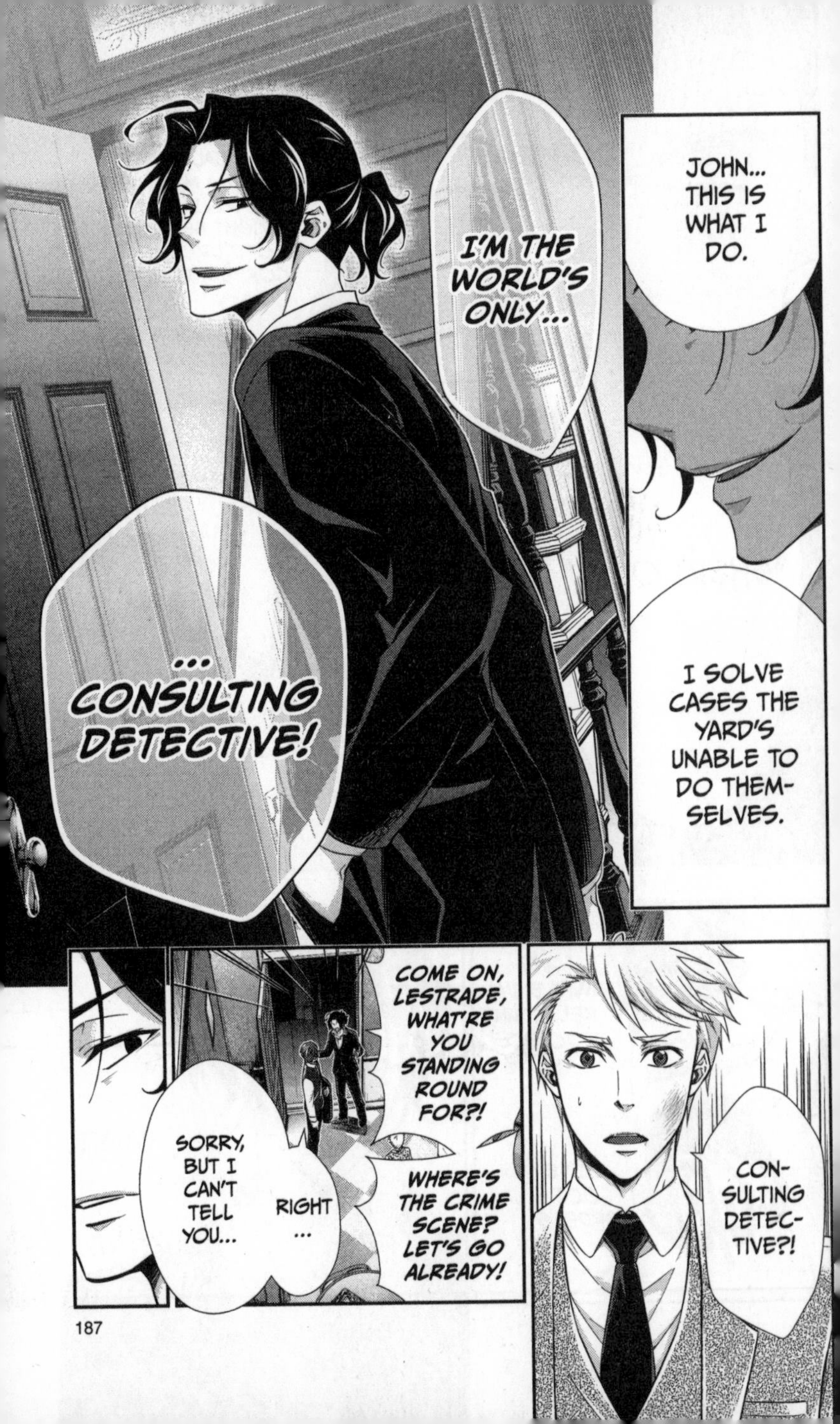
JOHN... THIS IS WHAT I DO.
I SOLVE CASES THE YARD'S UNABLE TO DO THEM-SELVES.
I'M THE WORLD'S ONLY...
...CONSULTING DETECTIVE!
CON-SULTING DETEC-TIVE?!
COME ON, LESTRADE, WHAT'RE YOU STANDING ROUND FOR?!
WHERE'S THE CRIME SCENE? LET'S GO ALREADY!
RIGHT...
SORRY, BUT I CAN'T TELL YOU...

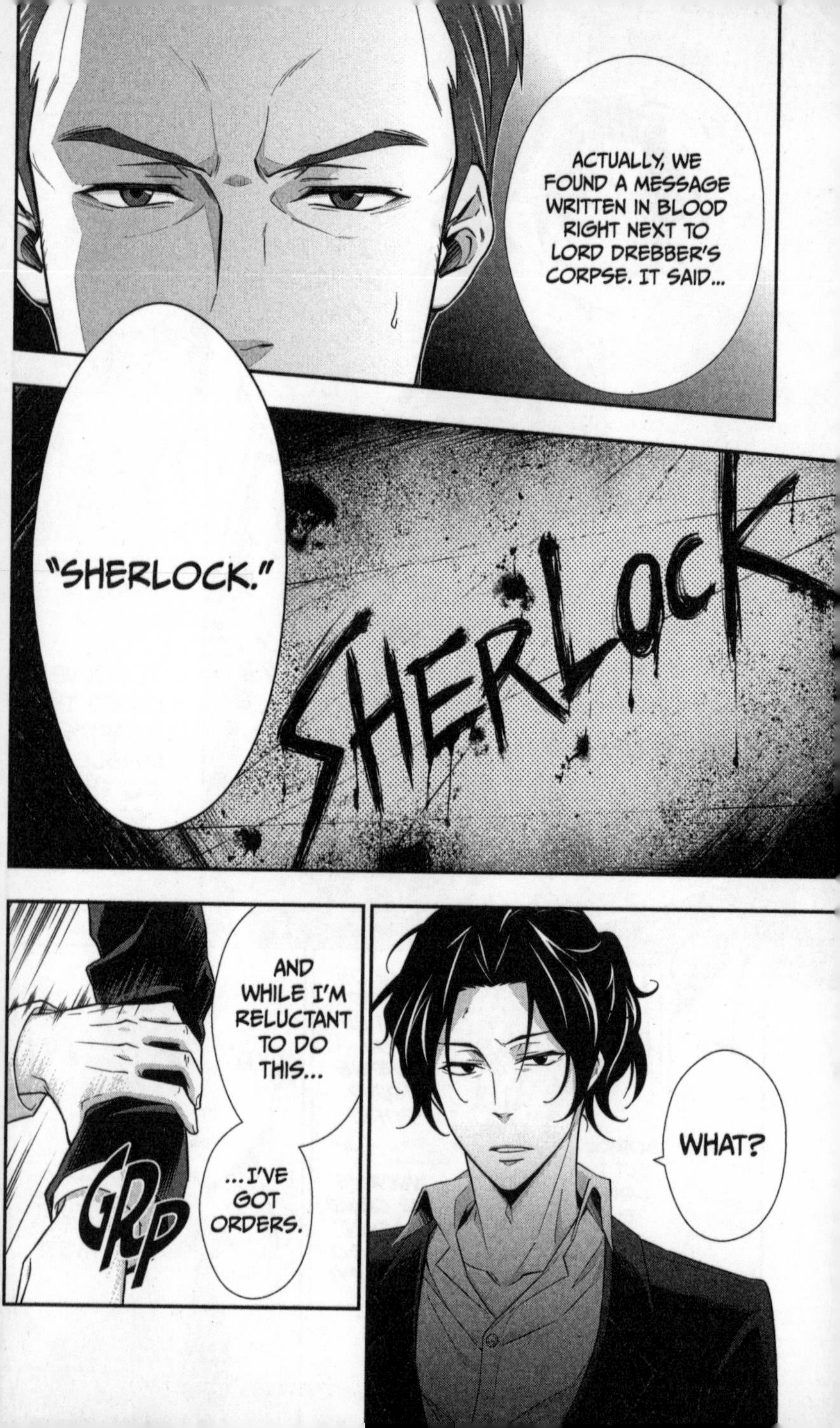
ACTUALLY, WE FOUND A MESSAGE WRITTEN IN BLOOD RIGHT NEXT TO LORD DREBBER'S CORPSE. IT SAID...
"SHERLOCK."
SHERLOCK
WHAT?
AND WHILE I'M RELUCTANT TO DO THIS...
...I'VE GOT ORDERS.
GRIP

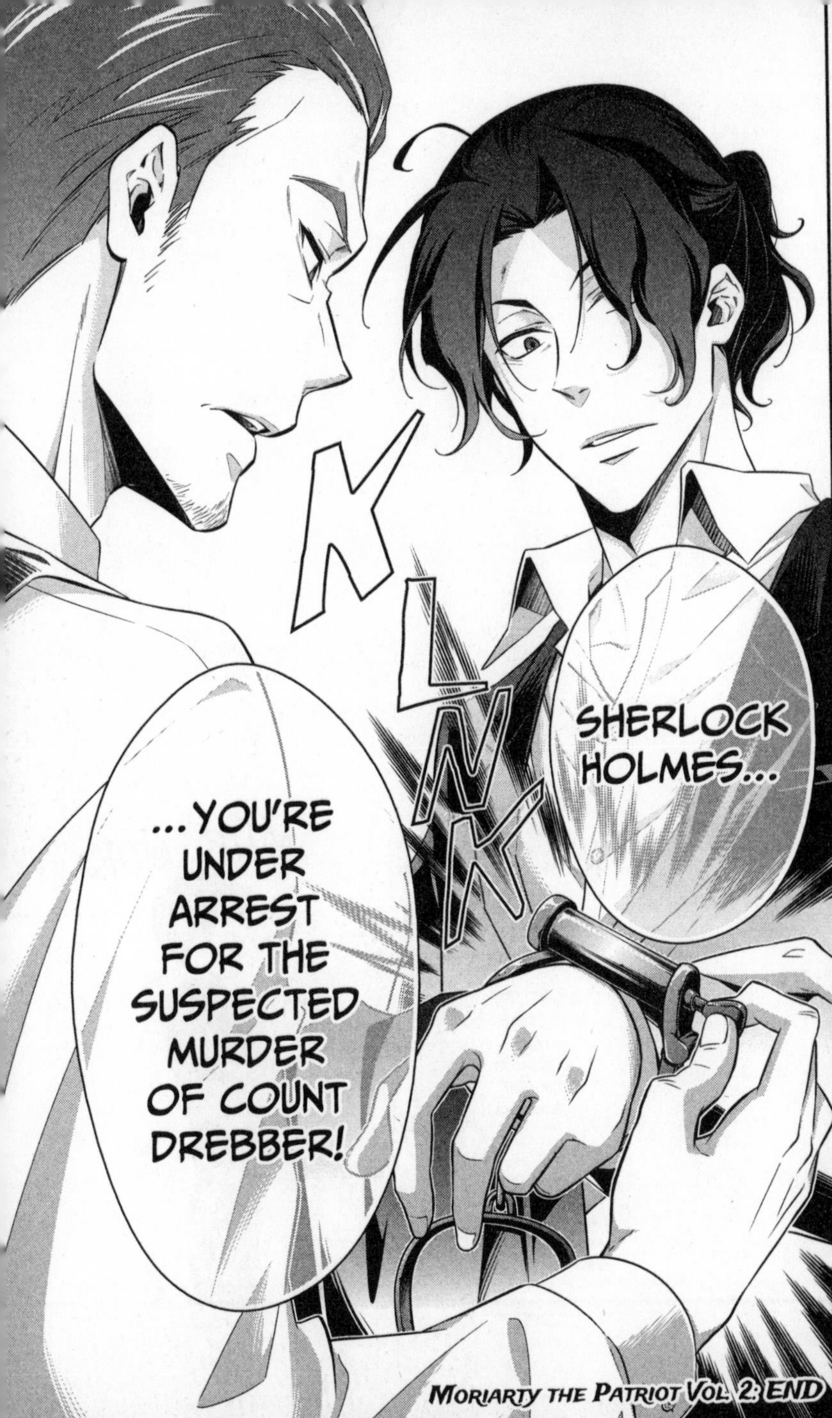
SHERLOCK HOLMES...
...YOU'RE UNDER ARREST FOR THE SUSPECTED MURDER OF COUNT DREBBER!

MORIARTY THE PATRIOT VOL. 2: END

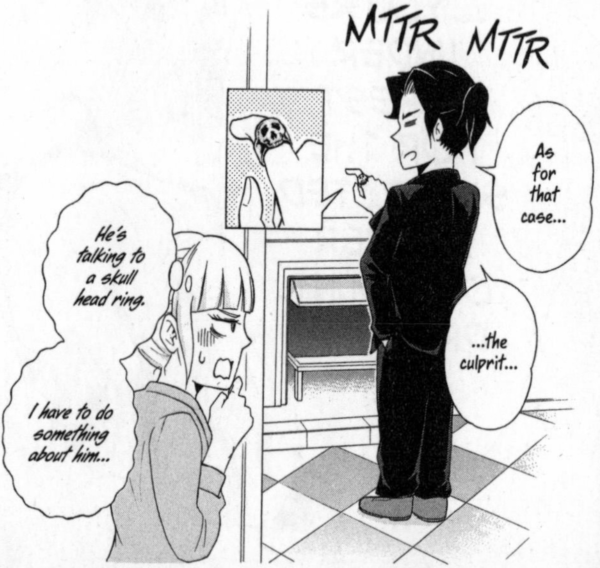
MTTR MTTR
As for that case...
...the culprit...
He's talking to a skull head ring.
I have to do something about him...

MORIARTY
THE PATRIOT

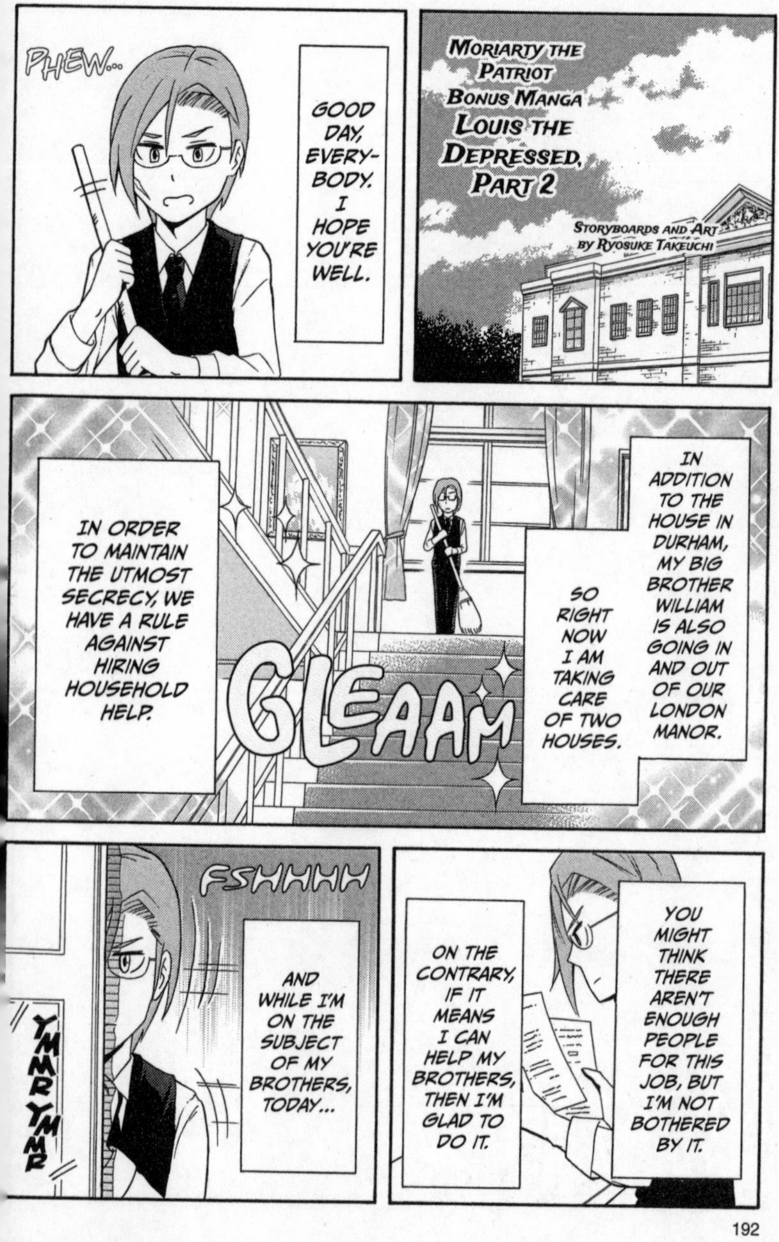
Moriarty the Patriot Bonus Manga
Louis the Depressed, Part 2
Storyboards and Art by Ryosuke Takeuchi
PHEW...
GOOD DAY, EVERYBODY. I HOPE YOU'RE WELL.
IN ADDITION TO THE HOUSE IN DURHAM, MY BIG BROTHER WILLIAM IS ALSO GOING IN AND OUT OF OUR LONDON MANOR.
SO RIGHT NOW I AM TAKING CARE OF TWO HOUSES.
GLEAAM
IN ORDER TO MAINTAIN THE UTMOST SECRECY, WE HAVE A RULE AGAINST HIRING HOUSEHOLD HELP.
YOU MIGHT THINK THERE AREN'T ENOUGH PEOPLE FOR THIS JOB, BUT I'M NOT BOTHERED BY IT.
ON THE CONTRARY, IF IT MEANS I CAN HELP MY BROTHERS, THEN I'M GLAD TO DO IT.
FSHHHH
AND WHILE I'M ON THE SUBJECT OF MY BROTHERS, TODAY...
YMMRYMMR

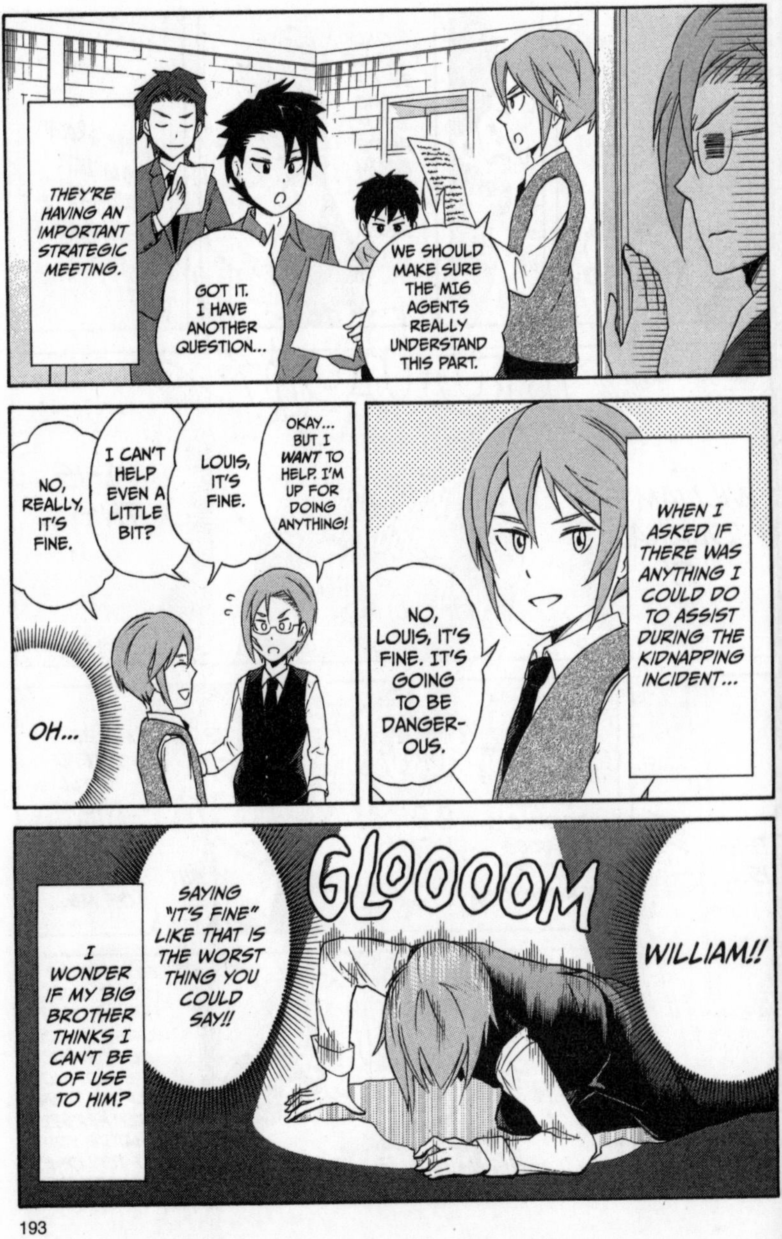
WE SHOULD MAKE SURE THE MI6 AGENTS REALLY UNDERSTAND THIS PART.
GOT IT. I HAVE ANOTHER QUESTION...
THEY'RE HAVING AN IMPORTANT STRATEGIC MEETING.
WHEN I ASKED IF THERE WAS ANYTHING I COULD DO TO ASSIST DURING THE KIDNAPPING INCIDENT...
NO, LOUIS, IT'S FINE. IT'S GOING TO BE DANGER-OUS.
OKAY... BUT I WANT TO HELP. I'M UP FOR DOING ANYTHING!
LOUIS, IT'S FINE.
I CAN'T HELP EVEN A LITTLE BIT?
NO, REALLY, IT'S FINE.
OH...
WILLIAM!!
GLOOOOM
SAYING "IT'S FINE" LIKE THAT IS THE WORST THING YOU COULD SAY!!
I WONDER IF MY BIG BROTHER THINKS I CAN'T BE OF USE TO HIM?

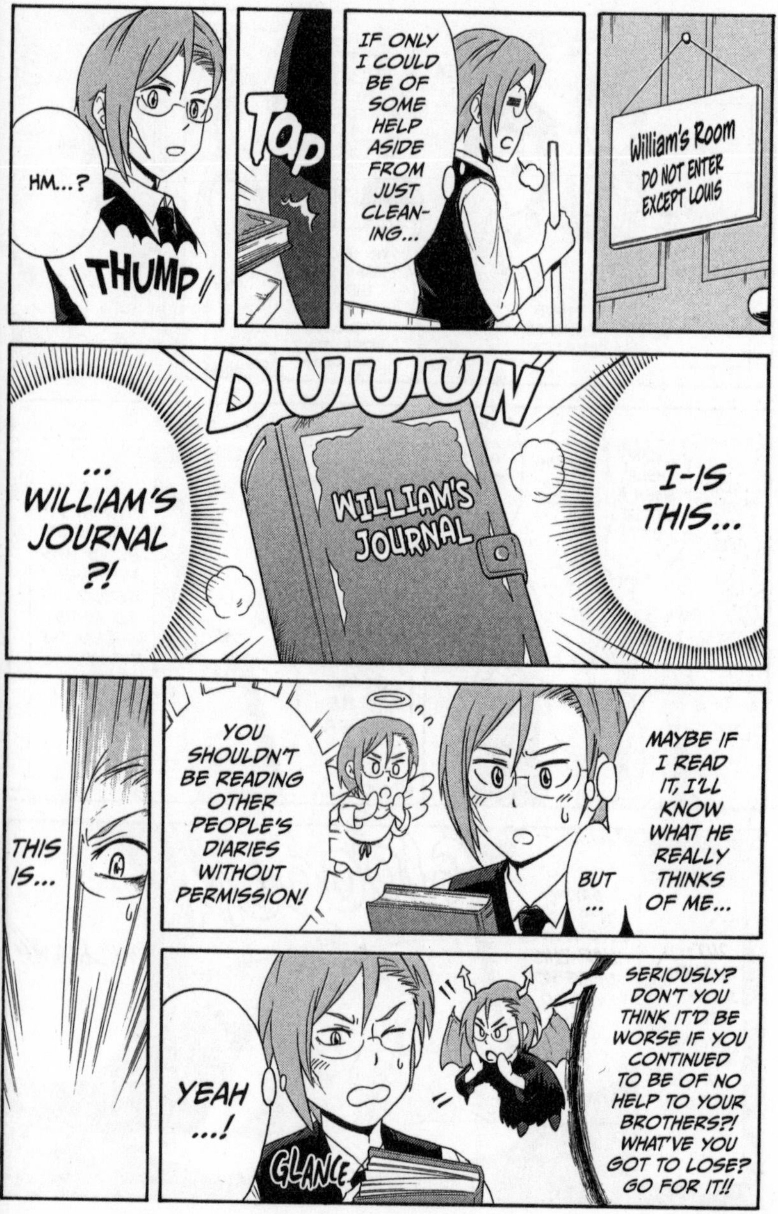
William's Room
DO NOT ENTER EXCEPT LOUIS
IF ONLY I COULD BE OF SOME HELP ASIDE FROM JUST CLEANING...
Tap
HM...?
THUMP
DUUUN
I-IS THIS...
WILLIAM'S JOURNAL
... WILLIAM'S JOURNAL ?!
MAYBE IF I READ IT, I'LL KNOW WHAT HE REALLY THINKS OF ME...
BUT ...
YOU SHOULDN'T BE READING OTHER PEOPLE'S DIARIES WITHOUT PERMISSION!
SERIOUSLY? DON'T YOU THINK IT'D BE WORSE IF YOU CONTINUED TO BE OF NO HELP TO YOUR BROTHERS?! WHAT'VE YOU GOT TO LOSE? GO FOR IT!!
GLANCE
YEAH ...!
THIS IS...

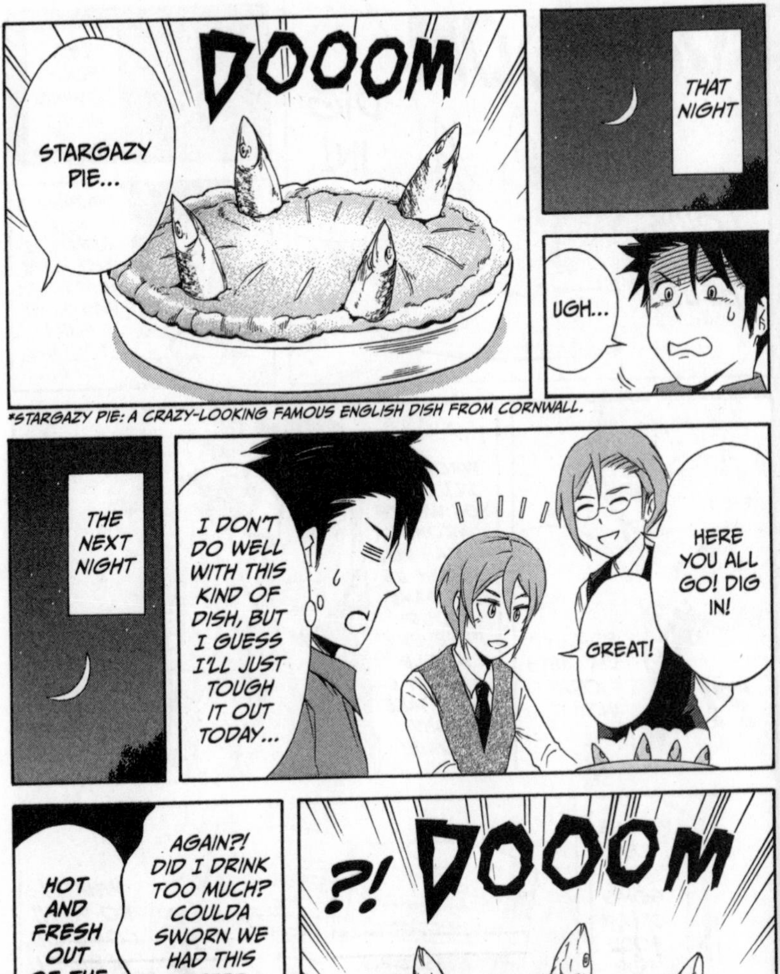
THAT NIGHT
UGH...
DOOOM
STARGAZY PIE...
HERE YOU ALL GO! DIG IN!
GREAT!
I DON'T DO WELL WITH THIS KIND OF DISH, BUT I GUESS I'LL JUST TOUGH IT OUT TODAY...
THE NEXT NIGHT
DOOOM
?!
AGAIN?! DID I DRINK TOO MUCH? COULDA SWORN WE HAD THIS YESTER-DAY...
HOT AND FRESH OUT OF THE OVEN!!
GREAT, LOUIS!

*STARGAZY PIE: A CRAZY-LOOKING FAMOUS ENGLISH DISH FROM CORNWALL.

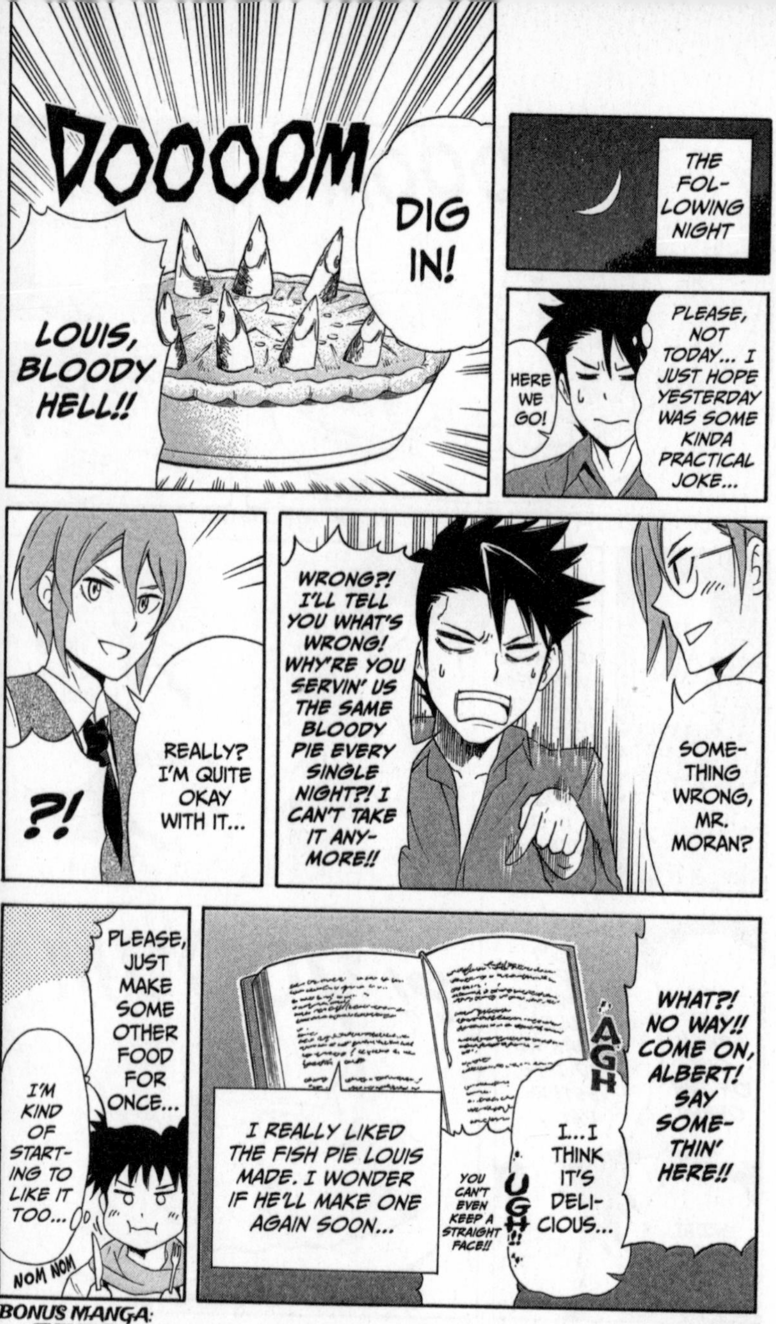

THE FOLLOWING NIGHT
PLEASE, NOT TODAY... I JUST HOPE YESTERDAY WAS SOME KINDA PRACTICAL JOKE...
HERE WE GO!
DIG IN!
DOOOOM
LOUIS, BLOODY HELL!!
SOMETHING WRONG, MR. MORAN?
WRONG?! I'LL TELL YOU WHAT'S WRONG! WHY'RE YOU SERVIN' US THE SAME BLOODY PIE EVERY SINGLE NIGHT?! I CAN'T TAKE IT ANYMORE!!
REALLY? I'M QUITE OKAY WITH IT...
?!
WHAT?! NO WAY!! COME ON, ALBERT! SAY SOMETHIN' HERE!!
AGH
I...I THINK IT'S DELICIOUS...
UGH!!
YOU CAN'T EVEN KEEP A STRAIGHT FACE!!
I REALLY LIKED THE FISH PIE LOUIS MADE. I WONDER IF HE'LL MAKE ONE AGAIN SOON...
PLEASE, JUST MAKE SOME OTHER FOOD FOR ONCE...
I'M KIND OF STARTING TO LIKE IT TOO...
NOM NOM

BONUS MANGA: THE END

MORIARTY
THE PATRIOT

To be continued in vol. 3

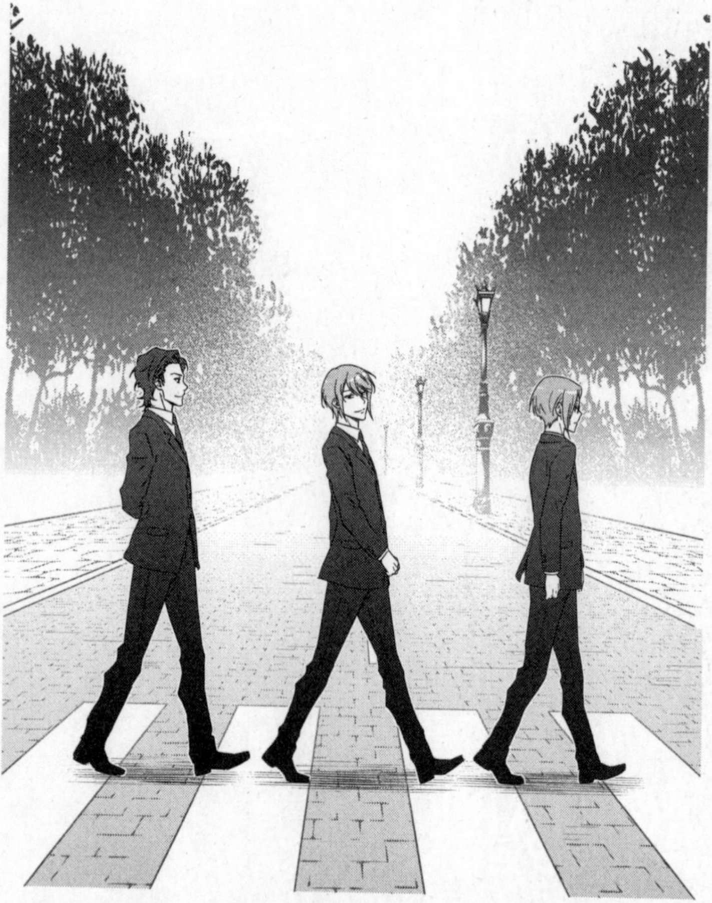

RYOSUKE TAKEUCHI

Sherlock Holmes's character and personality change depending on the translator, actor, art, configuration, setup, stage, etc. And I think exploring those differences is also part of the fun of the character. So I hope you can think of the Holmes in this series as just one of the many flavors of Holmes out there.

HIKARU MIYOSHI

I was so happy I could draw this volume's cover character so soon! More and more characters will be making their appearance, and the concept and manga art are going to be a little more difficult, but I'm still having fun drawing every single chapter for this series. I think it'll all be worth it, and it would make me happy if each of you finds even just one character you like.

RYOSUKE TAKEUCHI was born November 20, 1980, in Hyogo, Japan, and is a manga artist and writer. He got his big break in 2011 with *ST&RS*, his first serialized *Weekly Shonen Jump* series. He later did the storyboards for *All You Need Is Kill*.

HIKARU MIYOSHI is a manga artist whose previous work includes *Inspector Akane Tsunemori*, which was based on the popular anime *Psycho-Pass*.

Takeuchi and Miyoshi began collaborating on *Moriarty the Patriot* in 2016.

MORIARTY
THE PATRIOT

2

SHONEN JUMP Edition

BASED ON THE WORKS OF Sir Arthur Conan Doyle
STORYBOARDS BY Ryosuke Takeuchi
ART BY Hikaru Miyoshi

TRANSLATION (´･∀･`)♯ｱ?
TOUCH-UP ART & LETTERING Annaliese "Ace" Christman
DESIGN Joy Zhang
EDITOR Marlene First

YUKOKU NO MORIARTY © 2016 by Ryosuke Takeuchi, Hikaru Miyoshi
All rights reserved.
First published in Japan in 2016 by SHUEISHA Inc., Tokyo.
English translation rights arranged by SHUEISHA Inc.

The stories, characters and incidents mentioned
in this publication are entirely fictional.

Printed in Italy

Published by VIZ Media, LLC
P.O. Box 77010
San Francisco, CA 94107

10 9 8 7 6 5 4 3 2
First printing, January 2021
Second printing, April 2021

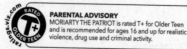

PARENTAL ADVISORY
MORIARTY THE PATRIOT is rated T+ for Older Teen
and is recommended for ages 16 and up for realistic
violence, drug use and criminal activity.
ratings.viz.com

viz.com

DEATH NOTE
ALL-IN-ONE EDITION

Story by **Tsugumi Ohba**   Art by **Takeshi Obata**

Light Yagami is an ace student with great prospects, and he's bored out of his mind. But all that chan[ges] when he finds the Death Note, a notebook dropped [by] a rogue Shinigami death god. Any human whose na[me] is written in the notebook dies, and now Light [has] vowed to use the power of the Death Note to rid [the] world of evil. But when criminals begin dropping de[ad,] the authorities send the legendary detective L to tr[ack] down the killer. With L hot on his heels, will Light [lose] sight of his noble goal...or his life?

Includes a NEW epilogu[e] chapter!

All 12 volumes in ONE monstrously large edition!

...uji Itadori is resolved to save the world from **cursed spirits** but he soon learns that the best way to do it is to slowly lose his **humanity** and become one himself!

JUJUTSU KAISEN

STORY AND ART BY
GEGE AKUTAMI

In a world where **cursed spirits** feed on unsuspecting humans, fragments of the legendary and feared demon **Ryomen Sukuna** were lost and scattered about. Should any demon consume Sukuna's body parts, the power they gain could **destroy the world** as we know it. Fortunately, there exists a mysterious school of **Jujutsu Sorcerers** who exist to protect the precarious existence of the living from the **supernatural!**

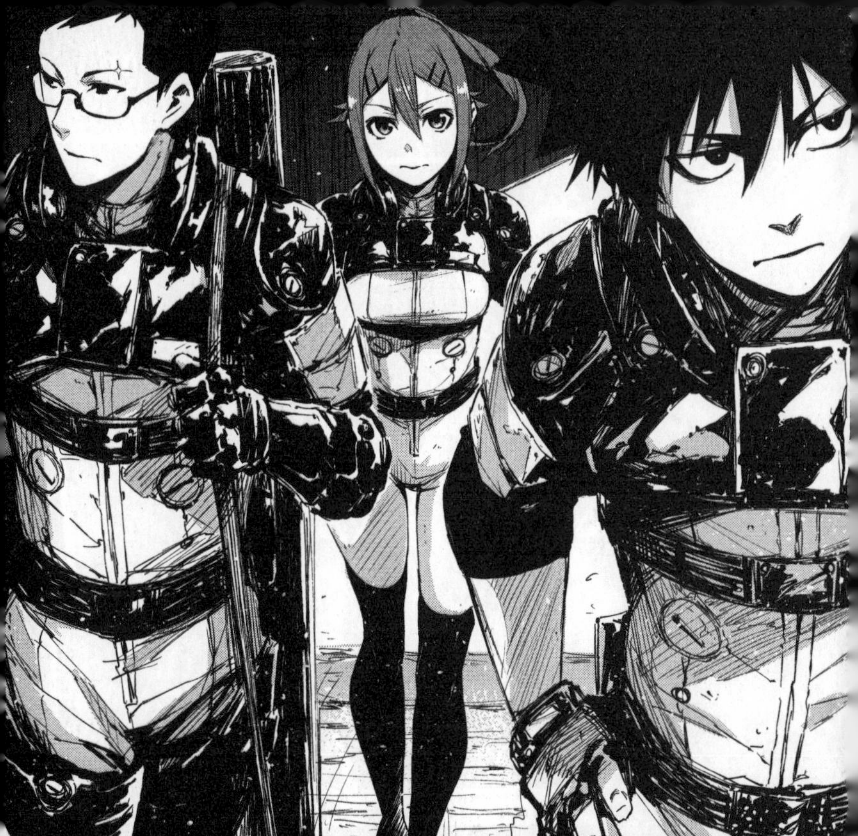

BLACK TORCH

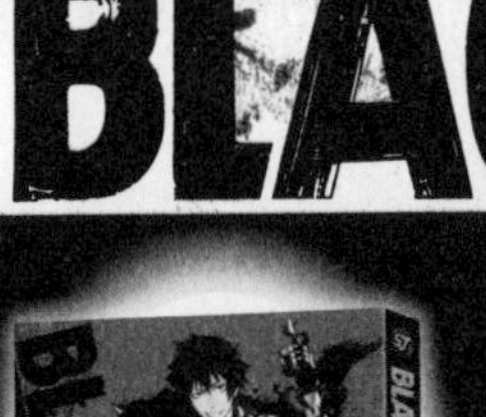
BLACK TORCH
BLACK TORCH
TSUYOSHI TAKAKI
1

Ninja and animal lover Jiro Azuma's life is chan
forever when he finds himself in the middle of a wa
ninjas vs. demons.

Jiro Azuma is descended from a long line of ninja, an
can talk to animals. One day he rescues a unique b
cat named Rago, a supernatural being, and is drag
into a mystical war.

THE PROMISED NEVERLAND

STORY BY KAIU SHIRAI
ART BY POSUKA DEMIZU

mma, Norman and Ray are the brightest
ids at the Grace Field House orphanage.
d under the care of the woman they refer
o as "Mom," all the kids have enjoyed a
mfortable life. Good food, clean clothes
d the perfect environment to learn—what
ore could an orphan ask for? One day,
hough, Emma and Norman uncover the
ark truth of the outside world they are
forbidden from seeing.

YOU'RE READING THE
WRONG WAY!

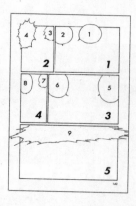

MORIARTY THE PATRIOT reads from right to left, starting in the upper-right corner. Japanese is read from right to left, meaning that action, sound effects and word-balloon order are completely reversed from English order.